Content Reading Instruction

A Communication Approach

Mark W. Conley
Michigan State University

McGraw-Hill, Inc.
New York   St. Louis   San Francisco   Auckland   Bogotá
Caracas   Lisbon   London   Madrid   Mexico   Milan
Montreal   New Delhi   Paris   San Juan   Singapore
Sydney   Tokyo   Toronto

This book was developed by Lane Akers, Inc.

Content Reading Instruction
A Communication Approach

2 3 4 5 6 7 8 9 0 DOC DOC 9 0 9 8 7 6 5 4 3 2

ISBN 0-07-557716-X

This book was set in Caledonia by General Graphic Services, Inc.
The editor was Lane Akers;
the photo editor was Anne Manning;
the photo researcher was Rona Tuccillo.
Project supervision was done by The Total Book.
R. R. Donnelley & Sons Company was printer and binder.

Photo Credits: p. xvi, Joel Gordon; p. 2, Elizabeth Crews/Stock, Boston; p. 20, Joel Gordon; p. 22, Ulrike Welsch; p. 52, Elizabeth Crews/Stock, Boston; p. 88, Ulrike Welsch; p. 114, Elizabeth Crews/The Image Works; p. 140, Susan Lapides/Design Conceptions; p. 142, Elizabeth Crews/Stock, Boston; p. 176, Joel Gordon; p. 218, Kathy Sloane/Photo Researchers; p. 260, Elizabeth Crews; p. 288, Spencer Grant/Stock, Boston; p. 290, Tony Velez/ The Image Works; p. 322, Sven Martson/Comstock; p. 358, Barrera/ TexaStock; p. 360, Peter Bates/The Picture Cube; p. 376, Joel Gordon. Other photo credits are shown with the accompanying photos.

Library of Congress Cataloging-in-Publication Data

Conley, Mark William.
    Content reading instruction: a communication approach / Mark W.
Conley.
        p.   cm.
    Includes bibliographical references and index.
    ISBN 0-07-557716-X. — ISBN 0-07-557718-6 (instructor's manual)
    1. Content area reading.   I. Title.
LB1050.455.C65   1992
428.4′071′2—dc20   91-20165

About the Author

Mark W. Conley is assistant professor of teacher education at Michigan State University. He was an English and reading teacher at the middle-school and high-school levels prior to earning a Ph.D. in secondary reading from Syracuse University. Dr. Conley taught courses in content area reading and secondary reading at the University of Alaska–Anchorage and Eastern Michigan University before going to Michigan State, where he teaches courses in content area reading to beginning and practicing teachers. He also teaches English to middle-school students in an urban professional development school. Dr. Conley is the author of many journals, articles, and book chapters. He coedited and wrote *Research Within Reach: Secondary School Reading* published by the International Reading Association. He was named Researcher of the Year in 1990 by the Michigan Reading Association, and, in 1991, he received the Elva Knight research award from the International Reading Association.

To Teachers
and Our Kids

Contents

Preface

Content Reading Instruction: A Communication Approach is designed for courses in teacher education variously labeled Content Area Reading or Secondary Reading. Its purpose is to help you teach your students to read and communicate more effectively in whatever subject area you happen to be teaching. To accomplish this goal, I have produced a text with the following characteristics.

CONTENT COVERAGE

Because students from so-called nonprint subjects such as art, music, physical education, and industrial arts face many of the same problems of comprehension, motivation, and limited knowledge as students from the print-dominated subjects, this text covers all the content areas. By showing how reading strategies can be integrated with other language modes (listening, speaking, writing, and observing), it is possible to improve comprehension in any subject area. This attention to both print and nonprint subjects is what most distinguishes this text and has led me to title it a *communication* approach.

INSTRUCTIONAL EMPHASIS

The word *instruction* appears in the title to highlight the emphasis on what teachers think and do to help students become more literate. Each of the instruction-oriented chapters (5–11), which are the heart of the book, has a common format: setting goals, planning for instruction, and teaching a lesson. They not only describe specific teaching strategies, but also develop students' sense of how, when, and where to adapt these strategies to various contexts and subject areas.

PEDAGOGICAL FEATURES

An abundance of subject-specific examples, including sample dialogues, have been scattered throughout the book. In addition, cases illustrating instructional decision-making are provided toward the end of each of the teaching chapters (6–11 and 13). All of these examples, dialogues, and cases have been gathered or created in collaboration with real content area teachers. Finally, chapter-opening objectives, rationales, and concept maps are provided so that readers can quickly sense both the direction and justification for studying the information presented.

ACKNOWLEDGMENTS

Many people contributed to the preparation of this book. Harold Herber is originally responsible for my interest in content reading. A number of school district curriculum specialists, including Kathy Wilson of the Anchorage school district and Joan Lessard of the Fairbanks North Star School District, made it possible for me to try out many of the ideas in the book with classroom teachers. Bill Mester, Superintendent of the Mead (WA) School District, and Fran Mester, a teacher in the Spokane School District, are responsible for much of my current thinking about teacher decision-making and the role of content reading in schools. Many classroom teachers in my undergraduate and graduate classes have helped me grow and have contributed to the examples that appear throughout the text.

The following reviewers have contributed thoughtful critiques that have improved the final version of this text: Patricia Anders, University of Arizona; Barbara Guzzetti, Arizona State University; Ann McCourt, University of Delaware; David O'Brien, Purdue University; Laura Roehler, Michigan State University; and Dixie Lee Spiegel, University of North Carolina.

Special acknowledgment goes to Laura Roehler and Gerry Duffy from Michigan State University, who gave me the original boost and confidence to write a book. Thanks to Lane Akers who gave me patient encouragement and guided me wisely from the start. Finally, I owe a great deal of thanks to my wife, Sigrid, and to the kids, Brendon, Kelly, and Erin. While working for three years in the basement writing this book, I could always count on one of them to pull me out of writer's block, make me forget how tired I had become, or help me remember what it is all about.

Mark W. Conley

Content Reading Instruction
A Communication Approach

Section I

Introduction

Section I contains a single chapter introducing you to the goals for a communication approach to content reading instruction. At the end of this section, you should be able to understand the purposes and themes that appear throughout the book and be able to answer questions such as:

1. What is content reading?

2. What is a communication approach to content reading?

3. What kinds of instruction make up a communication approach to content reading?

"No longer will it be sufficient to teach some facts of geography, a little algebra, or the mechanics of language. The school subjects will become means for learnings that transcend them."

From J. Goodlad (1984). A place called school (p. 244). New York: McGraw-Hill.

1

Content Reading and Communication

CHAPTER OBJECTIVES

After reading this chapter, you should be able to:

1. Understand the goals for instruction for helping students learn effectively from their reading.

2. Explain what it means to take a communication approach to content reading instruction.

RATIONALE

For many years, news about students and reading has not been good. Students leave school without knowing how to perform simple reading tasks: many cannot scan a phone book to find emergency numbers or read an employment application. Equally disturbing are recent declines among all students in the ability to understand whole passages of text (Applebee, Langer, & Mullis, 1988; NAEP, 1986). Solutions to the crisis in literacy are no longer restricted to teaching basic reading skills and using remedial readers. All students require instruction in reading. Without the ability to use reading to engage in a variety of ways of thinking, our students will be incapable of communicating and surviving in our print-based society.

Too often, responsibility for solving these problems is placed solely on elementary and remedial reading programs. *Elementary reading programs* (programs designed to teach beginning readers) are sometimes expected to teach students everything they should ever need to know about reading by the time they enter the middle school level. This expectation is unrealistic because the reading and communication needs of students change dramatically as they progress through school and eventually into the outside world. The reading curriculum for most elementary students focuses mostly on *learning-to-read strategies* (such as pronouncing words or comprehending paragraphs and stories). Learning-to-read strategies offer students a broad foundation for learning, but not the specific kinds of strategies that are necessary for reading in subjects like mathematics, science, English, social studies, vocational education, or music. For example, some students experience increasing difficulty with reading in the upper grades as the reading demands become more complex and specialized.

Students who are unsuccessful with reading are often placed in *remedial reading programs* (programs designed to help problem readers improve). Remedial instruction

CHAPTER ORGANIZER

An organizer is a visual way of thinking about a set of concepts and ideas. It is a device—a study technique—designed to help people remember. A chapter organizer is provided for each of the chapters in this book. Each chapter organizer represents one of many ways of organizing important concepts.

You can use the organizer as it is presented or you can create your own. If you decide to use the organizer, either write notes directly on the organizer or make a copy of it. As you read, watch for terms on the organizer. Jot down a few words or phrases that will help you understand, explain, and remember. To create your own organizer, make a list of important words and phrases (headings and italicized words are important). Then organize the words and phrases in ways that make sense. When studying, review not only the meanings but also the relationships among the words and phrases.

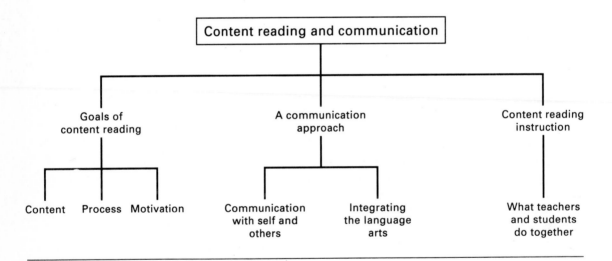

typically focuses on the learning-to-read strategies students have not yet acquired (Allington & Johnston, 1989). To expect remedial programs to give students all they need to know about reading is also unrealistic. While some students in remedial reading programs could profit from revisiting what they did not learn, they still must learn to adapt to new and more challenging subject-matter concepts.

Content reading is a field in education devoted to helping students acquire specific strategies for reading in various subject areas, termed *reading-to-learn strategies*. Reading-to-learn strategies (involved in such activities as mathematical problem-solving or using a manual to set up a machine) provide ways for thinking and communicating in different subjects (Singer & Donlan, 1980). These strategies help students continuously increase their knowledge, update their skills, and improve communication with the world around them.

Teachers at all levels—elementary, middle, and high school—have a stake in focusing on content reading. Reading plays a significant, supportive role in developing deep, subject-matter understanding. For example, students concentrating on a debate in an English class need assistance in figuring out what information is important from a variety of written sources. Students exploring ecosystems in science require help in separating their misconceptions from scientific theory as they read, observe, and reflect. Students in a choral music class often need help in integrating musical scores and symbols with the finer points of musical performance. In each of these situations, opportunities abound for showing students how to use reading to gain information or to communicate with others about what they know.

It is not necessarily automatic or easy to integrate subject-matter teaching with opportunities for teaching students about reading-to-learn. Inevitably, teachers are faced with difficult decisions about textbooks, students, and instruction. This book has been written to assist teachers with many of these decisions, and to support teachers across the curriculum as they help students engage in more effective content reading and communication.

THE GOALS OF CONTENT READING

Content reading has three important goals for students; (1) understanding essential content, (2) learning how to read-to-learn, and (3) developing motivation for lifelong reading. Each goal is described below.

Understanding Essential Content

Content reading gets part of its name from the first priority of subject-matter teachers: to teach content. Simply defined, *content* is that which teachers want students to understand. Every subject (or *content area*) has its own content or defining sets of facts, concepts and principles. For example, as students go through the school day, they gain familiarity with the past (social studies, history), learn how to use complex symbols to solve problems (mathematics), and discover new ways to express themselves (writing, music, and art). Content is neither static nor solid. The content of a subject grows and/or changes continuously through the discourse or conversations of larger communities in and outside of school.

The ongoing challenge to schools is to ensure that students are well-prepared to actively join a continuously changing world. To do this, teachers need to help students understand not only the traditional content of a subject but also ways in which the content evolves. This is a kind of "deep" content understanding that prepares students to take part in the real-world conversations that contribute to serious thinking in various subjects.

Students are not always afforded classroom experiences that result in a depth of content knowledge. In an eighth-grade science class, I once observed two students as they were busily completing a laboratory exercise. The lab consisted of pouring acids on different types of metals. Questions in a lab book focused on observations about the chemical reactions: the students noted changes in color and the appearance of smoke, residues, or heat. One question in the lab book asked if the students were surprised by the reaction of an acid with a particular type of metal. Both students dutifully wrote: "Yes I was surprised." I asked the lab partners how they arrived at that answer. One replied: "My partner said that's the right answer." The other explained: "That's what the teacher told us to put down."

This anecdote suggests some of the problems students face when learning content. They do not automatically distinguish important from less important facts, nor are they able to construct the concepts that facts help us understand. Students spend a great deal of time listening to teachers, reading textbooks, writing answers to questions, and taking tests and quizzes. In addition, they are expected to decide independently what is important about the content and what teachers want them to know. Without guidance, many students fail to develop useful knowledge.

Understanding essential content means knowing how to distinguish between what is essential in a subject and what is not. It means learning implications and applications that transform loose clusters of facts into meaningful knowledge and then being able to communicate that knowledge in meaningful ways.

Learning How to Read-to-Learn

Research in the past several decades has produced an explosion of knowledge about reading-to-learn. These insights contrast dramatically with previous perceptions that reading is an act of pronouncing words or regurgitating an author's message. *Reading-to-learn* is defined as an *interactive* process in which meaning is *constructed* in the mind of the reader. Reading-to-learn is an interactive process in the sense that reading is an act of communication with a writer. The perspectives and knowledge of the reader interact with the language and perspectives of the writer. It is a constructive process in the way that readers draw from a number of sources of information to build their own message, from sources within themselves (such as prior knowledge), on the printed page, and in the context where reading occurs.

To illustrate for yourself the interactive and constructive nature of reading-to-learn, compare the experience of reading the poem below with reading the baseball rule that follows it.

TO SATCH

By Samuel Allen

Sometimes I feel like I will never stop
Just go on forever
Till one fine mornin
I'm gonna reach up and grab me a handfulla stars

Swing out my long lean leg
And whip three hot strikes burnin down the heavens
And look over at God and say
How about that!

BASEBALL RULE 2.00—DEFINITION OF TERMS

A *strike* is a legal pitch when so called by the umpire, which—

(a) Is struck at by the batter and is missed;
(b) Is not struck at, if any part of the ball passes through any part of the strike zone;
(c) Is fouled by the batter when he has less than two strikes;
(d) Is bunted foul;
(e) Touches the batter as he strikes it;
(f) Becomes a foul tip.

What past images or experience did the poem conjure up? Did the poem call up previous experiences with baseball or with poetry? Did the baseball rule remind you about other times when you were faced with legalistic language, such as at the license bureau or filing your taxes? Did reading either piece remind you of experiences at the ballpark or in some government office? How did your feelings change as you read each piece? If any of these questions or experiences crossed your mind, you were interacting with the texts, constructing your own sense of what each meant to you, and not merely extracting verbatim some author's message.

For many students, the processes underlying reading-to-learn go on all the time, yet teachers and students can be largely unaware when this is happening or how to make the processes work more efficiently. If a student's interaction with a text is productive and positive, the result could be comprehension. If, on the other hand, this interaction is somehow blocked, the result could as easily be frustration and failure.

By the eighth grade, many students have only a very basic understanding of reading-to-learn. Many are proficient at pronouncing words and understanding factual information. A large percentage of students, however, are unable to apply what they know (Applebee, Langer, & Mullis, 1988; NAEP, 1986). Many students are inexperienced in applying reading to varying kinds of situations, from experiments in science to problem-solving in vocational education. Though the curriculum becomes more complex and differentiated as students get older, few students understand how to adapt their reading comprehension to different subject-matter tasks or situations. Students do not readily change their approach to reading with each new task or situation as easily as you probably did in reading the baseball poem and the baseball rule.

Knowing how to read-to-learn means knowing how to adapt flexibly depending on available knowledge, the language of the text, and the different purposes for reading (for instance, to gain information, for pleasure). Teachers are the key to creating the conditions that help students understand what it means to read-to-learn. Teachers can provide students with frequent and rich opportunities for reading in a particular subject while offering them clear suggestions on how to shift their approach to reading from one situation to the next. The chapters that follow all address ways to develop students' knowledge about reading-to-learn.

Developing Motivation for Lifelong Reading

Motivation involves the desire to learn. In many classrooms, the refrain is "Why are we learning this?" or "Will this be on the test?" In others, students are passive; they prefer classroom activities that are easy and even repetitive (Goodlad, 1984). Students will participate in class based on the rewards they expect to receive for their participation (Sedlak et al., 1986). For some students, minimal participation is the price they pay for teachers to leave them alone. For others, passing a test is the only reason to read (Mathewson, 1976).

A common misconception is that motivation is a concern for only the poorest readers. To be sure, students who can't read often descend into a cycle of failure, from failure in reading to problems with motivation, from problems with motivation to failure in reading. Some students who seem unable to read really can, but won't. These readers have more skills than they communicate to their teachers (Herber, 1978). Yet another concern is the good reader who reads just to get a passing grade—and never develops a sustained interest in reading or in the content he or she is studying.

Motivation affects all readers

Elizabeth Crews/The Image Works

Many who teach a specific subject would like students to become motivated enough to choose careers and develop lifelong interests based on experiences with reading and learning in that subject. Teaching a subject as merely an assortment of facts guarantees that this won't happen. When students see purposes behind what they are reading, when they use reading to discover their own purposes, motivation results.

Developing motivation for lifelong reading means acquiring a desire to read for personal satisfaction and enjoyment. When reading becomes a more personal and purposeful act, students continue to read throughout their lives. They value what they read and they know they can be successful.

A COMMUNICATION APPROACH

This book emphasizes a *communication approach* to content reading. A communication approach transforms reading-to-learn into reading-to-communicate. Whereas reading-to-learn focuses on using reading to gain information and get pleasure out of reading, reading-to-communicate means using language (reading, writing, speaking, and listening) to explore information and feelings and interact with the surrounding world.

The reason for reading is communication (Hennings, 1978). It is a part of daily functioning, from buying groceries to operating a computer. It is part of recreation, from watching television to playing a sport. Reading is so deeply ingrained in everyday communication that people often don't notice they are doing it. How often do people say to themselves, "I'm going to do some reading now" before paying some bills or settling in to read the morning paper? For most adults, reading-to-communicate is both necessary and automatic.

In schools, however, students' experiences with reading often do not automatically involve meaningful communication. For some teachers, textbooks are the curriculum (Alvermann & Hayes, 1989), but many students do not readily read textbooks in ways that foster communication. The tools that most teachers use to get students to read from texts—worksheets, study guides, and quizzes—do not always prepare students to articulate what they are learning.

Out of frustration with either the limitations of textbooks (see Chapter 2) or students' inability to use them (Chapter 3), some teachers downplay textbooks in favor of lectures, note-taking, and visual aids. However, textbooks and reading activities usually still play a role as ways to complete assignments or provide supplemental information (Alvermann & Moore, 1991). When reading becomes integrated with other classroom activities and students are not prepared specifically to deal with relevant texts, they may be required to engage in higher-level communication tasks before they are ready (for example, listening to a lecture and taking notes simultaneously, coordinating information found in notes with text information).

Students must develop the comfort and competence they need in order to read effectively for communication (Mikulecky, 1982). To help students achieve this, teachers must take a communication approach to content reading instruction. This approach to content reading instruction involves teaching the student how to: (1) communicate with oneself and others and, (2) integrate reading with other language skills including writing, speaking, and listening. These two goals are explained in the following sections.

Communicating with Self and Others

Reading-to-communicate with oneself involves a personal dialogue, a kind of "inner speech" (Moffett & Wagner, 1984). *Reading-to-communicate with others* consists of the public dialogue between teachers and students and the verbal exchange among students. The first goal of a communication approach to content reading is to provide students with multiple opportunities for personal as well as public dialogues so that their communication with self and others is enriched and enhanced.

A reader's inner speech is closely aligned with thinking and reasoning. It is the reader's inner voice that asks while reading: "What do I already know about this?" "Is this the best way to read this?" and "Does this make sense?" A reader's inner voice helps in devising an approach to reading, evaluating whether or not the approach is successful and coming up with alternatives when meaning becomes blocked (Garner, 1987). Sometimes teachers share their personal thinking—sometimes referred to as *thinking out loud*—while reading, solving a problem, or reflecting on an issue. By making their personal thinking public, teachers provide opportunities for the development of students' own inner voices. Also, teachers can engage students in various forms of writing, such as journals (see Chapter 10), and poetry to help students learn how to think and relect on their own.

Ideally, teaching and learning should be rich in opportunities for public dialogue, for the whole class and small group discussions that are a regular part of instruction, and for the multiple interactions between teachers and students and among students and each other. Public dialogues are often used by the teacher to prepare students for different ways of communicating information. Because of rapid changes in the workplace and in the world in general, students will require both knowledge and the ability to communicate information to solve familiar and new problems (Employability Skills Task Force, 1989). In the future, students will need to read and communicate in a variety of ways, from acting on information found in training materials and manuals to working with information appearing on a computer screen. Ideally, in-school experiences with reading and communicating should prepare students for lifelong experiences in a changing world. Through talk and by example, teachers can show students how to apply flexibly many kinds of ideas to many different tasks and situations.

Public dialogues also help students learn to share feelings. Many adults talk about what they read, identifying with the experiences of characters in a novel, expressing surprise over something read in a newspaper, or exploring in a self-help book the joys of living or the sorrows associated with death and dying. Again, through talk and by example, teachers can show students how reading and communicating help people think about and express different feelings.

The public dialogue that occurs during instruction potentially enhances a reader's inner voice. As students learn more about the thoughts and perspectives of others, they gain more insight into their own worldview and feelings. For example, consider this

Elizabeth Crews/Stock, Boston

Communication in classrooms involves public dialogues

dialogue in which an English teacher gets students to think about an ethical dilemma raised by a novel the class is reading together:

TEACHER: So the team kept winning by using a secret player who had failing grades but had a great throwing arm. Was that the right thing to do?

JEFF: Sure, why not? They were getting away with it.

TEACHER: But what if all the other teams used a secret player? One team could use a twenty-year-old running back and another could use a player taking steroids. Is it OK to fool people that way?

JEFF: It depends on if they get caught.

MARIA: Wat a minute! How would you feel if you were on the other team? It's cheating no matter how you slice it!

JEFF: Yeah, but cheating happens all the time. Besides, the team wouldn't have won if they didn't break the rules.

TEACHER: We haven't finished the book to see what happens. Suppose they win by breaking the rules. Would it feel the same compared to winning without breaking the rules?

JEFF: Nope. But at least they would win. I always feel better when I win than when I lose.

ROBERT: That's crazy, Jeff! You can't tell me winning is everything. It's much better to win something straight out then to get there by cheating.

TEACHER: Let's bring this back to earth. How about some examples from your own lives of when you won but didn't exactly feel right about it.

RON: We played a hockey game once and one of the kids got hurt real bad on the final goal. That didn't feel so good.

ANN: We cheated in a basketball game once and got caught.

TEACHER: What happened?

ANN: Nobody really did anything to us, but we felt embarrassed because everybody knew.

TEACHER: OK, so we have some ideas to work with here. Jeff is still saying that is it better to win no matter how you do it, some of you are saying that winning isn't everything, and others are saying that it doesn't always feel good to win, especially if you get caught cheating. It helps to get these ideas out in the open when we're reading or just living life. We may not agree but we can see what issues are going to be important. Let's read some more to see what the team decides to do about the secret player.

JEFF: I'm still not convinced the team is wrong. But I'll keep going so I can make up my own mind.

TEACHER: Fair enough!

Notice how the teacher engages students in some real-life problem-solving, examining different aspects of the problem (cheating versus winning), getting information both from the book and from students' experiences and feelings, having them speculate on what might happen if they and the characters in the novel follow similar paths. Ideally, as students experience this kind of public dialogue repeatedly and in different situations, they will develop their own inner sense of how to deal with similar problems and dilemmas. They can learn to live with ambiguity, reading and communicating with others when they need to expand their perspectives. Other students who—like Jeff—are much more certain about what they know and believe can learn to withhold judgment, reading and communicating to decide whether or not they should confront their existing views. These are some of the many ways that students' public expressions can become part of the inner voice that guides them as they read, communicate, and learn.

Integrating the Language Arts

Reading, writing, speaking, and listening—referred to as the *language arts*—are forms of language deeply rooted in what a person comes to know and feel (Petrosky, 1982). The language arts are the basis for thinking and meaning-making. The second goal of a communication approach to content reading is to integrate the language arts so that students learn many avenues for constructing meaning on their own.

Reading, writing, speaking, and listening are related through two underlying, interrelated language processes: *comprehending* and *composing* (see Figure 1.1). When students comprehend, they reconstruct and explore the structure and meaning of ideas expressed by an author or speaker. When students compose, they develop ideas and express their thoughts and feelings. Through comprehending, students *take in* concepts, reshaping and reflecting; through composing, students *generate* concepts, relating and expressing (Squire, 1984).

FIGURE 1.1

Integrating the Language Arts

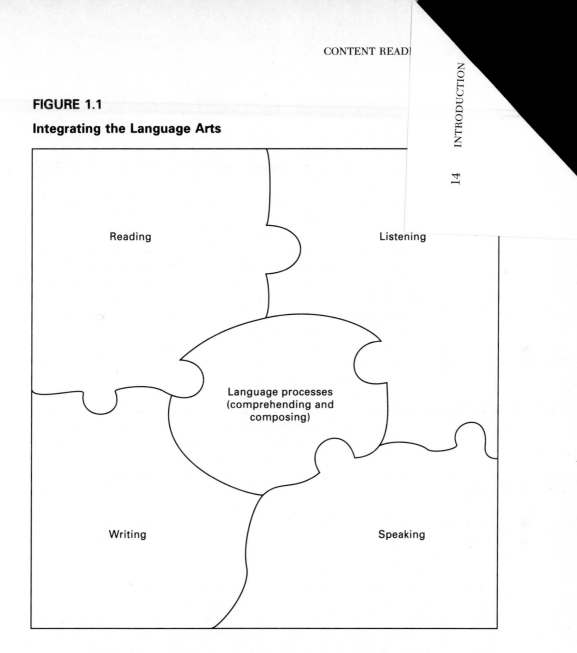

In the past, it has been popular to speak about reading and listening as comprehending and to group writing and speaking under composing. The more recent view is that each of the language arts involves a combination of comprehending and composing (McGinley & Tierney, 1989). Consider what happens while you are reading. Not only are your eyes scanning the page, comprehending the information, but also you are composing and constructing your own sense of what the reading means to you. Now think about what happens while you are writing. You brainstorm and compose and, as the writing emerges, you comprehend and revise what you have written. Finally, consider what happens while speaking and listening during a conversation. When listening, you take in the language of the speaker while simultaneously composing your own meanings and interpretations. When speaking, you compose your thoughts into speech while simultaneously thinking about the effect you are having on the listener. The language arts are intimately connected.

The language arts are also essential ways of knowing and producing ideas across the curriculum, from so-called print-based areas such as mathematics and English to content areas less dependent on reading such as vocational education and music. For example, in mathematics students may struggle to comprehend a problem. To assist them, the teacher might ask students to compose some questions that help to clarify the problem or provide more information. Students in an English class may freeze at the thought of writing for information or for pleasure. To unlock their ability to write, the teacher might encourage students to talk with each other, brainstorming possible topics, purposes, and audiences (see Chapter 10). In vocational education class, students are frequently confronted with a problem involving a machine or directions in a manual or on a blueprint. To help students develop lifelong learning in the shop, teachers might guide students in knowing when it is best to work from a manual or blueprint versus consulting a coworker or supervisor. Finally, students in a music class may fail to distinguish between merely playing notes and expressing themselves musically. By making comparisons between music and various types of everyday communication (for example, polite conversation versus a vigorous debate or argument), teachers can sensitize students to the nuances of musical expression.

The language of any content area is both rich and complex. Students are not necessarily skillful in integrating reading, writing, speaking, and listening to foster their own learning in or out of school. However, knowing how the language arts work in a content area, as an integrated set of powerful learning tools, is one of the best ways for students to gain access to and apply knowledge of a subject. This book provides many opportunities for teachers to explore the language arts for subject-matter teaching.

WHAT IS A COMMUNICATION APPROACH TO CONTENT READING INSTRUCTION?

A *communication approach to content reading instruction* is what teachers and students do together to develop deep understandings of content, better and varied ways to process information, and lifelong motivation to read and learn. It is what teachers and students do together to support reading and communicating for different purposes, integrate reading with other forms of language, and foster communication with oneself and others. While these goals could be the goals of any teacher, in the past teachers have shown a reluctance to become involved with content reading. Reasons for this involve teachers' preconceptions and even some misconceptions about content reading.

For example, Singer (1979) found that teachers disagreed with items on a survey that suggested that every teacher is a teacher of reading. On the other hand, the teachers agreed that it is the teacher's job to teach students how to learn from their textbooks. In more recent studies, middle and high school teachers revealed misconceptions, confusing content reading instruction with elementary or remedial reading instruction (O'Brien & Stewart, 1990). Some teachers resist content reading instruction because they feel that generic reading activities (such as mapping out concepts) are a less than satisfactory solution to subject-specific concerns (such as doing science labs or solving story problems) (Ratekin et al., 1985). Other teachers avoid content reading instruction because of constraints placed on them in schools (O'Brien & Stewart, 1990). For instance, when teachers feel pressured to cover a great deal of content, the efficient solution is to replace reading materials and classroom discussion with teacher talk and passive note-taking. When this happens, content reading instruction takes a backseat. Without a well-developed understanding of how content reading instruction relates to real classrooms or an acknowledgment of school-based constraints, teachers tend to view content reading instruction as having little value.

A communication approach to content reading instruction *is not* about teaching isolated reading skills or instruction divorced from the realities of classrooms. It *is* concerned with what teachers can do to help students read-to-learn and read-to-communicate. It *is* concerned with how teachers can employ specific forms of instruction to meet the needs of readers across the curriculum.

SUMMARY

Literacy problems in this country have multiplied. The responsibility for showing students how to read-to-learn and read-to-communicate lies mostly with the subject-matter teacher. A communication approach to content reading focuses on teaching students about the personal and public ways we use reading for communication, as well as the powerful learning that comes from integrating the language arts.

This book provides practical ways to teach students about learning from texts and communicating in school and beyond. By practicing the communication approach espoused here, teachers can teach content while teaching content area reading. No instructional time is given up or lost just teaching reading. Through the ideas presented in this book, students not only learn the content, they learn it better.

SPECIAL PROJECTS

Course-Based

1. Are you a good reader? Write your own personal definition of reading. What are some unique ways that you use reading for communication?

Field-Based

2. Interview an expert in your content area. Ask him or her to (1) define reading, and (2) explain the role of reading in his or her daily routine. Does your expert's formal definition of reading correspond with his or her everyday reading habits? How would you account for any differences?
3. Observe a teacher in your content area. During a lesson, record the instances when students are reading. What types of reading are involved? For what purposes? How are other forms of language (writing, speaking, listening) used in conjunction with reading?

SUGGESTED READING

These books are for those who wish to know more about content reading and content reading instruction:

DUFFY, G. (1990). *Reading in the middle school,* 2d ed. Newark, DE: International Reading Association.

ESTES, T., & VAUGHAN, J. (1985). *Reading and learning in the content classroom.* New York: Allyn and Bacon.

HERBER, H., & NELSON, J. (1991). *Teaching content areas: Reading, writing and reasoning.* Englewood Cliffs, NJ: Prentice-Hall.

JONES, B., PALINCSAR, A., OGLE, D., & CARR, E. (1987). *Strategic teaching and learning: Cognitive instruction in the content areas.* Reston, VA: Association for Supervision and Curriculum Development.

LAPP, D., FLOOD, J., & FARNAN, N. (1989). *Content area reading and learning: Instructional strategies.* New York: Prentice-Hall.

MANZO, A., & MANZO, U. (1990). *Content area reading: A heuristic approach.* Columbus, OH: Charles Merrill.

VACCA, R., & VACCA, J. (1989). *Content area reading.* Glenview, IL: Scott-Foresman.

These books incorporate a communication approach:

MOORE, D., MOORE, S., CUNNINGHAM, P., & CUNNINGHAM, J. (1986). *Developing readers and writers in the content areas.* New York: Longman.

READANCE, J., BEAN, T., & BALDWIN, S. (1985). *Content area reading: An integrated approach.* Dubuque, IA: Kendall/Hunt.

These reviews provide a good start for those interested in research on content reading:

ALVERMANN, D., & MOORE, D. (1991). Secondary school reading. In R. Barr, M. Kamil, P. Mosenthal, & P. D. Pearson (Eds.), *Handbook of reading research,* Vol. II (pp. 951–983). New York: Longman.

ALVERMANN, D., MOORE, D., & CONLEY, M. (1987). *Research within reach: Secondary school reading.* Newark, DE: International Reading Association.

ALVERMANN, D., & SWAFFORD, J. (1989). Do content area strategies have a research base? *Journal of Reading, 32,* 388–394.

MOORE, D., READANCE, J., & RICKELMAN, R. (1983). An historical exploration of content area reading instruction. *Reading Reasearch Quarterly, 18,* 419–438.

This book includes a chapter that discusses new ways of viewing the relationship between remedial reading programs and content area classrooms:

SLAVIN, R., KARWEIT, N., & MADDEN, N. (1989). *Effective programs for students at risk,* chap 1. Boston: Allyn and Bacon.

These references describe emerging perspectives on literacy in various subject-matter areas:

ANDERSON, C., & ROTH, K. (1989). Teaching for meaningful and self-regulated learning of science. In J. Brophy (Ed.), *Advances in research on teaching,* Vol. I. Greenwich, CT: JAI Press.

BRANDT, R. (1988). *Content of the curriculum.* Reston, VA: Association for Supervision and Curriculum Development.

GAGNON, P., & THE BRADLEY COMMISSION (1989). *Historical literacy.* New York: Macmillan.

GROSSMAN, P. (1990). What are we talking about anyhow? Subject-matter knowledge for secondary teachers. In J. Brophy (Ed.), *Advances in research on teaching,* Vol. II. Greenwich, CT: JAI Press.

NATIONAL COUNCIL OF TEACHERS OF MATHEMATICS (1989). *Curriculum and evaluation standards for school mathematics.* Reston, VA: National Council of Teachers of Mathematics.

This book attempts to define literacy, both generally and specifically:

VENEZKY, R., WAGNER, D., & CILIBERTI, B. (1990). *Toward defining literacy.* Newark, DE: International Reading Association.

These books discuss constraints that affect content area teachers and their concerns about literacy at various school levels:

GOODLAD, J. (1984). *A place called school.* New York: McGraw-Hill.

LIPSITZ, J. (1984). *Successful schools for young adolescents.* New Brunswick, NJ: Transaction Books.

SEDLACK, M., WHEELER, C., PULLIN, D., & CUSICK, P. (1986). *Selling students short: Classroom bargains and academic reform in the American high school.* New York: Teachers College Press.

SIZER, T. (1985). *Horace's compromise: The dilemma of the American high school.* Boston: Houghton Mifflin.

REFERENCES

ALLEN, S. (1972). To Satch. In P. McFarland, M. Kavanagh, W. Jamison, & M. Peckham (Eds.), *Moments in literature.* Boston: Houghton Mifflin.

ALLINGTON, R., & JOHNSTON, P. (1989). Coordination, collaboration, and consistency: The redesign of compensatory and special education interventions. In R. Slavin, N. Karweit, & N. Madden (Eds.), *Effective programs for students at risk.* Boston: Allyn and Bacon.

ALVERMANN, D., & HAYES, D. (1989). Classroom discussion of content area reading assignments: An intervention study. *Reading Research Quarterly, 24,* 305–335.

ALVERMANN, D., & MOORE, D. (1991). Secondary school reading. In R. Barr, M. Kamil, P. Mosenthal, and P. D. Pearson (Eds.), *Handbook of reading research,* Vol. II (pp. 951–983). New York: Longman.

APPLEBEE, A., LANGER, J., & MULLIS, I. (1988). *Who reads best?: Factors related to reading achievement in grades 3, 7, and 11.* Princeton, NJ: Educational Testing Service.

EMPLOYABILITY SKILLS TASK FORCE (1989). *Progress report to the Governor's Commission on Jobs and Economic Development.* Lansing, MI: Michigan State Board of Education.

GARNER, R. (1987). Strategies for reading and studying expository text. *Educational Psychologist, 22,* 3, 299–312.

GOODLAD, J. (1984). *A place called school.* New York: McGraw-Hill.

HENNINGS, D. (1978). *Communication in action: Dynamic teaching of the language arts.* Chicago: Rand McNally.

HERBER, H. (1978). *Teaching reading in content areas.* Englewood Cliffs, NJ: Prentice-Hall.

HOLMES GROUP (1990). *Tomorrow's schools: Principles for the design of professional development schools.* East Lansing, MI: The Holmes Group.

MATHEWSON, G. (1976). The function of attitude in the reading process. In H. Singer & R. Ruddell (Eds.), *Theoretical models and processes of reading.* Newark, DE: International Reading Association.

MCGINLEY, W., & TIERNEY, R. (1989). Traversing the topical landscape: Reading and writing as ways of knowing. *Written Communication, 6,* 3, 243–269.

MIKULECKY, L. (1982). Job literacy: The relationship betwen school preparation and workplace actuality. *Reading Research Quarterly, 17,* 3, 400–419.

MOFFETT, J., & WAGNER, B. (1984). *Student-centered language arts and reading, K-13: A handbook for teachers.* Dallas: Houghton Mifflin.

NATIONAL ASSESSMENT OF EDUCATIONAL PROGRESS (1986). *Literacy: Profiles of America's young adults.* Princeton, NJ: Educational Testing Service.

O'BRIEN, D., & STEWART, R. (1990). Preservice teachers' perspectives on why every teacher is not a teacher of reading: A qualitative analysis. *Journal of Reading Behavior, 22,* 2, 101–129.

PETROSKY, A. (1982). From story to essay; Reading and writing. *College Composition and Communication, 33,* 1, 19–36.

PROFESSIONAL BASEBALL PLAYING RULES COMMITTEE (1987). *Official baseball rules.* New York: The Times Mirror Company.

RATEKIN, N., SIMPSON, M., ALVERMANN, D., & DISHNER, E. (1985). Why teachers resist content reading instruction. *Journal of Reading, 28,* 5, 432–437.

SEDLAK, M., WHEELER, C., PULLIN, D., & CUSICK, P. (1986). *Selling students short: Classroom bargains and academic reform in the American High School.* New York: Teachers College Press.

SINGER, H. (1979). Slogans and attitudes. *Journal of Reading, 22,* 8, pp. 756–757.

SINGER, H., & DONLAN, D. (1980). *Reading and learning from text.* Boston: Little, Brown.

SQUIRE, J. (1984). Composing and comprehending: Two sides of the same basic process. In J. Jenson (Ed.), *Composing and comprehending.* Urbana, IL: ERIC Clearinghouse on Reading and Communication Skills and the National Conference on Research in English.

Section II

Assessing Textbooks, the Reading Process, and Student Motivation

Whenever you plan a lesson, gaps exist between the information found in textbooks and what students are ready and willing to learn. For some lessons, the information is complex and unfamiliar and students are less than motivated. These situations call for substantial preteaching and guidance. For other lessons, the information is easily accessible and students want to learn. These situations allow instead an emphasis on critical thinking.

Three factors influence the size of gaps between textbooks and students: characteristics of textbooks (Chapter 2), what students know about the reading process (Chapter 3), and student motivation (Chapter 4). The purpose of this section is to help teachers understand and assess these factors so that gaps can be reduced. Instruction is the vehicle for reducing gaps and is the subject of Chapter 5.

At the end of this section, you should be able to tell how knowledge about texts, students, and instruction can be used to guide planning decisions. In addition, you should be able to answer the following questions:

1. What makes textbooks and other kinds of reading difficult?

2. What factors influence whether or not students can or will read?

3. What is instruction? What are some ways to plan content reading instruction to develop independence in students' understanding of content, their knowledge about the reading process, and their motivation?

QUESTION: What makes reading hard or easy?

"Some reading is hard because of the way the author chose to write the book."

"When you have the knowledge, it is always easy."

"The *big* words make it hard."

"Reading is easy when you are interested in what you are reading and you understand the words they are using. If I am not interested in what I am reading, it's a littler harder."

"Reading is hard and easy. It depends on what subject you are reading."

Responses of a seventh-grade science class.

2

Using and Assessing Textbooks

CHAPTER OBJECTIVES

After reading this chapter, you should be able to:

1. Describe various purposes of texts and other content materials and what makes them difficult for students.

2. Estimate the difficulty and potential of a content area text with a specific group of students in mind.

RATIONALE

The picture most people have of school *texts* (short for *textbooks*) is large, hardcover books such as literature anthologies or science books. In this book, "texts" are printed material of any length that teachers use to teach content, including newspapers, magazines, and paperbacks as well as how-to manuals and various kinds of documents, such as forms to fill out or schedules to follow.

When planning to teach, most content teachers start by thinking about texts, not about reading or reading instruction (Hinchman, 1985). It's not that teachers don't care about reading or the reading needs of their students, but the reading of texts is important for achieving an important end: helping students comprehend course content.

In the past, frequent attempts have been made by researchers to help teachers use textbooks more effectively. Many of these efforts are based on the concept of *readability*, which refers to the level of difficulty students experience in comprehending a textbook or other type of reading material (Klare, 1984).

More recently, the concepts *friendly text* and *inconsiderate text* have entered the discussion. These terms emphasize the two-way communication between readers and textbooks: the reader attempts to construct meaning from the text, and the text contains features that more or less communicate an author's message. Friendly texts contain features that enhance this communication; inconsiderate texts contain features that interfere (Anderson & Armbruster, 1984).

The implications of these concepts—readability, and friendly versus inconsiderate texts—are controversial. To some people, texts must be made more readable so that students can spend more time reading and less time struggling to gain access to the content (Anderson & Armbruster, 1984). To others, inconsiderate texts are a fact of life, and teachers need to show students how to read them (Herber, 1984). Between these two

CHAPTER ORGANIZER

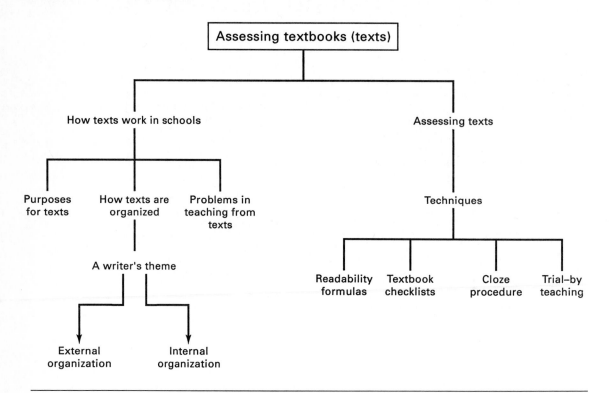

points of view lie the decisions classroom teachers must make about the best ways to teach course content and for what reasons.

This chapter introduces many issues surrounding the use of texts, demonstrates ways to predict how students will react to texts, and tells how you can get ready to reduce gaps between texts and students.

HOW TEXTS WORK IN SCHOOLS

This section describes how texts work both in the ideal, (what teachers hope for) and in real classrooms (when teachers are faced with everyday constraints). It begins with a discussion of the *purposes* of texts. Next, the *organization* of texts is explained. Finally, specific problems in teaching from texts are examined.

The Purposes of Texts

Texts, through their role in developing knowledge in content areas, potentially contribute to many important purposes. Purposes for reading in different content areas are set according to differences in knowledge and ways in which knowledge gets used and

Laima Druskis/Photo Researchers

Texts serve many different purposes in school

applied. Purposes for texts in various content areas are suggested in Figure 2.1. The identification of these purposes is the result of recent research exploring the types of knowledge teachers need for using texts effectively (Anderson & Roth, 1989; Grossman, 1987; Parsons, 1987; Schoenfeld, 1986; Wilson & Wineburg, 1988).

In Figure 2.1 notice how the purposes in each content area stress learning beyond the factual level, the kind of learning characterized as "high literacy" with an emphasis on problem solving and making real-world connections (Bereiter & Scardamalia, 1987). These purposes reflect a new commitment to make learning school subjects meaningful in school and beyond. In school, texts should serve as vehicles for comprehension, as a means for achieving higher-level understandings; they should not exist as the central focus of instruction. Reading and writing based on texts can serve to develop both deep subject-matter understanding (comprehension of subject-specific purposes) and interdisciplinary connections (awareness of how various subject-matter purposes interrelate) (McGinley & Tierney, 1989).

Texts can promote lifelong learning, encourage responsibility and equality of educational opportunity, offer particular types of knowledge, and impart specific skills. These goals probably transcend the comprehension of any single text. Rather, both teachers and students need to apply a variety of texts in a variety of ways (Shulman, 1987).

The purposes of texts described here lay the groundwork for the exciting and relevant school curriculum envisioned by Soreson (1978): students in social studies viewing

FIGURE 2.1

Purposes of Texts in School Subjects

Social Studies

Describing the human world

—Making facts and concepts meaningful within a historical context

Explaining social and historical patterns

—Exploring chronlogical patterns and causation

Acting in social contexts

—Functioning as a socially responsible person, a worker and consumer, and a citizen

Mathematics

Comprehending symbols and problems

—Attaching meaning to symbols; giving reasons for procedures; evaluating reasonableness of answers

Doing calculations or solving problems

—Performing mathematical operations

Using mathematical knowledge

—Seeing real-world applications

Appreciating mathematical knowledge

—Engaging in mathematics as a reasonable, rather than arbitrary, activity; enjoying the discovery of mathematical patterns

Science

Describing real-world objects, systems, or phenomena

—Classifying, measuring, examining systems and subsystems

Explaining real-world objects, systems, or phenomena

—Using scientific laws or theories

Predicting future observations

—Speculating through science and past observation

Controlling real-world objects, systems, or phenomena

—Taking responsibility for the environment; applying technology to improve upon natural phenomena

English (purposes of literature and writing)

Reporting information (exposition) and telling stories (narrative)

—Using language to comprehend and communicate

Explaining human characteristics and behavior

—Comparing actions and motivation; exploring the influence of setting and of characters on each other; seeing recurring patterns in literature and human behavior

Applying reading and writing in meaningful contexts

—Seeing personal and real-world connections; developing imagination

Persuading others or helping them to understand a point of view

—Establishing and communicating goals; providing objective support for arguments

Physical Education

Contributing to motor, cognitive, and social development

—Developing exercise, health, and moral concepts

Building skills in a variety of physical activities

—Illustrating competitive and noncompetitive skills

Encouraging lifelong health and fitness

—Understanding the value of weight control and physical activity

FIGURE 2.1 *(Cont.)*

Art and Music

Fostering interpretations of art and music based on personal experience

—Relating paintings and musical compositions to experience and feeling

Perceiving art and music in terms of human themes and social contexts

—Seeing art and music as reflections on life and society

Understanding aesthetics—beauty and quality—in art and music

—Developing objectivity and appreciation

Vocational Education

Knowing the names and functions of various tools

—Relating tools to the jobs that are performed

Integrating knowledge and skill

—Interpreting a work situation or job; responding with the appropriate knowledge and skill

Adapting to changes in the workplace

—Building the ability to learn more in the face of changing working conditions

Foreign Languages

Developing facility with the technical aspects of language

—Knowing how languages are structured

Improving communicative competence with languages

—Building the ability to use languages to make meaning

Increasing cultural awareness and appreciation

—Making connections between language and culture

Source: Many of these subject-matter purposes were originally conceived by faculty and staff of the Academic Learning teacher preparation program at Michigan State University.

---

opposing perspectives on the same historical period, writing their own histories; science students posing problems apart from the text and obtaining and interpreting data; physical education students making up rules and playing their own invented games. For this vision to be realized, however, teachers need to understand clearly how texts are organized and the problems associated with teaching from texts.

The Organization of Texts

The *organization* of a text consists of a writer's theme and the external as well as the internal features of a text. Well-organized texts provide a good foundation for purposeful teaching. Poorly organized texts are frustrating because of the effort it takes to construct meaning from them: the more incoherent and confusing the organization, the more the reader (and teachers) must struggle. With a well-organized text, students read with a minimum of effort and few misconceptions, provided, of course, that students know something about the topic and are motivated. (These student-related factors are discussed in Chapters 3 and 4).

The following sections explain how texts are organized and how text organization affects what students come to understand.

A Writer's Theme   Most well-organized texts adhere to some overarching *theme*. A theme is a generalization that serves to relate or unify large chunks of text information (Bisanz et al., 1978). Themes hold together the facts and concepts, characteristics, and events a writer wants to convey (Calfee & Chambliss, 1987).

Good writers use themes to organize their knowledge. For example, suppose a historian decides to write a chapter about the Civil War. The historian knows generally how wars start. He or she also knows the specific causes and events leading up to the actual war. In writing about the Civil War, the historian could decided to develop this theme:

> The Civil War was fought because of economic, social, and political differences between the North and the South.

Another writer might be concerned about physical conditioning. He or she wants to stress low-impact exercises that improve the conditioning of the heart as opposed to aggressive, high-impact exercises that sometimes cause injuries to the legs and feet. In writing a book, this writer might be guided by this theme:

> Brisk walking can be a more beneficial aerobic exercise than jogging.

Through themes, different writers choose to emphasize different kinds of knowledge for different purposes.

Sometimes good writers state their themes at the beginning of a text; other times, they state themes explicitly in a later paragraph. *Explicit themes* announce what the passage will explain, document, or elaborate. Sometimes, themes appear as questions that the text will answer. Once identified, themes help readers make predictions about upcoming text content. When themes are clearly spelled out in a text, both good and poor readers tend to comprehend more effectively (Moes et al., 1984).

In some cases, themes are not stated explicitly. *Implicit themes* (themes that are not directly stated) are found most often in stories but sometimes in informational material presented in list form (for instance, lists of chemicals, formulas, tools). When themes are implicit, students are forced to come up with their own way of organizing the text information. Finding a theme (as opposed to identifying one that is already in the text) makes reading much more difficult. Students have few clues as to the importance of various kinds of text information. They lack an organizing framework for remembering large chunks of text. When students experience difficulty in identifying an author's theme, it is often because the theme is buried in the complex concepts and structure of a text (Hare, Rabinowitz, & Schieble, 1989).

Text writers do not always build themes in ways that assist students with their reading. Some writers spend so much time giving background information that they fail to develop and elaborate upon a clear theme throughout the text. Other writers present a theme at the outset, but stray so much from the main point that their writing becomes nearly incomprehensible (Cox & Kazarian, 1985).

Fortunately, as students get older, they tend to get better at generalizing from their reading and identifying themes on their own (Lehr, 1988). Teachers can be enormously helpful in making students aware of the importance of themes, how to recognize themes when they are stated explicitly, and how to construct themes when they are implicit. When students are taught about the theme of a text before they read, their ability to comprehend and recall information increases (Risko and Alverez, 1986).

A Text's External Organization   A text's *external organization* consists of the format and design features that help communicate the author's theme: the headings, section breaks, and paragraphs that make up the text. External organization also includes such features as the preface, table of contents, appendixes, bibliography, and index. In addition, some texts use maps, graphs, charts, illustrations, and review questions. Obviously, not all texts take advantage of these features. Well-organized texts use these elements in ways that are consistent with the writer's overall theme.

External features like headings can help students discriminate between important and less important content (Hare & Lomax, 1985). For example, look at the headings in the texts in Figure 2.2. What does the heading structure tell you about how the information in each text has been organized? Notice how headings from the history text are organized to depict many different, complex ideas. The physical education text uses a very simple heading structure to contrast different physical activities.

Other external features can pose some significant problems for students. For example, the details on some graphs are difficult to read or interpret. Some charts contain confusing information that is not explained well by the accompanying textual information. Many students do not know how to integrate maps or illustrations into their text reading. Others are unaware of the value of a glossary or index.

Teachers need to help students make the best use of external text features. Early in the school year, teachers should familiarize students with the table of contents, index, and glossary of a text. Teachers can model ways to answer review questions as well as ways to use illustrations, charts, and graphs as students encounter them (Reinking, 1986). When students gain an understanding of the content of a text, teachers can ask them to come up with other ways of organizing textual information. By taking time to teach external text features, teachers build students' independence in using texts.

FIGURE 2.2

Examples of the external organization of texts (heading structure)

History Text	*Physical Education Text*
"The Civil War and Reconstruction"	"Games for Two"
Comparison with the Revolutionary War	High Activity
Strategy: Naval Operations	Toe Fencing
The War in the West	Medium Activity
The War in the East	Quick Draw
Behind the Lines	Low Activity
Government in Wartime	This Is My Nose

Source: History text from H. Bragdon and S. McCutchen (1981). *History of a free people.* New York: Macmillan. Physical education text from the New Games Foundation (1981). *More new games.* New York: Doubleday.

A Text's Internal Organization   The internal organization of a text consists of *facts* and *concepts,* and their relationship and organization within various kinds of texts.

Facts are records of events (Novak & Gowan, 1984). An event can be a chemical reaction, the playing of a clarinet, or the writing of a short story. Contrary to what many people think, facts are only as reliable as the persons or instruments that record events. For example, many a school science experiment goes awry when the instrumentation fails to record the facts.

A *concept* describes a relationship among facts. For instance, "respiration" is a concept that describes many different ways that organisms get oxygen to living cells. Another concept, "causes of war," draws together historical, social, and economic forces that contribute to wars and invites comparisons from one war to another. In texts, facts typically change from chapter to chapter, but concepts show up again and again. As Novak (1977) suggests, "concepts are what we think with" (p. 18). Concepts are what readers and writers use to cluster and categorize, to make sense of the world and communicate.

The arrangement of facts and concepts in a text can make a big difference in what students eventually understand. At the sentence level, the *syntax* (ordering and grammatical function of words and phrases) can influence the difficulty of a text. For example, compare the following sentences:

1. The economy of many third world countries depends on economic and social conditions in other parts of the world.
2. Third world country economics depends on other parts of the world and social and economic conditions.

While the first sentence conveys a fairly complex set of ideas, it does so in a straightforward, unambiguous manner. The second sentence, constructed from the same words as the first, loads up concepts so that two or three words affect the eventual meaning of a fourth (for instance, "third world country economics"). Notice how changing the phrasing of the latter half of the second sentence changes both the meaning and the difficulty of the sentence.

At the paragraph or passage level, other important text features hold facts and concepts together and help the reader learn and remember. For example, good writers use *cohesive ties,* words like "because," "therefore," and "however," which tell how a text is organized. Many writers pay special attention to building some *redundancy* into texts, repeating important facts and concepts often within transitions and summaries. Without the special kind of help that comes from cohesive ties and well-written transitions and summaries, texts can be exceptionally difficult to comprehend.

Facts and concepts are organized differently in relation to one another in *expository* (informational) materials found in most science, mathematics, and vocational education texts when compared with *narrative* (story-type) materials found in English anthologies and history texts, and accompanying some musical compositions. Well-written *expository* texts inform or persuade. To accomplish these purposes, writers organize information hierarchically, so that more important, broader concepts typically come before less important, specific facts (Meyer, Brandt, & Bluth, 1980). Within this hierarchy, writers also use the following *text patterns* (ways of relating facts and concepts to one another) to communicate a theme:

Cause-effect: Explaining how facts and concepts (as effects) are caused by other facts and concepts

Compare-contrast: Noting similarities and differences among facts and concepts

Time order: Sequencing or ordering facts and concepts

Enumeration: Listing information so that later facts and concepts explain and elaborate on earlier facts and concepts

Examples of these patterns appear in Figure 2.3. The patterns can be signaled by specific words, such as "because" (cause-effect), "different from" (compare-contrast), "before" (time order), and "most important" (enumeration). Good readers know how to use these cues to build meaning from a text (Spyridakis & Standal, 1987). Notice in Figure 2.3 how facts and concepts build on one another to develop these patterns.

Well-written *narrative* texts are organized to tell a story. To accomplish this purpose, story writers organize information hierarchically, and the hierarchy is composed of basic story elements (Mandler & Johnson, 1977; Thorndyke, 1977). These elements include:

Setting: The environment in which the story occurs

Episodes: Sequences of events, including an initiating event, an internal response, an attempt, a consequence, and a reaction

>*Initiating event:* An event or an action that prompts a main character to achieve a goal
>
>*Internal response:* A main character's inner reaction or desire in response to the initiating event
>
>*Attempt:* Overt actions carried out by a main character to achieve a goal
>
>*Consequence:* The result of a main character's actions (either achieves or does not achieve the goal)
>
>*Reaction:* Emotions or actions that result from achieving or failing to achieve the goal

Figure 2.4 presents a map of the story elements for "To Build a Fire," a story about a man's unsuccessful struggle for survival in the Arctic wilderness. Note that in the hierarchy of a story, different story elements are combined to construct a theme. Taken together, story elements reflect the ideal internal organization of narrative texts.

Problems in Teaching from Texts

Problems in teaching from texts can be traced to three sources: problems in texts, readers' past negative experiences with texts, and problems in ways texts are used.

Problems in teaching from texts often come from missing or overly implicit themes and confusing external text features and internal patterns. The best of readers can falter when texts are disorganized and inconsistent. Expository texts tend to be more difficult for readers to comprehend than narrative texts. Expository texts are often written in an impersonal tone, with authors sometimes more intent on presenting information than making connections. In comparison with narrative writers, expository writers are also

FIGURE 2.3

Hierarchical Patterns in Expository Tests

	Cause-Effect Pattern: Social Studies
Main concept	The Civil War was fought because of economic, social, and political differences between the North and the South.
Supporting concept	Because slavery supported the economy of the South, the South was reluctant to abolish it.
Fact	John Brown led a slave revolt at Harper's Ferry.
	Compare-Contrast Pattern: Science
Main concept	Vertebrates are different in structure when compared with invertebrates.
Supporting concept	Unlike invertebrates, vertebrates have backbones.
Fact	Humans and frogs have backbones.
	Time Order Pattern: Mathematics
Main concept	When solving an equation, the student needs to perform some operations before others.
Supporting concept	Perform the operations in parentheses first.
Fact	$25/4 = 6.375$
	Enumeration Pattern: Vocational Equation
Main concept	Most important, you have to keep a cool head and use what you know about first aid to ensure shop safety.
Supporting concept	You must get the injured worker stabilized and out of danger.
Fact	Pressure applied to a wound stops bleeding.

---

more likely to employ complex and changing organizational patterns. Narrative writers usually do a better job building concepts across lengthy passages (Perera, 1986).

Another problem in teaching from texts relates to students, because many students have limited exposure to different kinds of texts. Up until the middle school years, students spend most of their time reading narrative texts while getting few opportunities to read expository texts (Schmidt et al., 1984). Later chapters in this book provide teaching techniques that broaden readers' experiences with various kinds of texts.

Problems in teaching from texts also come from the ways teachers use texts. Many teachers overemphasize texts. Intentionally or unintentionally, teachers can become so focused on texts that higher-level themes and purposes are sacrificed. Research has

FIGURE 2.4

Hierarchical Story Structure

	Story: To Build a Fire
	Author: Jack London
Theme:	A law of nature is "survival of the fittest."
Setting:	Arctic Alaska
Episode:	A man and his dog brave sub-Arctic temperatures but the man loses his chance to survive when he fails to build a fire.
Initiating event:	The man breaks through some ice and gets wet on his way back to camp.
Internal response:	He curses his luck.
Attempt:	He tries to build a fire and dry out his footgear.
Consequence:	A tree bough dumps snow on the burning fire and he can't get the fire going again.
Reaction:	The man grows delirious and freezes to death. His dog survives and moves off to find the camp.

As students get older, they become confronted with many kinds of texts

Mark Antman/The Image Works

demonstrated that teachers rarely cover topics not found in texts, while topics included in a text are rarely omitted (Stodolsky, 1988). Reasons for this range from school district mandates to situations where teachers may not feel knowledgeable about a subject (O'Brien & Steward, 1990). Whatever the reason, the tendency is to rely on texts exclusively even when the texts have some serious shortcomings (Stodolsky, 1988).

Some teachers rush through texts without making sure that students develop more than a factual understanding. In a study of how teachers use texts, one teacher voiced a preference for "controlled" discussions, discussions in which the text is used to refocus attention, as opposed to discussions where students explore different sides of an issue (Alvermann, 1986). By using texts this way, teachers virtually guarantee only a factual understanding of a text. Motivation suffers when students are not afforded opportunities to apply their reading in a meaningful way or develop a critical point of view.

Teachers who are knowledgeable about a subject and their texts can overcome these problems and make good instructional decisions. Knowledgeable teachers do not view all text topics as equally important. They tend to pay attention to the content and organization of a text as well as to their students' level of understanding. Because texts sometimes omit essential information, knowledgeable teachers can compensate by selecting from and supplementing a text (Wilson & Wineburg, 1988).

Teachers need to know as much as they can about their subjects and their texts in order to overcome the problems described here. This entails going beyond the mechanical or the factual, learning how to assess texts, and then using them selectively.

ASSESSING TEXTS

Assessing texts is crucial for day-to-day planning and teaching. Teachers who have assessed their texts can compensate instructionally for organizational problems or students' inexperience with texts. Text assessment also helps teachers select more readable texts. In order for teachers to select the most readable texts and use them for daily instructions, teachers must know the potential purposes of those texts, their organization, and the probable ease or difficulty with which students can use texts to construct meaning. There are many factors to consider and many ways to consider them.

The following sections discuss and illustrate various ways to assess texts, including the use of: (1) *readability formulas,* (2) *textbook checklists,* (3) the *CLOZE procedure,* and (4) *trial-by-teaching.*

Readability Formulas

Readability formulas provide estimates of difficulty primarily confined to measurements of word and sentence length. In the past, readability formulas have been used extensively for text selection (Klare, 1984).

Most readability formulas are based on the simple idea that longer words and sentences are more difficult than shorter words and sentences. Another criterion concerns the frequency of uncommon versus common words. Passages with uncommon words (like "newton-meter") are viewed as more complex than passages with many common words (like "energy").

This section offers practice using two standard readability formulas, the *Fry Graph* and the *Raygor Readability Estimate.* Each formula is described and illustrated and then followed by a few words of caution.

The Fry Readability Graph   The Fry Readability Graph (or Fry Graph) is one of the most widely used formulas for estimating readability in both business and education (Fry, 1977). The graph is based on word length and sentence length. Word length is determined by the number of syllables in a sample passage. Sentence length is determined by the number of sentences in a sample passage. Usually, three (or more) sample passages are used to calculate readability. More passages are used if a great deal of variability appears in the sample passages. An average of word and sentence length is determined across all the sample passages and then compared to the readability graph. The Fry Graph and directions for its use appear in Figure 2.5.

The Raygor Readability Estimate   Alton Raygor (1977) devised a reliable and easy way to estimate readability. While other formulas involve more complex calculations, such as syllable counts (for example, the Fry graph), or comparisons between texts and extensive word lists (for example, the Dale-Chall Readability Formula, 1948), the Raygor calculates only the number of long words and the length of sentences. The number of long words is determined by counting all words having six or more letters. Sentence length is determined in the same way as the Fry. An average of the number of long words and the average length of sentences is calculated across three sample passages and then applied to the Raygor graph to find the readability.

In a study comparing the Fry with the Raygor, it was found that the Raygor takes less time and is simpler without sacrificing accuracy (Baldwin & Kaufman, 1979). The Raygor Estimate appears in Figure 2.6.

Words of Caution   Readability formulas are only *rough* estimates of how readable a text is. They measure some aspects of difficulty, but neglect many factors that influence readability. For example, a readability formula would classify the following short sentence as readable, even though it is not particularly easy to understand (from Marshall, 1979, p. 543):

There was a run on the bank.

Readability formulas do not say much about the complexity of the content or the prior knowledge or motivation the reader brings to the text (Campbell, 1979; Clewell & Clifton, 1983).

Publishers use readability formulas to rewrite texts to make them more readable. To do this, they shorten words and sentences. This practice does not guarantee the result will

FIGURE 2.5

Fry Readability Graph

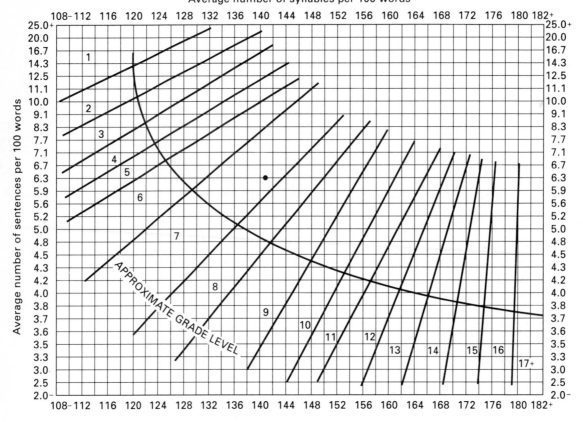

Directions for Administration

1. Count out three 100-word passages at the beginning, middle, and end of a text selection. *Do* count proper nouns, initials, and numbers. (A word is defined as a group of symbols with space on either side, so Mark, JRB, 1990, and & are each counted as one word. A syllable is a pronounced syllable. Therefore, 1990 has four syllables and & has one syllable.)
2. Count the number of sentences in each 100-word passage, estimating to the nearest tenth for partial sentences.
3. Count the total number of syllables in each 100-word passage. An easy way to count is to put a mark above every syllable over one in each word.
4. Enter the graph with the average number of sentences and the average number of syllables for the three samples. Plot the point where the averages intersect on the graph. The grade level nearest the spot marked is the best estimate of the difficulty of the selection.

Example:

Passage	Sentences	6+ Words
A	6.0	15
B	6.8	19
C	6.4	17
Total	19.2	51
Average	6.4	17

Note mark on graph. Grade level is about 5.

Source: S. Baldwin & R. Kaufman (1979). A concurrent validity study of the Raygor Readability Estimate. *Journal of Reading, 23,* 148–153. This graph is not copyrighted.

---

be any less complex or confusing. Compare the original and the rewritten sentences below:

Original

The triangle is a right triangle because it has one 90° angle.

Rewritten

The triangle is a right triangle. It has one 90° angle.

The rewritten version contains shorter sentences yet omits an important connection (the defining relationship between right triangles and 90° angles) which the reader has to supply. Ironically, when texts are revised according to the results of readability formulas, readability usually suffers; readers must work harder to fill in the gaps (Davison, 1984). Text revisions based on readability formulas can also seriously distort content concepts. For example, any scientist would cringe when reading this description of a cell (from Armbruster, Osborn, & Davison, 1985, p. 20):

A cell is made of living stuff. A cell can grow. It takes in food. It changes the food into more living stuff. . . .

To deal with these shortcomings—and place readability formulas in proper perspective—Joan Nelson-Herber (1985) offers the following guidelines:

1. Learn to use a simple readability formula as an aid in evaluating text material for student use.

2. Wherever possible, provide text materials containing the essential facts, concepts, and values of the subject at varying levels of readability within the range of the students.

3. Don't assume that matching readability level of material to reading achievement level of students results in automatic comprehension.

FIGURE 2.6

Raygor Readability Estimate

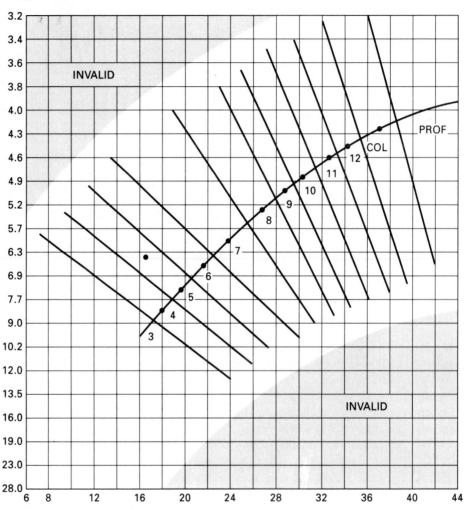

Directions for Administration

1. Count out three 100-word passages at the beginning, middle, and end of a text selection. Count proper nouns but not numbers.
2. Count the number of sentences in each 100-word passage, estimating to the nearest tenth for partial sentences.
3. Count the number of words with six or more letters.
4. Average the sentence length and word length measures over the three samples and plot the average on the graph. The grade level nearest the spot marked is the best estimate of the difficulty of the selection.

Example:

Passage	Sentences	6+ Words
A	6.0	15
B	6.8	19
C	6.4	17
Total	19.2	51
Average	6.4	17

Note mark on graph. Grade level is about 5.

Source: S. Baldwin & R. Kaufman (1979). A concurrent validity study of the Raygor Readability Estimate. *Journal of Reading, 23,* 148–153. This graph is not copyrighted.

---

4. Don't assume that rewriting text materials according to readability criteria results in automatic reading ease.

5. Recognize that using a readability formula is no substitute for instruction.

A Textbook Checklist

Textbook checklists are the primary vehicle for assessing many of the factors that readability formulas ignore, including the compatibility between a reader's prior knowledge and the concepts found in a text, the way new concepts are introduced, the clarity of a text's organization, and whether or not the text is motivating (Irwin & Davis, 1980). This section presents one example of a textbook checklist, the *Irwin-Davis Readability Checklist* (see Figure 2.7).

The Irwin-Davis Checklist consists of thirty-six questions. In response to each question, a teacher rates a text on a scale of 1 to 5. The scores are then summarized and analyzed to inform teaching decisions or decisions about the appropriateness of a text. Questions appearing on the checklist are research-based and cover an entire range of external as well as internal text features. The questions are grouped under four headings:

1. *Understandability.* Fourteen questions address
   a. The match between students' prior knowledge and the text information
   b. Ways in which new concepts are presented and defined
   c. The clarity of headings, sentence complexity, the presence of irrelevant details
   d. The quality of teachers' manuals
2. *Learnability.* Six questions address the degree to which the text has been organized to help students learn and remember.
3. *Reinforcement.* Nine questions concern opportunities for practice, summarizing, and creative thinking in texts and supplementary materials.
4. *Motivation.* Seven questions focus on motivation issues, such as the availability of interesting and relevant activities, the potential for applying text information, and the range of appealing role models.

FIGURE 2.7

The Irwin-Davis Readability Checklist

Textbook Title _____

Publisher _____

Copyright Date _____

Directions: This checklist is designed to help you evaluate the readability of your classroom texts. It can best be used if you rate your text while you are thinking of a specific class. Be sure to compare the textbook to a fictional ideal rather than to another text. Your goal is to find out what aspects of the text are or are not less than ideal. Finally, consider supplementary workbooks as part of the textbook and rate them together. Have fun!

Rate the questions below using the following rating sytem:

5 - Excellent
4 - Good
3 - Adequate
2 - Poor
1 - Unacceptable
NA - Not applicable

Understandability

A. _____ Are the assumptions about students' vocabulary knowledge appropriate?

B. _____ Are the assumptions about students' prior knowledge of this content area appropriate?

C. _____ Are the assumptions about students' general experiential backgrounds appropriate?

D. _____ Does the teacher's manual provide the teacher with ways to develop and review students' conceptual and experiential backgrounds?

E. _____ Are new concepts explicitly linked to the students' prior knowledge or to their experiential backgrounds?

F. _____ Does the text introduce abstract concepts by accompanying them with many concrete examples?

G. _____ Does the text introduce new concepts one at time with a sufficient number of examples for each one?

H. _____ Are definitions understandable and at a lower level of abstraction than the concept being defined?

I. _____ Is the level of sentence complexity appropriate for the students?

J. _____ Are the main ideas of paragraphs, chapters, and subsections clearly stated?

K. _____ Does the text avoid irrelevant details?

L. _____ Does the text explicitly state important complex relationships (e.g., causality, conditionality, etc.) rather than always expecting the reader to infer them from the context?

M. _____ Does the teacher's manual provide lists of accessible resources containing alternative readings for the very poor or very advanced readers?

N. _____ Is the readability level appropriate (according to a readability formula)?

Learnability

A. _____ Is an introduction provided for in each chapter?

B. _____ Is there a clear and simple organizational pattern relating the chapters to each other?

C. _____ Does each chapter have a clear, explicit, and simple organizational structure?

D. _____ Does the text include resources such as an index, glossary, and table of contents?

E. _____ Do questions and activities draw attention to the organizational pattern of the material (e.g., chronological, cause and effect, spatial, topical, etc.)?

F. _____ Do consumable materials interrelate well within the textbook?

Reinforcement

A. _____ Does the text provide opportunities for students to practice using new concepts?

B. _____ Are there summaries at appropriate intervals in the text?

C. _____ Does the text provide adequate iconic aids such as maps, graphs, illustrations, etc. to reinforce concepts?

D. _____ Are there adequate suggestions for usable supplementary activities?

E. _____ Do these activities provide for a broad range of ability levels?

F. _____ Are there literal recall questions provided for the students' self-review?

G. _____ Do some of the questions encourage the students to draw inferences?

H. _____ Are there discussion questions which encourage creative thinking?

I. _____ Are questions clearly worded?

Motivation

A. _____ Does the teacher's manual provide introductory activities that will capture students' interest?

B. _____ Are chapter titles and subheadings concrete, meaningful, or interesting?

C. _____ Is the writing style of the text appealing to the students?

D. _____ Are the activities motivating? Will they make the student want to pursue the topic further?

E. _____ Does the book clearly show how the knowledge being learned might be used by the learner in the future?

F. _____ Are the cover, format, print size, and pictures appealing to the students?

G. _____ Does the text provide positive and motivating models for both sexes as well as other racial, ethnic, and socioeconomic groups?

Readability Analysis: Summary

Weaknesses
1. On which items was the book rated the lowest?
2. Did these items tend to fall into certain categories?
3. Summarize the weaknesses of this text.
4. What can you do in class to compensate for the weaknesses of this text?

Assets
1. On which items was the book rated the highest?
2. Did these items fall into certain categories?

FIGURE 2.7 *(Cont.)*

3. Summarize the assets of this text.
4. What can you do in class to take advantage of the assets of this text?

Source: J. Irwin & C. Davis (1980). Assessing readability: The checklist approach. *Journal of Reading, 24,* 2, 129–130. Copyright 1980 by the International Reading Association. Reprinted with permission of Judith W. Irwin and the International Reading Association.

Words of Caution   Textbook checklists are an improvement over readability formulas in that they begin to take into account the relationship between reader and text. Checklists, however, can be subjective. It is possible to fixate on less crucial aspects of texts (for example, whether or not a chapter has headings) rather than more important ones (for example, whether or not chapter headings are clear enough to help a reader build ideas). Checklists also offer no guarantee about how students will actually respond to a text. Texts that are clearly organized and appropriate to a teacher may be overly complex and incoherent to students.

It is important to recognize these shortcomings and not rely on checklists. Any attempt to gather information about texts is incomplete without feedback from students.

CLOZE *Procedure*

In the *CLOZE procedure,* words are systematically deleted from a passage and readers supply the missing words. Taylor (1953) originally coined the term "CLOZE" to express how readers naturally bring to "closure" passages in which words have been deleted. An advantage of this technique over others is that teachers can directly obtain information about students' understandings of a text.

The CLOZE procedure has four stages: (1) preparation of the text, (2) administration, (3) scoring, and (4) interpretation (Pikulski & Tobin, 1982). Specific steps within each stage are detailed in Figure 2.8.

Words of Caution   The CLOZE procedure incorporates the central factors responsible for difficulty in reading: the reader and the text. However, because of this, it is not always easy to decide how to interpret information based on these measures. What appears to be a problem with text could be a problem in the reader's interpretation. What appears to be a problem may not be a problem at all. Like the textbook checklist, CLOZE suffers from a certain amount of subjectivity.

For example, compare the student responses to the sentence below in which one word has been deleted, as in the CLOZE procedure:

purple

You have learned that energy is the ability to do _____.

movement

FIGURE 2.8

The CLOZE Procedure

Preparation of the Text

1. Select a passage of approximately 250–300 words. This passage should a,
   to be representative or typical of the content of the book. If a book become
   progressively more difficult, try to select a passage from the second quarter
   the book.
2. Inspect the passage to ensure that it is not heavily dependent on information
   presented earlier in the text. If it contains a number of anaphoric words or
   phrases (e.g., it, this, these, points) which have referents found only in earlier
   sections of the text, another passage should be selected.
3. Keep intact the first and last sentences.
4. Randomly choose one of the first five words in the second sentence. Beginning
   with this word, omit every fifth word until 50 words have been deleted. A word
   is defined as any group of letters set off by spaces. Thus, a number such as
   1980 should be deleted as if it were a single word. However, hyphenated words
   are generally considered two separate words (e.g., three-dimensional), except in
   instances where the prefix cannot stand alone (e.g., co-opt).

Administration

5. If students have had no previous experience with CLOZE, it is advisable to do a
   practice exercise.
6. Explain the task to students, directing them to read all of the sentences before
   they try to fill in the blanks.
7. Students should be encouraged to work as long as they please, though you
   may wish to set a time limit when it appears that students' efforts are no longer
   productive.

Scoring

8. Count as correct every exact word students supply. Do not count synonyms
   since it will affect the reliability of the scores and cause needless argument over
   the scores.
9. Multiply the number correct by 2 to obtain the CLOZE percentage score.

Interpretation

10. Students who obtain CLOZE scores of at least 50 percent are at an
    independent level in relation to the material. They should be able to read the
    material with relative ease. No teacher guidance should be necessary.
    Consequently, the material should be appropriate for homework assignments
    and other types of independent projects.
11. Students scoring between 30 and 50 percent are at an *instructional* level in
    relation to the material. They should be able to use the material for
    instructional purposes. However, some guidance may be necessary to help
    them master the demands of the material.

FIGURE 2.8 *(Cont.)*

12. Students having scores of less than 30 percent are at a *frustration* level in relation to the material. They will usually find the material much too challenging. Since there is almost no potential for success, the material should definitely be avoided.

Source: J. Pikulski & A. Tobin (1982). The Cloze Procedure as an informal assessment technique. In J. Pikulski and T. Shanahan (Eds.), *Approaches to the informal evaluation of reading.* Newark, DE: International Reading Association.

In teaching a unit on energy, a teacher would be pleased if students placed "work" in the blank (this is the classic definition of energy). The teacher would undoubtedly be very concerned about students who placed "purple" in the blank because their response signals not only unfamiliarity with the content, but also a lack of knowledge about how language is organized.

What about students who insert the word "movement"? According to the CLOZE procedure, the answer would be incorrect. But the answer reveals some understanding of the concepts underlying energy. What looks like a problem may actually become useful prior knowledge in a lesson.

Another concern is the relationship between the CLOZE procedure and classroom practice. CLOZE resembles few, if any, classroom practices content area teachers use to help students gain meaning from texts. Students in content area classes are rarely exposed to text passages that have been systematically altered by deleting words, and they are rarely asked to fill in blanked-out slots in their texts. CLOZE is particularly weak in offering information about how students read beyond the sentence level (Shanahan, Kamil, & Tobin, 1982). CLOZE also is not appropriate for making decisions about individual students. Consequently, it is unfair to use results from CLOZE to make predictions about what individual students may do with texts under all sorts of instructional conditions.

Trial-by-Teaching

In *trial-by-teaching,* teachers teach text-based lessons and directly observe and analyze their students' experiences in reading and comprehending. Trial-by-teaching offers insight into how readers construct meaning from a particular text, information that is invaluable for making planning and teaching decisions.

Trial-by-teaching involves making observations, conducting interviews, and collecting student work samples (Moore, 1984). Each of these methods is described briefly.

Observations Teachers can gather a great deal of rich information about students and their work with texts through *observations*. Prime opportunities for observation occur when students are reading a text, completing text activities, or discussing text information.

So what do teachers look for when they are observing students' work with texts? When students in a class are reading, notice students' ability to focus their attention on the text for extended periods of time. If the time they spend engaged seems extremely short, followed by periods of frustration and off-task behavior, there may be some problems with the text. Students sometimes indicate problems by frequently raising their hands and asking for help with the activities provided in the text. During discussions, listen for students' capacity to discuss major points in the text, their ability to talk about the text in their own language, and their tendence to relate concepts from one section of the text to the next. What students say during discussions may offer some clues about the clarity and organization of a text.

Interviews   Interviewing students about what they found easy or difficult in a text is another option. Ask students to point out specific instances where the text was helpful or confusing. Compare their responses with observations made during a lesson. Again, listen for ways student talk about a text. Inability to talk clearly about a text or make connections could be signs that a text is overly complex.

Work Samples   Collect work samples from students to reveal how well they interact with a text. Have students answer questions based on textual information, or use the text as part

Teachers can learn a great deal by observing students' work with texts

Ulrike Welsch

of a writing assignment. Evaluate students' work according to their ability to incorporate the text into their responses. Attempts to avoid the text could be signs that a text is difficult. On the other hand, if the text is well-integrated into students' work, the text may be useful for teaching.

Words of Caution   Used once or twice, trial-by-teaching won't guarantee students' future reading performance. There are too many aspects of a text and its relationship with students that change from one section of a text to another (for example, the knowledge and motivation related to a topic). Used continuously, trial-by-teaching can provide an ongoing foundation for planning and teaching decisions. The more teachers watch their students interact with a text and invite students' critical reactions, the more insight teachers gain into the true potential of a text.

SUMMARY

In this chapter, the focus has been on texts. The information in texts makes up the content of most content area classes. When teachers know the purposes of texts and what makes texts difficult, they can use texts more effectively. Readability formulas, textbook checklists, observations, and interviews all contribute to daily planning and the process of selecting more readable texts. None of the current methods for examining or using texts are totally reliable. Techniques that reliably assess readability can omit important factors or ignore the student. Techniques that incorporate the student's perspective can be difficult to interpret. The best approach to the text assessment is one that combines a number of techniques. Decisions about texts, whether for planning or purchasing, should converge on the reader's relationship with the text.

In the next chapter, these points will be further developed through ways of gathering and applying information about students.

SPECIAL PROJECTS

Course-Based

1. Identify a section of a text (or other reading materials) that is at least a chapter in length. Select, combine, and apply the measures from this chapter that are most appropriate. Is the text readable? Friendly? Will it help achieve high-level subject-matter purposes? (See Figure 2.1.) If you were a member of a text adoption committee, what would be your recommendation? Should your school purchase the text?

Field-Based

2. Interview a teacher about the purposes and organization of the text he or she uses. Observe the teacher using the text. How did considerations about the text and its relationship with students influence the teacher's instructional decisions? How did he or she compensate for any problems in the text? Build on its strengths?

SUGGESTED READING

The following references are for those who wish to know more about the purposes and organization of texts in content area classrooms:

DAVIES, F. (1986). The function of the textbook in sciences and the humanities. In B. Gillham (Ed.), *The language of school subjects*. Portsmouth, NH: Heinemann Educational Books.

MCDIARMID, G., BALL, D., & ANDERSON, C. (1988). Subject-specific pedagogy. In M. Reynolds (Ed.), *The knowledge base for beginning teachers*. Washington, DC: American Associate of Colleges of Teacher Education.

MEYER, B. (1984). Organizational aspects of text: Effects on reading comprehension and applications for the classroom. In J. Flood (Ed.), *Promoting reading comprehension*. Newark, DE: International Reading Association.

SCHALLERT, D. (1987). Thought and language, content and structure in language communication. In J. Squires (Ed.), *The dynamics of language learning*. Urbana, IL: National Conference on Research in English.

The following sources concern approaches to assessing text difficulty:

ROTHERY, A. (1986). Readability in math. In B. Gillham (Ed.), *The language of school subjects*. Portsmouth, NH: Heinemann Educational Books.

SINGER, H. (1986). Friendly texts: Description and criteria. In E. Dishner, T. Bean, J. Readance, & D. Moore (Eds.), *Reading in the content areas: Improving classroom instruction*. Dubuque, IA: Kendall/Hunt.

ZAKALUK, B., & SAMUELS, S. J. (1988). *Readability: Its past, present, and future*. Newark, DE: International Reading Association.

The following discuss students' comprehension of various kinds of texts;

MUTH, K. (1989). *Children's comprehension of text: Research into practice*. Newark, DE: International Reading Association.

SANTA, C., & HAYES, B. (1981). *Children's prose comprehension: Research into practice*. Newark, DE: International Reading Association.

The following references summarize current research on text difficulty:

ALVERMANN, D. (1987). Learning from text. In D. Alvermann, D. Moore, & M. Conley (Eds.), *Research within reach: Secondary school reading*. Newark, DE: International Reading Association.

HOLDZKOM, D. (1987). Readability. In D. Alverman, D. Moore, & M. Conley (Eds.), *Research within reach: Secondary school reading*. Newark, DE: International Reading Association.

KLARE, G. (1984). Readability. In P. D. Pearson, R. Barr, M. Kamil, & P. Mosenthal (Eds.), *Handbook of reading research*, Vol. I (pp. 681–744). New York: Longman.

REFERENCES

ALVERMANN, D. (1986). Discussion versus recitation in the secondary classroom. In J. Niles & R. Lalik (Eds.), *Solving problems in literacy: Learners, teachers, and researchers*. Rochester, NY: The National Reading Conference.

ANDERSON, C., & ROTH, K. (1989). Teaching for meaningful and self-regulated learning in science. In J. Brophy (Ed.), *Advances in research on teaching*. Vol. I (pp. 265–309). Greenwich, CT: JAI Press.

ANDERSON, T., & ARMBRUSTER, B. (1984). Content area textbooks. In R. Anderson, J. Osborn, & R. Tierney (Eds.), *Learning to read in American schools: Basal readers and content texts.* Hillsdale, NJ: Erlbaum.

ARMBRUSTER, B., OSBORN, J., & DAVISON, A. (1985). Readability formulas may be dangerous to your textbooks. *Educational Leadership, 42,* 7, 18–20.

BALDWIN, S., & KAUFMAN, R. (1979). A concurrent validity study of the Raygor Readability Graph. *Journal of Reading, 23,* 148–153.

BEREITER, C., & SCARDAMALIA, M. (1987). An attainable version of high literacy: Approaches to teaching higher-order skills in reading and writing. *Curriculum Inquiry, 17,* 1, 9–29.

BISANZ, G., LAPORTE, R., VESONDER, G., & VOSS, J. (1978). On the representation of prose: New dimensions. *Journal of Verbal Learning and Verbal Behavior, 17,* 3, 337–357.

CALFEE, R., & CHAMBLISS, M. (1987). The structural design features of large texts. *Educational Psychologist, 22,* 4, 357–378.

CAMPBELL, A. (1979). How readability formulae fall short in matching student to text in the content areas. *Journal of Reading, 22,* 683–689.

CLEWELL, S., & CLIFTON, A. (1983). Examining your textbook for comprehensibility. *Journal of Reading, 27,* 219–224.

COX, B., & KAZARIAN, M. (1985). The development of concepts in middle-grade U.S. history textbooks. In J. Niles & R. Lalik (Eds.), *Issues in literacy: A research perspective.* Rochester, NY: The National Reading Conference.

DAVISON, A. (1984). Readability—appraising text difficulty. In R. Anderson, J. Osborn, & R. Tierney (Eds.), *Learning to read in American schools: Basal readers and content texts.* Hillsdale, NJ: Erlbaum.

FRY, E. (1977). Fry's readability graph: Clarification, validity, and extension to level 17. *Journal of Reading, 21,* 242–251.

GROSSMAN, P. (1987). *A tale of two teachers: The role of subject matter orientation in teaching.* A paper presented at the annual meeting of the American Educational Research Association, Washington, DC.

HARE, V., LOMAX, R. (1985). Readers' awareness of subheadings in expository text. In J. Niles & R. Lalik (Eds.), *Issues in literacy: A research perspective.* Rochester, NY: The National Reading Conference.

HARE, V. RABINOWITZ, M., & SCHIEBLE, K. (1989). Text effects on main idea comprehension. *Reading Research Quarterly, 24,* 1, 72–88.

HERBER, H. (1984). Subject matter texts—Reading to learn: Response to a paper by Thomas H. Anderson and Bonnie B. Armbruster. In R. Anderson, J. Osborn, & R. Tierney (Eds.), *Learning to read in American schools: Basal readers and content texts.* Hillsdale, NJ: Erlbaum.

HINCHMAN, K. (1985). Reading and the plans of secondary teachers: A qualitative study. In J. Niles & R. Lalik (Eds.), *Issues in literacy: A research perspective.* Rochester, NY: The National Reading Conference.

IRWIN, J., & DAVIS, C. (1980). Assessing readability: The checklist approach. *Journal of Reading, 24,* 3, 124–130.

KLARE, G. (1984). Readability. In P. D. Pearson, R. Barr, M. Kamil, & P. Mosenthal (Eds.), *Handbook of reading research.* New York: Longman.

LEHR, S. (1988). The child's developing sense of theme. *Reading Research Quarterly, 23,* 3, 337–357.

MANDLER, J., & JOHNSON, N. (1977). Remembrance of things parsed: Story structure and recall. *Cognitive Psychology, 9,* 111–151.

MARSHALL, N. (1979). Readability and comprehensibility. *Journal of Reading, 22,* 542–544.

MCGINLEY, W., & TIERNEY, R. (1989). Traversing the topical landscape: Reading and writing as ways of knowing. *Written Communication, 6,* 3, 243–269.

MEYER, B., BRANDT, D., & BLUTH, G. (1980). Use of top-level structure in text: Key for reading comprehension of ninth grade students. *Reading Research Quarterly, 16,* 1, 72–103.

MOES, M., FOERTSCH, D., STEWART, J., DUNNING, D., ROGERS, T., SEDA-SANTANA, I., BENJAMIN, L., & PEARSON, P. D. (1984). Effects of text structure on children's comprehension of expository material. In J. Niles & L. Harris (Eds.), *Changing perspectives on research in reading/language processing and instruction.* Rochester, NY: The National Reading Conference.

MOORE, D. (1984). A case for naturalistic assessment of reading comprehension. In E. Dishner, T. Bean, J. Readance, & D. Moore (Eds.), *Reading in the content areas: Improving classroom instruction.* Dubuque, IA: Kendall/Hunt.

NELSON-HERBER, J. (1985). Readability: Some cautions for the content area teacher. In J. Harker (Ed.), *Classroom strategies for secondary reading,* 2d ed. Newark, DE: International Reading Association.

NOVAK, J. (1977). *A theory of education.* Ithaca, NY: Cornell University Press.

NOVAK, J., & GOWAN, D. (1984). *Learning how to learn.* New York: Cambridge University Press.

O'BRIEN, D., & STEWART, R. (1990). Preservice teachers' perspectives on why every teacher is not a teacher of reading: A qualitative analysis. *Journal of Reading Behavior, 22,* 2, 101–129.

PARSONS, M. (1987). Talk about painting: A cognitive-developmental analysis. *Journal of Aesthetic Education, 21,* 1, 37–55.

PERERA, K. (1986). Some linguistic difficulties of school textbooks. In B. Gillham (Ed.), *The language of school subjects.* London: Heinemann Educational Books.

PIKULSKI, J. & TOBIN, A. (1982). The Cloze Procedure as an informal assessment technique. In J. Pikulski & T. Shanahan (Eds.), *Approaches to the informal evaluation of reading.* Newark, DE: International Reading Association.

RAYGOR, A. (1977). The Raygor Readability Estimate: A quick and easy way to determine difficulty. In P. D. Pearson (Ed.), *Reading: Theory, research, and practice.* Rochester, NY: Twenty-Sixth Yearbook of the National Reading Conference.

REINKING, D. (1986). Integrating graphic aids into content area instruction: The graphic information lesson. *Journal of Reading, 20,* 2, 146–151.

RISKO, V., & ALVEREZ, M. (1986). An investigation of poor readers' use of a thematic strategy to comprehend text. *Reading Research Quarterly, 21,* 3, 298–316.

SCHMIDT, W., CAUL, J., BYERS, J., & BUCHMAN, M. (1984). Content of basal text selections: Implications for comprehension instruction. In G. Duffy, L. Roehler, & J. Mason (Eds.), *Comprehension instruction: Perspectives and suggestions.* New York: Longman.

SCHOENFELD, A. (1986). On having and using geometric knowledge. In J. Hiebert (Ed.), *Conceptual and procedural knowledge: The case of mathematics.* Hillsdale, NJ: Erlbaum.

SHANAHAN, T., KAMIL, M., & TOBIN, A. (1982). Cloze as a measure of intersentential comprehension. *Reading Research Quarterly, 17,* 2, 229–255.

SHULMAN, L. (1987). Knowledge and teaching: Foundations of the new reform. *Harvard Educational Review, 57,* 1–22.

SORESON, S. (1978). Education and the structure of the disciplines. In I. Westbury & N. Wilkof (Eds.), *Science, curriculum, and liberal education: Selected essays.* Chicago: University of Chicago Press.

SPYRIDAKIS, J., & STANDAL, T. (1987). Signals in expository prose: Effects on reading comprehension. *Reading Research Quarterly, 22,* 3, 285–298.

STODOLSKY, S. (1988). *The subject matters*. Chicago: University of Chicago Press.

TAYLOR, W. (1953). Cloze procedure: A new tool for measuring readability. *Journalism Quarterly, 9, 3,* 206–223.

THORNDYKE, P. (1977). Cognitive structures in comprehension and memory of narrative discourse. *Cognitive Psychology, 9,* 77–110.

WILSON, S., & WINEBURG, S. (1988). Peering at history through different lenses: The role of disciplinary perspectives in teaching history. *Teachers College Record, 89, 4,* 525–539.

"Reading is the process of constructing meaning from written texts. It is a complex skill requiring the coordination of a number of interrelated sources of information."

From R. Anderson, H. Hiebert, J. Scott, & I. Wilkinson (1985). Becoming a nation of readers: The report of the Commission on Reading (p. 7). Washington, DC: The National Institute of Education.

3

Understanding and Assessing the Reading Process

CHAPTER OBJECTIVES

After reading this chapter, you should be able to:

1. Describe what good readers know about the reading process.

2. Explain how individual differences in students' knowledge about the reading process influences comprehension.

3. Evaluate how well students read to learn from content area texts.

RATIONALE

Research has demonstrated repeatedly how a teacher's expectations make a big difference in a student's success or failure (Brophy, 1985). Especially important are the effects of a *self-fulfilling prophecy.* In this context, self-fulfilling prophecy is based on teacher expectations, for good or ill, about student achievement. When a teacher expects less, students can "live down" to that teacher's expectations. On the other hand, when a teacher encourages success, students who are at risk of failure or even good students can rise to greater and greater heights of achievement.

Sometimes, teachers' assumptions concerning what students know about the reading process contribute to negative self-fulfilling prophecies. Based on little information, some teachers assume that certain students are hopelessly weak in reading. These students are rarely challenged to excel academically, and their existing low self-esteem and helplessness can be deepened and reinforced. Again, based on little information, some teachers overestimate their students' reading strengths, sometimes challenging students before they are ready or have been adequately prepared. Students whose reading strengths have been overestimated can rapidly become frustrated and unwilling to expend any effort to succeed on their own (Eccles & Wigfield, 1985).

To avoid negative self-fulfilling prophecies and promote positive and realistic expectations, teachers must know as much as they can about students' existing knowledge and capabilities. To prepare all students for reading-to-learn, teachers need to acquire a positive and balanced understanding of what students may or may not know about the reading process. Based on this knowledge, teachers can make better decisions about how to maximize learning opportunities for all.

CHAPTER ORGANIZER

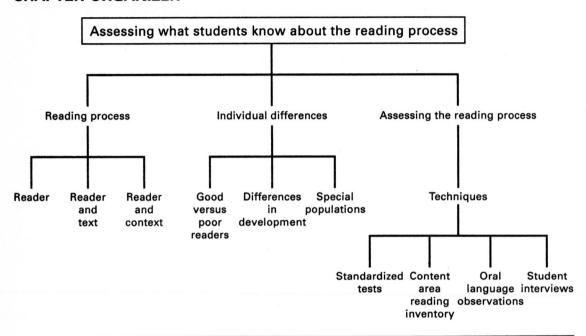

This chapter focuses on what students know about the reading process. By describing the reading process and how students differ in their knowledge about reading, the chapter addresses the teaching goal of developing a positive and balanced understanding in students. It also illustrates ways to gather and interpret information about how students use reading-to-learn.

THE READING PROCESS: AN INTERACTIVE VIEW

Proficient reading is interactive: good readers combine knowledge they already possess with information in texts and with features of the context in order to construct meaning. An understanding of these factors—the *reader,* the *text,* and the *context*—and how they interact is essential for knowing how students use reading-to-learn and reading-to-communicate. This section describes features of the reader, the text, and the context in detail and explains their role in an interactive view of reading.

The Reader

Expert readers draw on many resources inside themselves. These resources can be grouped into two categories: *prior knowledge* and *metacognition.*

Prior Knowledge   A student's *prior knowledge* includes his or her knowledge about a topic, familiarity with the language used in a text (both text structure and content), and understanding of how to think about and discuss concepts under study. In the past decade educational research has emphasized the importance of a student's prior knowledge in teaching and learning. For example, in science education, Roth (1987) suggests that effective science teaching requires "knowledge about students' ways of understanding the content" (p. 547). In writing about art education, Parsons' (1987) argues that good teachers help students appreciate art through their own (the students') past experiences. Researchers and teachers representing many different content areas have agreed that prior knowledge is critical for all kinds of learning.

Reading researchers have defined *reading comprehension* as the interaction of various kinds of prior knowledge with new textual information (Anderson & Pearson, 1984). To illustrate the impact of prior knowledge on comprehension, read the following brief paragraph and see if you can determine what it is about:

> Single sector reads and writes are cached. Data bases with records smaller than 512 bytes, batch files, and source files for language processors will be affected. The disk file directory and the FAT are cached and always resident once read from disk. Other files have their sectors purged if they are not frequently accessed.

Knowing that the topic was about computers and software might have aided your comprehension somewhat. At what point(s) did your prior knowledge break down and the paragraph became difficult to comprehend? Lacking experience with the topic (the operation of cache computer memory) or the language used (for example, the terms "cache" and "FAT"), it is unlikely that much interaction between prior knowledge and new information could occur. As a result, you may have comprehended very little of the information in the paragraph.

Because of variations in prior knowledge, not everyone experiences the same kinds of difficulty or success while reading. Consider how comprehension would vary if the paragraph above were read by a new computer user, an experienced computer hobbyist, or a professional computer programmer. Chances are that differences in their knowledge about computers would make the experience of comprehending the paragraph different for each individual.

Schema theory provides a cognitive (in the head) explanation for the role of prior knowledge in comprehension. A *schema* consists of a set of mental slots for storing concepts in memory (Rumelhart, 1981). Readers have different *schemata* (plural for schema) for all sorts of knowledge. Some examples from research include a restaurant schema (Shank & Abelson, 1977), a geography schema (Collins et al., 1975), and even a *Star Wars* schema (Means & Voss, 1985). In school, readers have schemata for the content and organization of texts. A schema for context contains knowledge about topics, events, and situations described in texts. A schema for the organization of texts includes knowledge about how authors use themes and organize concepts, in either expository or narrative form (Armbruster, 1986).

Classroom studies show that students who have prior knowledge about the content and the organization of a text comprehend more successfully than students with little or no

Good readers use their prior knowledge to read and learn

Sven Martson/Comstock

prior knowledge. In one study, readers who knew more about the content and organization of a set of social studies passages were better able to judge what was important in the passages than students who had less prior knowledge (Ohlhausen & Roller, 1988). Readers with more prior knowledge tend to focus on broad, relevant concepts when they read, thus helping them pick up on broad themes as well as smaller yet important details. In contrast, less knowledgeable readers tend to fixate on less significant words, sentences, dates, numbers, or lists of facts. When it comes time to recall what they have read, less knowledgeable students are often overwhelmed and cannot remember. Having a clear and relevant knowledge base available dramatically assists with comprehension.

As important as what readers know is how readers use what they know. Schema theory outlines two processes involving the use of prior knowledge during comprehension (Rumelhart & Norman, 1977). *Assimilation* is the process in which existing prior knowledge causes the reader to recognize and remember some facts and not others. *Accommodation* is the process in which a schema is used to reconstruct and interpret information in text and in the reader's head to form new concepts.

How these processes work during comprehension can be illustrated by considering an example of a schema and what happens when a reader encounters new textual information. A possible schema for the concept "nations" in social studies appears in Figure 3.1. Notice how this schema has slots that represent various attributes of nations (for example, economics, politics, types of nations). This is the kind of schema that a social studies teacher might like students to have as they encounter new information throughout

FIGURE 3.1

A Schema for the Concept "Nations"

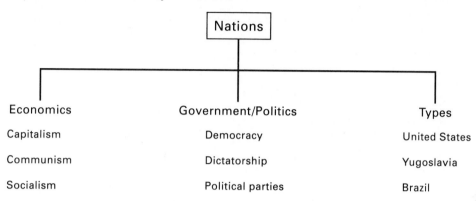

the year. It provides a solid base upon which to add new information and make comparisons (for instance, between capitalistic and socialist nations).

New nations and their features are assimilated only if certain conditions are met. Students must fully understand the nature of the slot into which a nation or feature might belong, and they need to know enough about the new information to fit into an existing slot. For example, suppose students are studying England. As students understand England's role as a sovereign nation with a monarchy and a parliamentary democracy, this new information could be incorporated within existing slots. England could be added to the "types" slot, and the terms "monarchy" and "parliamentary democracy" could be added to the "government/politics" slot. If students are uncertain about the slot or the new concepts, none of this assimilation will happen. The slot representing government and politics could be ambiguous or students could become puzzled about a country that has a monarchy and a parliament simultaneously. Learning through assimilation depends on having (or creating) some congruence between what students already know and the new information they are about to learn. Teachers are responsible for finding out what students know and helping them fit new information into existing slots.

Some situations call for accommodations within the schema. Accommodations involve creating new slots or dissolving some existing ones. To illustrate this process, suppose information about England's class system (lives of commoners and the aristocracy) is introduced and compared with American aspirations for a classless society (everyone has equal opportunity). While this information is indirectly related to economic, governmental, and political features of countries, these new aspects call for the creation of a new category, one that takes into account the societal features of nations. The schema for nations might now look like the diagram in Figure 3.2.

Teachers who understand the role of prior knowledge in processes of assimilation and accommodation are in a good position to help students learn. The implications for instruction are profound. In some cases, students might know a great deal about what they are reading. The teacher's responsibility in these situations shifts to helping students make the most out of what they know. Students in a vocational education class, for example, may

FIGURE 3.2

A Schema for the Concept "Nations"—Revised

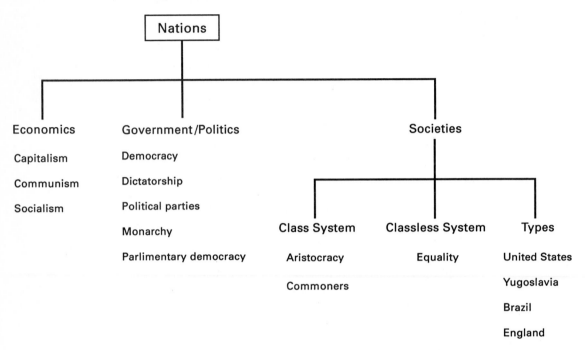

have acquired a great deal of knowledge on their own about small engine repair. Most of their knowledge might come from observation rather than direct experience or from reading manuals. The teacher's approach in this situation focuses on assimilation for the most part, as students refine what they already know. But the teacher also must help students accommodate new kinds of information that may conflict with what they know. Students must also adapt to new ways of learning, both from manuals and from working directly with small engines.

In other cases, students may not know much about a topic. In these situations, teachers must provide some background or help students dig deep to call up any relevant knowledge or experiences. For example, seventh graders in a science class may know little about molecular theory. The teacher might prepare students by asking them to think about the question: "How small is the smallest particle of matter?" He or she might divide some clay in half several times and pose the question: "How many times could the clay be divided until the smallest particle of clay remains on the lab table?"

These brief classroom examples demonstrate the importance of teachers in developing students' knowledge—enriching existing schemata and creating new slots—upon which they can base new learning. Chapter 5 builds on the ideas described here to show how students' prior knowledge shapes classroom planning and teaching decisions.

Metacognition   *Metacognition* is the name given readers' ability to take different approaches to what they read, monitor their success, and make adjustments when meaning breaks down (Baker & Brown, 1984). Far from a straight ahead, linear journey, comprehension is more like passing through a maze. Good readers are *strategists:* they know how to adapt their approach to comprehension as they pass through the maze, avoiding blockages, sometimes backtracking, and trying out different paths.

Good readers know that differences in content area, text, and purpose call for differences in ways to read. For example, novels about the old west are frequently found in both English and social studies classes. An English class might emphasize broad themes about human nature and society. In contrast, a social studies class might deal with the history and culture of the old west. In one class, a novel might be required reading, while in the other it might be assigned as extra credit to enrich the class text. In one class, the novel might be the subject of a test or an in-class essay, while in the other it might be the centerpiece of a planned class discussion. Sensitive to these differences, good readers adjust their approach to reading, calling upon different kinds of prior knowledge, reading for broad concepts and themes in some cases and for a much more detailed understanding in others. These kinds of conscious, strategic adaptations to different reading situations are at the heart of metacognition.

Besides the ability to use strategies, metacognition also involves the ability to make corrections when comprehension breaks down. Good readers *monitor* their own success with comprehension. When an approach to reading isn't working, good readers know it and make appropriate adjustments. In contrast, less experienced readers or those who have problems reading are sometimes not aware when they are not comprehending, and they know few alternatives for bailing themselves out.

When good readers have comprehension problems, they apply a range of alternatives referred to as *fix-it strategies* (Baker & Brown, 1984). Fix-it strategies include the following (from Collins & Smith, 1980):

- Ignore and read on.
- Watch for the problem to be resolved by future information.
- Make an educated guess.
- Reflect on what has already been read.
- Reread the current sentence or paragraph.
- Consult an expert source, like a glossary, encyclopedia, or the teacher.

Being metacognitive means knowing how to adapt to different reading situations, monitor one's own success, and apply fix-it strategies when meaning is somehow blocked. It means knowing how to cope effectively with reading when the reading gets tough.

The Reader and the Text

Reading is an interactive process between what is written on the page and what readers know about their world and about their own reading (Spiro, 1980). Meaning resides in the text only to the extent that the text itself affects what readers consider when constructing

FIGURE 3.3

Relationships between Different Types of Text Comprehension and Beyond-Text Comprehension

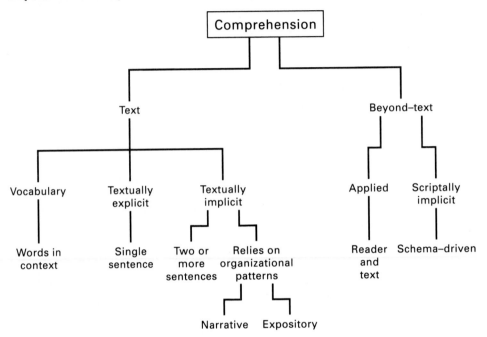

meaning. This type of meaning is referred to as *text comprehension*. Meaning also resides in the reader to the extent that readers use their own knowledge to construct meaning. This second type of meaning is referred to as *comprehension beyond text*. Figure 3.3 contains a map (or schema) for the concepts discussed in this section. Refer to this map as new concepts are introduced.

Text Comprehension   During *text comprehension*, readers make sense out of the language authors chose to convey a theme. The language of texts consists of the content as well as the organizational features that make texts friendly or unfriendly. The language of texts plays a role in three important aspects of text comprehension: (1) understanding vocabulary, (2) recognizing and identifying important facts, and (3) making text-based interpretations. To experience how each of these factors plays a role in text comprehension, read this math problem and the questions that follow.

MATH PROBLEM

You decided to save money the painless way: 1 cent the first week, 2 cents the second week, 3 cents the third week, and so on for sixteen weeks. Your friend makes an educated guess and estimates you will save more this way than if you save $60 every week for sixteen weeks.

QUESTIONS

a. What are the steps in your plan to save money?
b. Why is your friend's estimate inaccurate?

Like many math problems, this one uses relatively familiar vocabulary terms, and words that are unfamiliar are not particularly challenging. Comprehension of the problem, however, is dependent on an understanding of the word "estimate." Approaching the problem would involve considering two different ways of thinking about the information in the problem (estimating and calculating). This example, in which a small number of vocabulary words play a critical role in comprehension of an entire text, is fairly typical of vocabulary in most subject areas. Vocabulary words derive their meaning not in isolation, but rather from the context in which they appear; in this way they give meaning to the entire text. Ways of identifying and teaching vocabulary that support text comprehension are described in Chapter 6.

Another part of text comprehension involves recognizing important facts. Comprehension based on the first type of question in the math problem is *textually explicit* (Pearson & Johnson, 1978). Textually explicit comprehension occurs when readers assimilate facts on the printed page, sometimes referred to as "reading the lines." The first question in the problem involves textually explicit comprehension because the response it calls for is explicit, factual, and located in the first sentence of the problem.

Text comprehension also involves interpretation. The second type of question in the math problem requires comprehension that is *textually implicit*. Textually implicit comprehension occurs when readers interpret information that is not obvious, sometimes referred to as "reading between the lines." The second question requires estimations that are only suggested by the problem: the likelihood of accumulating a substantial number of dollars by saving only a few cents a week. Textually implicit comprehension also involves readers in a consideration of expository and/or narrative text patterns. Recall from Chapter 2 that text patterns are part of the internal organization of a text, including cause-effect relationships, comparisons, sequences of events, and enumeration of ideas. In order to comprehend the entire math problem above, the reader must understand the comparison between saving a few pennies at a time with saving dollars every week. The second question involves textually implicit comprehension because the response is implicit, entails comparisons between different kinds of text information, and is constructed from a number of concepts throughout the problem. Ways of guiding students with textually explicit and implicit comprehension are the subject of Chapter 7.

Comprehension Beyond Text   *Comprehension beyond text* means going beyond the author's language to construct meaning. There are two types of beyond-text comprehension: *applied and scriptally implicit.*

Applied comprehension occurs when readers integrate text information with their prior knowledge to produce a new principle or generalization (Herber, 1978). Students who read the math problem above and say: "People who save money like that kid would have to wait too long to buy anything important" are engaging in applied comprehension. *Scriptally implicit* comprehension happens when readers use their own schema (sometimes referred to as a "mental script") to construct meaning (Pearson & Johnson, 1978). Students who read the math problem above and say: "I wonder what is the best way to save money for a new computer" are engaging in scriptally implicit comprehension.

These categories share a focus on how readers use text and prior knowledge to accommodate new information. They differ, however, in the relative emphasis placed on the text versus the reader. Readers engaged in applied comprehension balance and synthesize text information and prior knowledge. Readers involved in scriptally implicit comprehension place more weight on prior knowledge than on text, yet the text still inspires what they come to understand.

The importance of beyond-text comprehension extends across the curriculum. English teachers rely on beyond-text questions to teach students about universal themes as they are depicted in literature. Science teachers ask beyond-text questions (for example, "How do animals get rid of waste?") to teach students about science and the environment. Beyond-text principles in vocational education, especially ones related to safety, guide students as they move from the shop manual to the machine. Beyond-text comprehension is the basis for reasoning (Chapter 8) and study (Chapter 9) across the curriculum.

The Reader and the Context

The *context* for reading includes many of the factors already discussed, such as the reader's prior knowledge, features of the text, and tasks students are asked to perform (Spiro, 1980). It includes a reader's motivation to read (see Chapter 3). Context also involves *social features* of a reading situation, such as the participants (for example, a teacher and students) and the discussion or talk that sometimes accompanies the acts of reading and comprehending. These factors change and affect reading differently from situation to situation.

Several misconceptions have plagued reading instruction in the past: (1) reading occurs as an isolated act, and (2) meaning lies in words, sentences, and paragraphs alone. The following sentences are a simple illustration of why these misconceptions are not true (from Spiro, 1980, p. 249)

1. Ronald Reagan lost his cool, but the former president soon regained it.
2. Ronald Reagan lost his cool, but the current president soon regained it.

In each sentence, who is the former president and who is the current president? Both sentences are well-formed and coherent, yet how would the comprehension of these sentences change if the sentences were read in 1978? In 1984? In 1992? In each case, the identity of the current and former president changes not only because of what the words say, but also because of the perspective and prior knowledge of the reader. What the reader brings to the text creates one kind of context in which the words are understood.

The *social context* is the setting in which reading occurs, the individuals involved, the time and location, and the expectations and language used (Harste & Mikuleky, 1984). In the case of the sentences about Ronald Reagan, the language provides a basis for understanding, but the social context shapes the eventual meaning. Are the sentences read in a classroom? A newspaper? History book? Magazine? If they are read in a classroom, what related activities will students engage in? What are the teacher's expectations? What assistance will be provided? If read in a magazine, are the sentences read for information? For pleasure? Will the information be shared? All these questions concern important and influential aspects of the social context.

Classrooms are a special kind of social context. Reading takes on significance based on the nature of the subject matter, a teacher's perspective on texts, expectations for students, and relationships between the classroom and the real world. In classrooms where rote memorization of isolated facts is the norm, the social context is narrow, impeding and constraining what students might learn. In classrooms where the goal is deep, subject-matter understandings with applications to the outside world, the social context is often broad and supportive.

Ideally, meaning is *socially constructed* (Collins, Brown, & Newman, 1987). People reading the same text often give each other tremendous support for comprehension just by talking with one another. In classrooms, teachers and students help each other comprehend texts through rich and varied kinds of communication. For instance, notice how meaning is socially constructed in this exchange where a student in an English class questions why a story turned out the way it did:

JON: Wait a minute. I don't understand why the story turned out like that. It just didn't make sense.

TEACHER: What didn't make sense?

JON: I don't know. It just doesn't make sense to me.

TEACHER: Now, let's think a minute. We have said before that in good stories, writers help us get to know the characters as people. Is there something about the characters that makes the ending a problem?

JON: The author didn't really tell enough about the kid (character). Maybe that's the problem. I just can't figure out why anybody would do what he did. It wouldn't happen that way in my neighborhood. Nobody would turn someone in like that.

TEACHER: So what you're saying is that you're having a problem with the characters being realistic?

JON: Yeah. That—the characters—really make a difference in whether the story works out.

People
reading the
same text
give each
other support
in
understanding
the text

Elizabeth Crews/Stock, Boston

Notice how the teacher asks questions that guide the student to construct an understanding. Notice also that the teacher is not merely leading the student to a prescribed answer. Socially constructed meanings are developed together among participants, and not just through teachers playing "Guess what's in my head?"

Teachers and students need to work together to create contexts that (1) support teaching and learning and (2) develop an understanding of how reading and comprehension change from one situation to the next. These themes guide many of the ideas presented in this book. Chapter 11 focuses specifically on ways to develop effective classroom discussions.

INDIVIDUAL DIFFERENCES

A persistent challenge to any content area teacher is to be aware of individual differences in students related to reading, and to use this awareness wisely to guide instruction. On one hand, emphasizing differences can lead to harmful stereotyping. On the other hand, teachers who continuously examine differences in their students can ensure that all students receive many opportunities to learn.

This section focuses on individual differences by: (1) describing how students differ in their knowledge about reading, (2) explaining differences in ways students develop in their reading and language ability, and (3) detailing important characteristics of students who comprise "special populations" of readers in content area classrooms.

Good versus Poor Readers

The main difference between *good and poor readers* is that poor readers lack the knowledge about reading that allows them to be interactive. When good readers encounter a problem in their reading, they examine the approach they are using, evaluate other strategies they know in comprehending texts, and select and adapt their approach according to what is needed to acquire meaning.

Poor readers sometimes rely on misconceptions about reading, such as trying to memorize the text when the text does not make sense. When poor readers make mistakes, they have few strategies to fall back on to correct them (Johnston, 1985). They may be able to compensate for their lack of knowledge about reading (for example, pronouncing every word), but a single, ineffective approach to reading may be the only one a poor reader has available.

Teachers should take into account individual differences among their students

Michael Weisbrot/Stock, Boston

Consider the response of a tenth grader (a poor reader) who was asked how he comprehended a very complex social studies textbook:

> "When I get a reading assignment, I look at the titles and the pictures and I start telling myself a story. The story is about the chapter. If I tell myself a good story, I can get enough information for a 'D' on the test. That's passing."

Activities like this one allow poor readers to compensate for what they do not know about reading. Other compensating behaviors include listening to classroom discussions and copying notes from the blackboard. These activities are effective sometimes, but are insufficient when a different approach to reading is required. For example, suppose the social studies student wishes to do more than pass. He or she needs to know alternatives to approaching reading in social studies (such as skimming versus reading in depth) and ways to choose among them.

Profiles of good, average, and poor readers are summarized in Figure 3.4. Keep in

FIGURE 3.4

Profiles of Readers According to Differences in Knowledge about Reading

Good Readers

Superior readers possess a great deal of knowledge about reading from direct experience. They are especially good at factual learning and are capable of forming sophisticated interpretations. These students need to refine what they know by learning how to think critically and creatively about how concepts in content areas can be applied outside of school.

Average Readers

These students know basic pronunciation skills and are accurate and fluent in their oral reading. Some can be slow in their reading: given time, they can comprehend as well as most good readers. Some may read too fast, sacrificing comprehension. Most know enough about reading to comprehend well at a literal level, yet they need to learn more about how to form interpretations, evaluate what they read, and read flexibly.

Poor Readers

Because they have yet to make sense out of what they read, problem readers can experience difficulty in virtually every curriculum area. These students are still struggling to understand basic, learning-to-read skills. Many of these students are highly adaptable (they compensate for their shortcomings sufficiently to succeed in some subjects). However, they tend to overly depend on single approaches to reading, such as pronouncing words or memorizing text.

mind that these profiles only reflect general tendencies (adapted from Singer & Donlan, 1980).

Development and Reading

Differences in the ways students develop are related directly to: (1) students' evolving knowledge about language, and (2) the kinds of instruction they receive in school.

Many children enter school with an impressive amount of knowledge about language, especially in the areas of speaking, listening, and even writing. In a careful study of the language development of preschool children, Harste, Woodward, and Burke (1984) documented the types of knowledge young children exhibit. Their findings indicate the following with respect to what young children know:

- Language is functional in that it can be used to accomplish things (such as labeling or encouraging action).
- Language means different things to different people.
- Writing is a symbol system that signals various types and shades of meaning.
- Language learning involves prediction and risk-taking.

Anyone who doubts these findings need only observe a three-year-old use language to hang onto a favorite toy, or figure out which tube in the bathroom contains the toothpaste. Based on experience with language, young children develop not only an awareness of letters and sounds but specific knowledge about how language is used to generate meaning.

As children enter school, their early experiences with language are a driving force behind development in reading and writing. For example, through oral language experiences, some students develop the ability to identify topics, categorize facts and concepts, and seek explanations. They may even know how to construct a simple outline. These activities all play a part in successful early literacy development. For some students, however, differences between their natural language and what they learn in school can be a source of early failure (Heath, 1982).

Many schools continue to emphasize early reading as an abstract rather than a natural or functional process. Students are taught to break down language into isolated bits. Phonics, the study of sound-symbol relationships, and word identification and sentence comprehension are the goals of an abstract early reading curriculum rather than ways to accomplish real purposes. Students who cannot reconcile differences between their existing, functional view of language and reading presented as an abstract process often become poor readers. The persistent challenge for teachers in all grades is to find ways to build on students' knowledge about language and its functions.

While basal readers (texts designed to teach reading) are the predominant focus at the elementary level, students are now exposed to content concepts at younger and younger ages. Science, history, physical education, and music concepts are introduced as early as preschool. Field trips and labs serve as the earliest vehicles for content learning.

As students progress through the upper elementary grades and middle school, content area texts become the focus. These materials differ from most elementary reading

Teachers should build on students' developing knowledge, skill, and motivation

David Pratt/Positive Images

materials in organization and function. Elementary reading texts are primarily narrative in their organization (written like stories). Middle school and especially high school materials are mostly expository in structure (written to convey information), even when the content is English or social studies (Goodlad, 1984).

For good readers, the transition to a content-based curriculum is comfortable because their knowledge about language and reading has grown richer and more complex. They have experience with different types of texts and know how to monitor and refine their approach to comprehension. They understand the social nature of comprehension to the degree that they won't be silent when meaning breaks down.

The transition is rocky for students who have gained only limited knowledge about the reading process. They are bombarded with reading materials and do not know how to respond to the new demand to use reading-to-learn from subject-matter texts. When meaning breaks down, these students rarely know what questions to ask, even to the extent of asking for help.

Figure 3.5 summarizes the differences in readers that are influenced by development. Remember that students' language development and instruction are key factors in the normal development of reading ability.

Special Populations

Special populations include three groups: (1) *bilingual students*, (2) *gifted students*, and (3) *learning disabled students*. The special educational needs of these groups have been

FIGURE 3.5

Profiles of Readers According to Differences in the Development of Knowledge about Reading

Adolescent Readers (High School Age)

High school readers are almost entirely focused on learning school subjects. Many (but not all) have learned to apply their knowledge about reading to learning in content areas.

Early-Adolescent Readers (Middle School Age)

Subject-matter texts comprise most of their reading materials. For some students, knowledge about how to read has become complex. However, the emphasis at this level shifts dramatically to reading-to-learn subject matter. For some students (those still learning to read), this shift can be too abrupt.

Young Readers (Elementary School Age)

Younger children already know a great deal about how language works through experiences with speaking and listening. Reading and writing development depends on experiences in and outside of school that build on what students already know about language. Science, social studies, and mathematics subjects are covered, but usually in the form of narrative materials and nonprint activities.

---

recognized: for example, the *Bilingual Education Act of 1968* supports the unique needs of bilingual students who have limited proficiency in English. There is no law mandating gifted education programs, yet federal policy recommends special instruction for gifted students (Ysseldyke & Algozzine, 1984). The educational rights of learning disabled students were guaranteed in 1975 by *Public Law 94-142*.

These students—bilingual, gifted, and learning disabled—are distinguished by differences in reading ability, motivation, and development. The nature and special needs of each group are described in the following sections.

Bilingual Students   *Bilingual* literally means "two languages." Bilingual students have a primary language, the language of their birth. They have been exposed to a second language either by coming to this country or because the language spoken at home differs from the language spoken at school.

Some bilingual students prefer to speak their primary language; others speak English most of the time, while at home their parents or grandparents attempt to maintain the primary language. Provided development in the primary language has been normal, bilingual students are usually successful with reading-to-learn in school subjects, even if a transition from another language to English is required (Mohan, 1986).

Some bilingual students, however, have limited proficiency in their primary language that can hinder their proficiency in English. Because these students lack basic knowledge about language, especially reading and writing, their success in an all-English content area curriculum is often blocked. Because language-related learning has yet to become meaningful for these students, school can be a frustrating experience (Ovando & Collier, 1985).

Most bilingual students also have a *multicultural background:* that is, they live simultaneously in two cultures. Their knowledge about reading and language and their beliefs and values reflect a constant interaction between American culture and their own diverse cultural backgrounds. For example, some students come from countries that stress authoritarian relationships in school: teachers provide the information students are required to learn, and students are responsible for reproducing it. Some students are accustomed to a standardized curriculum with a uniform set of instructional methods (Ovando & Collier, 1985). Students who have had more structured school experiences could become confused or even resistant when teachers encourage them to read flexibly. For these students, interactive reading may represent a new and formidable challenge.

Teachers can help bilingual students by providing many opportunities for communication. It is especially important to incorporate what students may already know about language, culture, and subject matter into everyday teaching. By providing communication opportunities that build on what students know, teachers not only develop students' language proficiency and subject-matter learning, they acknowledge the strengths in language and culture that students bring with them. This makes it more likely that bilingual students will feel valued for who they are as they adapt to a new language and culture.

A practice that provides communication opportunities rich in language and culture involves the use of *dialogue journals* (Dolly, 1990). Dialogue journals involve ongoing written conversations between teachers and students and among students themselves. Each participant makes an entry regularly (daily or weekly) in a spiral notebook and then turns it over to a partner, who responds by reacting to or expanding on journal topics. Students with particularly low proficiency in English can start the process by drawing pictures or even cartoons. Gradually, words and sentences are incorporated. Participants in dialogue journals try to carry on a conversation, rather than being concerned with revision or correcting sentence-level errors. This kind of writing ensures that students are reading and writing text geared roughly to their reading abilities. In addition, it helps nonnative learners to develop language facility within a more realistic communicative context. Dialogue journals are an active and functional way for *all* students to develop competence and experience with reading and writing.

To further develop bilingual students' ability to read-to-learn, teachers should:

- Emphasize flexibility in reading (reading faster or more slowly, depending on the text and purpose for reading).
- Provide necessary background information for reading or writing.
- Ask students to restate what they have learned in their own words.

Most of all, bilingual students need opportunities to talk and explore, especially in conjunction with reading and writing (Thonis, 1989). The more teachers can provide these kinds of experiences, the better students will master not only English but also school subjects (Mohan, 1986).

Gifted Students *Gifted students* are knowledgeable and usually voracious readers. Most gifted students read skillfully by first grade, gobbling up almost twenty books per month (Anderson, Tollefson, & Gilbert, 1985). As gifted students grow older, they grow dramatically in knowledge about reading and in motivation. They enjoy problem-solving and have a high tolerance for ambiguity: problems with more than one solution do not bother them. They are much more self-motivated than teacher-motivated (Bates, 1984).

The special educational needs for gifted students center on preferences for specific types of instruction. Gifted students prefer to work alone on activities that encourage independent learning, a learning style not consistent with the structure of many classrooms (Bates, 1984). Pulling gifted students out of the regular classroom for specialized instruction is not the best solution to this problem. Gifted students need to learn how to interact with their less capable peers. Though most gifted students are well adjusted, high-achieving, and well-rounded, some experience emotional and social problems (Torrence, 1986). Instruction that balances independent work and interaction with other students helps gifted students achieve academically and socially.

To help gifted students excel in their reading and learning, teachers should:

- Encourage student research on *real* problems, problems with connections to students' interests, no existing solution, and a potential for making contributions to the sciences, arts, or humanities (Davis & Hunter, 1990).
- Offer generous opportunities for discussion and sharing of work.
- Engage gifted students in teaching and tutoring other students.
- Ask gifted students to prepare instructional materials for use in a whole class (Bates, 1984).

You may discover other practices like these that challenge and support gifted students in their reading and learning.

Learning Disabled Students *Learning disabled* students experience problems with learning in one or more of the following areas: reading, mathematics, or spelling. These students do not always have reading problems. Those learning disabled students who are problem readers often do not know much about reading and are unable to process information efficiently (Kolligian & Sternberg, 1987). The inability to process information is what distinguishes generally poor readers from students with a reading-related learning disability.

Learning disabled students with reading problems process information from texts in uniquely inefficient and idiosyncratic ways. For example, some students spend so much time on detailed tasks, such as pronouncing words or determining their meaning, they fail to judge whether the effort is appropriate or efficient (Kolligian & Sternberg, 1987; Samuels, 1987). Unlike poor readers, who might recognize a failure to comprehend, some learning disabled readers may persist on smaller, less essential activities, unaware that these activities hinder comprehension. Because of repeated failure, learning disabled students reveal some of the same motivation problems as poor readers. Many believe their difficulties are insurmountable.

Labeling criteria for learning disabled students vary substantially from state to state, and even from school to school. This has led many researchers to call for a reexamination of the criteria (Reynolds, Wang, & Walberg, 1987; Blachman, 1988). Classroom teachers need to be involved in the process of discovering which students are truly disabled and require assistance. This is especially important, given emerging trends to integrate learning disabled students into regular classrooms (termed the *Regular Education Initiative*) (Gartner & Kerzner, 1987).

Recent proposals call for a three-step approach to the needs of learning disabled students: (1) collaboration between special educators (specialists concerned with learning disabilities) and content teachers, (2) assessment based on the demands of the regular education curriculum, and (3) special assistance for disabled readers in regular classroom settings (Reynolds, Wang, & Walberg, 1987). Researchers generally agree that the same kind of quality instruction that benefits regular education students also helps learning disabled students, with one difference: teachers need to be more sensitive and alert to the needs of learning disabled students, and to pay greater attention to matching students' needs with specific teaching strategies (Wong, 1989).

To provide assistance to learning disabled students with reading problems, teachers should:

- Discuss texts and assignments before students begin reading.
- Cue students to the use of learning strategies (when, where, and how a strategy might successfully be applied) for reading texts.
- Use, and teach students to use, graphic organizers and other visual ways of depicting and relating textual concepts (see Chapter 6).

These practices help learning disabled students gain access to the knowledge found in texts as well as develop their ability to read-to-learn.

ASSESSING THE READING PROCESS

Teachers can assess students' understanding of the reading process through a variety of approaches. Traditionally, teachers have had to rely solely on commercially available *standardized reading tests* to gauge their students' reading abilities. Standardized reading tests are paper and pencil tests on which students are asked to complete a range of reading-related tasks, from pronouncing words to reading sentences and paragraphs and answering comprehension questions. Standardized tests have many advantages, especially when it comes to ease of test administration, scoring, and interpretation for large groups of students (Farr & Carey, 1986).

Lately, researchers have been advocating reading assessments that are grounded more directly in classroom instruction (Wiggins, 1989). So-called *authentic tests* are constructed so that there is a close relationship between learning tasks (activities that students complete during instruction) and testing tasks (activities that students complete on a test) (see, for example, Valencia, McGinley, & Pearson, 1990). Compared with standardized tests, authentic tests involve more open-ended kinds of tasks. Students might be asked to generate hypotheses, prepare questions, gather information, and/or make judgments. Because authentic tests tend to be much more involved and tied to specific classroom contexts than standardized tests, authentic tests tend to work better with small numbers of students (on a class or individual level).

The following sections depict a range of assessment approaches devoted to students' knowledge about the reading process, including: (1) *standardized tests,* (2) a *content area reading inventory,* (3) *oral language observations,* and (3) *student interviews.* Standardized tests represent the tradition of large-scale, commercial approaches to reading assessment. The content area reading inventory, oral language observations, and student interviews represent attempts to move toward more authentic, classroom-based reading assessment.

The same type of thinking about assessment emphasized in the last chapter applies here: no single assessment approach is by itself sufficient. The goal here is to learn how to use different assessment approaches to develop an accurate and rich picture of students' reading strengths and weaknesses.

Standardized Tests

Standardized tests are used to measure reading performance. *Reading performance* is the extent to which students comprehend what they read. A list of commonly used standardized tests appears at the end of this chapter. Standardized tests are so named because they are administered according to a specific (or standard) set of procedures. They are also known as *norm referenced tests* because students' scores are compared against the standard or normal performance of a larger population of test-takers, referred to as the *norming population.* The norming population is supposed to represent most students who eventually take the test (Farr & Carey, 1986).

Standardized tests in reading follow a consistent format: to assess comprehension performance, students read short passages and answer questions about the passages. Other areas of assessment, or subtests, include vocabulary (recognizing the correct meaning of a word in or out of context), reading rate (reading passages and answering questions within a limited amount of time), and study skills (assessing ability to locate information and use reference books like the encyclopedia and the dictionary) (Farr & Carey, 1986).

Standardized tests yield several types of scores, the more useful of which is a *percentile rank score.* A percentile rank is a proportion that represents the relative number of students who scored at or below a particular score out of the entire testing population. For example, *Student A* may have a percentile rank score of 70. This means that 70 percent of the students who took the test received a score that was equal to or less than this student's score; 30 percent of the students who took the test did better than this student.

Consider this second example. *Student B* received a percentile rank score of 40. This means that 40 percent of the students who took the test received a score that was equal to or less than this student's score; 60 percent of the students who took the test did better than this student.

The following guidelines can be used to form tentative interpretations about reading ability from percentile rank scores. Students whose percentile rank scores range from 65 to 100 may be good readers. Students with scores from 35 to 64 may be average readers. Students with scores from 0 to 34 may be poor readers.

Words of Caution   Standardized tests are often widely misinterpreted, and they portray a very limited view of the reading accomplishments of most students. Some standardized tests greatly underestimate as well as overestimate students' knowledge about the reading process (Hiebert & Calfee, 1989). Inaccurate scores sometimes come from students' perspectives on standardized tests. Many students perceive little personal benefit from performance on standardized tests and they simply do not try very hard. Some students could be highly motivated and successful in any content area, yet they perform poorly on a standardized test (Johnston, 1983; 1986). Other students might perform quite well on the general reading tasks on a standardized test only to experience problems with the uniquely specialized reading tasks that are found in many content areas (for example, setting up an experiment in science while reading a lab manual or reading a blueprint in vocational education).
       Other problems that cloud student performance on and teacher interpretation of standardized tests include (Johnston, 1983):

* Sometimes test questions can be answered without referring to test passages.
* Answers to some test questions may require rare types of prior knowledge about test passages.
* The relationship between test questions and what is being assessed is not always clear.
* The complexity of passages and questions can interact to produce wide variations in difficulty throughout a test.
* The norming population for the test may not be representative of all students taking the test.
* Tests given in English may not accurately reflect what bilingual students know about reading or school subjects.
* Standardized tests are only one-day samples, and students' performance on them can fluctuate from one day to another.

Standardized tests provide first impressions. For a more accurate assessment, teachers should always compare the results of standardized tests with the results of other kinds of assessment.

The Content Area Reading Inventory

A *content area reading inventory (CARI)* is a silent assessment of students' interactive reading. Typically, a CARI is administered to classroom groups of students. Teachers construct this assessment to find out how readers apply reading skills to textual subject matter. A CARI has several advantages over other measures. First, in comparison with standardized tests, a CARI incorporates several additional yet important aspects of reading-to-learn, such as prior knowledge, metacognition, and the influence of context on reading. Second, a CARI is a more authentic assessment, since it is based on the actual text the class is using. This makes it is easier to explain to students the purposes for responding to the inventory. In addition, the information teachers gain from a CARI can be used directly to plan instruction.

A CARI usually consists of three sections. Section I addresses factors associated with *the reader:* prior knowledge and metacognition. Students complete this section of the inventory before they read. As they read a brief passage from their subject-matter text, students are asked to complete two more sections. Section II assesses the interaction between *the reader and the text:* text comprehension, including vocabulary, textually explicit and implicit information and beyond-text comprehension, including applied and scriptally implicit understandings. Section III, focusing on the *reader and the context,* deals with factors that affect a reader's ability to comprehend, learn, and communicate in different reading situations: the reader's ability to understand directions, ask clarifying questions, communicate with peers, and communicate in written form.

Figure 3.6 depicts a completed CARI for a biology class. Look carefully at how the teacher converted the item descriptions given above into questions for the inventory.

FIGURE 3.6

A Content Reading Inventory for a Biology Class

"Kinds of Animals"

Section I: The Reader

Directions: Using your previous knowledge and experience with reading, answer each of the following questions.
  A. Prior Knowledge
  1. What types of experiences outside school would most help you understand your reading in biology?
     Working in a science or medical lab, working with a doctor or veterinarian.
  2. Why is it important to study the characteristics of different animals?
     We can learn more about animals and ourselves.
  3. What is a phylum?
     A phylum contains animals that have characteristics different from animals in another phylum (taught in a previous lesson).
  4. Name one way scientists consider insects and mice to be different.
     Insects have a hard outer covering and no backbone. Mice have a backbone and are more complex organisms.
  5. Name one way scientists consider sponges and earthworms to be alike.
     Neither has a backbone.
  B. Metacognition
  6. If you were reading your science chapter and you came to a paragraph you did not understand, what could you do to figure it out? Correct answers could vary:

FIGURE 3.6 *(Cont.)*

Read further to get more information. (fix-it strategy)
Reread and think about what has been read. (fix-it strategy)
Read another book on the same topic. (fix-it strategy)
Incorrect or incomplete responses:
Pronounce all the words.
Try to memorize the words I could not understand.

7. If you were not given much time to read your science chapter, what could you do to get the information?
   Figure out how the chapter is organized, read chapter headings, and skim for important facts. (fix-it strategy)
8. If you were asked to research a topic from your science text, what library resources could you use?
   Reader's Guide to Periodical Literature, encyclopedias, science journals like Discovery. (consulting an expert source)
9. If you came to a word you did not know in a chapter, and reading the chapter did not help you figure it out, what other place in the text could you look to find the definition?
   The glossary. (fix-it strategy, consulting an expert source)
10. How does an author or a science text usually let you know that a word is new and important?
    By placing the word in boldface letters or in italics. (fix-it strategy, consulting an expert source)

Directions: Read the sections in the text about animal classification, sponges, worms, and insects (pages 67–72). Based on your reading, answer the questions in Sections II and III on a separate sheet of paper.

Section II: The Reader and the Text

11. What is the difference between vertebrates and invertebrates?
    Vertebrates have backbones; invertebrates do not. (vocabulary)
12. Why are sponges classified as animals and not plants?
    Sponges do not make their own food like plants; they eat small organisms in the water. (textually explicit)
13. Explain in your own words what a parasite is, as it is used in this sentence: "A parasite is an organism that gains food and protection from another living organism."
    A parasite is an animal that does not go out and get its own food. Instead, it lives off other animals. (vocabulary)
14. Name one thing you can do around the house to avoid disease caused by worms.
    Cook pork thoroughly. (applied)
15. How could the characteristics of earthworms help people who garden?
    Earthworms have segmented bodies. As earthworms burrow through the ground, the segments loosen the soil. (applied)

16. What is the purpose of the chart on page 71?
    To compare the characteristics of different animals. (textually implicit)
17. Which animal is more complex, sponges or insects? Explain your answer.
    Insects are more complex. Sponges are sacks of cells, while insects have hard-shelled bodies with many parts. An insect's parts are made for specific purposes, like biting or poisoning other animals. Animals that are more differentiated are more complex. (textually implicit)
18. How did the organization of the chapter help you answer question 17 on page 70?
    The chapter compares the characteristics of insects with the characteristics of sponges. (text implicit)
19. Name one insect you know about that is not mentioned in Chapter 4.
    Answers will vary, but the answer must be an insect. (scriptally implicit)

Section III: The Reader and the Context

20. What pages would you have to read if you were told to read Chapter 5 tonight?
    Pages 73 through 80.
21. Why would it be a good idea to wait for the teacher's directions before doing the earthworm activity on page 71?
    Correct:
    The teacher might have some special directions, or might need to explain directions or ideas.
    Incorrect:
    I never wait.
22. If you were absent and the class had already finished Chapter 4, what could you do to catch up?
    Correct:
    Talk to the teacher or a classmate, copy notes, and read the chapter.
    Incorrect or incomplete:
    Read the chapter. (This is incomplete because the student will not be aware of what the teacher emphasized or what the class has learned.)
23. The insect lab on page 72 is very complicated. How could you and your lab partner work together to make the lab easier to complete?
    Correct:
    One person could read the directions while the other does the activities.
    Incorrect:
    Skip some of the steps.
24. If a plan were made to destroy all of the insects in a local swamp, what kinds of information from the chapter might help in writing a letter to fight the plan?
    Insects are more beneficial than harmful. They are food for other animals in the food chain, they eat other insects to control their own population, and they eat dead plant and animal material to keep the environment clean.

To design your own CARI, follow these steps. First, select a brief (four- or five-page) passage from the textbook students will be reading. Choose a passage that you think is reflective of the kind of reading students will be doing most of the year (neither too difficult or unfamiliar nor too easy). Identify what you feel is the writer's theme or main message. For the biology inventory, the theme is: As animals become more differentiated, their functions become more complex.

Plan to write between twenty and twenty-five questions for the inventory, about ten for Section I, ten for Section II, and five for Section III. All the questions should be related to the theme you have identified for the passage. Construct an answer key as you make up the questions. Creating an answer key along with the questions is the best way to guard against vague questions and ensure that a range of question types appear on the inventory.

For prior knowledge questions, focus on knowledge and experiences that will help students understand the passage. In the biology inventory, for example, the teacher encouraged students to think about outside school experiences they might have had that would help them understand biology. Other prior knowledge questions are less experiential and more passage-specific, such as asking students to compare one type of animal with another. Some questions can tap into prior learning, such as the question on the biology inventory about a phylum. Metacognition questions address readers' ability to apply fix-it strategies and monitor their own progress. Most of these questions pose reading-related problems or challenges and ask students what they would do in response.

To construct questions dealing with the reader and the text, scan the passage for important vocabulary terms that are likely to be unfamiliar to students and for textual and beyond-text concepts that you think are essential. Form questions, ensuring that students can answer the questions with information in the text and/or with prior knowledge. Some reader and context questions are constructed by asking students how they would complete a typical assignment involving the text. Others deal with oral directions, ways of dealing with absences from class, and how students might communicate with one another and others to apply textual information.

To administer a CARI, explain the purposes of the inventory to students (to gather information that will help you teach and assist them in learning). Have students complete Section I before they read the text passage. As they read, have students complete Sections II and III. Scoring is a matter of counting as correct every student answer that is as close as possible to the corresponding answer on the answer key. Be flexible in scoring responses that have several plausible responses (such as metacognition and context items).

Scores from the CARI can be interpreted in a number of ways. One way is to look at the whole scale and calculate the overall percent of correct responses. This percentage can be interpreted in the following manner (adapted from McWilliams & Rakes, 1979):

Percent of Correct Responses	*Knowledge about Reading-to-Learn*
86–100	Good
64–85	Average
0–63	Poor

Groups of questions as well as individual items can be analyzed to gather valuable information for planning and teaching. For example, if students in a class miss a majority of questions within a category (such as prior knowledge or text comprehension), teachers can focus extra attention on the category while designing instruction (for instance, building background information or providing extra guidance while students are reading). Patterns of response to individual items might yield some trouble spots. For example, incorrect responses to item 6 on the biology inventory suggest that students may have little knowledge about how to compensate for comprehension problems. Incorrect answers to items 4 and 5 or 15 and 17 may reveal some basic misconceptions about science. Teachers who know about these problems can demonstrate some alternative ways to comprehend, and can work on changing students' misconceptions.

Words of Caution   Though a CARI is more authentic than standardized tests, Farr and Carey (1986) raise several important unanswered questions: Are teachers adequately trained to design assessments such as a CARI? What kinds of information should these assessments yield? How should teachers use them? Like the teacher-made assessments described in Chapter 2 (text checklists and trial-by-teaching), "homemade" assessments such as a CARI can suffer from a certain amount of subjectivity.

While it may not be possible to avoid these questions and concerns entirely, there are a few ways to make the CARI a valuable assessment tool. Keep focused on desired outcomes as you write the questions and answers, and, as when working with standardized tests, always interpret the results of the CARI alongside the results of other tests.

Oral Language Observations

Oral language observations determine the degree to which students are able to use language—especially speaking and listening—to construct meaning. Not restricted to observations of *oral reading* (when students read a text out loud), oral language observations are based on students' oral language performance across a range of instructional and assessment activities.

Oral language observations are valuable for what they reveal about the diversity of students' abilities in using and integrating oral language with other ways of communicating. Not all students are comfortable expressing themselves in many ways. For example, some students like to read and write, but they may be uncomfortable talking with the teacher or other students. Some students are comfortable talking with others, but they freeze when it comes to reading or writing. Many students who are poor readers and writers can also be poor speakers and listeners. Figure 3.7 depicts some general profiles of students who differ in their oral language ability.

The variations shown here (Figure 3.7) can affect all sorts of activities, from classroom discussions to classroom assessment. Doing oral language observations helps teachers determine students' particular communication strengths and weaknesses. This helps teachers make better instructional decisions as well as evaluate how and what students are learning.

FIGURE 3.7

Profiles of Students According to Differences in Oral Language Ability in Content Areas

Good Oral Language Ability

These students are highly proficient in speaking and listening when it comes to personal and content area topics. When some topics are unfamiliar, they can usually paraphrase, tying together what they do know. They possess a good oral, subject-matter vocabulary and use concrete as well as abstract concepts during discussion.

Average Oral Language Ability

These students have a basic command of language for personal and content area purposes. They talk easily about familiar topics, but can be at a loss when the content is unfamiliar. Most are familiar with concrete but not abstract terms in oral vocabulary.

Low Oral Language Ability

These students have limited ability to speak about and listen to personal as well as content area topics. These students may also reflect problems with forming simple sentences and asking questions. Some may be bilingual speakers. They are limited in their oral vocabulary.

So how do teachers conduct oral language observations? They can observe either in specially created situations or during everyday teaching. Teacher-designed situations involve *role-playing* or *simulations* (see Chapter 8). Lectures, demonstrations, and whole-class and small-group discussions are all everyday situations in which teachers can observe students talking and listening to each other. Teachers should make an effort to observe and study students at work on a variety of classroom activities, since activities can differ in the kinds and amount of oral language required (Glazer & Searfoss, 1988). Compare students' oral language performance in situations involving reading and writing with situations in which students are talking with one another. Observing students in a range of situations will give you an indication of how well they integrate oral language with different kinds of instructional activities.

Other specific ways teachers can assess as well as develop students' oral language include:

- Calling on students to summarize important points from a lecture
- Having students repeat directions for an activity to partners
- Soliciting student volunteers to teach other students who have been absent
- Encouraging students to suggest questions to ask during a discussion
- Asking students to explain their opinions

Watch students as they engage in these activities. Compare your observations with the profiles in Figure 3.7 to determine the range of differences in oral language ability that exist within each of your classes. You can use this information to take advantage of students' strengths (for example, by placing students who have good oral language skills in leadership roles) while supporting and encouraging students who may have some weaknesses (for example, by role-playing to demonstrate how students can work together during small-group discussions).

Words of Caution   Especially as students get older, oral language performance needs to be interpreted in light of developmental changes and students' past experiences. For instance, when asked to read orally, older students frequently do not sound proficient because most of their experiences as older readers focus on silent reading and comprehension. They simply may not be as accustomed to oral reading as they may have been in elementary school (Bruder & Biggs, 1988). Many older students and adults report that they feel embarrassed and nervous when reading out loud or speaking in front of large groups. Often, these negative feelings are attributed to situations in which teachers or other students publicly corrected mistakes with reading or speaking (Biggs & Bruder, 1986).

To avoid these problems, assess oral language ability under many different conditions, from speaking to students one-on-one to observing performance in both small-group and whole-class settings. Do not rely on observations of oral reading alone. By comparing performance across different situations, teachers should get a good picture of students' oral language abilities.

Student Interviews

Student interviews are a way to encourage individual students to talk about what and how they are learning (Nicholson, 1985). There are many insights that are just beneath the surface of most kinds of classroom interaction that can be discovered through a few interview questions.

In a student interview recently conducted in a seventh-grade English class, the teacher wanted to find out what students thought they had learned in a short story unit the class had just completed. She asked students what they thought they had learned, and what were their favorite and least favorite activities. She also asked them to recommend stories and instructional activities for the coming semester. By asking these questions the teacher discovered that students (1) learned more than she thought they had, (2) felt like they were working hard at reading and writing but they enjoyed what they were doing, and (3) wanted to do more story writing so they could keep learning how to put their feelings down on paper. This kind of information is invaluable both in evaluating prior instruction and in planning for the future.

To get the most out of student interviews, try to create opportunities to talk with one or several students at a time. While one-on-one chatting with students may not be easy to accomplish given the constraints of most classrooms, the payoff is a greater understanding of students' thinking about the classroom and their communication ability. Start the interview with *friendly questions*, initially avoiding academic questions to make students feel comfortable ("How's your day going?"). Next, ask specific *content questions* ("What do you understand about 'x'?"), *process questions* ("That's interesting. How did you figure that out?"), questions about the task at hand ("What are you supposed to do here?"), and *motivation questions* ("What is it you like most about doing 'x'?" or, "How do you think doing this will help you in the future?"). As students answer these questions, it is important to ask *probe questions*. Probe questions call for clarification and encourage students to reflect on their own answers ("What made that activity hard to do?" or "What did you mean when you said 'x'?"). Try to keep students on track to learn as much as possible about their views and their ability to articulate them, and then move on to other areas of interest or other students.

Teachers who have used these techniques find that it helps them keep track of students' implicit "theories" about reading-to-learn and how they are learning and communicating. Students often reveal gaps in prior knowledge, difficulties in understanding certain assignments, tendencies to fill in answers without a sense of the reasoning behind their responses, or even problems in seeing either the immediate or long-term relevance in a topic or task. In addition, many teachers are pleasantly surprised when students reveal that they have learned a great deal during instruction.

Words of Caution   It can be a real challenge to get students to articulate what it is they are learning and how. Initially, students may not be responsive when interviewed because they see teachers as an authority. Being interviewed requires a certain comfort level and willingness to collaborate. In your first attempts to interview students, they may be surprised at your interest or they may be reluctant to talk much. Pull back if students seem too uncomfortable. Avoid going through all the steps of the interview for the first few times. Sometimes, it is best to try to approach students regularly with one or two good questions, altering what you ask depending on the circumstances (observations of students, the task on which students are working). In this way, you can keep track of students' perspectives and suggestions as well as build good rapport throughout the year.

SUMMARY

This chapter has described differences in how students understand and apply the reading process in content areas. Students who have more prior knowledge about what they are reading tend to be more successful than students who know considerably less. Good readers are strategists. They know about language, how to monitor their own comprehension, fix problems, and adapt their approach when necessary. Students who are verbal and write well are in a better position to comprehend than those who experience difficulties with language.

Reading assessment should be multifaceted. Various assessments, in spite of individual shortcomings, must be combined so that a rich and more authentic picture of students' strengths and weaknesses emerges. Results from standardized as well as teacher-constructed tests and observations help teachers avoid harmful stereotyping and aim for success among all types of students. With student success as a goal, the next chapter turns to the topic of assessing students' motivation.

SPECIAL PROJECTS

Course-Based

1. Selecting from the measures described in this chapter, design an approach to assess the reading process students in your class. Take into account the need to test what students know about reading, what they know about a subject, and how they process information from texts in different situations.

Field-Based

2. Convert the content area reading inventory so that it can be used as an interview. Interview two students who contrast in some way (such as grades, observed motivation, level of class participation). In what ways do the students differ in their understanding of reading and subject matter? Try to account for these differences in terms of what you know about individual differences and how reading develops. How might your findings affect how you teach your subject?

SUGGESTED READING

This is a comprehensible resource on readers and reading:

ANDERSON, R., HIEBERT, H., SCOTT, J., & WILKINSON, I. (1985). *Becoming a nation of readers: The report of the Commission on Reading.* Washington, DC: The National Institute of Education.

These texts discuss the needs and instruction for special population students:

CARRELL, P., DEVINE, J., & ESKEY, D. (1989). *Interactive approaches to second language reading.* New York: Cambridge University Press.

OVANDO, C., & COLLIER, V. (1985). *Bilingual and ESL classrooms: Teaching in multicultural contexts.* New York: McGraw-Hill.

REID, K. (1988). *Teaching the learning disabled: A cognitive developmental approach.* Boston: Allyn and Bacon.

SELLIN, D., & BIRCH, J. (1981). *Educating gifted and talented learners.* Rockville, MD: Aspen Systems.

These are useful references on assessment of student reading ability:

FARR, R., & CAREY, R. (1986). *Reading: What can be measured?*, 2d ed. Newark, DE: International Reading Association.

GLAZER, S., SEARFOSS, L., & GENTILE, L. (1988). *Reexamining reading diagnosis: New trends and procedures.* Newark, DE: International Reading Association.

JOHNSTON, P. (1983). *Reading comprehension assessment: A cognitive basis.* Newark, DE: International Reading Association.

LESLIE, L., & CALDWELL, J. (1989). *Qualitative reading inventory.* Glenview, IL: Scott, Foresman.

These books describe specific ways to assess verbal and written language:

COOPER, C., & ODELL, L. (1977). *Evaluating writing: Describing, measuring, judging.* Urbana, IL: National Council of Teachers of English.

UNDERHILL, N. (1987). *Testing spoken language.* New York: Cambridge University Press.

REFERENCES

ANDERSON, R., HIEBERT, H., SCOTT, J., & WILKINSON, I. (1985). *Becoming a nation of readers: The report of the Commission on Reading.* Washington, DC: The National Institute of Education.

ANDERSON, R., & PEARSON, P. D. (1984). A schema-theoretic view of basic processes in reading. In P. D. Pearson, R. Barr, M. Kamil, and P. Mosenthal (Eds.), *Handbook of reading research,* Vol. I, (255–292). New York: Longman.

ANDERSON, M., TOLLEFSON, N., & GILBERT, E. (1985). Giftedness and reading: A cross-sectional view of differences in reading attitudes and behaviors. *Gifted Child Quarterly, 29,* 4, 186–189.

ARMBRUSTER, B. (1986). Schema theory and the design of content area textbooks. *Educational Psychologist, 21,* 4, 253–267.

BAKER, L., & BROWN, A. (1984). Metacognitive skills and reading. In P. D. Pearson, R. Barr, M. Kamil, and P. Mosenthal (Eds.), *Handbook of reading research,* Vol. I (353–394). New York: Longman.

BATES, G. (1984). Developing reading strategies for the gifted: A research-based approach. *Journal of Reading, 27,* 7, 590–593.

BIGGS, S., & BRUDER, M. (1986). *Reading histories of adult poor and non-readers in Pittsburgh: An attempt to establish where reading failure begins.* A paper presented at the International Conference on Language and Adult Literacy, New York.

BLACHMAN, B. (1988). The futile search for a theory of learning disabilities. *Journal of Learning Disabilities, 21,* 5, 286–288.

BROPHY, J. (1985). Teacher-student interaction. In J. Dusek (Ed.), *Teacher expectancies.* Hillsdale, NJ: Erlbaum.

BRUDER, M., & BIGGS, S. (1988). Oral reading and adult poor readers: Implications for practice. *Journal of Reading, 31,* 8, 736–741.

COLLINS, A., BROWN, J., & NEWMAN, S. (1987). The new apprenticeship: Teaching students the craft of reading, writing and mathematics. In L. Resnick (Ed.), *Cognition and instruction: Issues and agendas.* Hillsdale, NJ: Erlbaum.

COLLINS, A., & SMITH, E. (1980). *Teaching the process of reading comprehension* (Tech. Rep. No. 182). Urbana: University of Illinois, Center for the Study of Reading.

COLLINS, A., WARNOCK, E., AIELLO, N., & MILLER, M. (1975). Reasoning from incomplete knowledge. In D. Bobrow & A. Collins (Eds.), *Representation and understanding: Studies in cognitive science* New York: Academic Press.

DAVIS, S., & HUNTER, J. (1990). Historical novels: A context for gifted student research. *Journal of Reading, 33,* 8, 602–607.

DOLLY, M. (1990). Integrating ESL reading and writing through authentic discourse. *Journal of Reading, 33,* 5, 360–365.

ECCLES, J., & WIGFIELD, A. (1985). Teacher expectations and student motivation. In J. Dusek (Ed.), *Teacher expectancies.* Hillsdale, NJ: Erlbaum.

FARR, R., & CAREY, R. (1986). *Reading: What can be measured?* Newark, DE: International Reading Association.

GARTNER, A., & KERZNER, D. (1987). Beyond special education: Toward a quality system for all students. *Harvard Educational Review, 57,* 4, 367–395.

GLAZER, S., & SEARFOSS, L. (1988). Reexamining reading diagnosis (preface). In S. Glazer, L. Searfoss, and L. Gentile (Eds.), *Reexamining reading diagnosis.* Newark, DE: International Reading Association.

GOODLAD, J. (1984). *A place called school.* New York: McGraw-Hill.

HIEBERT, E., & CALFEE, R. (1989). Advancing academic literacy through teachers' assessments. *Educational Leadership, 46,* 7, 50–54.

JOHNSTON, P. (1983). *Reading comprehension assessment: A cognitive basis.* Newark, DE: International Reading Association.

JOHNSTON, P. (1985). Understanding reading disability: A case study approach. *Harvard Educational Review, 55,* 2, 153–177.

JOHNSTON, P. (1986). Steps toward a more naturalistic approach to assessment of the reading process. In J. Algina (Ed.), *Advances in content-based educational assessment.* New York: Ablex.

HARSTE, J., & MIKULEKY, L. (1984). The context of literacy in our society. In A. Purves & O. Niles (Eds.), *Becoming readers in a complex society.* Chicago: The University of Chicago Press.

HARSTE, J., WOODWARD, V., & BURKE, C. (1984). *Language stories and literacy lessons.* Portsmouth, NH: Heinemann Educational Books.

HEATH, S. (1982). What no bedtime story means: Narrative skills at home and at school. *Language in Society, 2,* 49–76.

KOLLIGIAN, J., & STERNBERG, R. (1987). Intelligence, information processing, and specific learning disabilities. *Journal of Learning Disabilities, 20,* 1, 8–17.

MCWILLIAMS, L., & RAKES, T. (1979). *Content inventories: English, social studies and science.* Dubuque, IA: Kendall/Hunt.

MEANS, M., & VOSS, J. (1985). Star wars: A developmental study of expert and novice knowledge structures. *Journal of Memory and Language, 24,* 746–757.

MOHAN, B. (1986). *Language and content.* Reading, MA: Addison-Wesley.

NICHOLSON, T. (1985). The confusing world of high school reading. *Journal of Reading, 28,* 6, 514–527.

OHLHAUSEN, M., & ROLLER, C. (1988). The operation of text structure and content schemata in isolation and in interaction. *Reading Research Quarterly, 23,* 1, 70–88.

OVANDO, C., & COLLIER, V. (1985). *Bilingual and ESL classrooms: Teaching in multicultural contexts.* New York: McGraw-Hill.

PARSONS, M. (1987). Talk about painting: A cognitive-developmental analysis. *Journal of Aesthetic Education, 21,* 1, 37–55.

PEARSON, P. D., & JOHNSON, D. (1978). *Teaching reading comprehension.* New York: Holt, Rinehart and Winston.

REYNOLDS, M., WANG, M., & WALBERG, H. (1987). The necessary restructuring of special and regular education. *Exceptional Children, 53,* 5, 391–398.

ROTH, K. (1987). Curriculum materials, teacher talk and student learning: Case studies in fifth grade science teaching. *Journal of Curriculum Studies, 19,* 6, 527–548.

RUMELHART, D. (1981). Schemata: The building blocks of cognition. In J. Guthrie (Ed.), *Comprehension and teaching: Research reviews.* Newark, DE: International Reading Association.

RUMELHART, D., & NORMAN, D. (1977). Accretion, tuning and restructuring: Three modes of learning. In J. Cotton & R. Klatzky (Eds.), *Semantic factors in cognition.* Hillsdale, NJ: Erlbaum.

SAMUELS, S. J. (1987). Information processing abilities and reading. *Journal of Learning Disabilities, 20,* 1, 18–22.

SHANK, R., & ABELSON, P. (1977). *Scripts, plans, goals and understanding.* Hillsdale, NJ: Erlbaum.

SINGER, H., & DONLAN, D. (1980). *Reading and learning from text.* Boston: Little, Brown.

SPIRO, R. (1980). Constructive processes in prose comprehension and recall. In R. Spiro, B. Bruce, & W. Brewer (Eds.), *Theoretical issues in reading comprehension.* Hillsdale, NJ: Erlbaum.

THONIS, E. (1989). Bilingual students: Reading and learning. In D. Lapp, J. Flood, & N. Farnan (Eds.), *Content area reading and learning.* Englewood Cliffs, NJ: Prentice-Hall.

TORRENCE, E. (1986). Teaching creative and gifted learners. In M. Wittrock (Ed.), *Handbook of research on teaching.* New York: Macmillan.

VALENCIA, S., MCGINLEY, W., & PEARSON, P. D. (1990). Assessing reading and writing. In G. Duffy (Ed.), *Reading in the middle school,* 2d ed. Newark, DE: International Reading Association.

WIGGINS, G. (1989). Teaching to the (authentic) test. *Educational Leadership, 46,* 7, 41–47.

WONG, B. (1989). Banish fears and sorrows in beginning secondary teachers: Some suggestions for teaching learning-disabled and gifted students. In D. Lapp, J. Flood, & N. Farnan (Eds.), *Content area reading and learning.* Englewood Cliffs, NJ: Prentice-Hall.

YSSELDYKE, J., & ALGOZZINE, B. (1984). *Introduction to special education.* Boston: Houghton Mifflin.

TEST REFERENCES

CALIFORNIA TEST BUREAU. (1986). *California achievement tests.* New York: McGraw-Hill.

FARR, R., PRESCOTT, G., BALOW, I., & HOGAN, T. (1986). *Metropolitan achievement tests.* Cleveland, OH: Psychological Corporation.

GARDNER, E., RUDMAN, H., KARLSEN, B., & MERWIN, J. (1981). *Stanford achievement test.* New York: Psychological Corporation.

HIERONYMOUS, A., LINDQUIST, E., & HOOVER, H. (1982). *Iowa tests of basic skills.* Chicago: Riverside Publishing.

"With my kids, motivation is like a guard at a door: motivation can invite everything in, or it can shut the door and keep everything out!"

A mathematics teacher discussing the impact of motivation on her students.

4

Assessing Students' Motivation

CHAPTER OBJECTIVES

After reading this chapter, you should be able to:

1. Explain how motivation affects the gap between students and their texts.

2. Describe individual differences in motivation and sources for these differences.

3. Select and design ways to assess student motivation.

RATIONALE

Motivation is part of a complex cycle in reading and learning in content areas. When students are motivated and knowledgeable, the door is open, learning is inviting, and students achieve. The more students achieve, the more motivated they are to let everything in. Unfortunately, this cycle also works against students: they can be so unmotivated that the door shuts and they no longer try. For these students, the door shuts not only on present learning, but also on any future success.

Motivation affects reading-to-learn in content areas in both general and specific ways. Reading attitudes and reading interests generally influence motivation to read in nearly any setting. Motivation to read in a particular subject is much more specific: for example, some students like history and hate math, while others like math and hate history. Though general reading attitudes and interests, especially poor ones, are bound to affect student achievement over time (Athey, 1976), motivation to read in a particular subject has more of an impact on day-to-day teaching and learning (Eccles & Wigfield, 1985).

This chapter is about student motivation. It explains different kinds of motivation and how each affects reading and learning. Next, the chapter discusses individual differences in motivation and how these differences emerge. The chapter concludes with assessment techniques for determining students' motivation to read-to-learn in content area classrooms.

READING ATTITUDES AND INTERESTS

Reading attitudes are feelings that cause students to approach or avoid a reading situation. Attitudes influence the desire to read. Positive reading attitudes are essential for success in

CHAPTER ORGANIZER

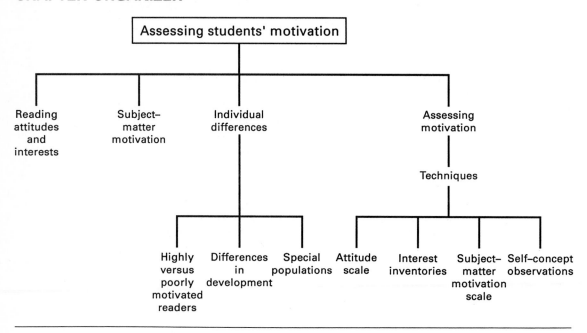

any content area; negative attitudes about reading usually accompany reading failure (Athey, 1976). When students have favorable attitudes toward reading, they tend to increase in achievement and they read more (Alexander & Filler, 1976).

Past experiences with reading at home or at school influence reading attitudes. When parents model reading (reading books and newspapers), when they read to their children and encourage them to read, positive attitudes result (Wigfield & Asher, 1984). Favorable attitudes also develop when teachers read with their students and show that they value reading. Persistent success with reading in school also promotes more positive attitudes toward reading.

Reading interests are preferences students have toward what they read. Reading materials are not in themselves intrinsically interesting or uninteresting. Instead, interest depends on a specific interaction between a reader and reading material.

To a limited extent, students have predictable preferences for certain types of books (Carlsen, 1979; Carter & Harris, 1982). For example, as a group, early adolescents prefer books about characters like themselves, while older adolescents like to read about universal human issues, such as injustice. As a group, males would rather read about sports and science fiction, while females would rather read about animals and romance.

To avoid stereotyping, teachers should use caution when applying these general patterns to individuals within groups. Individual interests are so diverse that predictions about what an individual student will like are unreliable when based solely on group membership. Readings that are interesting to some individuals can be deadly to others. However, any student who learns to associate pleasure with reading can be motivated to read from subject-matter texts (Fader et al., 1976; Mathison, 1989).

Some variations in interest at the individual level may be due to the close relationship between interest and prior knowledge about a topic. In a study of high-achieving seventh and eighth graders, Baldwin, Peleg-Bruckner, and McClintock (1985) demonstrated how interest level changes according to the amount of knowledge students have about different topics. The more students know about a topic, the more interest they show in learning. The more knowledge and interest, the better students comprehend what they are reading. Conversely, the less students know about a topic, the less interest they show. And the less knowledge and interest, the less students comprehend.

Unfortunately, teachers do not always recognize their own critical role in the development of reading attitudes and interests. For example, reading and writing activities are sometimes used for punishment. While these activities are not harmful in themselves, their use as punishment communicates the message that reading and writing (and, for that matter, any other work in the content area) can be the unpleasant consequences of misbehavior.

Teachers should adopt specific practices that promote more positive reading attitudes and interests. Teachers can provide situations in which reading is functional, emphasize students' reading strengths and abilities rather than picking on errors and shortcomings, and suggest different kinds of recreational reading. In the classroom, Mathison (1989) offers the following suggestions for generating interest:

- Use analogies and personal anecdotes to make the strange familiar or the familiar strange (for example, compare the structure of the heart to a city map or talk about odd personal experiences that are similar to the experiences of characters in a story).
- Disrupt readers' expectations and introduce conflicting information.
- Challenge students to resolve paradoxes and dilemmas.

Teachers can share some of these practices with parents so students develop more positive attitudes toward and lifelong interest in reading.

Teachers can also serve as role models, sharing with students books, magazines, or news articles they are reading. Some teachers and even entire schools implement *uninterrupted sustained silent reading* (often termed *USSR*) programs, in which everyone, adults as well as students, engages in recreational reading during a specified period of the day (Berglund & Johns, 1983). Many teachers stockpile a wide range of magazines that are subject matter–related or of general interest to students (see Appendix B, at the end of this text, for a listing of possibilities) (Olson, Gee, & Forester, 1989). The idea here is to create an environment where interest and positive attitudes are natural and enjoyment is the ultimate goal.

Elizabeth Crews

Teachers can help students take a greater interest in reading

SUBJECT-MATTER MOTIVATION

This section discusses three factors that comprise subject-matter motivation: self-concept, value, and metacognition.

Self-Concept

Simply defined, *self-concept* involves the view students have of themselves in relation to others (Quandt & Selznick, 1984). Students with a positive self-concept expect the best from themselves. They have high *self-esteem:* positive feelings of self-worth and a faith in their own abilities. These students persist with assignments. They are *internally motivated,* preferring assignments that are personally challenging. They like to figure things out on their own.

In contrast, students with a negative self-concept tend to give up when they are confronted with something difficult. *Learned helplessness* is a quality of students who believe from past experience that they have little or no control over their own capacity to succeed (Eccles & Wigfield, 1985). Students with a low self-concept are *externally motivated:* they constantly seek approval from the teacher or through grades and they rarely work independently. A major problem with this orientation is that when these students fail, they often lay blame outside themselves ("The teacher is mean" or "The

The degree of motivation matters most for poor readers. When good and poor readers are interested in what they are reading, both groups do better than when they have little motivation. Because of their inability to process information from texts, poor readers often view their reading as unattainable and uninteresting. However, poor readers also compensate for their lack of knowledge about reading through motivation. Poor readers will tackle some very sophisticated books and stick with them simply because the books hold their interest (Osako & Anders, 1983).

Figure 4.2 depicts some profiles of highly, average, and poorly motivated readers (from Harter & Connell, 1984). How might these differences be reflected in a typical content area classroom?

Development and Motivation

The power of motivation, for good or ill, gets stronger with age. Young children are often highly motivated, if only because they lack a complete understanding of what it takes to succeed. Even when they are graded, younger students often do not understand what grades mean (Harter & Connell, 1984). As they get older, students gain more knowledge about reading and the complexity of the tasks they face in school. This knowledge, combined with a greater emphasis on competition and grading, tends to make older students less motivated (Stipek, 1984).

FIGURE 4.2

Profiles of Readers According to Differences in Motivation

Highly Motivated Readers

Students who are motivated to read and learn in content area possess good self-concepts, little anxiety, and strong personal responsibility (intrinsic motivation) for their own success.

Readers with Average Motivation

These students are often anxious about their own success. Some have good self-concepts, while others feel they fail much of the time. Range of responsiblity goes from strong internal motivation to blaming others for failures.

Poorly Motivated Readers

These students have a poor self-concept and high anxiety about most tasks they are asked to complete. Many attribute failures not to their own efforts but to the actions of others (e.g., "The teacher gave me that bad grade"). Many, because they are poorly motivated, are rarely successful, and, because they are rarely successful, they are poorly motivated.

The crucial time for motivation is during the middle school years (Lipsitz, 1984). The middle school can be particularly tough because students are adapting to new academic standards and changing social relationships. Students who are normally motivated to read and learn can suddenly turn off to schooling as a result of increased anxiety. For some students, the fact that they must now expend extra effort means (to them) that they have less of a capacity to succeed. Peer approval at this level also becomes important. Students who find themselves in a peer group that does not value school will maintain lower grades just to maintain their status in the group (Harter & Connell, 1984).

As students make the transition from the middle school to the high school, they develop the ability to view their learning in terms of long-term goals. They see relationships between studying certain subjects and going to college and having a career (Stipek, 1984). Not all older students arrive at this realization or become more motivated. For example, an eleventh grader was disgusted with her American History class, yet she also expressed a desire to become a lawyer. She could see no connection between success in her American History class and her eventual goal. For many students, the higher their grade level, the more they are able to compare what they know with what they do not know. If they have been successful, this comparison leads to greater confidence and more success. If they have not been successful, their self-evaluation produces anxiety and more failure (Harter & Connell, 1984).

The power of motivation, for good or ill, gets stronger as students get older

Gans/The Image Works

FIGURE 4.3

Profiles of Readers According to Differences in the Development of Motivation

---

Adolescent Readers (High School Age)

For some students at this level, motivation results from understanding how studying some school subjects relates directly to college or career goals. Other students still find little value in reading or in school.

Early-Adolescent Readers (Middle School Age)

Students begin to understand the true complexity of reading and related school activities. They can be motivated or unmotivated based on what they think they can achieve in a more complex school environment.

Young Readers (Elementary School Age)

Motivation for these students is relatively simple: they can be more willing to try based solely on their interests or encouragement from teachers.

Figure 4.3 summarizes differences in students based on the development of motivation.

Special Populations

There are specific concerns about motivation related to teaching bilingual students, gifted students, and learning disabled students. These concerns are related in the next section.

Bilingual Students   Evidence suggests that for bilingual students, self-concept and motivation is poorer than that of the general population. In addition to contributing to poor academic performance, the anxiety of living in two cultures can be deadly: while suicide is the second most common cause of teenage death in the United States, it is ten times more prevalent among some minority culture groups than in the general population (Tempest, 1985).

Clearly, the priority for these students is to reduce their anxiety and help them develop better self-concepts. Gilliland (1986) offers teachers the following set of recommendations for helping students from other cultures build positive self-concepts. Teachers should:

- Communicate high expectations for success.
- Cooperate with students to establish realistic, immediate goals.
- Learn about the good qualities of students' cultures so that those qualities can be incorporated into teacher praise.
- Recognize individual strengths and use them to help students learn.

- Develop an atmosphere of mutual respect in the classroom.
- Build skills necessary for achievement.
- Teach communication and decision-making skills.

Soldier (1989) adds that teachers should use culturally relevant materials and learning experiences whenever possible. While these principles are applicable to virtually any student, they are especially critical for the motivational needs of bilingual students.

Gifted Students   Motivation in gifted students centers on the extent to which challenges are built into the curriculum. Many gifted students feel that the traditional curriculum is obsolete. These students thrive on a curriculum focusing on creative problem-solving, forecasting and planning the future, research and computer skills, and methods for scientific exploration and inventing (Torrence, 1986).

Many gifted students are more self-motivated than teacher-motivated. As a result, few will wait for teachers if inadequate challenges exist in the curriculum. For some gifted students, this means presenting challenges for themselves, supplementing what they are learning with their own independent work. For others, this means boredom and alienation from mainstream schooling.

Teachers need to determine whether the curriculum reading and the accompanying reading activities are sufficiently demanding and enriching for gifted students. If they are, gifted students will likely be highly motivated.

Learning Disabled Students   Because of repeated failure, learning disabled students reveal some of the same patterns of learned helplessness as poor readers. Many believe their difficulties with reading are insurmountable.

Studies have shown that students with learning disabilities have lower self-concepts than normally achieving students (Cooley & Ayres, 1988). Learning disabled students are more likely to explain their successes in terms of external factors ("The teacher helped me") than in terms of their own effort or ability. At the same time, these students are more likely to explain their failures in terms of things beyond their control, such as innate ability (or disability). Both of these explanations naturally lead to lowered motivation (Weiner, 1979). These students often feel that because they have little impact on their own academic success, and failure is inevitably beyond their personal control, nothing can be gained by continuing to try.

By building concepts and processes related to learning in a subject and helping learning disabled students recognize when they are successful, teachers can break this cycle of failure. Simply praising these students is not enough. Praise without attention to real success in the classroom eventually dooms learning disabled students to experience more failure. Balancing a concern for content learning, reading process, and motivation is a much better prescription for success for learning disabled students.

ASSESSING MOTIVATION

This section presents four techniques to assess motivation: (1) a *scale of general attitudes toward reading,* (2) a *subject-matter motivation scale,* (3) *interest inventories,* and (4) *self-concept observations.* Think about ways these techniques can be combined with assessment techniques from Chapters 2 and 3 to gain a better understanding of the gap between the textbooks, what students know about the reading process, and their motivation.

Reading Attitude Scale

Tullock-Rhody and Alexander (1980) designed a scale that can be used to assess attitudes toward reading (called the *Rhody Scale*). Using this scale gives teachers a general idea about whether or not students are willing to pick up a book and read it. It may be particularly useful to teachers who may want students to do independent reading outside of class.

Items on the Rhody scale cluster into the following groups, for more detailed interpretation: school-related reading (items 11, 18), library reading (items 9, 20), recreational reading (items 5, 7, 22, 24, 25), and general reading (items 1, 2, 3, 6, 7, 8, 12, 13, 14, 15, 16, 19, 21, 23). The scale, as well as directions for scoring, appear in Figure 4.4

Words of Caution   An attitude scale like the Rhody Scale does not say much specifically about students' motivation or reading performance in various subject-matter classes. For example, a student may love reading but have particular motivation difficulties in mathematics or music. In contrast, a student may dislike reading in general but be a voracious reader in some subjects. Combining an attitude scale with other assessment techniques provides a much more complete indicator of what students like to do and learn.

Interest Inventories

Interest inventories are designed to assess students' reading preferences. Interest inventories can be fun to construct, and they provide useful information about students. Before designing one, it is important to think carefully about your goals and what you might do with the information. Some teachers have created simple profiles of individual students and their interests and formed classroom interest groups.

There are many ways to design an interest inventory. Two kinds of interest inventories are presented here: a general interest inventory (Figure 4.5) and a more specific prior knowledge/interest inventory (Figure 4.6).

General Interest Inventory   A *general interest inventory* is useful for determining students' general likes and dislikes. Readance, Bean, and Baldwin (1985) suggest that general inventories, like the one in Figure 4.5, help teachers match student interests to different kinds of reading. For example, Roger Kahn's *The Boys of Summer* might be a good match for a student indicating an interest in history and sports.

FIGURE 4.4

Rhody Secondary Reading Attitude Assessment

Directions: This is a test to tell how you feel about reading. The score will not affect your grade in any way. You read the statements silently as I read them aloud. Then put an X on the line under the letter or letters that represent how you feel about the statement.

SD—Strongly Disagree
 D—Disagree
 U—Undecided
 A—Agree
SA—Strongly Agree

	SD	D	U	A	SA
1. You feel you have better things to do than read.	___	___	___	___	___
2. You seldom buy a book.	___	___	___	___	___
3. You are willing to tell people that you do not like to read.	___	___	___	___	___
4. You have a lot of books to read in your room at home.	___	___	___	___	___
5. You like to read a book whenever you have free time.	___	___	___	___	___
6. You get really excited about books you have read.	___	___	___	___	___
7. You love to read.	___	___	___	___	___
8. You like to read books by well-known authors.	___	___	___	___	___
9. You never check out a book from the library.	___	___	___	___	___
10. You like to stay at home and read.	___	___	___	___	___
11. You seldom read except when you have to do a book report.	___	___	___	___	___
12. You think reading is a waste of time.	___	___	___	___	___
13. You think reading is boring.	___	___	___	___	___
14. You think people are strange when they read a lot.	___	___	___	___	___
15. You like to read to escape from problems.	___	___	___	___	___
16. You make fun of people who read a lot.	___	___	___	___	___
17. You like to share books with friends.	___	___	___	___	___
18. You would rather someone just tell you information so that you won't have to read to get it.	___	___	___	___	___
19. You hate reading.	___	___	___	___	___
20. You generally check out a book when you go to the library.	___	___	___	___	___
21. It takes you a long time to read a book.	___	___	___	___	___
22. You like to broaden your interests through reading.	___	___	___	___	___
23. You read a lot.	___	___	___	___	___

	SD	D	U	A	SA
24. You like to improve your vocabulary so you can use more words.	___	___	___	___	___
25. You like to get books for gifts.	___	___	___	___	___

SCORING: To score the Rhody Secondary Reading Attitude Assessment, a very positive response receives a score of 5, and a very negative response receives a score of 1. On items 4, 5, 6, 7, 8, 10, 15, 17, 20, 22, 23, 24, and 25, a response of "strongly agree" indicates a very positive attitude and should receive a score of 5. On the remaining items, a "strongly disagree" response indicates a very positive attitude and should receive a 5 score. Therefore, on the positive items, "strongly agree" receives a 5, "agree" receives a 4, "undecided" receives a 3, "disagree" receives a 2, and "strongly disagree" receives a 1. The pattern is reversed on the negative items. The possible range of scores is 5×25 (125) to 1×25.

Source: Reprinted from R. Tullock-Rhody & J. Alexander (1980), with permission of Regina Tullock and the International Reading Association.

FIGURE 4.5

A General Interest Inventory

Directions: The purpose of this inventory is to find out what you like to read. After every topic listed below there is a blank space. On each space, grade each topic A, B, C, D, or F based on how much you would like to read about the topic. An A means "It's wonderful; I like it!" An F means "It's terrible; I hate it!"

Careers _____	Biography _____
Adventure _____	Aerospace _____
Family _____	Mathematics _____
Sports _____	Humor _____
Science _____	Crime _____
Fantasy _____	Animals _____
Nature _____	History _____
Plays _____	Mysteries _____
Science fiction _____	Poetry _____
Romance _____	Nonfiction _____
Novels _____	The supernatural _____

FIGURE 4.6

A Prior Knowledge/Interest Inventory for a Science Fiction Story Unit

---

Part I: This section tests what you already know about Science Fiction, the unit we are about to study in English. For each question, circle the best answer.

What You Already Know

1. Which of the following is a leading author of science fiction stories?
   a. Edgar Allen Poe
   b. James Thurber
   c. Ray Bradbury
   d. O. Henry

2. Which of the following is a major difference between science fiction and other types of stories?
   a. Science fiction stories have themes.
   b. Science fiction stories are never related to real life.
   c. Science fiction writers are scientists.
   d. Science fiction writers try to make an imaginary world real.

3. How are science fiction and other types of stories alike?
   a. They are true.
   b. They have themes about good versus evil.
   c. They take place in the same time.
   d. They only deal with human characters.

4. Which of the following is a television show based in science fiction?
   a. *The Cosby Show*
   b. *Highway to Heaven*
   c. *Star Trek: The Next Generation*
   d. *The Wizard of Oz*

5. Which of the following is true of science fiction stories?
   a. Science fiction stories contain predictions about the future.
   b. Science fiction stories do not make predictions about the future.
   c. Science fiction stories are based on proven scientific theories.
   d. Science fiction stories prove scientific theories.

6. While reading a science fiction story, which of the following story elements would be most important for understanding the story?
   a. Setting
   b. Characters
   c. Initiating event
   d. The author's point of view

7. Which of the following describes a science fiction plot?
   a. A team of climbers scales the world's tallest mountain.
   b. A man gets revenge on a former friend by sealing him up in a wine cellar.
   c. A man must choose between two doors; behind one is a lady and behind the other is a tiger.
   d. An air force pilot becomes the first half-human, half-machine.

8. Identify the science fiction story from the following list:
   a. ''To Build a Fire''
   b. ''The Tell-Tale Heart''
   c. ''The Ransom of Red Chief''
   d. ''All Summer in a Day''

9. A major award for writing science fiction stories is:
   a. The Bernie Award
   b. The Hugo Award
   c. The Roddenbury Award
   d. The Spielburg Award

10. Which of the following characters would you least expect to see in a science fiction story?
    a. A robot
    b. An astronaut
    c. A gunfighter
    d. A scientist

Part II: The purpose of this section is to find out what kinds of things you would be interested in reading during our study of science fiction stories. Circle the number that best represents how you feel about each topic.

Your Interests	Love It	Like It	So-So	Not So Hot	Hate It
Robots	5	4	3	2	1
Computers	5	4	3	2	1
Travel to other planets	5	4	3	2	1
Life on other planets	5	4	3	2	1
Scientific discoveries	5	4	3	2	1
Wars	5	4	3	2	1
Telepathy or ESP	5	4	3	2	1
The environment	5	4	3	2	1
Aliens	5	4	3	2	1
Time travel	5	4	3	2	1

Scoring: Prior knowledge scores from 0 to 3 are low, from 4 to 6 are medium, and from 7 to 10 are high. Interest scores from 5 to 15 are low, from 16 to 35 are medium, and from 36 to 50 are high.

Prior Knowledge/Interest Inventory   A *prior knowledge/interest inventory* represents one way to modify and adapt a general interest inventory for different purposes. The inventory in Figure 4.6 takes into account the close relationship between prior knowledge and topic interest (Baldwin, Peleg-Bruckner, & McClintock, 1985).

Part I consists of prior knowledge questions that are factual and derived from the unit students are about to study. Part II consists of items about related interests. On the inventory in Figure 4.6, Part II items were developed by subdividing the general topic, science fiction, into subtopics such as "travel to other planets" and "the environment." These subtopics could be subdivided even further. For example, "travel to other planets" could be subdivided into "rockets," "space shuttles," "traveling at the speed of light" and "living in space." The "environment" could be subdivided into "the land," "ocean life," and "life in the air."

The uses and advantages of a prior knowledge/interest inventory are many. Most important, teachers can gauge whether interest or disinterest is related to prior knowledge and then plan accordingly. Teachers need to pay special attention to prior knowledge and interest when both factors are extremly high or extremely low. These are the conditions under which prior knowledge and interest most influence comprehension (Baldwin, Peleg-Bruckner, & McClintock, 1985). If students know little about a topic and express disinterest, teachers need to offer appropriate background information and continue building interest. When knowledge and interest are high, teachers must still guide students in seeking information or ways of thinking yet to be considered.

Words of Caution   Like the Content Area Reading Inventory described in the last chapter, interest inventories can be somewhat tricky to construct, and they are less effective when they lack direction. Always develop an interest inventory with a clear sense of what you want to know about students' reading interests.

FIGURE 4.7

A Scale to Assess Subject-Matter Motivation

Directions: Use the scale below to rate how you feel about learning in art. Your responses will not affect your grade in any way. You read the statements silently as I read them aloud. Then circle the letter or letters that represent how you feel about the statement.

SD - Strongly Disagree
  D - Disagree
  U - Undecided
  A - Agree
SA - Strongly Agree

1. If an assignment is difficult in *art,* I wait until other students figure it out before I try it.

                    SD   D   U   A   SA

2. I like to go on to new work in *art* that is at a more difficult level.

                    SD   D   U   A   SA

3. The only reason to complete my work in *art* is to get finished and get good grades.

                    SD   D   U   A   SA

4. I like to figure out assignments in *art* on my own.

                    SD   D   U   A   SA

5. If I keep trying in *art,* I can be successful.

                    SD   D   U   A   SA

6. Just trying hard does not always work in *art.*

                    SD   D   U   A   SA

7. I like to do extra projects because I can learn about things in *art* that interest me.

                    SD   D   U   A   SA

8. If I have a problem with an assignment in *art,* I hardly every know what to do to figure it out.

                    SD   D   U   A   SA

9. In *art,* enjoying my assignments and doing well are important to me.

                    SD   D   U   A   SA

10. I get my work done in *art* just to keep the teacher happy.

                    SD   D   U   A   SA

11. My best experiences in school have been in *art* class.

                    SD   D   U   A   SA

12. In comparison with others, I do not do well in *art.*

        SD   D   U   A   SA

13. When I learn things in *art,* it usually makes me want to learn more.

        SD   D   U   A   SA

14. When I miss *art* class, I lose out on learning some interesting information.

        SD   D   U   A   SA

15. In *art,* I know many ways to figure out what I do not understand.

        SD   D   U   A   SA

16. In *art,* I don't always know what the teacher is asking me to do.

        SD   D   U   A   SA

17. If an assignment in *art* is difficult, it may be because I need to approach it a different way.

        SD   D   U   A   SA

18. What I am learning in *art* will never apply to my own life.

        SD   D   U   A   SA

19. I like it when the teacher assigns easy work in *art.*

        SD   D   U   A   SA

20. I can usually complete assignments in *art* because I know what to do.

        SD   D   U   A   SA

21. I don't like my *art* class as much as I like my other classes.

        SD   D   U   A   SA

22. I can be absent from *art* class and not miss anything important.

        SD   D   U   A   SA

23. When I get stuck on an assignment in *art,* I always ask the teacher for help.

        SD   D   U   A   SA

24. What I am learning in *art* class could someday make my life better.

        SD   D   U   A   SA

Scoring: To score this scale, a very positive response receives a score of 5, and a very negative response receives a score of 1. On items 2, 4, 5, 7, 11, 12, 13, 14, 15, 17, 20, and 24, a response of "strongly agree" indicates very high motivation and should receive a score of 5. On the remaining items, a "strongly disagree" response indicates very high motivation and should receive a 5 score. Therefore, on the positive items, "strongly agree" receives a 5, "agree" receives a 4, "undecided" receives a 3, "disagree" receives a 2, and "strongly disagree" receives a 1. The pattern is reversed on the negative items. The possible range of scores is 5 × 24 (120) to 1 × 24.

Subject-Matter Motivation Scale

Figure 4.7 depicts a *subject-matter motivation scale*. When students enter a class for the first time, it would be helpful to teachers to gain some understanding of the extent to which students are motivated to read and learn in a subject. The subject-matter motivation scale meets this need.

The scale was constructed based on current research on motivation, taking into account how students' motivation varies in different subjects. Items on the scale cluster into three areas: self-concept (items 2, 3, 4, 7, 10, 13, 19, 23), value (items 9, 11, 12, 14, 18, 21, 22, 24), and metacognition (items 1, 5, 6, 8, 15, 16, 17, 20). The scale is easily converted for use in other content areas by replacing the word "art" in each item with the name of another subject.

Words of Caution   Motivation can be volatile, especially for certain age groups such as middle school readers. Students can change radically from day to day, from subject to subject, and from topic to topic. For this reason, there is a need to assess motivation often and flexibly. While the subject-matter motivation scale helps establish a baseline understanding of students' motivation, it should be combined with ongoing observations of students to keep track of how motivation fluctuates across the year. Continuous updating of knowledge about student motivation requires combining techniques like the subject-matter motivation scale with teacher observations.

Self-Concept Observations

Quandt and Selznik (1984) suggest observing the following aspects of students' behavior to determine whether they are motivated based on a positive versus a negative self-concept:

1. *Comments students make about themselves.* Negative comments about themselves or their ability to read could indicate motivation problems. Watch for a sincere, consistent pattern before forming conclusions about what students say.

2. *Reactions students have to instruction.* Facial expressions, body movements, gestures, and groans or sighs can indicate lack of motivation and poor self-concept.

3. *Interactions between students and peers.* If students stay to themselves or are ridiculed by others, they may become unmotivated.

4. *Willingness of students to volunteer.* If students seldom volunteer, it could be an indication of a problem.

5. *Level of students' confidence.* Watch for the extent to which students ask about their own progress. This can be a sign of insecurity. Be careful in your interpretation. Students who never ask questions of this nature can also be insecure.

Words of Caution   Teacher observations are better suited for ongoing assessment, though the observations described here consider only one dimension of motivation, self-concept. Other dimensions of motivation should be considered and incorporated, such as how much students value a subject. In addition, teachers might want to examine ways to build positive reading attitudes and interests.

SUMMARY

Positive attitudes and interests are the basis for the will to read in all school subjects. Students who are motivated to perform in a content area have a good self-concept, value what they are learning, and are aware of their own subject-specific skills. Differences in motivation are often the result of past school experiences. Success builds success. Students who have had positive experiences with reading and subject-matter learning are more likely to continue their success than students who have been less successful. The continuing challenge for teachers is to reliably assess and build motivation, especially in students who are persistently disinterested and fail. The next chapter considers ways to meet this challenge, and other challenges related to content reading, through instruction.

Observation can help teachers understand their students' motivation

Ulrike Welsch

SPECIAL PROJECTS

Course-Based

1. Design an interest inventory that surveys interests along with aspects of the reading process, such as prior knowledge, the reader's interaction with the text, and the influence of context.

Field-Based

2. Administer the Rhody Secondary Interest Inventory and the subject-matter inventory to a group of students. Compare the results.

3. Arrange to observe a content area classroom. What kinds of activities appear to be motivating to students? What evidence do you see that students are motivated? Watch for instances of mock participation (when students go through the motions but have really become mental dropouts). What are the reasons for this behavior?

SUGGESTED READING

These references discuss motivation. Some offer methods for assessing and building motivation in students.

CIANI, A. (1981). *Motivating reluctant readers.* Newark, DE: International Reading Association.

FADER, D., DUGGINS, J., FINN, T., & MCNEIL, E. (1976). *The new hooked on books.* New York: Berkley Publishing Company.

MATHISON, C. (1989). Activating student interest in content area reading. *Journal of Reading, 33,* 3, 170–177.

STIPEK, D. (1988). *Motivation to learn: From theory to practice.* Englewood Cliffs, NJ: Prentice-Hall.

These articles provide comprehensive reviews of research on motivation:

PRAWAT, R. (1989). Promoting access to knowledge, strategy, and disposition in students: A research synthesis. *Review of Educational Research, 59,* 1, 1–42.

WIGFIELD, A., & ASHER, S. (1984). Social and motivational influences on reading. In P. D. Pearson, R. Barr, M. Kamil, & P. Mosenthal (Eds.), *Handbook of reading research,* Vol. I (pp. 423–453). New York: Longman.

Appendixes A and B, at the end of this text, contain bibliographies and references of reading materials of interest to young readers.

These educational journals regularly review books that might be of interest to young readers:

Journal of Reading and *The English Journal* (for middle and secondary school readers)

Language Arts and *The Reading Teacher* (for elementary school readers)

REFERENCES

ALEXANDER, J., & FILLER, R. (1976). *Attitudes and reading.* Newark, DE: International Reading Association.

ASHTON, P., & WEBB, R. (1982). *Teachers' sense of efficacy: Toward an ecological model.* A paper presented at the annual meeting of the American Educational Research Association, New York.

ATHEY, I. (1976). Reading research in the affective domain. In H. Singer & R. Ruddell (Eds.), *Theoretical models and processes of reading.* Newark, DE: International Reading Association.

BALDWIN, S., PELEG-BRUCKNER, Z., & MCCLINTOCK, A. (1985). Effects of topic interest and prior knowledge on reading comprehension. *Reading Research Quarterly, 20,* 4, 497–504.

BERGLUND, R., & JOHNS, J. (1983). A primer on uninterrupted sustained silent reading. *The Reading Teacher, 36,* 6, 534–541.

BLOOM, D. (1983). Classroom reading instruction: A socio-communicative analysis of time on task. In J. Niles & L. Harris (Eds.), *Searches for meaning in reading/language processing and instruction.* Rochester, NY: The National Reading Conference.

BROPHY, J. (1981). Teacher praise: A functional analysis. *Review of Educational Research, 51,* 1, 5–32.

CARLSEN, G. (1979). *Books and the teenage reader.* New York: Bantam Books.

CARTER, B., & HARRIS, K. (1982). What junior high students like in books. *Journal of Reading, 26,* 42–46.

COOLEY, E., & AYRES, R. (1988). Self-concept and success-failure attributions of nonhandicapped students and students with learning disabilities. *Journal of Learning Disabilities, 21,* 3, 174–178.

COVINGTON, M., & OMELICH, C. (1987). "I knew it cold before the exam": A test of the anxiety blockage hypothesis. *Journal of Educational Psychology, 79,* 4, 393–400.

DAVIDSON, J. (1985). What you think is going on, isn't: Eighth-grade students' introspections of discussions in science and social studies lessons. In J. Niles & R. Lalik (Eds.), *Issues in literacy: A research perspective.* Rochester, NY: The National Reading Conference.

ECCLES, J., ADLER, T., & MEECE, J. (1984). Sex differences in achievement: A test of alternative theories. *Journal of Personality and Social Psychology, 46,* 26–43.

ECCLES, J., & WIGFIELD, A. (1985). Teacher expectations and student motivation. In J. Dusek (Ed.), *Teacher expectancies.* Hillsdale, NJ: Erlbaum.

FADER, D., DUGGINS, J., FINN, T., & MCNEIL, E. (1976). *The new hooked on books.* New York: Berkley Publishing Company.

GARNER, R. (1989). Metacognition: Answered and unanswered questions. *Educational Psychologist, 24,* 2, 143–158.

GILLILAND, H. (1986). Self-concept and the Indian student. In J. Reyhner (Ed.), *Teaching the Indian child: A bilingual/multicultural approach.* Billings, MT: Eastern Montana College.

HARTER, S., & CONNELL, J. (1984). A model of children's achievement and related self-perceptions of competence, control, and motivational orientation. In J. Nichols (Ed.), *Advances in motivation and achievement.* Greenwich, CT: JAI Press.

HUNSLEY, J. (1987). Cognitive processes in mathematics anxiety and test anxiety: The role of appraisals, internal dialogue, and attributions. *Journal of Educational Psychology, 79,* 4, 388–392.

LIPSITZ, J. (1984). *Successful schools for young adolescents.* New Brunswick, NJ: Transaction Books.

MATHISON, C. (1989). Activating student interest in content area reading. *Journal of Reading, 33,* 3, 170–177.

NICHOLS, J. (1984). Conceptions of ability and achievement motivation. In R. Ames & C. Ames (Eds.), *Research on motivation in education.* New York: Academic Press.

NICHOLS, J., PATASHNICK, M., & NOLEN, S. (1985). Adolescents' theories of education. *Journal of Educational Psychology, 77,* 6, 683–692.

OLSON, M., GEE, T., & FORESTER, N. (1989). Magazines in the classroom: Beyond recreational reading. *Journal of Reading, 32,* 8, 708–713.

OSAKO, G., & ANDERS, P. (1983). The effect of reading interest on comprehension of expository materials with controls for prior knowledge. In J. Niles & L. Harris (Eds.), *Searches for meaning in reading/language processing and instruction.* Rochester, NY: The National Reading Conference.

PELIAS, M., & PELIAS, R. (1988). Communication apprehension in the basic course in performance of literature. *Communication Education, 37,* 2, 118–126.

QUANDT, I., & SELZNICK, R. (1984). *Self-concept and reading.* Newark, DE: International Reading Association.

RAFFINI, J. (1986). Student apathy: A motivational dilemma. *Educational Leadership, 44,* 1, 53–55.

READANCE, J., BEAN, T., & BALDWIN, S. (1985). *Content area reading: An integrated approach.* Dubuque, IA: Kendall/Hunt.

SOLDIER, L. (1989). Language learning of Native American students. *Educational Leadership, 46,* 5, 74–76.

STIPEK, D. (1984). The development of achievement motivation. In R. Ames & C. Ames (Eds.), *Research on motivation in education.* New York: Academic Press.

TEMPEST, P. (1985). The Navajo student and the Tennessee Self Concept. *Journal of American Indian Education, 24,* 3, 1–7.

TORRENCE, E. (1986). Teaching creative and gifted learners. In M. C. Wittrock (Ed.), *Handbook of research on teacher education,* 3d ed. (pp. 630–647). New York: Macmillan.

TULLOCK-RHODY, R., & ALEXANDER, J. (1980). A scale for assessing attitudes toward reading in secondary schools. *Journal of Reading, 23,* 7, 609–613.

WEINER, B. (1979). A theory of motivation for some classroom experiences. *Journal of Educational Psychology, 71,* 3–25.

WIGFIELD, A., & ASHER, S. (1984). Social and motivational influences on reading. In P. D. Pearson, R. Barr, M. Kamil & P. Mosenthal (Eds.), *Handbook of reading research,* Vol. I. (pp. 423–453). New York: Longman.

"I am the director. I need to direct them in the direction I want them to go. If I don't, that is like relinquishing my responsiblity in the lesson. But I'm also the facilitator. Sometimes, I let them guide me more and not be so hung up on directing them toward one idea or direction."

Comments made by a social studies teacher on her role during instruction.

5

Instruction

After reading this chapter, you should be able to:

1. Explain how instruction guides students in constructing meaning from texts.

2. Assess the effects of instruction in your classroom.

3. Make decisions about the instructional approach needed, given different kinds of instructional situations.

RATIONALE

Instruction is the bridge between texts and students. It is what teachers actively do to help students learn.

Just as the experience of reading changes depending on the situational context, the nature of instruction changes depending on variations in texts, students' understanding of the reading process, and students' motivation. In some situations, teachers are blessed with a clearly written text and knowledgeable, motivated students. In other situations, teachers are faced with incomprehensible texts or students who don't know or care about a subject or topic. Teachers in either situation think and act differently when it comes to instruction.

In more ideal situations, teachers are in a better position to use texts to teach content (recall from Chapter 1 that *content* refers to the knowledge or concepts that make up a subject; it is the subject matter that teachers want students to learn). They can also take more time to help students understand how to read-to-learn (recall that *reading-to-learn* refers to interactions between the reader, the text, and different contexts; knowing how to read-to-learn means knowing how to adapt the reading process to various conditions or situations in order to comprehend).

Teachers (and students) in less-than-ideal situations can find themselves in a real bind. With difficult texts and less knowledgeable or unmotivated students, teachers often spend a great deal of time building background knowledge and motivation. Teachers in these situations often complain about how much time it takes to teach content or how students seem to know so little about reading and learning from texts. Sometimes, students in these situations become difficult to manage because they are struggling and do not see the relevance of the text or the approach a teacher might be taking. Teachers facing

CHAPTER ORGANIZER

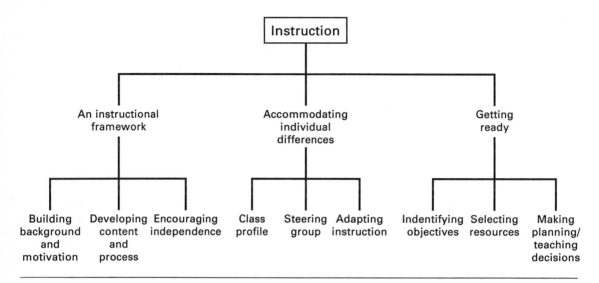

these problems must build enough content knowledge, understanding of the reading process, and motivation that students begin to see connections between learning in a subject and their own eventual success.

Instruction is a continuous cycle of problem-solving, crafting, improvising, and reflecting (Yinger, 1986). Effective teachers are sensitive to even the slightest changes in texts and students. They frequently adapt their instruction and continuously reflect on the effects of their teaching.

This chapter offers knowledge about instruction. It builds on ideas from previous chapters about texts, the reading process, and student motivation to focus on decisions about instruction. It explains how instruction can be used to reduce gaps between textbooks and students and demonstrates ways to gather feedback about your own instructional practices. Finally, the chapter provides an overview of classroom decisions that guide content reading instruction.

WHAT IS GOOD INSTRUCTION?

Good instruction consists of active participation by teachers and students in classroom activities focused on comprehension and learning. Because it is so dependent on the context or environment a teacher is able to create, good instruction is complex.

In some classrooms, only the appearance of good instruction is present. Sometimes, teachers fall into the trap of making instructional activities, such as discussions or reading and writing assignments, so complex that students spend all their time trying to *do* the activities rather than learning the concepts that the activities are supposed to convey. In some cases, students are so skilled at going through the motions during instruction, they fill out ditto sheets or draw aimlessly while they wait unnoticed for others in the class to produce the answers.

Good instruction depends on placing instructional activities in their proper perspective. The activities teachers select for instruction only set the stage. Used superficially, instructional activities become a barrier to deeper understandings, a way of wasting time. Used wisely, instructional activities provide clear pathways to comprehension and learning.

Instruction facilitates comprehension by helping modify existing knowledge or create new knowledge when students read texts (Anderson & Pearson, 1984). Instruction facilitates learning by helping students both internalize different kinds of knowledge and communicate what they know. During instruction, teachers use language (explanations, discussions, textual information, oral and written directions) to help students comprehend and learn (Shulman, 1986). The language teachers use provides a temporary *scaffold* to challenge and support students' existing knowledge and motivation (Vygotsky, 1978). A teacher's scaffold builds background and motivation for the content and processes students are about to encounter. As instruction progresses, teachers develop, monitor, and refine what students know. Gradually, students construct their own scaffolds. When this happens, teachers fade into the background, providing independent practice.

These ideas suggest a basic framework for good instruction.

AN INSTRUCTIONAL FRAMEWORK

Good instruction consists of three major stages: (1) *building background and motivation,* (2) *developing content and process,* and (3) *encouraging independence.* These stages comprise an *instructional framework* (see Figure 5.1).

The purpose of the instructional framework is to provide support for the thinking and decision-making that comprise good instruction. It is important to keep in mind that stages of this framework overlap. Teachers never really cease building background and motivation. Developing content and process and encouraging independence are ongoing tasks.

The following sections explain the instructional framework depicted in Figure 5.1. As you read the following sections, refer to the figure. The explanations that follow focus on lesson planning; however, the same principles apply to planning units of study (see Chapter 13).

Building Background and Motivation

Early moments of a lesson are critical for building background and motivation. Before students read, teachers need to foster student motivation through participation and relate new topics to any past experiences or previous learnings.

FIGURE 5.1

An Instructional Framework

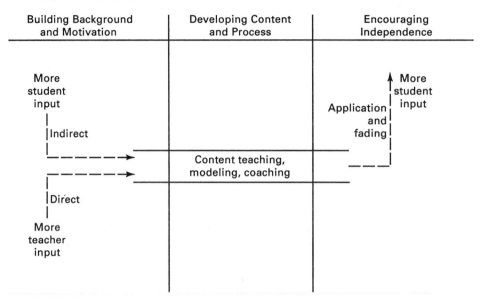

Building Background and Motivation	Developing Content and Process	Encouraging Independence

Teachers should provide students with a frame of reference

Joel Gordon

Vacca (1985) offers a set of principles devoted to building students' readiness for what they are about to read. Content teachers should:

- Select motivational approaches that will arouse a particular group of students for a particular lesson.
- Provide students with a frame of reference for learning the concepts they will encounter and acquire.
- Explain specific skills students will need in order to handle the subject matter (for example, specific ways of thinking about a topic or set of concepts).
- Help students become familiar with key vocabulary.

Teachers who do not follow these principles are often frustrated because students do not complete assignments. A still too common refrain from teachers is: "Read the chapter and answer the questions at the end." Some students are bold enough to report that it makes more sense to wait and hear what the teacher has to say before bothering to read. That way, they can discover the teacher's purpose—and still decide if it makes sense to do the reading. Like ourselves, students rarely read unless they know something about what they are going to read and possess a need or desire.

There are many ways teachers can give students a sense of purpose before they read. Mapping and charting out concepts, asking questions about students' prior knowledge (see Chapter 6), and using a study guide (Chapters 7 and 8) are among many useful alternatives. In using these activities, teachers should strive to build a positive classroom environment, encouraging students to get involved, and providing positive feedback and appropriate praise while building on students' interests. They should explain and model necessary skills and provide opportunities throughout instruction for practice and application.

Teachers should also consider the effects of wide versus narrow gaps between texts and what students already know and are motivated to learn (recall the discussion of these factors in the previous chapters). Depending on the size of these gaps, teachers will want to consider taking more of a direct versus an indirect approach to building background and motivation (see Figure 5.1).

Direct Approach   A *direct approach* is called for when students know little about the content and related reading processes in a lesson. A direct approach is defined as teachers providing overt assistance (that is, giving information, modeling, and explaining ways to think, read, and learn). The following examples help illustrate what is meant by a direct approach to instruction.

First consider eighth-grade students in a social studies class in the northeast United States reading in their texts about westward expansion in the late 1800s. The text may be somewhat difficult, presenting only a dry discussion of facts followed by five or ten questions focusing only on text comprehension. Students in this situation may not be interested in the content of the lesson because they feel that the setting and the time period have nothing to do with them. They may know few, if any, reading processes for approaching the text, such as making some connection to concepts they already know or constructing a way of organizing the textual information by using a set of concepts (for example, using the concepts "expansion" and "change" to remember important concepts in the reading).

To assist students in this situation, the teacher might talk about what the United States was like before the westward expansion in terms of geography, population, and economics. He or she could teach concepts such as "expansion," asking students to think about ways their own neighborhoods have expanded and changed over the years. Before students read, the teacher could ask students to watch for ways the west expanded and changed over the years. The intent of this preparation would provide a clear framework for students to read and comprehend the textual information.

Compare the situation in a social studies class with the early experiences of middle school students in an instrumental music class. Students at this level may have had few, if any, experiences with a musical instrument. They may know very little about how to read music. They may or may not be motivated to learn but will certainly need to be persistent and patient until they develop greater facility with all that is involved in playing the instrument.

To assist students in the early stages, an instrumental music teacher must do almost all the talking. The content he or she must convey consists of the inner workings of the instrument as well as the rudiments of breath control and mouth, hand, and body position. Students must be exposed to the system of reading notes. Reading processes involve not only recognizing and interpreting notes and expression marks but also coordinating music reading with music performance.

As should be clear from these examples, a direct approach consists of teachers providing most of the background, explanations, and the tools for reading and learning. A direct approach should be considered in situations involving new or complex content and when students have little or no prior knowledge or motivation.

Indirect Approach   An indirect approach is necessary when students know relatively more about the content and processes in a lesson or when motivation is high. Teachers take an *indirect approach* when they use and refine students' existing prior knowledge and motivation to introduce a lesson. When prior knowledge is available and students are motivated to talk about what they know, teachers must play a role different from that required in a direct approach. The following examples illustrate an indirect approach.

Many students enter a science lesson on plant nutrition believing that plants literally eat dirt. This conception may come from watching someone plant flowers around the house or from personal experiences with gardening. Other students, from school or their reading, may already know that plants manufacture food in their leaves while gathering vitamins and minerals from the soil. Neither group of students may be aware of the contribution of photosynthesis to plant nutrition (Roth, Anderson, & Smith, 1987).

In this situation, the teacher might engage students in talking about how plants grow. As the knowledge of the class becomes apparent, the teacher refines students' thinking by recording their ideas on the blackboard, pointing out conflicting explanations, and then having them read. As students read and discuss the textual information, any misconceptions are replaced with scientifically accurate concepts about plants. Students who were inaccurate in their original conceptions now understand how plants really get their nutrition. Students who already knew something about the topic gain a richer understanding, such as knowing the scientific processes underlying plant nutrition. The

An indirect approach to instruction should be considered when the knowledge and perspectives that students already possess need to be shaped and refined

Joel Gordon

approach is indirect because the teacher provides opportunities for students to wrestle with their own existing conceptions—rather than providing conceptions for students as in a direct approach.

Now consider a situation that plagues many vocational education teachers. Many students come to class, for example, in building trades or machine tools, thinking they already know a great deal about tools, machines, and safety. Unfortunately, many students may not know as much as they think, leading to injuries and a waste of materials. Direct teaching (or preaching!) does not help with this problem: students very quickly tune teachers out. Indirect teaching in which students talk about what they know first is a better option. Getting students to present their opinions first helps teachers identify and respond specifically to any misconceptions. At the same time, students feel that their opinions count and they can become more accepting of what the teacher has to say.

An indirect approach consists of working with and building upon what students already know, erasing misconceptions in some cases and enriching prior knowledge in other cases. An indirect approach to instruction should be considered when the knowledge and perspectives that students already possess need to be shaped and refined.

Developing Content and Process

As students read, teachers need to provide guidance in building content knowledge as well as knowledge about the reading process. *Content teaching, modeling,* and *coaching* are the instructional activities best suited for accomplishing these purposes (see Figure 5.1).

Content Teaching   Recall that content is the knowledge of the subject matter that teachers want students to understand. According to Roehler and Duffy (1989), meaningful *content teaching* occurs when teachers (1) actively engage students in the gradual construction of meaning (2) through a series of interactions with the content in which (3) new information is integrated with old information.

Consider this example of *actively engaging students in the gradual construction of meaning*. A mathematics teacher wanted students to think about differences in small versus large numbers. She posed a problem for students: how much money would a professional basketball player lose if he were suspended for one game? Addressing the problem first involved asking a series of questions: How much money do professional basketball players make? Do they get extra money for playoff games? Do they receive bonuses? How long is a player's contract? Does the salary include benefits? How does a suspension affect benefits? To answer these questions, students needed to do some reading and research. The teacher helped students gather their information, refine their questions when necessary, and relate information to the questions. As students worked, several began to invent mathematical formulas that took into account the important factors (for example, amount of 1 suspended game = total salary divided by number of years in the contract, divided by number of games in a year). This gradual approach allowed the teacher and her students to avoid mindless calculation, developing instead deeper mathematical understanding in a rich problem-solving context. The gradual construction of meaning, as this example illustrates, involves starting with a concept and building students' understanding carefully over time.

Now consider this example of *moving students through a series of interactions with the content*. A physical education teacher wanted students to think more deeply about some of the aspects of his weight training program (such as bench-pressing, aerobic exercise, stretching, and nutrition). One of his frustrations was that students tended to come in and work on weight lifting and Nautilus equipment without thinking carefully about taking care of their bodies and exercising wisely. Some injuries had resulted, and students were not making the progress that they could have been. He talked with students about the problem and asked them to research and prepare a five-minute talk for the class about one of the weight room activities. His hunch was that as students read about proper training and they talked about it with other students, the combination of increased information and oral and written language would enlighten students about their work in the weight room. This example illustrates several ways of moving students through a series of interactions with the content, by involving students in using different kinds of language (reading, writing, speaking, and listening) to explore and learn about the content, and by motivating students to interact with one another as part of the learning task.

Finally, consider this example of *integrating new information with old information*. A history teacher was responsible for teaching students about the Great Depression. He wanted students to feel what it is like to wrestle with real historical problems, especially ones that seem to keep coming back to haunt us in modern times. He designed a series of instructional activities that encouraged students to relate problems of the past with problems of the present. One activity entitled "You Are the President" engaged students in decision-making and discussions about the stock market failure, farm foreclosures, and unemployment in the 1930s. Discussions were based on excerpts from *The Grapes of*

Wrath and photographs from the period. New information was combined with prior knowledge, and new understanding was forged when the class connected problems of the Great Depression with modern economics and social ills (Wilson & Wineburg, 1988). When students integrate new and old information in this manner, they are better prepared over a lifetime to apply what they have learned.

The approach to content teaching described and espoused here is characterized by use of multiple sources of information, frequent opportunities to read and learn, and a classroom environment rich in language and communication. Other ways of teaching content effectively—ways that share these characteristics—are explained and illustrated throughout this text.

Modeling   *Modeling* involves showing how an expert might perform a task (such as comprehending or learning how to do an instructional activity) while explaining how and why the task is done that way (Collins, Brown, & Newman, 1987). Through modeling, teachers strive to demonstrate and develop in students mastery of a subject as well as greater metacognitive awareness of how reading can be used to comprehend content.

The teacher in the previous social studies example modeled historical thinking. He explained Franklin Roosevelt's proposed legislation as a way of thinking about possible solutions and courses of action related to problems during the Great Depression. Students then considered the merits of legislation as a way of solving economic and social problems (Wilson & Wineburg, 1988).

Consider how a vocational education teacher might model the reading process in the shop. While reading a shop manual out loud, he or she might guess what different words mean, summarize lists of procedures, and predict the function of various tools and machines. He or she might also model what to do when parts of the manual don't make sense or how to use the manual as a reference while working in the shop.

Teachers model the power of reading to construct meaning by:

- Explaining reading-related processes
- Demonstrating ways to monitor and evaluate comprehension
- Showing students how to apply fix-it strategies (see Chapter 3)

The goal of these activities is to foster in students strategic thinking when reading to comprehend and learn in content areas.

Coaching   When teachers engage in *coaching,* they observe ways students read and learn. They note difficulties, help when necessary, and offer suggestions on how to avoid problems or refine ideas. When teachers provide coaching, they give hints, adapt tasks on which students are working or select other ones, or show students why a particular approach to learning is ineffective (Collins, Brown, & Newman, 1987).

In English class, coaching might take the form of helping students focus in on decisions about audience, purpose, and form as they learn how to write (see Chapter 10). Students might write a little and then talk with teachers or other students about their intentions and how they are reflected in the writing. Teachers or other students might provide coaching by asking questions about parts of the writing that are not clear or whether the writing style is well-suited to the intended audience and purpose. In physical education, students might verbally summarize and demonstrate the steps of a particular physical activity (such as a serve in volleyball), while the teacher or other students observe, troubleshoot, and offer advice.

Schoenfeld (1988) suggests that when coaching, teachers should approach students with the following general questions in mind:

- What are you doing?
- How are you doing it?
- Why are you doing it that way?
- How will your approach make you successful?

Teachers can use students' answers to these questions to decide whether students are developing accurate concepts and understanding the answer-finding process.

Encouraging Independence

Teachers encourage student independence through *application* and *fading* (see Figure 5.1).

Application   Application consists of giving students opportunities to practice and apply what they have learned independently. If students cannot apply what they have learned to new or unusual situations in and outside of school, then they may not have learned anything of value. Two types of application are especially important: *application of content knowledge* and *application of the reading process* (Herber, 1978).

Application of content knowledge occurs through activities designed to help students generate concepts and generalizations on their own. Several content area examples illustrate this kind of application:

- After reading a mystery story in an English class, students write mysteries for each other.
- In a physical education class, students read about the effects of nutrition on fitness, plan and adopt a personal menu, and later report on its effects.
- In some science classrooms, students design and present the results of an experiment to satisfy their curiosity about a recently studied scientific concept.

Typically, these activities share an emphasis on the real-world functions of lesson information and on students communicating what they have learned.

Application of the reading process occurs through activities designed to help students review and apply the reading processes used throughout a lesson. The simplest way to do this is to ask a class: "What ways (or kinds of thinking) did we use to figure out what we needed to know?" If the teacher developed specific methods for thinking about subject matter or using reading to figure out unfamiliar content, students should be able to explain the methods and suggest ways to use them in the future (Conley, 1990).

Several examples of application of the reading process are:

- In a mathematics class, students thought about what they learned in a previous lesson before moving on to the next lesson.
- After cleaning up the shop, students discussed how they solved problems by using manuals, charts, or diagrams.
- In a history class, students talked about ways to map out concepts in order to better remember important textual information.

The emphasis in applying the reading process is on helping students transfer their understanding of reading from one lesson to the next.

Fading   *Fading* is the stage during instruction when teachers gradually give students more responsibility for and control over learning (Collins, Brown, & Newman, 1987). Teachers fade out of the limelight usually during application activities at the end of a lesson. The purpose of fading is to complete the process of helping students practice and internalize what they have been learning.

Transfer of control is appropriate on one condition: teachers must be reasonably certain that students really understand the content and reading processes covered and can apply them. If students aren't ready, teachers need to consider reteaching and reinforcing the content and processes not yet acquired. Reinforcement techniques appear in later chapters.

ACCOMMODATING INDIVIDUAL DIFFERENCES

Good instruction also makes accommodations for individual differences. Teachers accommodate by adjusting instructional activities so that all students are continually challenged and not frustrated. Based on a case study of one effective teacher working with special population students, Dillon (1989) makes the following general recommendations for meeting individual needs:

- Varying teaching styles for better communication
- Working one-to-one, when possible
- Posing problems and instilling a desire to learn
- Modeling behaviors and processes that students are expected to acquire
- Building students' background knowledge
- Anticipating problems and adapting lessons to students' changing needs

Teachers should apply these principles to many different kinds of instructional situations.

It is difficult to make these accommodations, however, without an accurate sense of strengths and weaknesses of students in each classroom. What makes this task so formidable is the number of students involved. Teachers with no planning time or 100 to 150 students per day have precious little time to collect enough information to tailor instruction to each individual. Two approaches can help: (1) developing a class profile, and

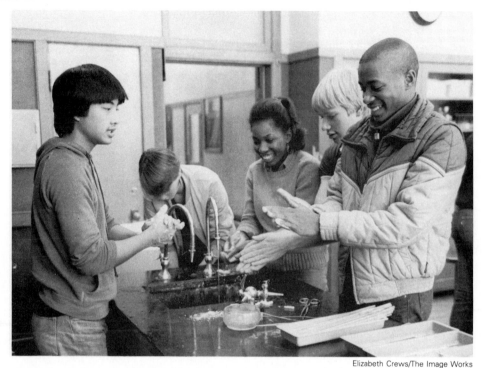

Accommodating individual differences means making adjustments to instruction so that *all* *students* are challenged

Elizabeth Crews/The Image Works

(2) identifying a classroom steering group. These approaches build on the assessment techniques explained in previous chapters.

Developing a Class Profile

A sample *class profile* appears in Figure 5.2. It was constructed first by identifying the factors most important for students' success and achievement in the class. Next, assessment techniques were selected and administered. Finally, results were summarized for each student.

Note how the top of this profile consists of information about the class textbook. Other assessment techniques can be substituted for the ones used in this sample. For instance, a CLOZE score could be used instead of the textbook checklist. Results could be summarized in terms of whether students found the text easy, frustrating, or just right. A general attitude scale could be used in place of the subject-matter scale to assess motivation.

Well-designed profiles assist teachers in making judgments about individuals and an entire class at a glance. Jennifer, for example, is a good student who nonetheless may need continual challenge to keep her interest. Justin tends to have adequate prior knowledge for what he is reading, yet his comprehension is less than desirable. The reason for Justin's poor performance may lie in his lack of motivation, his language and writing ability, or a

FIGURE 5.2

A Sample Class Profile

Teacher ___Duffy___ Grade/Subject _10th Grade History_ Class Period _6th_

Textbook _This is America's Story_ Readability ___11.0 (Raygor)___

Textbook Evaluation Checklist _60 pts. (difficult text)_

Notes _Heavy vocabulary load for this group. Chapters skip around a lot. Many concepts not relevant to the kids._

Assessment Measures

1. Achievement: _Iowa Tests of Basic Skills_
2. Prior knowledge: _Content Area Reading Inventory_
3. Metacognition: _Content Area Reading Inventory_
4. Comprehension: _Content Area Reading Inventory_
5. Oral language ability: _Oral Language Observations_
6. Writing ability: _Writing Sample_
7. Motivation: _Subject-Matter Motivation Scale_

Profile codes:

Performance

H = High

M = Medium or average

L = Low

Special populations

B = Bilingual

G = Gifted

S = Special education

Scale

Student Name	Achievement	Prior knowledge	Metacognition	Comprehension	Oral language	Writing ability	Motivation	Special populations
Jennifer	M	H	H	M	H	M	L	G
Chris	L	H	L	L	L	L	L	S

combination of these factors. Although this classroom of students comprehends well, they could use guidance in their writing.

A class profile helps teachers meet individual student needs by providing a "snapshot" of the areas where students need extra help. For instance, teachers may discover that many students require instruction in reading long passages, while a somewhat smaller group is highly motivated and skilled with longer reading assignments. Teachers can create classroom groups in which students with certain strengths can help students who require extra help.

It is necessary to restate the tentative nature of these judgments. As noted in earlier chapters, assessment techniques on which a class profile is based do not tell the whole story about students. A class profile can be an important tool in making judgments about students and instructional decisions, but only when it is combined with ongoing, day-to-day observations.

Identifying a Classroom Steering Group

One way to simplify the task of adjusting instruction for individual differences is to identify a steering group. Most teachers naturally single out a group of students in a class on which they base both planning and instructional decisions. Researchers refer to this group as the *steering group* (Dahllof, 1971).

Steering groups consist of five or six students who the teacher considers to be *truly representative* of all students in a class. To create a representative group, teachers identify students who vary according to a number of factors (such as achievement, motivation, comprehension, writing ability, and even social skills). When considered as a whole, the students chosen as the steering group should reflect the full range of strengths and weaknesses in a class. For example, students who are strong in achievement balance others who are weaker. Students who are highly motivated balance those whose motivation varies or whose motivation is low. At times, these students may work together. Many times, however, members of a steering group will be spread throughout the class. What makes them a group is the notion that these diverse students collectively represent the diversity of the whole class. The students depicted in Figure 5.3 are good candidates for a steering group; as a group, they reflect a range of performance on a number of factors. Observing the performance of the members of a steering group during instruction provides an indicator of performance for various students throughout a class. Teachers observe students' performance to evaluate the complexity of the classroom tasks and assignments, whether goals for instruction are realistic, and if time to complete work is adequate. By observing students in the steering group, teachers might discover that instruction is appropriate for some students and not others. High achievers in the steering group might become bored with some types of instruction; low achievers or students with low motivation might falter when instruction becomes particularly challenging. While these observations might not generalize to everyone in the class, they could help teachers make better decisions about increasing or reducing complexity, modifying goals, or altering allotted time (Dahllof, 1971).

Be aware that the performance of a steering group does not necessarily reflect the performance of all individuals. A steering group provides a *rough* gauge of individual

FIGURE 5.3

A Classroom Steering Group

Student Name	Achievement	Prior knowledge	Metacognition	Comprehension	Oral language	Writing ability	Motivation	Special populations
Theresa	H	H	H	M	H	M	H	—
Matt	H	H	H	H	H	M	H	G
Carlos	M	H	L	M	M	L	M	B
Suzanne	M	M	M	M	H	M	M	—
Christine	L	M	L	L	M	L	L	—
Mike	L	L	L	L	H	L	L	S

performance. Hypotheses based on observations of the steering group should always be confirmed or confronted by observing students who are not members of the steering group. Teachers should also consider changing the membership of the steering group periodically so that the focus can be on different students throughout the year.

ORGANIZING FOR INSTRUCTION

Effective instruction is intentional. This section discusses three intentional processes in preparing for instruction: (1) identifying content and behavioral objectives (for process and motivation), (2) selecting resources, and (3) making planning and teaching decisions.

Identifying Objectives

Objectives are useful tools for making planning and teaching decisions. A clear set of objectives should point to the concepts to be learned as well as to the behaviors teachers expect from students as a result of instruction (Novak, 1977). An objective that focuses on concepts is called a *content objective*. Objectives that emphasize behaviors are termed *behavioral objectives*. Content objectives represent content goals for a lesson. Behavioral objectives reflect the process and motivation goals that support content learning.

Content Objective   A *content objective* summarizes the concepts teachers want students to learn through instruction. One way to develop a content objective is to ask: "If students studied this content successfully, what concepts would they identify as most important?" or "What statement from students would indicate they understand the content?" (Earle, 1976; Phelps, 1984).

During planning, a content objective is an organizational device—a generalization that guides the design of a lesson (or unit) with a consistent focus. While teaching, a content objective guides instructional decisions that close the gap between what students already know and the content they need to learn.

FIGURE 5.4

Sample Content Objectives for Individual Lessons

Tenth-Grade Science

A single cell carries on all the same life functions that humans do.

Eighth-Grade English

You don't have to fight someone to keep your self-respect.

Middle School Mathematics

Using a percent to calculate a discount price can be misleading.

First-Year French

Shopping in France differs from shopping in the United States.

Physical Education

Warm-up and cool-down activities can be general and specific to the running activity in which you are involved.

Tenth-Grade Social Studies

Because of differences in their historical traditions, the North and South will always be in conflict.

Eleventh-Grade Health

Mental health is an illness that affects us all; society has a responsiblity to help the mentally ill.

High School Art

An artist uses form and color to express different feelings.

Middle School Music

A rock tune has a different musical effect on an audience than a march.

Vocational Education

Shop safety requires a cool head and knowledge about first aid.

Business Education

It takes more than money to run a successful small business.

6

Vocabulary Instruction

CHAPTER OBJECTIVES

By the time you finish this chapter, you should be able to:

1. Prioritize and select for emphasis the words and concepts that are important for students to know.

2. Plan and teach using specific instructional activities for building vocabulary concepts, developing processes for independent vocabulary learning, and fostering enjoyment in learning new words.

RATIONALE

Learning the names for things can be a powerful experience. As the quote at the beginning of the chapter suggests, vocabulary is one of the key elements for understanding an entire subject. When the language of a subject is learned, students see what they had not seen before and they can communicate in ways that are unique from one subject to the next.

All too often, *difficult words* are the sole focus of vocabulary teaching, with difficulty determined by the size of a word rather than by students' familiarity with a concept. This is an overly simple and generic approach to a complex issue. A lengthy word can be easy to comprehend and apply, if students are already familiar with what the word represents. On the other hand, short words such as "love," "irony," "power," and "ellipse" pose problems because, for many students, each word represents an abstraction. What complicates matters even further is that concepts hidden behind these terms change from situation to situation. For example, consider the multiple meanings of the word "square," as it is used in mathematics (a four-sided figure), building trades (a tool for measurement), or casual conversation (a nerd). The importance of learning a word cannot be determined through generic means, such as selecting longer rather than shorter words for teaching, or without reference to the context in which the word appears. Vocabulary instruction should focus on concepts that are both unfamiliar and essential to the context in which they are being applied.

Problems related to vocabulary instruction vary across content areas. In English, social studies, and science, teachers face the problem of too many words to teach. When teachers in these areas select words for instruction, they often focus on difficult words or words highlighted by a textbook. Not surprisingly, when using these criteria, teachers compile lengthy vocabulary lists. These lists may not adequately reflect what teachers feel

CHAPTER ORGANIZER

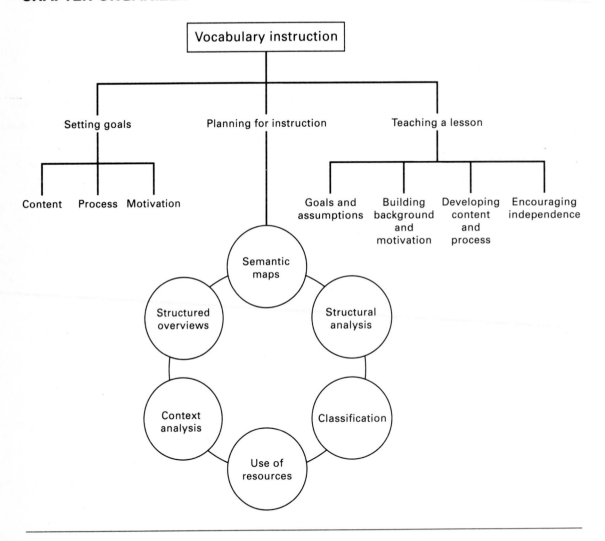

is important about content. In addition, it is usually impossible, given time constraints, to teach all the vocabulary words and still give students an understanding of the content.

In mathematics, music, physical education, and vocational education, teachers face a much different problem. Consider this example from trigonometry:

$$\frac{\sqrt{c + d}}{5 - \sqrt{c + d}}$$

This equation contains few symbols, yet the concepts represented are sophisticated. In some content areas, students have serious vocabulary problems when trying to comprehend a small number of words or symbols that represent many complex concepts.

Still another problem concerns concepts not explicitly represented by words in print. This problem occurs in nearly every content area. For example, in teaching literature, English teachers use language that never appears in a short story or novel, such as "metaphor" or "plot." In physical education, teachers use different kinds of language for physical activity, such as "check swing," "jump shot," "underhand serve." Students can fail to comprehend because the content they need to learn is not explained or explicitly represented in texts or other classroom resources or activities.

Students need to know about words and their meanings if they are to learn successfully in any content area. The problem of limited word knowledge is significant because of the strong relationship between vocabulary and comprehension (Anderson & Freebody, 1981). If students are unfamiliar with most of the words they encounter, they will have trouble learning (Stahl, Jacobson, Davis, & Davis, 1989). Given these problems, the challenge is: How can content area teachers enable students to understand vocabulary so that they can comprehend and communicate in a subject?

This chapter confronts the challenge of vocabulary instruction. It discusses criteria for identifying essential vocabulary and explains and illustrates ways to teach words and concepts so that students know how to use the language of different content areas to read and communicate in and out of school.

SETTING GOALS

Planning for vocabulary teaching requires special kinds of thinking about goals for content (which words to teach), process (which vocabulary processes to emphasize), and motivation (how to develop student interest). These decisions are the subject of this section.

Content Goals

The content goals for vocabulary are to: (1) select vocabulary terms that are important in a specific context, and (2) teach vocabulary at an appropriate level (definition or meaning).

Words are important in a context when they are basic to understanding larger subject-matter concepts and principles. For example, middle and secondary school students already know how to eat. They develop the basic knowledge and ability to eat without knowing the term "nutrition." The goal in many science and health classes, however, is to teach students what it means "to eat well." To achieve this goal, students must acquire and communicate with a common language based on the content to be learned. Emphasizing nutrition and other related concepts during vocabulary instruction helps teachers and students distinguish old concepts from new, encouraging students to progress from a junk-food mentality to a better understanding of the body and relationships between a balanced diet and good health.

Students "know" vocabulary terms on a number of levels. *Definition* and *meaning* often are used interchangeably though each actually reflects a different way of knowing a word. Students know definitions when they are able to associate or match words with a specific fact or quality. For instance, with practice students could easily match the terms "digestion" and "nutrition" with their textbook definitions:

- *digestion:* the process of changing foods into nutrients that an organism can absorb.
- *nutrition:* the sum of the processes by which living things take in and use food substances.

Definitional knowledge, however, is insufficient when students must understand the terms in a more functional way, such as knowing how "digestion" and "nutrition" apply to eating or choosing a health-related career.

To achieve deeper understanding, students need to know the meanings behind vocabulary terms. Students know vocabulary meanings when they can appropriately apply concepts to the content they are learning. The ultimate test of students' ability to apply vocabulary is a test of *transfer*. Ideally, when students study meanings, they should be able to apply them in current lessons and transfer their understanding to later lessons. Consider the recurrence of "respiration" in the science curriculum. Students learn early in the year that the term applies to processes by which plants exchange oxygen and carbon dioxide between cells and the environment. Later in the year, knowing about plant digestion gives students a start in understanding how human beings digest food. Since they already know that respiration involves an exchange of oxygen and carbon dioxide, students should be able to transfer what they know to help them learn about respiratory exchanges in the human body.

Unfortunately, teachers cannot be sure that students will transfer their vocabulary knowledge from one lesson to another. When asked about previously taught concepts, some students respond with blank stares or disbelief. The reason for this may be *traditional vocabulary instruction*. Traditional instruction focuses on large numbers of words, taught mostly on a definition level. When students are exposed to large numbers of vocabulary concepts and are given little time to study them, learning is often superficial and short-term. Trying to teach a large number of words on a meaning level is no way out of this dilemma. Though taking a meaning approach—as opposed to a definition approach—makes the learning deeper and more long-term for some words, developing meanings always takes more time and fewer words can be taught. If large numbers of words are fundamental to understanding the content, teachers can very quickly become bogged down in teaching individual word meanings.

Teachers are faced with a complex set of decisions. Because of the content of a lesson and the sequence of concepts across lessons, it may be best to teach some words on a definition level, saving more in-depth treatment for later lessons. In other lessons, it may be best to teach some words on a meaning level, because knowing the meaning will help students comprehend entire passages. How can teachers make these kinds of decisions?

Spencer Grant/Stock, Boston

Traditional vocabulary instruction focuses on large numbers of words

One way for teachers to make decisions about vocabulary is to ask themselves three questions about the words in a reading selection:

1. Which words are important to the content objective for the lesson?

2. Which words are unfamiliar?

3. Which words will students see again?

Recall from Chapter 5 that a content objective states approximately what students should understand by the end of a lesson. Words that meet the criteria for all three questions deserve special emphasis: these words are basic to understanding the content objective, unfamiliar to most students, and reappear later in the curriculum. By spending time on the meaning of these words, teachers increase the likelihood that students will apply them in immediate as well as future lessons.

Words that meet the criteria for only one or two questions deserve a different kind of emphasis. For example, some unfamiliar words are related to the content objective yet never reappear in the curriculum. Consider this example from a social studies lesson dealing with how the federal government is organized (for example, federal, legislative, judicial branches). The teacher developed the following content objective for the lesson: Our government is organized so that there is a balance of power. The text contrasted

FIGURE 6.1

Selecting and Prioritizing Vocabulary for a Science Lesson

Content objective: Acids are unique because of their makeup and uses.

Students: Mixed Group of 8th Graders

Which words are important to the content objective?	Which words are unfamiliar?	Which words will students see again?
Acid tastes		Acid
Sweet		
Sour		
Salty		
Bitter		
Molecules		Molecules
Ions		Ions
Colorless		
H^+ ions	H^+ ions	H^+ ions
Hydrochloric acid (HCl)	Hydrochloric acid (HCl)	
Indicators (pH)	Indicators (pH)	Indicators (pH)
Weak acids	Weak acids	Weak acids
Vinegar		
Lemon juice		
Vitamin C		
Strong acids	Strong acids	Strong acids
Battery acid	(H_2SO_4)	
(H_2SO_4)	Nitric acid	
Nitric acid	(HNO_3)	
(HNO_3)		

Selection Decisions

Words to teach on a meaning level	Words to teach on a definition level	Words for brainstorming or review
H^+ ions	Hydrochloric acid	Molecule
Weak acids	HCl	Ion
Strong acids	H_2SO_4	
Indicators	Nitric acid	
pH	HNO_3	

"bicameral" with "unicameral" legislatures. The teacher decided to teach the meaning of bicameral because, in his mind, the concept met all the criteria for emphasizing the meaning of a word. Unicameral, on the other hand, was dealt with on a definition level because (1) it was important to the content objective (in showing one way to organize the government), (2) it was unfamiliar to students, and (3) it was unlikely to reappear in the curriculum (Nebraska has the only unicameral or single-chamber legislature in the country).

Other words are familiar and recurring; some of them may have been taught in previous lessons. In the social studies class just described, "government" was a recurring word. Students had just completed study of monarchies in Europe. Now they were turning to democracies. Familiar words, relatable to the content objective, can be used to initiate brainstorming or review. For instance, the social studies teacher began discussion by asking students what they had learned about governments up to that point. This approach allows teachers to build, review, and refine the meanings of a small number of conceptually related vocabulary terms while providing connections from one lesson to another.

Figure 6.1 depicts the way one science teacher made decisions about which vocabulary words are important to teach. Keep in mind that these decisions are subjective: this teacher made her decisions based on an understanding of her students at a particular point in the curriculum. Note also how her judgments about familiarity are based on students' familiarity with specific concepts important in the lesson, rather than on general familiarity. For example, students have a general awareness of the differences between weak and strong acids, but they have not yet studied the specific chemical differences developed in the lesson. Teachers who follow the steps depicted here can prioritize and teach vocabulary according to what is important to the overall content of a lesson.

Process Goals

There is one process-oriented goal for teaching vocabulary: to help students become strategists when applying different vocabulary processes. A *vocabulary process* is a way of figuring out and applying the meaning of an unknown word. Some of the more common vocabulary processes good readers use are defined and illustrated in Figure 6.2.

Recall from Chapter 3 what it means to be a *strategist* when reading (selecting, adapting, and monitoring reading processes). Being a strategist with vocabulary means being flexible in selecting, combining, and adapting any number of processes for comprehending unfamiliar words. Vocabulary processes must be matched appropriately to different kinds of words. For example, a word such as "Darwinism" is not easily compared or contrasted with other words (classification), nor is it possible to derive much meaning by breaking the word into parts (structural analysis). Instead, to determine the meaning of the term, students need to rely on the context in which the word appears and possibly outside resources, such as a textbook glossary. Usually, no single vocabulary process is sufficient for determining word meanings. In Figure 6.2, note how the use of classification is alone insufficient for finding the full meaning of "democracy."

Typically, to construct the meaning of a vocabulary word, students must apply several processes. Good readers can accomplish this in seconds! Poor readers often don't know when a word is important and/or that an important word is unfamiliar. Many students can develop a strategic approach to vocabulary learning, if teachers take time to explain vocabulary processes as they teach word meanings. For example, many teachers use the vocabulary processes in Figure 6.2 to teach unfamiliar terms. Teachers offer students a strategic approach by informing students how word meanings are being developed, by labeling, discussing, and modeling the techniques as ways good readers construct word meanings.

FIGURE 6.2

Vocabulary Processes for Constructing the Meaning of an Unfamiliar Word (Note: Unfamiliar words are underlined in the examples)

Using prior knowledge: Comprehending the meaning of a word by thinking about what is already known about the word.

> *Example:* Ozone is a term that appears in the news all the time. Scientists are worried that if the ozone goes away, people will be harmed by the sun's rays.

> *Meaning:* (Developed through reading or discussion) Ozone is a gas in the air that provides protection.

Context analysis: Comprehending the meaning of a word by studying the words in the surrounding context, such as in a sentence or in an entire passage.

> *Example:* The lottery winner behaved ostentatiously at the party, flashing $100 bills and gold jewelry.

> *Meaning:* A word used to describe showy behavior, behavior that attracts notice.

Classification: Comprehending the meaning of a word by comparing and contrasting unfamiliar words with which it can be associated or grouped.

> *Example:* Democracy is like or can be compared with "monarchy" and "dictatorship" (recently studied forms of government).

> *Meaning:* Since "monarchy" and "dictatorship" refer to forms of government, democracy must be another form of government.

Structural analysis: Comprehending the meaning of a word by breaking words into familiar parts.

> *Example:* Bifocal

> *Meaning:* "Bi" means two of something.
> "Foc" appears in the word "focus," meaning "to see."
> Bifocal means a two-part eyeglass lens, one for far and another for near vision.

Use of resources: After determining the possible meaning of a word using one or more of the above processes, confirming the meaning by looking it up in a dictionary, thesaurus, or glossary.

> *Example:* From classification, it appears that democracy is a form of government.

> *Meaning:* The glossary says that a democracy is a form of government in which the power is exercised directly by the people of a country.

Motivation Goals

The two motivation goals for teaching vocabulary are to help students: (1) gain self-confidence in their own abilities to learn new words, and (2) discover enjoyment in learning new words in a content area.

Attention to vocabulary processes and strategic vocabulary learning supports the first goal. Students grow in self-confidence and independence as they see that newly learned words and vocabulary processes can be used to eliminate confusion and to comprehend broader concepts and principles. They realize that they don't have to feel victimized by the unfamiliar terms that keep cropping up in the text.

Contrary to some beliefs, students will choose to expand their own vocabularies when motivated to do so. In a recent study, students reported that it is fun to learn new words and to be able to use them for communicating (Haggard, 1986). The words students enjoyed, however, came from pleasure reading rather than from school textbooks. Most students have not discovered how to enjoy and communicate with the vocabulary of their content texts.

Teachers can start to build motivation for vocabulary learning by finding out what students find interesting. For some students, this might mean asking what they read outside of school and asking them to keep a journal of the interesting words they discover. For other students, this could take the form of creating a slang dictionary complete with words students often use that adults do not understand. By listening to students' use of

Many students learn new words from their pleasure reading

Elizabeth Crews/Stock, Boston

language and discovering what interests them, teachers can select more relevant words from school texts. For example, a student who learns about "hydroponics" from science fiction pleasure reading will probably be motivated by the inclusion of hydroponics in a unit on photosynthesis. Teachers may also discover ways to use students' existing vocabularies to make texts more interesting. For instance, students who have developed a rich slang vocabulary for people and how they act (for example, "that dude is bad," "he's always stangin' on other people") might enjoy applying their language to the study of characters in a novel. By working with words that have some intrinsic interest to students, teachers can show students ways in which useful and exciting words are all around them.

PLANNING FOR INSTRUCTION

This section describes specific ways to plan for vocabulary instruction, once words—and the processes necessary to teach them—have been identified. Planning is based on each of the five vocabulary processes described earlier: use of prior knowledge, context analysis, classification, structural analysis, and use of outside resources.

Use of Prior Knowledge: Structured Overviews and Semantic Maps

Structured overviews and *semantic maps* are part of a family of techniques termed "organizers." The purpose of an organizer is to help students use prior knowledge to gain new knowledge (Ausubel, 1977). Organizers are visual displays or "scaffolds" for concepts students are learning. Later chapters will discuss the many purposes organizers serve, including assessment (note the use of organizers to introduce concepts at the beginning of each chapter in this text). The terms "structured overview" and "semantic map" are often used to represent specific uses of organizers for vocabulary instruction.

Structured Overviews   A structured overview is a way to represent hierarchical relationships between facts and concepts in a text (Barron, 1979). The technique is most useful in situations requiring a direct approach to instruction, that is, when students know little about a topic and teachers need to develop some background knowledge before introducing vocabulary terms.

Figure 6.3 depicts examples of structured overviews from several different subject areas. Note the distinctive relationships between larger, higher-level concepts and smaller, lower-level concepts and facts.

To design a structured overview, start with the content objective for inspiration. Pull concepts from the content objective that seem to be most important. For example, a science lesson on how refrigerators work used the following content objective: Refrigerators cool food through a process of evaporation and condensation. The science teacher selected "refrigerators," and "cool food" as two major concepts in the lesson.

Next, examine the text for facts and concepts that support the major concepts. Sometimes, these supporting concepts can be found in chapter and section headings in the textbook. In the refrigerator lesson, the next level of concepts involves pressure being applied to freon in the back of the refrigerator. Other concepts are added by determining

FIGURE 6.3

Structured Overviews: (*a*) Vocal Music, (*b*) Social Studies, and (*c*) English

Vocal Music

Content objective: Singing from printed music means we have to understand all of the different signs and markers. (Created by Cathy Koch)

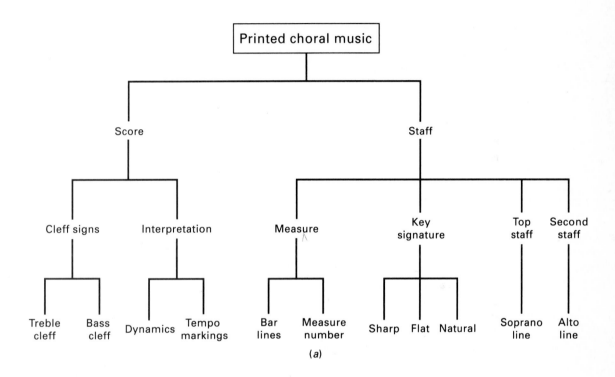

(*a*)

how and where the pressure is applied and the specific parts of the refrigerator that make the refrigerator do its job. Try to include some terms that are already familiar to students.

An important step is to position words on the overview that have been selected for vocabulary teaching. In the refrigerator lesson, "evaporation" and "condensation" were selected. The terms are located on the overview as supporting concepts that help students understand the action of the freon and the cooling of the refrigerator. A final step before teaching is to evaluate the overview. Does it effectively portray the relationships among concepts in the text? Can it be simplified? Will it be relatively easy to communicate clearly the meaning of key vocabulary terms? (Barron, 1979.) Steps for constructing a structured overview are summarized in Figure 6.4. The completed structured overview for the refrigerator lesson is also depicted.

In teaching from a structured overview, think carefully about how you will present the overview. Many teachers like to use an overhead projector; others prefer to build

FIGURE 6.1 *(Cont.)*

Social Studies

Content objective: The American economic system is based on a balance of wants and needs and goods and services. (Created by Sonia Arduser)

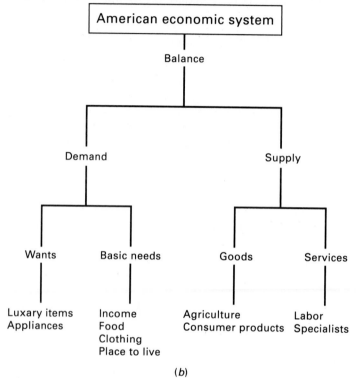

(b)

English

Content objective: A person's fantasies can offer escape from life's miseries.

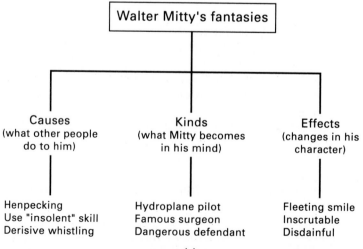

(c)

FIGURE 6.4

Procedures for Designing a Structured Overview

1. Select the most important concept(s) for a lesson. Make this decision based on the content objective.
2. Examine the text and add words that support these larger, higher-level concepts. Include any words that might already be familiar, or that have been previously taught.
3. Attach words to the overview that have been selected for vocabulary teaching. Words selected for meaning as well as definition emphasis may be included.
4. Evaluate the overview. Does it portray important relationships among lesson concepts? Does it show relationships between familiar terms and new vocabulary?

Content objective: Refrigerators cool food through a process of evaporation and condensation.

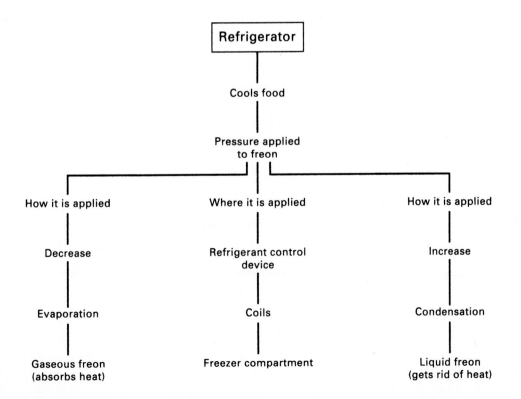

overviews gradually on the chalkboard. An overview can be entered at any point early in a classroom discussion. With the refrigerator example, a teacher might wish to explain how refrigerators cool food or describe the parts of a refrigerator. As more and more of the overview has been explained, teachers can introduce and teach the words selected for emphasis and attach them to the overview. It is important throughout this process to ask students periodically to summarize what they think concepts on the overview mean. This helps teachers keep track of students' developing understanding.

Semantic Maps   Semantic maps are more fluid and flexible in their shape and use than structured overviews. This makes them especially suitable for situations requiring an

FIGURE 6.5

Semantic Maps: (*a*) Mathematics, (*b*) Social Studies, and (*c*) Physical Education

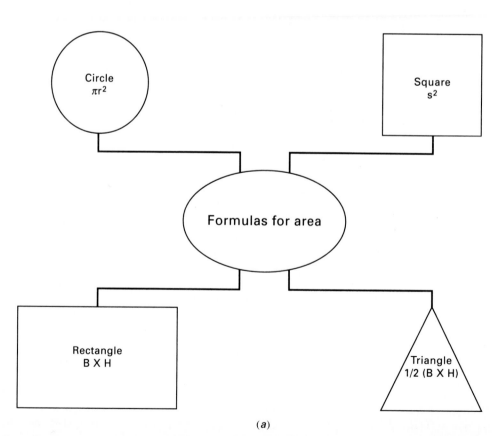

Mathematics

Content objective: The area of any figure can be found by using a formula.

Circle
πr^2

Square
s^2

Formulas for area

Rectangle
B X H

Triangle
1/2 (B X H)

(*a*)

Social Studies

Content objective: Historical propaganda has much in common with the way used cars are sold.

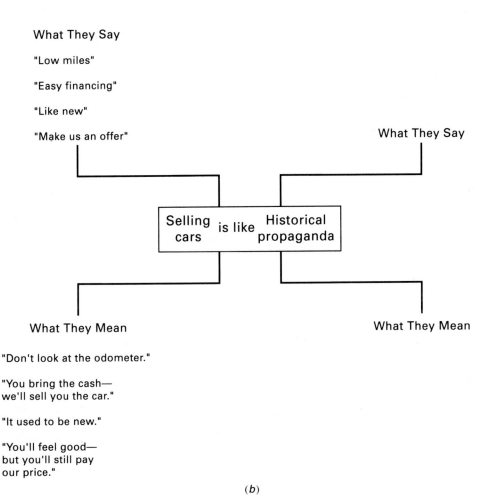

What They Say

"Low miles"

"Easy financing"

"Like new"

"Make us an offer"

What They Say

Selling cars   is like   Historical propaganda

What They Mean

What They Mean

"Don't look at the odometer."

"You bring the cash—
we'll sell you the car."

"It used to be new."

"You'll feel good—
but you'll still pay
our price."

(b)

indirect approach to instruction, that is, when students know something about the topic of a lesson and teachers attempt to capture and build on what they know.

Figure 6.5 depicts semantic maps from several different subject areas. Maps can take on a variety of shapes, from spider webs to trees to Venn diagrams. Maps are generally arranged in any shape that helps convey relationships among important concepts.

Teachers and students build maps during discussions, yet managing this process—and using it to teach vocabulary—requires some thinking before the lesson begins. First, teachers need to determine if a semantic map is a good technique for the content students are learning. If some of the key concepts are familiar to students, then mapping may be a good approach. This was the choice a science teacher made when she taught a lesson

FIGURE 6.5 *(Cont.)*

Physical Education

Content objective: With a little knowledge, a good hitter can become better and a weak hitter more effective.

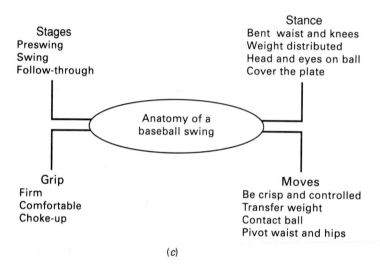

(c)

dealing with the forms and uses of energy. Many of the students had some familiarity with the concept "energy," but they did not know all the meanings the teacher wanted them to have. The teacher chose to use a semantic map because the meaning of "energy" was somewhat familiar.

Maps are constructed interactively through a process best described as *list-group-label* (Taba, 1967). Students brainstorm in response to starter concepts, like "energy," and teachers list what students say. Teachers then ask students to group terms that are alike. Next, students are asked to label the groups of terms. New vocabulary terms can be introduced at any point in this process, from the brainstorming stage or as words are grouped and labeled. As full participants in the mapping, teachers can also provide key terms and meanings behind important concepts.

It is important to sketch out ahead of time the likely configuration of the map and the eventual location of the vocabulary terms that will be taught. Steps for constructing a semantic map appear in Figure 6.6, along with a completed map. The map was designed ahead of time to capture what students might say about energy. The terms "electromagnetic" and "mechanical" were identified as key vocabulary concepts that students would learn at the appropriate time.

Context Analysis

Activities that stress *context analysis* typically involve placing vocabulary words in relevant sentences. Teachers can create original sentences or draw from students' reading. Drawing sentences from the reading has the advantage of teaching vocabulary terms in

FIGURE 6.6

Procedures for Designing a Semantic Map

1. Choose a familiar word (or words) to start the lesson. Use the content objective to guide your choice.
2. Think about words students will offer when asked to brainstorm for words that are related to the starter word(s). Write a brief list of those words (the list step).
3. Arrange words on the list to reflect possible groupings (the group step).
4. Write a label for each of the groups (the label step).
5. Place vocabulary words on the map that have been selected for teaching. Words that have been selected for meaning as well as definition emphasis can be included.
6. Evaluate the map. Does it portray important relationships among lesson concepts? Does it show relationships between familiar terms and new vocabulary?

Content objective: Even though there are many forms of energy, we could run out some day.

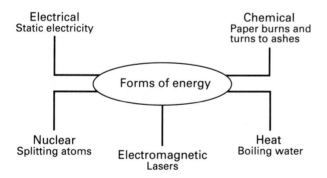

contexts students will later confront. Sometimes, terms are not well-defined by the sentences in which they are found. In these cases, it is best to design an original sentence (or sentences) that help develop a word's meaning.

To illustrate the point that context analysis activities need to be carefully evaluated, compare the contexts provided for the word "inalienable."

Weak Context

Rights that are *inalienable* cannot be given or taken away.

Strong Context

Everyone is born with *inalienable* rights, such as the right to live, the right to be free, and the right to be happy. No one can take these rights away.

Well-designed context analysis activities present a familiar context, guiding students to explore what they already know about a concept so they can assimilate the new term (Gipe, 1979). The first sentence is weaker because it provides only a general definition of the term. The second set of sentences is much stronger, because they name examples of some familiar inalienable rights.

Figure 6.7 depicts ways that context analysis is used across the curriculum.

While most of this section has dealt with context analysis activities presented in sentence form, one other related activity deserves mention: the use of demonstration and discussion to introduce the vocabulary students will encounter in their reading. This approach to context analysis is best explained through an example.

To give students a concept for "scientific observation," a science teacher spilled a bag of oranges on a lab table. He instructed lab partners to take an orange, examine it carefully, and write down any observations. Students were then instructed to place the oranges back into the bag. Finally, the teacher asked students to identify their original orange, using their written observations. The teacher used these experiences as a way to distinguish between casual observation, in which details are often overlooked, and scientific observation, in which details are critical for identifying and classifying different kinds of phenomena.

FIGURE 6.7

Context Analysis Across the Curriculum (Note: Vocabulary words are underlined)

English

Sentence context: I share <u>intimate</u> secrets only with my close, personal friends.

Meaning: _____

Consumer Math

Sentence context: When my weekly paycheck is $465.80, I get only $465. My boss always takes away the change and pays only to the <u>lowest whole number.</u>

Meaning: _____

Science

Sentence context: Steam rising from boiling water is one example of evaporation, a process where heat turns liquid into a gas.

Meaning: _____

Vocational Education

Sentence context: To see things as well as we do, robots use <u>vision sensing.</u>

Meaning: _____

This demonstrates an important principle of vocabulary development: activities that are personally involving both physically (they encourage hands-on participation) and emotionally (they are interesting and meet real-life needs) are the most effective. This principle can be applied in all sorts of ways, from using candy bars in mathematics in order to show how retail sales work to teaching students about aviation by visiting an airport. Creativity in context-based activities pays off in richer and more functional vocabulary understandings.

Classification

Classification activities build on ways that words can be compared and contrasted. Typically, students are given a small group of words (from two to six) and are asked to tell what the words have in common or how the words can be contrasted. The groups contain both familiar and new words. Students study the familiar words to derive the meaning of the new word.

Figure 6.8 presents some examples of classification activities for different subject areas. These activities build on comparisons between familiar and unfamiliar vocabulary words.

FIGURE 6.8

Classification Vocabulary Activities Emphasizing Comparisons (Note: Vocabulary words are underlined)

Social Studies

Directions: The underlined word in each of the following groups is important in our reading. Other words are already familiar to you. All the words are alike in some way. Study the familiar words to find out the meaning of the underlined word. Write the meaning on the blank below each set.

monarchy   <u>democracy</u>   dictatorship

Meaning: _____

Mathematics

Directions: Each of the items below contains a new vocabulary word and several number examples. Look carefully at each number example. On the blank below each item, write the meaning of the new term.

Word: <u>Whole numbers</u>

Number (0, 1, 2, 3, 4, 5)
Examples: (−5, −4, −3, −2, −1)

Meaning: _____

FIGURE 6.8 *(Cont.)*

Vocational Education

Directions: Each of the underlined words is a term that is important in our unit on fibers. Along with the new word, you will find two words that should be familiar. On the line below each set, list the properties that the fibers probably share.

cotton   wool   flax

Properties: _____

English

Directions: Each of the following sets of words describes one idea related to Montresor's plan for revenge in the story we are about to read, *The Cask of Amontillado.* Some of the words are already familiar; the underlined words are new. On the blank below each set, write a sentence that describes how the words might be part of Montresor's plan.

retribution   revenge   punish   pay back

Sentence: _____

_____

Another option with classification activities is to emphasize contrasts. Figure 6.9 illustrates these kinds of vocabulary development activities.

FIGURE 6.9

Classification Activities Emphasizing Contrasts (Note: Vocabulary words are underlined)

Social Studies

Based on the following examples, what is the meaning of the term underlined war?

Examples of undeclared wars	**Examples of declared wars**
Korean conflict	World War I
Vietnam	World War II
Grenada	

Mathematics

These are examples and nonexamples of irrational numbers. What is an irrational number?

Examples:	4.3131131113	*Nonexamples:*	3.3333̄
	$\sqrt{99}$		2.75
	Pi		4 1/8

Art

On the table at the front of the room, you will find two pieces of clay. One is labeled <u>greenware</u> and the other is called <u>leatherhard</u>. Feel the clay. Touch it to your face. In the spaces below, contrast the two types of clay.

Qualities of greenware: _____

Qualities of leatherhard: _____

English

How are parts of a story different from parts of an essay?

Parts of a story:	*Parts of an essay:*
Plot	Opening paragraph
Characters	Main ideas
Chain of events	Topic sentences
Climax	Details
Resolution	Closing

Structural Analysis

Structural analysis activities should emphasize the use of familiar word parts to construct the meaning of unfamiliar words. Teachers model these activities by showing students how to break words into familiar segments, and then build the meaning of an entire word by examining the meaning of the segments.

A typical approach to structural analysis involves memorizing long lists of prefixes and suffixes and/or Latin and Greek roots in isolation from situations. The hope is that students will recall and apply what they have learned in the past to understand unfamiliar terms. This approach fails for two reasons: (1) the large quantity of prefixes, suffixes, and roots necessitates a definition approach to teaching, and, as a result, (2) students tend to focus only on rote memorization. Odds are against this approach in supporting any transfer to the task of understanding unfamiliar words (Sternberg, Powell, & Kaye, 1983).

A better approach is one that models the structural analysis good readers perform when confronted with an unfamiliar word. Good readers are able to use structural analysis to make an educated guess about the meaning of a word, based on the meaning of different parts of the word. Figure 6.10 illustrates this approach.

Structural analysis often involves playful speculation about a word's meaning, which students enjoy. However, the process is not complete until students can successfully construct and apply the meaning. To do this, other vocabulary approaches are required, such as context analysis or the use of an outside resource.

Use of Outside Resources

Outside resources include the dictionary, thesaurus, almanac, encyclopedia, and textbook glossaries. These resources are best used when students have already developed a need to know and an initial sense of a word's meaning.

Again, the typical approach to this important part of vocabulary instruction is not

FIGURE 6.10

Using Structural Analysis to Construct the Meaning of a Word

Step 1: *Break the word into parts*

sym / bio / sis   in / surg / ent

Step 2: *Brainstorm for other words that contain these segments*

sym - sympathy,   in - into,
    symphony   income
bio - biology,   surg - surge
    biography,
    bionic
sis - analysis,   ent - adolescent
    synthesis

Step 3: *Determine the meanings of the word segments*

sym - together   in - in
bio - life   surge - move forward,
                                 rise up
sis - the act of,   ent - someone who is
    an action   (makes the word a noun)

Step 4: *Construct the meaning of the word*

"life acting together" or relationship   "someone who is rising up, a rebel"
between two organisms living closely
together, each benefiting from the
relationship

---

effective. Typically, students learn how to use the dictionary or textbook glossary in isolation rather than learning how to use these resources where and when it is necessary. Think about when an outside resource becomes essential. Normally, good readers consult an outside resource only when the potential meaning of a word has been established. For example, after a heated debate about whether any object in space can be called a satellite, two students reach for a dictionary to resolve their differences. Students need to understand how outside resources can help clarify and confirm some of the ideas they generate about unfamiliar words.

To teach students how to use outside resources, teachers should spend time developing an awareness of what different resources offer. For example, take the word "compound," and ask students to compare the information they find in the dictionary, the thesaurus, and a textbook glossary (see Figure 6.11).

Good readers select resources according to the information they need and the task(s) they are required to perform. *Dictionaries* work best when students are trying to clarify or

FIGURE 6.11

A Comparison of the Information Found in Different Resources for the Word "Compound"

Dictionary entry

compound (adj. kom'pound, kompound'; n. kom'pound; v. kempound'), adj. 1. composed of two or more parts or ingredients. n. something formed by combining parts, elements, etc. 3. a substance composed of two or more elements chemically united. 4. a word composed of two or more parts that are also words or word elements. v.t. to combine or mix. 6. to make by combining parts, elements, etc. 7. to intensify or make more serious 8. to pay (interest) on the accrued interest as well as the principle. 9. to agree, for payment, not to prosecute (a crime or felony).

Thesaurus entry

compound 1 vb syn join
         2 vb syn mix
         3 vb syn increase
         4 adj syn complex
         5 n syn mixture

Glossary entry

compound: substance composed of different kinds of atoms.

confirm the meaning of a word encountered during reading. A *thesaurus* will not serve this purpose: synonyms are presented, yet students still have to determine the meaning from looking at the thesaurus choices.

A thesaurus works best when students are trying to think about different ways to express themselves, such as when they are writing. Having already figured out what they want to say, students could use a thesaurus to make choices about saying things differently or more precisely. A dictionary will not serve this purpose: different definitions are presented for many different words, yet word meanings are neither categorized nor compared to permit decisions about different ways to say the same thing.

Textbook glossaries, located in the back of many content area textbooks, offer specialized information. For students in a science class researching chemical compounds, the definition in Figure 6.11 is useful. On the other hand, students in an economics class learning about "compound interest" would find the definition limited.

Students who learn how to use outside resources in isolation (apart from situations in which they need to learn new words) are likely to choose the wrong kind of resource or neglect available resources altogether. The goal of instructional activities devoted to outside resources should be to teach students how to pick and choose according to what they need. To teach students about the value and use of outside resources, teachers can: (1) demonstrate how they personally use outside resources to find out about words, and (2) emphasize the use of resources in places where students are most likely to find or use them (at home, on the job, or in a library).

TEACHING A LESSON*

This section presents a social studies lesson that incorporates many of the ideas presented in this chapter. In reading this section, think about how the principles of instruction illustrated here apply to planning and teaching a lesson in your content area.

Goals and Assumptions

The topic for the lesson is the Great Depression. The intended audience is a multigrade (grades 10, 11, 12), mixed-ability group of students studying American history. Students have already studied events during the boom and bust times after World War I. This lesson builds on these experiences, developing a link between past and present pressures on the economy.

The Great Depression is covered in the history textbook in about thirty-five pages. The focus of this lesson will be on the first five pages, in which basic concepts about the causes and consequences of the Depression are introduced. After reading the text, the teacher wrote the following content objective:

If the people, the government, and the businesses of the United States are not careful, a serious depression could happen again.

The statement makes the lesson functional from a historical perspective, helping students learn how to explain recurring historical patterns. To personalize the lesson, the teacher created the following question:

How safe is the money in your bank account?

This question encourages students to examine their role as consumers in an economy.

Having identified a focus for the lesson, the teacher next selected important vocabulary. Using the techniques described earlier in the chapter, the teacher made the following decisions:

*Thanks to Ken Nelson, a social studies teacher.

Words to Teach on a Meaning Level	Words to Teach on a Definition Level	Words for Brainstorming or Review
Great Depression (context)	Arkies	economy
downward slide (context)	Okies	capitalism
economic crash (context)	escapism	socialism
bank failure (context or prior knowledge)	intellectuals	communism
economic disenchantment (context or prior knowledge)	hoboes	
economic indicators (context or structural analysis)		

Note the assumptions (in parentheses) the teacher made about the best ways to teach words selected for meaning emphasis.

Finally, the teacher constructed a semantic map:

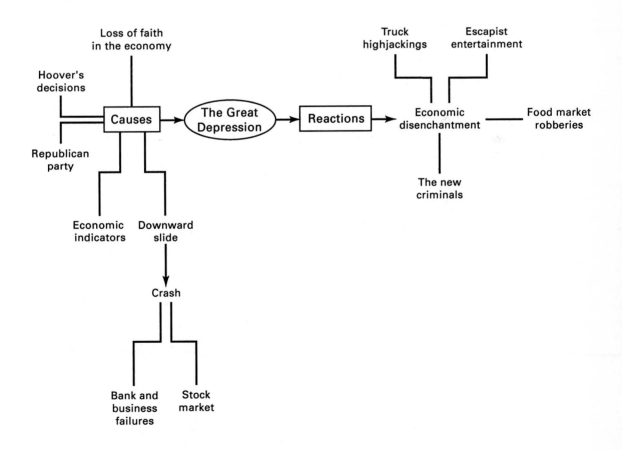

The map serves as the centerpiece for other instructional activities throughout the lesson. The teacher developed basic components, such as "the Great Depression," in the early stages of the lesson, while adding other concepts, such as "downward slide" and "economic disenchantment," as the lesson progressed.

Building Background and Motivation

Background and motivation for the lesson can be built in several ways.

The teacher writes the term "Great Depression" on the blackboard or projects it on the overhead. He or she asks the students: "How do you feel when you are depressed?" Responses might include "hopeless," "unable to go on," "stuck in a rut." As the concept of personal depression becomes clear, the teacher asks the students to speculate on what it means for an economy to be depressed. This approach gets students thinking about the causes of the Depression in terms of Americans' loss of faith in government and business.

A second way to begin the lession is to ask: "How safe is the money in your bank account?" Discussion could center on the Federal Deposit Insurance Corporation (FDIC), how the agency insures deposits up to a certain amount, and how the agency is currently running out of money from banks that have failed. The teacher can introduce issues surrounding the Great Depression by pointing out that the FDIC and other types of government control did not exist in 1929, thus making it more likely for banks and the stock market to fail. An important discussion question is: "Will another depression occur if governmental controls fail?" This approach gets students thinking about their own roles in the economy and why it might be important to study what happened during the Great Depression.

Selecting an approach, in this case, is a matter of preference. In the first case, students develop an initial understanding of the term "depression." In the second, students are exposed to economic issues that relate to the Great Depression, but they have not yet been taught what "depression" means. In either case, the teacher takes care to introduce the lesson with a combination of interest as well as concept development.

Developing Content and Process

This component of a vocabulary lesson develops: (1) an understanding of words students need to know on both meaning and definition levels (content), and (2) knowledge about how to understand unfamiliar words. Depending on the number of vocabulary words chosen, there are several different ways to organize instruction.

If there are few words to teach (say, five or less), it may be best to teach them during whole-class discussion. With fewer words, teachers can conduct a well-paced discussion while aiming for depth in students' understanding. The following example from the lesson on the Great Depression illustrates how a teacher can use whole-class discussion to develop the meaning of the term "downward slide":

TEACHER: We all know what it means to go down a slide or to slide downward. Has anyone experienced a slide where it felt like you could not stop yourself?
STEVE: We were on a muddy hill and once you started sliding, you couldn't stop.

TEACHER: Good example. Now think for a minute. We're going to talk about a "downward slide" in the economy. It's a lot like being on a muddy hill where you can't stop sliding. What do you suppose is a downward slide in the economy? Sherry?

SHERRY: It's probably where people start losing their jobs, the banks close down, and the stock market falls. Enough failures start to happen in the economy that everything slides down and starts to fail!

TEACHER: Good description. Now can anyone give me a sentence that summarizes what it means for the economy to be in a downward slide? Brandon?

BRANDON: It's when everything in the economy starts to fail and nobody can keep things from getting worse.

TEACHER: Very good.

Note the pattern in this approach; the teacher:

1. Builds a context by talking about a situation that is familiar to students

2. Introduces the new term

3. Encourages students to relate existing, familiar concepts (sliding down a hill) to concepts underlying the new term (economic slide)

4. Asks students to summarize what the new term means

With fewer words, teachers can conduct a well-paced discussion while aiming for depth in students' understanding

Rick Friedman/The Picture Cube

Teachers can take a similar approach when using other vocabulary processes, such as classification or structural analysis—build the meaning of the word (or words) using the appropriate vocabulary process, have students think about other related and familiar concepts, and help students summarize what they think new vocabulary terms mean.

If large numbers of words must be taught (say, more than five), it is best to opt for the use of some *paper and pencil activities* in conjunction with discussion of selected words. When students need to know large numbers of words, whole-class discussion of every vocabulary word or phrase is impractical. Paper and pencil activities, based on vocabulary processes, can help students achieve an in-depth understanding while dealing effectively with larger numbers of words. An important goal in using activities like this is to encourage students to use prior knowledge to develop word meanings. Figure 6.12 contains an example of a paper and pencil activity for teaching terms in the lesson on the Depression. Many students enjoy doing these activities during small-group, collaborative discussions (see Chapter 11).

FIGURE 6.12

A Paper and Pencil Activity for Developing the Meaning of Vocabulary Words

Directions: Read each paragraph. Then, based on the clues provided by the paragraph, decide what the underlined words mean. Discuss the meanings in your group. Write the meaning that your group decides is correct on the lines provided below each paragraph.

The school bookstore went bankrupt. The cafeteria has not made enough money to purchase food for next month. The school budget was voted down. The school district is in a downward slide.

Meaning: _____

_____

The number of school lunches sold, how many times the school budget has passed in recent years, the number of families moving in or out of the community, are all economic indicators for the school district.

Meaning: _____

_____

The bank's supply of money is low because people aren't paying their loans and mortgages and no new deposits are coming in. The demand for money is high because depositors want their money all at once. Conditions are perfect for a bank failure.

Meaning: _____

_____

During the Great Depression, people stopped trying to get jobs. Some turned to highjacking trucks, stealing from food markets, and robbing banks. These are all results of the <u>economic disenchantment</u> felt by many people in the United States.

Meaning: _____

_____

_____

    Teachers can develop students' knowledge about how to construct meaning from unfamiliar words by making explicit the vocabulary processes that underlie these activities. This means telling students what vocabulary processes are being emphasized and walking students through the mental steps required for using them. Consider this discussion of the use of context clues to learn "economic indicator":

TEACHER: The term "economic indicator" is important in this lesson on the Great Depression. We don't know what an economic indicator is, so we'll have to figure it out. This is a common problem in history: there are many words we may not know because of their use in a particular historical situation. Sometimes, the best way to figure out a word is to look at the words around it. We are going to look at some sentences that use the term and we'll study the clues provided by the sentences. This is called "looking at the context."

In this example, the teacher is both labeling and explaining the process necessary for understanding a new word. Going over the sentences together and practicing the process provides students with a model for how to understand words for themselves.

Encouraging Independence

Students gain independence with vocabulary learning when they have the desire and ability to master unfamiliar words and expand their existing vocabularies (Schwartz & Raphael, 1985). Desire comes from repeated success in learning new words. It also comes when teachers invite students to participate in choosing and learning vocabulary. For the sake of motivation and independence, Haggard (1986) recommends that students be given frequent opportunities to suggest words that the class should learn.

    The ability to master new words comes as students become strategists when applying and adapting vocabulary processes to learn words under many different conditions. Teachers can develop strategic ability in their students by explaining different kinds of vocabulary processes both within and across lessons. Three questions are important:

1. How does a reader decide when an unfamiliar word is important to know?

2. How does a reader choose the process or processes that aid in constructing the meaning of different kinds of terms?

3. How does a reader know when the meaning of a word has been successfully developed?

Teachers can help students answer these questions by taking time at the end of a lesson to review the vocabulary processes/strategies that helped construct the meaning of unfamiliar words. It is also important to review contexts in which a vocabulary process did *not* work. Teachers can share how they go about answering these questions, drawing from experiences both as a reader and a teacher. If this practice is repeated over time, students will gain a rich repertoire of vocabulary knowledge and ability.

SUMMARY

Vocabulary instruction involves more than teaching the hard words. Because of the quantity and/or compactness of concepts within content areas, teachers need to identify and distinguish words best presented on a definition level from words best taught on a meaning level. Helping students become strategists when learning vocabulary is an important goal. When students experience success in determining word meanings on their own, they are more likely to be interested in learning the language of a content area.

SPECIAL PROJECTS

Course-Based

1. Evaluate a textbook in your content area. What kinds of provisions are made for teaching vocabulary? Are the activities in the text more on a definition level or a meaning level? Design a lesson based on one section of the text to illustrate how you will make decisions about:
   a. Which words to teach
   b. How you will go about teaching them

Field-Based

2. Observe a teacher during a vocabulary lesson in your content area. Ask the teacher the following questions:
   a. How do you choose words to emphasize during your teaching?
   b. How do you create activities to teach vocabulary to your students?
   c. How do you know when students really understand the vocabulary they have been taught?

Consider the teacher's responses in light of the recommendations made in this chapter. How will you balance the need to teach many concepts with the time it takes to teach vocabulary meanings?

3. Plan a lesson in which you think vocabulary should be emphasized. Teach the lesson to a group of students. Evaluate your experience in terms of:

a. Your original assumptions about the kinds of vocabulary you needed to teach
b. The appropriateness of the vocabulary activities you created
c. How well students learned the words you taught them

SUGGESTED READING

These references offer examples of vocabulary activities similar to the ones presented in this chapter:

EARLE, R. (1976). *Teaching reading and mathematics.* Newark, DE: International Reading Association.

JOHNSON, D., & PEARSON, P. D. (1984). *Teaching reading vocabulary.* New York: Holt, Rinehart, and Winston.

MARZANO, R., & MARZANO, J. (1988). *A cluster approach to elementary vocabulary instruction.* Newark, DE: International Reading Association.

NAGY, W. (1988). *Teaching vocabulary to improve reading comprehension.* Newark, DE: The International Reading Association.

THELAN, J. (1984). *Improving reading in science.* Newark, DE: International Reading Association.

The April 1986 issue of the *Journal of Reading* is devoted entirely to practices for vocabulary instruction.

These publications are devoted specifically to creating and using structured overviews and semantic maps:

BARRON, R. (1979). Research for the classroom teacher: Recent developments on the structured overview as an advance organizer. In H. Herber & J. Riley (Eds.), *Research in reading in the content areas: The fourth report.* Syracuse, NY: Syracuse University Reading and Language Arts Center.

HEIMLICH, J., & PITTELMAN, S. (1986). *Semantic mapping: Classroom applications.* Newark, DE: International Reading Association.

The following articles present research reviews on vocabulary and vocabulary instruction:

ANDERSON, R., & FREEBODY, P. (1981). Vocabulary knowledge. In J. Guthrie (Ed.), *Comprehension and teaching: Research reviews.* Newark, DE: International Reading Association.

KARAZIM, L. (1982). Strategies of teaching vocabulary development in content areas. In J. Patberg (Ed.), *Reading in the content areas: Application of a concept.* Toledo, OH: University of Toledo College of Education.

MEZYNSKI, K. (1983). Issues concerning the acquisition of knowledge: Effects of vocabulary training on reading comprehension. *Review of Educational Research, 53,* 2, 253–279.

MOORE, D. (1987). Vocabulary. In D. Alvermann, D. Moore, & M. Conley (Eds.), *Research within reach: Secondary school reading.* Newark, DE: International Reading Association.

REFERENCES

ANDERSON, R., & FREEBODY, P. (1981). Vocabulary knowledge. In J. Guthrie (Ed.), *Comprehension and teaching: Research Reviews.* Newark, DE: The International Reading Association.

AUSUBEL, D. (1977). The facilitation of meaningful verbal learning in the classroom. *Educational Psychologist, 12,* 2, 162–178.

BARRON, R. (1979). Research for the classroom teacher: Recent developments on the structured overview as an advance organizer. In H. Herber & J. Riley (Eds.), *Research in reading in the content areas: The fourth report.* Syracuse, NY: Syracuse University Reading and Language Arts Center.

GIPE, J. (1979). Investigating techniques for teaching word meanings. *Reading Research Quarterly, 14,* 4, 624–644.

HAGGARD, M. (1986). The vocabulary self-collection strategy: Using student interest and world knowledge to enhance vocabulary growth. *Journal of Reading, 29,* 7, 634–642.

SCHWARTZ, R., & RAPHAEL, T. (1985). Concept of definition: A key to improving students' vocabulary. *The Reading Teacher, 39,* 2, 198–205.

STAHL, S., JACOBSON, M., DAVIS, C., & DAVIS, R. (1989). Prior knowledge and difficult vocabulary in the comprehension of unfamiliar text. *Reading Research Quarterly, 24,* 1, 27–43.

STERNBERG, R., POWELL, J., & KAYE, D. (1983). Teaching vocabulary-building skills. In A. C. Wilkinson (Ed)., *Classroom computers and cognitive science.* New York: Academic Press.

TABA, H. (1967). *Teacher's handbook for Elementary Social Studies.* Reading, MA: Addison-Wesley.

"Conceptual learning occurs when meanings about content area knowledge are (1) gradually constructed, (2) by the learners, (3) through a series of interactions with the content, (4) with new information integrated with old information (5) so that the result is conscious awareness of what is being learned, when it will be useful and how to use it effectively."

From L. Roehler and G. Duffy (1989). The content area teacher's instructional role. In D. Lapp, J. Flood, and N. Farnan (Eds.), Content area reading and learning: Instructional strategies. *Englewood Cliffs, NJ: Prentice-Hall, p. 116.*

7

Comprehension Instruction

CHAPTER OBJECTIVES

After reading this chapter, you should be able to:

1. Describe goals for comprehension instruction in terms of your own subject-matter teaching.

2. Plan and implement instructional activities devoted to deep and functional understandings of important content and greater awareness of how to comprehend and learn.

RATIONALE

As the quote at the opening of the chapter suggests, helping students comprehend can be a difficult task. To truly comprehend, students assume a role not unlike carpenters, building meanings gradually upon a base of their own knowledge. The result is functional: content area knowledge learned not for its own sake, but rather in support of students and their success both in and out of school. In many ways, teachers are like master carpenters, building scaffolds for students, showing them how to build meanings on their own.

The modern metaphor of a carpenter stands in contrast to traditional comprehension instruction, which is best compared with an assembly line. In the tradition of an assembly line, the teacher is an authority (supervisor) dispensing knowledge (jobs), with students (workers) absorbing the information that the teacher or textbook presents. The result of this kind of instruction is that students do not learn the material well, or learn it only for short periods of time. They get used to seeing only bits and pieces of information, without ever developing a sense of how content concepts fit together. Not only do they miss important aspects of the content, they do not develop the ability to figure out concepts on their own, nor do they see how learning the concepts might benefit them in the long run. It is no surprise that in some classrooms dominated by this tradition, students become either very passive or very bored.

Comprehension instruction consists of what teachers say and do to help students comprehend subject-matter concepts. Recall from Chapter 5 that instruction should actively engage teachers and students in communicating about subject matter, in providing a scaffold of concepts for students, helping them internalize new knowledge or modify old knowledge. The goal of good instruction is to support students in developing their own conceptions and independent thinking in a content area.

CHAPTER ORGANIZER

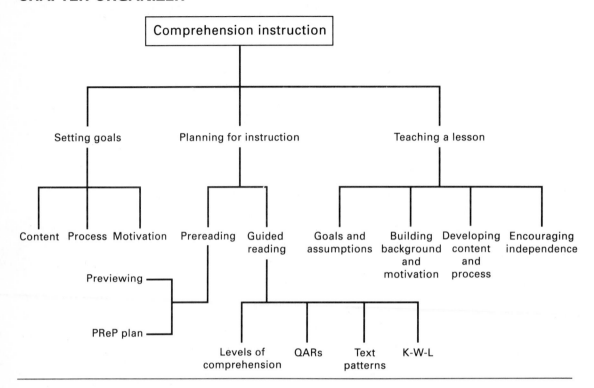

Historically, comprehension instruction has centered on recitation, or what one teacher describes as "getting information out on the floor." Recitation is a discussion routine in which teachers ask questions, students provide answers, and teachers provide reactions (Hoetker & Ahlbrand, 1969). Recitation often encourages students to give correct answers while discouraging wrong answers and even thinking:

TEACHER: Can someone give me a sentence that shows an example of the accusative case?

SALLY: You throw the ball.

TEACHER: Good. Now, can someone give me a sentence with an example of the dative case?

FRED: He sold the store.

TEACHER: No-o-o-o. Try again.

FRED: He sold him the store.

TEACHER: Very good, Fred. Class, we'll have a test on nominative and dative cases on Friday.

Note how this emphasis on answer-giving aims for only a surface awareness of the topics under study. Two students in this illustration provided the answer the teacher had in mind, but what evidence is there that these students really comprehended or could remember and apply the information beyond this lesson? And what do other students in the class know? Where practices like recitation persist, the emphasis is on memorizing lists of facts, and students are afforded few opportunities to learn.

Encouraging students to be meaning-makers rather than answers-givers requires an entirely different perspective to instruction, what has been called a *cognitive approach* (Roehler & Duffy, 1989). The term "cognitive" was chosen to represent the concept that comprehension and learning occur only when students' minds are actively engaged. Roehler and Duffy (1989) describe four actions teachers take when they adopt a cognitive approach to comprehension instruction:

1. *Plan.* Teachers review instructional materials in light of their own knowledge, create alternative ways for comprehending subject-matter concepts, and tailor activities to both the general and specific characteristics of their students.

2. *Motivate.* Teachers initiate, sustain, and direct students' motivation. This includes setting expectations, developing conscious awareness in students for how they are learning, and providing frequent opportunities for success.

3. *Provide information.* Teachers explain and model the content and the processes they want students to learn.

4. *Mediate.* Teachers ask questions and gradually transfer responsibility for learning to students. This includes responding to students' interpretations and adapting instructional information and approaches so that students can better comprehend.

Note how teacher questions and student responses are also part of this approach. The emphasis here, however, is on purposeful learning stemming from thoughtful planning and teaching decisions. At every step of the way, students, their understanding and motivation, are primary concerns.

It is not necessarily easy or automatic to shape instruction so that students are motivated and learning is in-depth. Pressures to cover content in disorganized textbooks conspire with problems in meeting student needs to make recitation a more appealing option when compared with other approaches to instruction. However, with ideas, classroom practice, reflection, and persistence, teachers can bring about radical transformations in their approach to the curriculum.

This chapter presents ideas for comprehension instruction (you will need to supply the other ingredients!). It describes goals for instruction, reviewing key elements of what it means to comprehend in a subject-matter area. Next, it explains several different ways to plan lessons in which comprehension is the focus. Finally, a complete lesson involving instruction is described and illustrated.

SETTING GOALS

Goals for comprehension instruction involve identifying and emphasizing important content, helping students learn to be strategists in their comprehension, and motivating students by providing frequent opportunities for success and by relating content to their own lives.

Content Goals

The content goals for comprehension are to: (1) teach students about important content, and (2) help students understand the many purposes of content both in and out of school.

As described in Chapter 3, comprehension focuses on important content: facts and concepts in a textbook as well as beyond-text principles and generalizations. When planning and teaching, teachers use their knowledge of the subject to make decisions about what is essential to know and what is not. Unfortunately, students are rarely let in on those decisions. If teachers could help students identify important information in a subject, students could spend more of their time comprehending and less on trial and error, guessing what teachers want them to know.

A second goal is to acquaint students with the information in a subject. (Now would be a good time to review the table of purposes in Figure 2.1). Comprehension is not only for school purposes; it is for purposes outside of school as well. Students who perceive that the goal of comprehension is to remember facts for a test will approach learning very differently than students who comprehend to apply what they have learned in realistic ways. Especially convincing is that students tend to retain information when they perceive a genuine purpose for that information: when students comprehend only for a test, they tend to forget everything almost before leaving the classroom; when students comprehend for purposes they understand and appreciate, they retain the information and usually want to learn more ("I want to find out more about government jobs," or "I wonder if I could help endangered animals").

To emphasize important content and its larger purposes, consider the following three steps while planning (the examples are from a class in consumer mathematics):

1. *Develop a content objective.* Content objectives spell out important facts, concepts, and principles for a lesson (see Chapter 5).

Example

A balance sheet consists of assets and debits.

2. *Revise the content objective* with in-school and out-of-school purposes in mind. Ask yourself: How could this information be used?

Example

You can keep track of your own finances by balancing your assets against your debits.

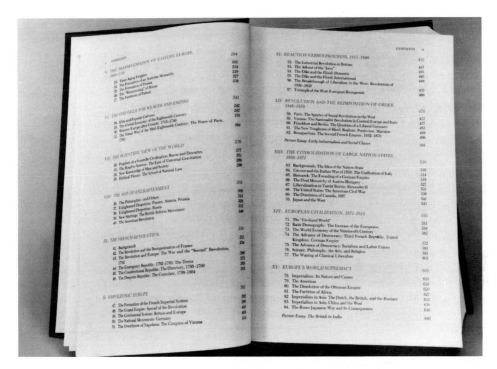

Teachers should help students understand what counts as important information

---

3. *Map out facts, concepts, and principles for the lesson.* Create a map (see Chapter 6), laying out what is important based on the textbook and on your own knowledge of the content. Use the content objective to guide your choices.

Example

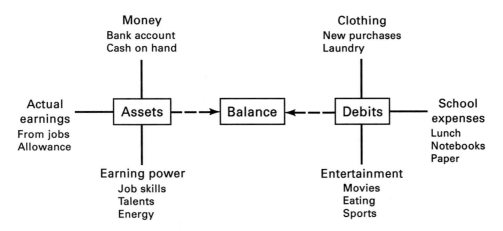

Process Goals

A process goal for comprehension instruction is: to help students develop strategies for applying different comprehension processes.

As explained in Chapter 3, comprehending involves such processes as pulling out and applying relevant prior knowledge and text information, perceiving and using the structure of text, asking and answering questions, and justifying one's thinking with evidence from the text and beyond. Comprehending strategically means selecting and adapting any one or combination of these processes to various kinds of printed information and purposes for learning. Vocabulary processes (Chapter 6) set the stage for comprehension to occur. Reasoning and studying processes (Chapters 8 and 9) build on comprehension. Viewed in this way, comprehension processes are central to communication and learning in a content area.

Comprehension processes have already been detailed in Chapter 3. Figure 7.1 briefly summarizes those processes, with examples from a student thinking aloud while learning about good nutrition in a health class.

Note particularly the emphasis on adapting to context during comprehension. Comprehending strategically means being able to examine situations where comprehension is required (reading a textbook, preparing a report, recreational reading), and selecting and modifying different processes to gain access to the information. It means monitoring the success (or failure) of processes and choosing other ones when a particular approach does not work.

Ultimately, students need to learn how to use comprehension processes independently to discover what is important in the content. They need to link up their knowledge of process, their knowledge of the content, and their understanding of the purposes for information in a subject. When this happens, students can make better decisions about what to comprehend, what processes to apply, and how much time to spend constructing the meaning.

Motivation Goals

The motivation goals for comprehension are: to afford students frequent opportunities for success with comprehension and to help students see connections between the content and their own lives.

Teachers set the stage for success by making sure that with content, the emphasis is on important and functional information. Opportunities for success come from teaching students about comprehension processes and then providing many opportunities for students to communicate what they are learning. As students comprehend and communicate with one another, they improve in confidence and self-concept. They develop a public awareness that they can comprehend as readily as others in the class.

Students tend to value a subject more when they see the relevance behind what they are learning. To be sure, it is not always possible to show students direct connections between the content and their lives, but a subject can become boring pretty quickly when all teachers say is: "You'll see how this is important some day." Whenever possible, teachers need to show students how concepts relate to real life. Frequently, this requires some creativity. For example, a calculus teacher presented students with a situation in

FIGURE 7.1

Comprehension Processes

Using prior knowledge: Activating and applying relevant background knowledge and past experiences.

Example:

> "This unit is about nutrition. I wonder what I would find out about my nutrition if I checked my refrigerator—butter, lots of eggs, and sweet stuff—not very good! I will probably learn if the food in my refrigerator is nutritious or not."

Metacognition: Awareness of processes used to comprehend, monitoring the success of processes, and applying fix-it strategies when comprehension breaks down.

Example:

> "I just figured out that there are different kinds of cholesterol, but I can't tell what the differences are just by reading this chapter. I'll check out the glossary and see if I can find out more."

Constructing meaning: Applying vocabulary knowledge, recognizing and identifying important facts, making text-based interpretations, and creating beyond-text generalizations.

Example:

> "So there is 'good' cholesterol and 'bad' cholesterol. The body makes some and food has some. Maybe I can change my diet to include low-fat, high-fiber foods so the good cholesterol outweighs the bad."

Adapting to contexts: Altering one's approach to comprehension depending on similarities and differences in texts and in ways of communicating with texts.

Example:

> "The section on vitamins looks like my science chapters. So much to remember! It's not at all like reading stories out of my literature book. Maybe I can group the vitamins, like my science formulas, to help me remember. One group could be 'helps digestion.' Another could be 'healthy blood.'"

which a new small business was just getting off the ground. The owner had to balance start-up costs with operating expenses and eventual profits. Students used derivatives to figure out just how much money it would take to keep the business going. Many discovered that, in some cases, investing more money would lead to losses and not profits! This kind of instruction keeps students interested and helps them see why studying a subject might be useful.

Teachers play a key role in the motivation that underlies comprehension. When teachers make planning and teaching decisions based on students' knowledge and interests and emphasize success and relevance in comprehension, students will become more involved and motivated about what they are learning.

PLANNING FOR INSTRUCTION

In the past ten years, research on comprehension instruction has mushroomed. Researchers from linguistics, educational psychology, teacher education, and different subject-matter areas have developed and evaluated many techniques for helping students comprehend more effectively. Many of the more promising instructional strategies for pre-reading and for guided reading are presented here. Before these strategies are described and illustrated, a few words of caution are in order.

Because insight on comprehension instruction comes from so many different research communities, there is a problem with "jargon." Though many researchers study the same phenomenon, different terms emerge, so that "literal" for one group is "textually explicit" for another. Individual groups, such as teacher educators or psychologists, develop their own unique language so they can communicate within their own groups. Problems arise whenever individuals try to communicate across groups—or when teachers try to incorporate several different kinds of comprehension activities into their classroom instruction. The result can be very confusing!

Keep in mind that what is important in the following activities is the purposes behind them—and not necessarily the labels that are used. It would be unfortunate if, as teachers and students engage in these activities, they spent more time figuring out labels than comprehending the content. In planning for instruction, try to identify a consistent language to use with your students so they can become aware of the comprehension processes that will most aid them in understanding the content.

Pre-Reading

Pre-reading, as an aspect of comprehension instruction, involves preparing students for what they are about to read. When teachers and students engage in meaningful pre-reading instruction, students develop clear purposes for learning and their comprehension is enhanced. Pre-reading includes: drawing out or providing prior knowledge about content and process, motivating students, and teaching important vocabulary. Previewing and the PReP plan are the pre-reading approaches explained here.

Previewing   Previewing (also known as "using a preview") is a method for building interest and prior knowledge before students read. Research has shown that previewing helps students improve not only their comprehension but also their attitudes toward expository (Graves & Prenn, 1984) as well as narrative (Graves, Prenn, & Cooke, 1985) kinds of text. Previewing works best when a direct approach to instruction is necessary, for example, when a teacher has determined ahead of time that students lack knowledge or motivation concerning the concepts or processes in an upcoming lesson.

In the research, previews consisted of 200-word scripts which teachers followed or read aloud. In practice, however, there are many ways to construct and use previews to accomplish the same purposes. Previews consist of four parts:

1. *Interest-building.* Teachers discuss with students what is to be learned and how it relates to what students know and care about. This discussion often includes a question phrased to generate curiosity.

Example

Today, we are going to learn about mystery stories. We will learn how they are written and how they affect us. Mystery stories are sometimes scary and often surprising. Have you ever tried to scare or surprise your friends with a story?

2. *Developing prior knowledge.* Students are provided with concepts they will need in order to understand the passage.

Example

A mystery story is almost always concerned with a crime and the capture of a criminal. The scare or the surprise comes from finding out who did the crime. All along the way, we are given clues to the identity of the criminal, which usually becomes known at the end of the story. Often, we are surprised when we find out.

3. *Providing a synopsis.* Teachers offer information about the text itself. For stories, this means introducing themes, major characters, and setting, if appropriate. For expository texts (see Figure 7.2) the author's main message and major concepts are related.

Example (for a story)

In the story you are about to read, a murder takes place on board a cruise ship. The murdered man, Mr. Weatherby, was a wealthy banker sailing with his lovely wife, Myrna, a former movie star. In the cabin across from the banker and his wife is a devilishly handsome Olympic swimmer, Biff. Down the hall is Sharkey, an accountant who recently retired from Mr. Weatherby's bank. As the story begins, a shot rings out from Mr. Weatherby's cabin. Biff's door slams shut, but reopens. Biff comes out, his robe revealing a small but noticeable red stain. Myrna screams and says the shot was fired from outside their cabin window. Just then, Sharkey is seen running away from his cabin. The ship's detective arrives on the scene.

4. *Offering strategies.* Students are given some tips for how to read the text to get the most out of it.

FIGURE 7.2

Previewing an Expository Text (From a Middle School Science Unit Exploring the Five Senses)

We use our senses every day. We tend to take our senses for granted, but thousands of people go through each day without one or more of their senses. How do we use our senses? What would it be like to be without our senses?

Our senses consist of sight, hearing, taste, smell, and touch. In the chapter you are about to read entitled Control Systems, you are going to learn that our senses are our way of relating to our environment. Our senses are all part of the body's nervous system. The nervous system is best compared to a busy newsroom, with messages coming in, news editors deciding what is important, and news writers preparing stories for broadcast. The senses send the messages, which our brain interprets. Next, our brain sends a response and we smell, see, hear, taste, and feel. In some cases, our senses lead to pleasurable feelings as we listen to a new song or taste a favorite dish. In other cases, our senses literally save our lives by signaling pain when we hurt ourselves. People who have lost one or more of their senses, either at birth or through some disease, illness, or accident, miss out on some of these advantages. However, humans are incredibly adaptable: the blind often develop a much better sense of hearing, and people who do not hear well learn to rely on their sense of sight.

As you read, think about how your senses guide you each day. Read to see how people learn to cope when they do not have one of their senses.

Example

In mystery stories, the authors always sprinkle in clues to throw us off and clues that tell us the identity of the murderer. Read to see what clues are offered and to see how the ship's detective solves the mystery.

The PReP Plan   The *PReP Plan* is another way to build interest and prior knowledge within a lesson devoted to comprehension (Langer, 1982). PReP stands for three kinds of questions teachers ask sequentially early in a lesson: (1) *Prior knowledge* (asking questions about initial associations and impressions), (2) *Reflection* (asking questions to refine what students know), and (3) *Prerequisite knowledge* (asking questions to get students ready to read, elaborating upon previous responses and making predictions about what they will read). In contrast to previewing, which works best when students know relatively little about a lesson topic, PReP works best when teachers have determined ahead of time that students know somewhat more about what they are going to learn. PReP is geared toward an indirect approach to instruction.

PReP is used for both instruction and pre-assessment. Instructionally, PReP serves as a way to develop central concepts, that is, concepts students must identify in order to comprehend the content objective of a lesson. During the first stage, devoted to prior knowledge, teachers ask students to make initial associations with the central concepts:

TEACHER: What comes to mind when you see the word "revenge"?
MARCUS: What we did last Halloween when some kids stole our candy!
NATHANIEL: What we did when we found out who spray-painted our house!

During the next stage, teachers ask students to reflect on their initial associations:

TEACHER: How did you get revenge?
MARCUS: We went and stole their candy.
NATHANIEL: My Dad called the cops!
TEACHER: Did you get revenge or did the problems keep going on?
MARCUS: The kids stole their candy back and we didn't get anything.
NATHANIEL: We got some nasty phone calls after that.
TEACHER: So it's hard to get revenge without someone getting back at you?
ALL: Right!

Finally, teachers develop students' prerequisite knowledge (knowledge required to read and comprehend):

TEACHER: Today, we're going to read a story, "The Cask of Amontillado," about someone who tries to get revenge. Let's see if he really gets complete and final revenge or if his problems continue. The story involves some wine, a catacomb (also known as a cave), and some bricks and mortar. One man tries to get revenge on another who embarrassed him. Who would like to predict what might happen? What sort of embarrassment do you think the one man committed to call for such an evil revenge?

Note how the teacher's questions attempt to get students motivated as they make predictions about what they will read in the story.

PReP is also useful for pre-assessment. The technique helps teachers determine how much prior knowledge students possess as well as the kinds of language students use when they talk about lesson concepts. Teachers need to be especially careful when making judgments about what students already know. It is easy to underestimate what students know because lesson concepts are embedded in everday language. Consider this exchange from a social studies lesson:

TEACHER: What do you think about when you hear the word "economy"?
RALPH: It's like—you know—you only got so much dough and you want to spend it on everything you see but you can't unless you get a job.

For teachers and other students, listening to this kind of answer can be very taxing! However, the student has captured the essential concepts of supply and demand that are the focus of the lesson. The real challenge in using PReP lies in listening for the gems of knowledge in some student responses, recognizing students' contributions, and, ultimately, helping students learn to better express their ideas (more about this in Chapter 11, devoted to classroom discussions).

The following is a three-point scale for making judgments about how well students know the content of a lesson (Langer, 1982):

1. *High degree of knowledge.* Students talk about major concepts as well as relationships among concepts.

Example

The early Indians needed food just like us, but their search for food was tied to their traditions and religions.

2. *Some degree of knowledge.* Students offer some examples and attributes of the concept.

Example

I know that the Indians had tribes.

3. *Little knowledge.* Students offer some loosely related firsthand experiences or suggest words that sound like the major concepts.

Example

My cousins made an Indian fort once.

PReP allows teachers to informally assess the degree to which students are ready to comprehend. If students' responses are generally in the 1 to 2 range, it is safe to continue on the same course, pulling out what students know and developing lesson concepts. If, on the other hand, responses are in the 2 to 3 range, teachers might switch to a more direct approach, developing concepts necessary to comprehend the lesson. Making this kind of switch midstream in a lesson may seem unnerving at first. However, students are afforded greater opportunity to develop deep understandings of the content when teachers are sensitive to what students do and do not know. PReP provides a foundation for developing this kind of sensitivity.

Special Considerations   Previewing and the PReP plan are both good ways to work with students' prior knowledge while preparing them for reading and comprehending. Each technique, however, relies on a different set of assumptions about the quantity and quality of prior knowledge that students already possess. Previewing is effective when students know very little about the concepts in a lesson, while the PReP plan works when students know relatively more.

If a teacher's assumptions are correct about what students do or do not know, then students are provided a good conceptual framework for what they are about to read. If, on the other hand, a teacher's assumptions about prior knowledge are incorrect (both

Joel Gordon

Guided reading helps students focus on comprehending different types of texts

techniques provide opportunities to test your assumptions), adaptions must be made. For instance, a teacher may begin a lesson with a preview only to discover that students know much more than he or she had assumed. The solution is to shift to more of an indirect approach, drawing out the prior knowledge that students already possess. A teacher who selects the PReP plan could just as easily discover that students are largely unaware of the concepts under study. Again, teachers need to be flexible, shifting to an approach incorporating more direct explanation as opposed to eliciting what students know. When it comes to pre-reading, it is important to plan ahead, but be prepared to alter your approach based upon what you learn about your students.

Guided Reading

Guided reading involves the use of supplemental materials (most often, study guides). Historically, the purpose of guided reading has been to help students focus on specific purposes and tasks, all geared toward comprehending many different types of texts (Moore, Readance, & Rickelman, 1983). A key to successful guided reading is flexibility, both in planning and in implementation.

The following guided reading activities are presented in a deliberate order, from those that are more content-oriented and require less student independence to those that are more process-oriented and require more student independence. Consider this sequence in thinking about how to adapt these activities to the needs of students.

Levels of Comprehension   *Guides for levels of comprehension* (Herber, 1978), also referred to as *three-level guides,* are effective for developing content concepts. Three-level guides consist of declarative statements written to conform to the comprehension emphasized at each of three levels: *literal, interpretive,* and *applied.* Literal statements reflect explicit text information. Interpretive statements focus on implicit text information. Applied statements emphasize beyond-text comprehension, combining information from the text with knowledge from across the curriculum and/or from the outside world (Herber, 1978). All statements are created with a content objective in mind, so that there is a consistent focus across all guide statements. Several examples of three-level guides appear in Figure 7.3

FIGURE 7.3

Examples of Guides for Levels of Comprehension (Three-Level Guides)

Social Studies

Content objective: The battle over women's rights did not end with women's suffrage.

Literal: Place a check next to the statement if it accurately *describes* what happened during the fight over the right for women to vote. Write your proof in the space beneath each statement.

_____ 1. Women became more highly educated.
_____ 2. Women demanded the right to decide who represented them in government.
_____ 3. The women's movement expanded to call for equal rights in education and property ownership.
_____ 4. Many men opposed the movement for equal rights.
_____ 5. Women and men organized marches and other protests.
_____ 6. The 19th Amendment to the constitution was approved in 1920, guaranteeing women the right to vote.

Interpretive: Place a check next to the statement if it *explains* why people fought over the right for women to vote. Write your proof in the space beneath each statement.

_____ 1. As women became more educated, they probably realized just how much their rights were ignored.
_____ 2. When women fought for their rights, men feared that they would lose their rights.

Applied: Each of the following statements reflects an *action* people are taking today on behalf of women's rights. Place a check next to the statement, if you support the action. Write reasons, from your reading and from what you know, in the space beneath each statement.

_____ 1. Battling against pornography.
_____ 2. Renewing the debate over the equal rights amendment.

_____ 3. Protesting over abortion.
_____ 4. Fighting for equal pay.

Science

Content objective: Why warts disappear remains a mystery.

Literal: Place an X in the blank if the statement *describes* a fact about warts. Write your evidence beneath each statement.

_____ 1. Warts are caused by viruses.
_____ 2. Some people use dandelion juice, potatoes, and cornbread crumbs as wart ointments.
_____ 3. Doctors use lasers and medicines to get rid of warts.
_____ 4. Many scientists (and people with warts) want to know what makes warts disappear.

Interpretive: Each of the following statements represents a *hypothesis* we might make about warts. Place an X in the blank if you can support the hypothesis. Write your reasons in the space beneath each statement.

_____ 1. An effective cure might be one that helps the immune system attack the wart virus.
_____ 2. Scientists need to compare how folkloric cures work in relation to how medical cures work to remove warts.

Applied: Place an X in the blank if the statement is a good *prediction* about what we will learn if we continue to study warts and viruses. Write evidence, from your reading and from what you know about science, in the space beneath each statement.

_____ 1. What some people dismiss as folkloric cures might actually work.
_____ 2. Science can be used to improve people's lives.

English

Content objective: It is not easy growing up (*The Outsiders*).

Literal: In this section, we get to know the characters. Place a check in the blank if the statement is a true *description* of the characters and events in the first chapter. Write evidence in the space beneath each statement.

_____ 1. Ponyboy wishes he looked like Paul Newman (but he doesn't really).
_____ 2. Darry is hard and firm and rarely grins at all.
_____ 3. Sodapop is always happy-go-lucky and grinning.
_____ 4. The Socs tried to cut Ponyboy's hair.
_____ 5. Darry saved Ponyboy.
_____ 6. Ponyboy cried after being attacked.

Interpretive: In this section, we understand *reasons* for why the characters do what they do. Place a check in the blank if the statement is a reason for what happens to the characters. Write evidence for your decisions in the space beneath each statement.

_____ 1. The brothers' parents were killed in a car accident.

FIGURE 7.3 *(Cont.)*

_____ 2. Darry thinks he is the boys' mother and father.

_____ 3. Greasers are poorer than Socs, but they are still proud and have big
dreams.

Applied: In this section, we *apply* our experiences to those of the characters. Place
a check in the blank if you agree with the statement. Write support for your
answers in the space beneath each statement. Use evidence from *The Outsiders*
and from your own experience.

_____ 1. It is not easy growing up.

_____ 2. Some people enjoy helping as much as some enjoy hurting other
people.

_____ 3. Everyone needs to feel a sense of belonging.

Chorus

Content objective: If you look good to the audience, you will sound good.

Literal: Place a check in the blank marked "The Reading" if you can support the
statement based on our reading about great performance techniques of famous
choral groups. Be ready to defend your decisions.

The Reading		The Video
_____	1. Each singer's posture is straight but not rigid.	_____
_____	2. The colors of clothing should be coordinated.	_____
_____	3. Hair should always be neat.	_____
_____	4. Teeth should be clean and free of food particles.	_____
_____	5. Face, hands, and fingernails are clean.	_____
_____	6. Everyone appears self-confident and enthusiastic.	_____

Interpretive: Place a check in the blank marked "The Reading" if it is a reasonable
conclusion you could make from the reading about great choruses. Be ready to
defend your decisions.

The Reading		The Video
_____	1. Straight body posture will produce a better sound.	_____
_____	2. Clothing that is messy or ill coordinated is distracting from the performance.	_____
_____	3. Messy hair can ruin a good performance.	_____
_____	4. A good smile is valuable to a performer.	_____

Applied: Place a check in the blank marked "The Reading" if you can support the
statement with the reading *and* from your past choral experiences. Be ready to
defend your decisions.

The Reading		The Video
_____	1. If you look good, you will sound good.	_____

Application activity: Now we will watch a video of our own performance. Place a
check in the blanks above marked "The Video" if the statements can be supported

by what you observe in our performance. Be ready with specific examples to support your decisions.

French (Literature)*

Content objective: La liberté est la chose plus important dans ce monde.

Literal level: Place a check next to the statement if it says what the author writes in the story. The statement may be word for word or reworded slightly. You must support your answers with at least one sentence from the text.

_____ 1. Les prisonniers dans les cachots du chateau d'if sont tres dangereux.
_____ 2. L'un apres l'autre, les prisonniers repondent à l'inspecteur que la
                nourriture est detestable et qu'ils désirent leur liberté.

Interpretive level: Place a check next to the statement if it represents what the author means by what he writes. You must support your decisions with two or more sentences from the text, whether or not you agree that the statement represents the text's deeper meaning.

_____ 1. Les visites de l'inspecteur général des prisons à la prison sont futiles.
_____ 2. A "cachot" is a dungeon.
_____ 3. Le chateau d'if a été un lieu de vacances en 1816.

Applied level: Now apply what you have read and your own personal experiences to respond to the following statements. Proof (evidence) for your responses must come both from the story and from what you know about your world. You must have at least one example from each source.

_____ 1. La liberté est la chose plus important dans ce monde.

*Thanks to Faith Kanatzidis, a French teacher.

There are several purposes behind the construction and use of a three-level guide. One purpose is to separate different types of comprehension to allow students to gain experience with one comprehension process at a time. The idea behind separating the levels is to build awareness of the different types of comprehension so that students can succeed in other types of situations, such as when teachers ask questions that reflect all three levels.

The three-level guide simplifies comprehension by using declarative statements or sentences rather than questions. Questions can be confusing because students often cannot tell what response is required. Many students do not understand differences in questions signaled by "what," "why," and "how." It is not uncommon for teachers to ask a "why" question (such as, "Why did the North win the Civil War?") only to receive a "what," or a factual, answer (such as, "The North fought for many years."). Because declarative statements do not contain "what," "why," and "how," students are not given the additional burden of discriminating among questions while they are comprehending the content of a lesson.

Another purpose of three-level guides is to give students the experience of justifying their own conclusions. Note in the examples in Figure 7.3 that each guide asks students to specify their proof or evidence. Not surprisingly, when first asked to do this, many students are unsure about what to provide or they check off all the statements without really thinking about them. This suggests that instead of relying solely on the structure of the guide to accomplish this purpose, teachers need to help students understand what it means to prove and to justify one's ideas.

Three-level guides are constructed by first identifying a content objective (see Chapter 5). Next, guide statements are written. Literal statements are phrased so that support for them can be found in a single place in the text (for example, in a single sentence or in a picture or diagram). Interpretive statements are written by gathering information from two or more places in the text (for example, combining the words from several sentences or summarizing entire paragraphs). Applied statements are generalizations that combine textual information with students' prior knowledge, experiences, or even previous learning. The sophistication or complexity of the guide is altered through the wording of the statements: using words closely paralleling the text (a simple guide) or paraphrasing and using broad summaries and applications (a more difficult guide).

The final step is to write directions for the guide. The guide should direct students to take two essential steps: (1) signify in writing that they have made a decision about the validity of the statements (often, a check mark serves this function), and (2) provide evidence or proof for their responses. Leaving out either of these features can change students' experiences with the guide dramatically. Figure 7.4 summarizes the steps for designing guides for levels of comprehension.

Special Considerations   Typically, three-level guides are used in conjunction with whole-class and small-group discussion. Whole-class discussion is used to introduce concepts (many teachers begin with a structured overview or semantic map). Students respond to guide statements in small-group, cooperative discussion. They are asked to check off statements for which group members can all find support. The requirement for

FIGURE 7.4

Steps for Preparing a Guide for Levels of Comprehension (Three-Level Guides)

1. Identify a content objective.
2. Write statements representing literal, interpretive, and applied levels of comprehension. Make sure all statements refer to the content objective.
3. Write directions for each level of the guide (literal—interpretive—applied). Make sure students are directed to respond in different ways at each level (for example, to look for facts at the literal level and to form interpretations at the interpretive level). Students should also be required to show they have made a decision about the statements (place a check, circle the item, etc.), and they must provide evidence for their decisions.

group consensus tends to bring diverse opinions together and forces students to wrestle with the content of a lesson. Whole-class discussion is used to compare responses from one small group to the next and to summarize different points of view.

An alternative is to have students respond to three-level guides individually and then hold a whole-class discussion; this is especially appropriate if students have had little experience with different kinds of discussion (see Chapter 11). Gradually, however, teachers should encourage students to discuss the guide material with each other, since peer discussion engages students in thinking about what it means to provide evidence and support for different kinds of concepts.

The strength of three-level guides is that they steer students beyond the facts in a text to comprehend higher-level concepts and principles. There are several things that three-level guides cannot do (but these can be accomplished with some adaptation or integration with other types of strategies). First, three-level guides are generic; teachers need to think about how best to adapt them so that specific subject-matter concepts are appropriately represented and communicated (see, for example, Conley, 1986). Second, three-level guides do not explicitly show students how to process information, justify their thinking, or answer questions. Comprehension processes are implicit in the creation and use of a three-level guide; teachers need to explain those processes if they want their students to have a more conscious awareness of how to learn. Finally, to use three-level guides appropriately, teachers must create a supportive classroom environment in which students are encouraged to work flexibly with different kinds of information and generate higher-level concepts. Teachers can build the right kind of environment for using three-level guides by encouraging discussions that are more student-centered than teacher-centered, and by teaching students how to shoulder more of the responsibility for using the guides so that teachers can help students refine their thinking (see Chapter 11).

Question-Answer Relationships   *Question-answer relationships,* known as *QARs* (Raphael, 1984), can also be incorporated into a guided reading approach to comprehension. The QAR is an instructional approach for sensitizing students to differences in types of questions (for example, asking for facts versus asking for reasons) and in the answers required.

QARs consist of two broad categories: *in-the-book* and *in-my-head* (Raphael, 1986). These names refer to the source of information in constructing both a question and an answer. In-the-book questions and answers deal with information in a text, while in-my-head questions and answers focus on prior knowledge and/or textual information. For example:

In-the-Book

Q. What happens when you combine equal concentrations of an acid and a base?

A. You get a neutral solution (page 140, sentence 4)

In-My-Head

Q. How are acids disposed of in your house?

A. (Answers depend on students' knowledge and experiences.)

These two large categories of questions and answers are each further divided into other kinds of questions.

The in-the-book category is divided into *right-there* and *think-and-search*. For right-there questions and answers, the words used to make up the question and the words used to answer the question are found in the same text sentence. For think-and-search questions and answers, words for the question and words for the answer are not found in a single sentence. Instead, readers must pull together different parts of the reading to answer the question. Consider these examples of right-there and think-and-search questions and answers:

Right-There

> Q. What is the formula for hydrochloric acid?
> A. HCl (page 147, sentence 2)

Think-and-Search

> Q. How can comparing the chemical formulas help distinguish an acid from a base?
> A. Acids have H^+ ions (e.g., HCl) and bases have OH^- ions (for example, NAOH) (from pages 143 and 148).

The in-my-head category is further divided into *author-and-you* and *on-my-own*. For author-and-you questions and answers, an answer comes from what students know, what is in the text, and how the two kinds of information fit together. For on-my-own questions and answers, students use only their own knowledge and experience. On-my-own questions can be answered without reading a text. These examples illustrate author-and-you and on-my-own questions and answers:

Author-and-You

> Q. What kinds of jobs do acids and bases perform in your house?
> A. (Answers come from students' understanding of acids and bases acquired from the text and their own knowledge and experiences)

On-My-Own

> Q. How do you take care of your car battery?
> A. (Answers come from students' experiences.)

To comprehend and learn how to use QARs, students are first taught to distinguish between in-the-book and in-my-head questions and answers during a brief discussion. Consider this excerpt:

TEACHER: In "To Build a Fire," how did the dog feel about his master?
ROBERT: He was loyal.
JENNY: He loved him.
TEACHER: How do you know that the dog felt that way? Can you prove it?
GEORGE: He curled up next to him and tried to keep him warm.
DAMON: He didn't leave him to freeze to death.

TEACHER: Can you show me where it said that in the story?

DAMON: It doesn't say he wouldn't leave him, but he does stay close to him.

TEACHER: Very good. That information was in the story. That's one place we can find answers to the questions we are asking.

Note the teacher's emphasis on supporting answers from the text as opposed to eliciting only correct answers from the floor. In the next segment, the teacher tries to draw from students' experiences:

TEACHER: Why doesn't the dog just walk out on the man? Isn't the dog risking his life as well? Does the text tell you why the dog doesn't just abandon his master?

JULIE: It doesn't say anything about that.

TEACHER: Then what do you think?

JULIE: If I was in danger, my dog would try to help me.

TEACHER: How do you know that?

JULIE: Because my dog is always trying to protect me. We take care of each other.

TEACHER: Good job. You used your own experience to come up with an answer. Whenever we read and answer questions, it is good to think about information we have in our own heads. That's another way we can understand and learn.

When students can distinguish clearly between in-the-book and in-my-head questions and answers, teachers can refine each category further. Right-there and think-and-search distinctions are usually made before moving on to teaching the difference between author-and-you and on-my-own. Throughout, the teacher should strive to make students aware of how to seek out different kinds of information. It is important to work category labels into discussions as a way of helping students develop this awareness:

TEACHER: When you found the information in the story about the dog's loyalty, did you find the information in one sentence? Two sentences?

GEORGE: It was more like all over the place!

TEACHER: Right. The proof is in many places, many events that happened. To really decide, you had to think about many different parts of the story. We call questions that make us think that way think-and-search questions. Sometimes we can find everything we need to answer a question in one sentence, but many times we have to search in a number of places to give a complete answer.

QARs do explicitly what three-level guides do implicitly: guide students to facts, concepts, and principles, while heightening students' awareness of different comprehension processes. The greatest advantage of QARs is that the technique helps students understand how different types of questions really require different types of information from the text and from their own knowledge. In addition, teachers can use QAR categories to show students the difference between poor questions and good questions (for example, "What is a good right-there question?" "What is a lousy think-and-search question?").

Experiences with QARs can help students begin to think about the kinds of questions that might be asked on an upcoming assignment or test.

Special Considerations   Research suggests that an emphasis on QARs needs to be more extensive if students are younger (elementary grades) and can be less extensive if students are older (middle and high school). Training for a week, with periodic reinforcement, is effective with younger students. Brief (ten-minute) sessions at the beginning of a lesson from time to time are sufficient to sensitize older students to QARs (Raphael, 1984).

There are also optimal times during instruction to develop different kinds of QARs. For example, questions asked prior to reading tend to be on-my-own types. During and immediately after reading, right-there and think-and-search questions are at the forefront. For application activities, on-my-own and author-and-you questions are the focus.

It is also important to reflect on the balance among different question types asked during each lesson. Too many right-there questions could indicate an overemphasis on facts at the expense of what students know. An overabundance of think-and-search questions could prove frustrating. Finally, teachers should reflect on the extent to which questions throughout a lesson build comfortably on one another (for example, how specific think-and-search questions relate to right-there questions posed earlier). To make sure questions are consistent, get into the habit of thinking about a content objective for each lesson involving QARs. It is easier to monitor the links from one question to the next when a coherent focus on content concepts has been established. Students stand a better chance of developing an awareness of the processes underlying QARs when teachers are careful about how—and in what logical sequence—they ask questions.

Text Patterns

Guides dealing with text patterns are termed *organizational patterns guides* or just *patterns guides* (Herber, 1978). Patterns guides highlight and emphasize a text's internal organization such that the concepts an author is presenting become more clearly represented. Recall that internal patterns consist of cause/effect, compare/contrast, time order, and enumeration (see Chapter 2). The following examples are intended to reinforce how these patterns are essential for communicating concepts across the curriculum.

In science classes, it is common for students to complete a lab experiment, achieve a set of results, and yet still not comprehend the entire point of the experiment. In these situations, students need to comprehend basic cause/effect relationships that provide the foundation for concepts in the lab. Recall that cause/effect relationships involve ways that facts, concepts, or events are caused by other facts, concepts, and events. Notions of cause and effect underlie many scientific hypotheses and explanations.

In mathematics, students often are expected to compare two sides of an equation and solve for an unknown variable or they are asked to convert numbers from one system to another (as in the case of converting fractions to decimals). In these situations, students need to comprehend compare/contrast relationships among concepts that form the equations. Recall that compare/contrast relationships involve similarities and differences among facts, concepts, and events. The inability of some students to compare or contrast mathematical expressions is one source of failure in many math classrooms.

In social studies, time order relationships matter not only at different points in time, but also with respect to recurring historical patterns. Recall that time order relationships consist of the sequence or order of facts, concepts, or events. During some historical periods, such as times of war, convolutions and confusion over how events unfold can often be the reasons underlying conflict. For example, during the Revolutionary War, the British claimed that colonial violence preceded violent British responses such as the Boston Massacre. On the other hand, colonists claimed that British violence and oppression came before colonists were forced to become violent. Note how in this example, the time order pattern, involving who was initially responsible for the violence, is also closely linked to a second pattern, causes and effects prior to the Revolutionary War.

English classes often involve enumeration patterns. Recall that an enumeration pattern consists of elaborations on previously stated concepts or events. In a novel, characters and events are often introduced long before their features and importance become clear. Students need some way to see that relationship between characters and events and what they signify. A patterns guide based on enumeration can meet this need. Some English teachers like to use patterns guides to deepen students' understanding of different story elements, such as an author's theme, features of the setting, actions of characters, and the importance of various plot events.

So what does an organizational patterns guide look like? Figure 7.5 contains a range of examples. Patterns guides have two parts: (1) a section that encourages students to examine relationships among concepts in terms of the pattern being emphasized, and (2) a section emphasizing the applied comprehension level.

FIGURE 7.5

Examples of Guides Emphasizing Text Patterns (Patterns Guides)

Social Studies

Content objective: For labor and management, public image is everything.

Pattern: Cause/effect

Part I: Below are some events and images. Place a check in the blank if you think the event on the left caused or created the image on the right. Base your decisions on your reading about unions and labor on pages 101–104. Write the name of the person or group responsible for the image in the space below each set of items.

Event	Image
_____ 1. Gompers organizes unions	Gompers is a troublemaker.
_____ 2. Being poor	Person lacks skill.
_____ 3. Sit-down strikes	Unions are bad for business.
_____ 4. High profits	Workers are ill-paid.

FIGURE 7.5 *(Cont.)*

_____ 5. Management refuses to negotiate	Management doesn't care about the workers.
_____ 6. Unions won the right to negotiate	Workers now could help run the plants as equals with managers.

Part II: Place a check next to the statements you can support from what you learned in Part I and from your knowledge about history. Be ready to support your answers.

_____ 1. It is only human to want more and more power.

_____ 2. Throughout history, appearances (or public images) are often deceiving.

_____ 3. No one really has control over one's public image.

_____ 4. People as well as governments live and die by public images.

English

Content objective: Caring for someone could save a life.

Pattern: Compare/contrast

Part I: Below are some phrases separated by a slash (/). Place a check in the blank to the left if the first phrase can be compared with the second based on the story "mischievous children." Write a brief explanation under each set of phrases.

(Hint: Think about how the phrases are the same or different with respect to characters and events in the story.)

_____ 1. The poor orphan / The other children

_____ 2. The first warning about the light / The second warning

_____ 3. The orphan's warning / Calling the orphan a liar

_____ 4. Hiding from the great beast / Following the beast into the cold

_____ 5. The orphan's fate / The fate of the other children

Part II: These statements use information in the story and say something about ourselves. Place a check next to the statements you think are true based on the story *and* your own experiences. Be ready to defend your decisions.

_____ 1. You should never call someone a liar.

_____ 2. Caring for someone could save a life.

Art

Content objective: There is a definite order in applying line and color in drawing.

Pattern: Time order

Part I: Below are words and phrases that are separated. The words and phrases in each line form a sequence. Decide if the words or phrases reflect the right sequence. That is, what is *named* first should *take place* first. If so, place a check on the line. Base your decision on the reading and my demonstration about line and color.

_____ 1. Color / Outline

_____ 2. Crosshatch / Shadow

_____ 3. Outline / Color
_____ 4. Create line variations / Create perspective
_____ 5. Form a design idea / Form a design

Part II: Next to each statement below, place a check if it can be supported by what you have learned about line and color *and* your own experiences with drawing. Be ready to give a drawing demonstration to support your answers.

_____ 1. How you use line and color can influence your work, for good or bad!
_____ 2. Outlining will always produce a stronger effect on color.

Mathematics

Content objective: Equations are part of everyday life.

Pattern: Enumeration

Part I: Write about a brief story problem using each of the following equations.

Equation: $3x - 3 = 15$

Story

Three of us wanted to go to the movies. We each had a free pass worth one dollar off the ticket price (a total of three dollars). The ticket lady charged us fifteen dollars to get in. To settle up, we had to figure out how much each of us owed.

Equation: $y + 6 = 9$

Story

_____

_____

Equation: $z - 8 = 17$

Story

_____

_____

Equation: $2r + 3 = -11$

Story

_____

_____

Part II: Below is a set of statements about how we use mathematics. Place a check next to the statements that you can prove. Give two or three real-life examples for each statement you have supported. The evidence should come from your knowledge about equations *and* your experiences with equations in real life.

_____ 1. If you know math, it is easier to be fair with money.
_____ 2. Whether they realize it or not, people find themselves in mathematical situations every day.

_____

To plan a lesson containing a patterns guide, choose a content objective. Then by examining the material to be read as well as the content objective, choose a text pattern. Remember that the purpose of a patterns guide is not merely to highlight content (reflected by the content objective) or to focus on process (reflected by the text pattern) but to develop an integrated understanding of the content concepts and the text patterns that form underlying relationships.

The first part of a patterns guide can be designed with a number of formats in mind. Figure 7.5 presents several examples. The more common format involves words or phrases separated by a slash:

Place a check next to the words and phrases separated by a slash (/), if they are compared in the reading. Be ready to tell how the words are compared.

_____ warts / zits

_____ laser treatment / onion juice

Another commonly used format involves columns:

Place a check in the blank to the left, if the word or phrase in Column A can be considered a cause of the word or phrase in Column B. Write reasons for your decisions.

	Column A	Column B
_____	virus	warts
_____	ointment	warts disappear

Still another format involves matching one set of words or phrases with another:

Match the words or phrase on the left with the words or phrases on the right, if the words or phrases are compared in the reading. Write reasons for your decisions.

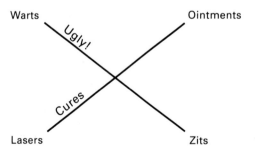

The choice of a format really depends on your choice of a pattern and the need to keep things simple. Be cautious about getting too creative, since it is easy to create a convoluted

FIGURE 7.6

Steps for Preparing a Patterns Guide

1. Identify a content objective.
2. Select a pattern that, if emphasized, helps students understand the content objective.
3. Decide on a format for Part I [words and phrases separated by a slash (/), columns, matching].
4. Create items for Part I and Part II based on consideration of the content objective *and* the pattern to be emphasized. Adjust the sophistication of guide items according to what students already know about patterns and the content to be learned.
5. Write directions for Part I and Part II. Make sure that students signify that they have made a decision about the items on the guide (circling, checking, etc.) and that they have evidence or proof for any decision.

patterns guide or one that focuses more on assessment than on instruction. For example, matching activities are commonly used on tests. When used for assessment, matching activities rarely require students to make judgments or specify reasons. Instead, students are accountable for providing answers that relate to lesson or unit outcomes. When used for instruction (à la patterns guides), matching activities invite reasoned decision-making.

Figure 7.6 summarizes the steps for creating a patterns guide.

Special Considerations   Students are not automatically ready to employ patterns to understand lesson concepts. What students know (or do not know) about text patterns must be incorporated into lesson planning. For some students, the terms "cause," "effect," "compare," and "contrast" may be familiar. For others, the terms may be completely foreign. Teachers need to assess how much their students know (see Chapter 2) and respond accordingly. Students already familiar with text patterns may need some brief reinforcement (such as a brief review of the meaning of different patterns). Students who are unfamiliar with text patterns benefit from pre-teaching, in which teachers explain and illustrate patterns (sometimes by seeking out patterns in material students have already learned).

Still another consideration when preparing a patterns guide concerns how changes in the wording of the items affect the sophistication of the guide. Compare the following sets of items:

warts / zits

skin protuberance / inflammatory skin swelling

A comparison based on the first set is stated directly in the reading, while the second set is never mentioned but implied. In addition, the first set contains simple, straightforward language, while the second set may be overly complex for some students or grade levels. Teachers who recognize these differences can adapt activities to alternatively support or challenge students. Teachers who inadvertently neglect differences in sophistication risk overly frustrating their students.

K-W-L

K-W-L is the name of a simple, three-step procedure for activating students' prior knowledge and then guiding their acquistion of concepts while they read. During the first two steps of the activity, teachers and students engage in discussion, followed by students' personal responses on a guide sheet (see Figure 7.7). Next, students read. Following their reading, students individually complete the third step, writing down what they learned. This is followed by another whole-class discussion to compare and contrast what students discovered in their reading. The initials K-W-L stand for the three steps in the activity. These steps are explained in the following sections.

Step K—What We Know   This section actually has two parts: brainstorming and categorizing. First, students brainstorm for what they already know about the major concepts in the lesson (part 1 on the guide sheet). As with semantic mapping, concepts chosen for this part are crucial: they should be familiar to students and specific enough to

FIGURE 7.7

K-W-L Guide Sheet

What We Know	What We Want to Find Out	What We Learn and Still Need to Learn
1.		

2. Categories of information we expect to use
        A.
        B.
        C.
        D.
        E.

generate many different yet relevant responses. For example, if the lesson is about sea turtles, use the starter word "sea turtles" as opposed to asking "What do you know about the ocean?" A general, enjoyable discussion about the ocean and beaches may never get students to think about specific kinds of prior knowledge that will help them understand the lesson concepts (Ogle, 1986). As different kinds of concepts are elicited, students transfer them to the guide sheet.

The second part of this step is to have students categorize the concepts they have generated (part 2 on the guide sheet). The purpose of this part is to get students to consider what kinds of information to expect when they read the passage. Accomplishing this often requires some oral modeling on the part of the teacher. Students are not accustomed to thinking about how to group concepts. Modeling one or two examples usually helps students get into the process. For example, a teacher might note that there are three or four pieces of information that describe how a turtle looks. The teacher then writes "how a turtle looks" on the guide sheet under the Categories of Information heading. The teacher continues by asking "Can you find other categories from the information we have listed?" (Ogle, 1986). Other categories are added to the guide sheet.

Step W—What We Want to Find Out   Just before they read, students generate questions they want answered. Questions are developed from information elicited during the brainstorming and categorizing that has just occurred. Again, teachers need to model the kinds of questions they would like students to begin asking. The tendency is for students to ask factual or tangential questions (such as, "What color is a turtle?" or "Is Fred's turtle still alive?"). Instead, students must learn to ask more purposeful or meaningful "why" and "how" questions (such as, "Why do turtles live so long?" or "How do turtles use their shell?").

Step L—What We Learn and Still Need to Learn   As they read, students stop themselves periodically to check and monitor their understanding. When they stop, students answer the questions that were raised during the W section. The emphasis at this stage is to help students recognize what they have learned as well as what they have not yet comprehended.

Students also raise additional questions as they encounter new information. For example, students might discover that turtle eggs are often stolen and eaten by predators. Thus, an important question is: "How many eggs are stolen and how many eggs go on to hatch?" The answer to this question tells a great deal about the survival of a species in the wild.

Special Considerations   The success of K-W-L is dependent on what students know about how to ask questions and the ability of teachers to make explicit the processes underlying each of the K-W-L steps. When students are asked to create their own questions, they often focus on facts. The reason is logical. In many classrooms, factual questions are more frequently asked (O'Flahaven, Hartman, & Pearson, 1988). As a result, students are more familiar with factual as opposed to interpretive or applied-type questions and they think those are the kinds of questions teachers value. To ensure that students get the most out of K-W-L, teachers may wish to engage students in other kinds of questioning activities, such as exposing them to levels of comprehension guides and QARs prior to work with K-W-L. As with the other activities in this chapter, a good rule to follow is to develop content objectives for lessons in which K-W-L is a central activity. During K-W-L, content objectives help focus the brainstorming and questioning activities on key content concepts.

A primary goal of K-W-L is to encourage students to be independent in applying underlying processes to a variety of reading situations. For this to happen, teachers need to provide modeling and clear explanations during each step. For example, while leading students through step K, teachers should demonstrate the importance of calling on prior knowledge before beginning a reading assignment. Similarly, teachers can emphasize the value of self-questioning. Ideally, teachers should provide explicit direction during students' early experiences with K-W-L and gradually shift responsiblity to students for employing the K-W-L steps. Eventually, students should be able to apply K-W-L on their own, with the teacher offering corrective feedback. As students master the technique, their motivation increases (Carr & Ogle, 1987). Once internalized, K-W-L is a powerful vehicle for learning and communicating in content areas.

TEACHING A LESSON

This section presents a mathematics lesson that incorporates many of the ideas presented in this chapter. In reading this section, think about how the principles of instruction presented here apply to planning and teaching a lesson in your content area.

Goals and Assumptions

This lesson is about triangles. The intended audience is a ninth-grade, mixed-ability group of students in a pre-algebra class. Students have already studied lines and angles and have done some simple measuring with rulers and protractors. This lesson builds on these experiences and moves students to consider features and purposes of two-dimensional figures.

The mathematics textbook deals with triangles in two pages. The first page of the text helps students recall the definitions for acute angles (less than 90 degrees), right angles (equal to 90 degrees), and obtuse angles (greater than 90 degrees). Next, it has students practice classifying whole triangles according to the types of angles within them. The chapter clues students that the angles of a triangle are equal to 180 degrees and gives an example of how to determine a third angle of a triangle if the other two angles are known. The second page of the text introduces the notion of classifying triangles according to the relationships of the sides (when sides are congruent or not congruent). Finally, the text provides a set of exercises for students to demonstrate their competence with the many concepts covered on the two pages of text.

Whew! The feeling many teachers get from mathematics texts is that far too many concepts are covered in too short a page range. Many hope that there is enough carryover from one lesson to the next (such as, students knowing the angle definitions) that the concept load will not be quite so heavy. Unfortunately, this is rarely the case. Teachers and their students often struggle from one lesson to the next to develop some coherent sense of what the mathematics content is all about and what purposes it serves.

Questions for planning include: (1) What content is important? and (2) What are the best ways to teach it so that students understand it (content), transfer their understanding under a variety of conditions (process), and appreciate the functions of the content in mathematical as well as real-world contexts (motivation)?

To begin addressing these questions, a content objective was written:

The size and shape of a triangle is directly related to the size and shape of its angles and sides.

This objective provides a simple (but not watered down) summary statement of the critical concepts in the lesson.

The objective does not address any real-world functions or applications of the concepts. This is not always possible or desirable in mathematics. For some concepts, it is necessary to strive for mathematical relevance (links from one math concept to another). For others, it is critical to stress real-world relevance (links from a math concept to real-world applications). For this lesson, a decision was made to focus on real-world connections, so the following question was developed:

How do people use triangles?

When used at some point during instruction, this question could cause students to reflect on the practical implications of their study of triangles.

The content objective and key question for instruction specify what content is important. The next set of decisions concern ways to develop a deep understanding of the content, how it can be used, and when and where it is useful. An adapted version of K-W-L was chosen to deal with these issues (see Figure 7.8).

FIGURE 7.8

K-W-L Guide Sheet for the Mathematics Lesson

What We Know about Triangles	What Math Tools We Have to Find Out	What We Learn and Still Need to Learn
1.		

2. How do people use triangles?

To engage students in realistic problem-solving, the following set of triangles was selected, along with the question, "Which triangle works best for building the roof of a house?"

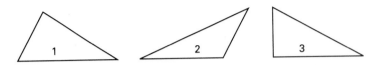

The eventual goal for applying concepts in this lesson is for students independently to choose a triangle and justify its use in constructing a roof.

Building Background and Motivation

The format for K-W-L makes it fairly simple to build background and motivation. To begin, the teacher shows students the triangles and asks the question, "What do we know about triangles?" One teacher taught this lesson, using a K-W-L guide sheet on an overhead projector. This is an excerpt from her discussion:

TEACHER: What do you know about triangles?
KENT: They have a point on top.
GEORGE: They are flat at the bottom.
TEACHER: OK, that's a good start. What else do you know?
TIFFANY: Three sides.
SHIWANA: They have a pyramid shape.
KENT: Yeah, a pyramid is really a triangle.
TELLY: I know something. They have 90-degree angles.
TEACHER: (Writes the answers on a K-W-L guide). Anything else?
THOMAS: They have touching sides.
TEACHER: They have touching sides? What do you mean?
THOMAS: The lines all come together.
TEACHER: OK, that's very interesting!

Note how the emphasis at this stage is on eliciting ideas. Note also that some elements of the PReP plan are operating, for example, when the teacher asks Thomas to explain his answer and asks other students to continue elaborating. Students' responses can also be evaluated in terms of PReP. In this excerpt, students offer an example (a pyramid) and several attributes of triangles (three sides, sides touch), and even a borderline misconception (triangles automatically have 90-degree angles). They do not relate concepts in a very sophisticated way: they do not talk about different kinds of triangles nor do they compare triangles to other shapes. Because of this feedback, it is safe to say that these students have some knowledge about triangles and neither a high nor low degree of knowledge. Armed with this information, the teacher can proceed through the lesson, building on concepts students already know (sides and angles) to develop richer conceptions of what triangles are all about.

What we know about triangles

Have a point

Flat on bottom

Three sides

Pyramid shape

90 degree angles

Touching sides

Lines come together

Getting students to think about the uses of triangles is a bit trickier, as this excerpt shows:

TEACHER: How do we use triangles?
THOMAS: I see 'em on buildings all the time.
TEACHER: That's interesting. Where do you see them?
THOMAS: All over. Mostly the roof, I guess.
SHIWANA: You got 'em all over your sweater!
TEACHER: You're right. I didn't really think about that. Where else do we use triangles?

How do people use triangles?

Roofs

Sweater

Paper tray

TELLY: That paper tray on your desk.

TEACHER: Right, there are objects in this room that have triangles built into them.

It is difficult for students and, indeed, most of us, to perceive all the different ways triangles function in everday living. Note how Thomas already recognizes the use of triangles for the roof of a building. While this is a good base of insight for the lesson, the teacher cannot conclude that all the students have made this connection, or that all students, including Thomas, have understood how the shape of a triangle relates to its function in supporting a roof.

Developing Content and Process

Normally, during the next step of K-W-L, students ask questions. However, general questions at this stage may not focus on specific aspects of the mathematics content or mathematical reasoning required in this context. Consequently, the teacher has students think first about the mathematical tools (concepts, procedures, models, symbols, and representations) that are required to find out more about triangles:

TEACHER: Today, we're going to learn about triangles and how people use them. What kinds of ideas have we already studied that could help us?

TELLY: We studied about the angles and the lines.

TEACHER: What about the angles and the lines?

TELLY: We measured them with the protractors and rulers.

TEACHER: Very good. What did we find out?

TIFFANY: How big the angles and lines are has something to do with the kind of angle it is. The shapes are different.

TEACHER: So protractors and rulers—measurement—might be important here too.

While this stage resembles the K—knowledge—step, it really is serving a different purpose: to get students to focus more specifically on the content knowledge critical for the understanding of triangles.

Next, the teacher helps students forge this mathematical information into a set of guiding questions. Note her use of modeling, her thinking out loud so that students can learn how to form their own questions:

TEACHER: I have a question about triangles that I thought about based on our study of angles. The question is: How are triangles formed? The way I came up with the question was to think about what was important in our study of angles. Remember how we figured out how angles are formed? Every time we came up with a new angle, that was an important question. Can you think of some other questions that might help us?

TIFFANY: We need to know how big are the angles.

TEACHER: OK, what made you think of that question?

TIFFANY: Well, the size of the angles made the angles different sizes. Maybe that's true with triangles.

What math tools we have to find out

Angles—Lines

Protractors

Rulers

How are triangles formed?

How big are the angles?

*How does the size of the
sides change the size of the triangles?*

THOMAS: That could be true about the sides too. My question is: how does the size
of the sides change the size of the triangles?
TEACHER: Very good. We'll have to see.

As the questions are generated, the teacher and students write them on the K-W-L guide
sheet. The guide sheet then serves as a useful framework for reading the math text and
exploring similarities and differences among various triangles based on observations about
angles and sides.

To further develop the concepts, students are provided many opportunities to
measure and compare different triangles. Through their experiences, they discover
several key features of triangles. These key features really define triangles, distinguishing
them from other shapes, such as a square or circle.

One discovery is of particular interest because of its relationship to what students
have learned about angles. Students have found that in some triangles, all the angles are
less than 90 degrees while in other triangles, one angle is more than 90 degrees. A third
type of triangle has one 90-degree angle. When compared, these triangles have very
different shapes in relation to one another. With help from the teacher, students classify
the triangles in terms of the angles within: triangles with angles less than 90 degrees are
acute; triangles with angles more than 90 degrees are obtuse; triangles with one 90-degree
angle are right triangles.

Ideally, the approach taken will help students remember these distinctions for a long
time. Rather than having teachers give students a set of labels and then try to develop a
very abstract set of concepts, students created their own questions. Experience with

What we learn and still need to learn

*Triangle #1–all angles
are smaller than 90° (acute)*

*Triangle #2–one angle
is more than 90°   (obtuse)*

*Triangle #3–one angle
equals 90°   (right)*

*Triangles have different
shapes because of
differences in the angles
inside them.*

measurement and observation becomes the vehicle for discovering answers and drawing conclusions. The teacher models the kinds of processes students need to employ and helps students acquire a language for the concepts learned.

Encouraging Independence

Now is the time to help students apply the concepts and processes they have learned, as well as explore mathematical and real-world implications.

A simple way to do this is to hold a discussion in which students speculate on the best triangle for the construction of a roof:

TEACHER: Which one should we use?

THOMAS: Most of them look like two right triangles pushed together.

TEACHER: OK, why do you suppose builders use that arrangement?

THOMAS: I don't know.

TEACHER: Shimonda, what do you think?

SHIMONDA: They use that kind of roof a lot, but I've seen other roofs that look like two obtuse angles shoved together.

TEACHER: What's the difference in the roofs?

BRENDA: The roofs with obtuse angles are not as steep as the roofs with right angles.

GEORGE: What about roofs with acute angles? Those would be really steep!

TEACHER: Let's draw some of the roofs and compare their advantages and disadvantages.

Notice that the emphasis here is on speculation and discovery. The teacher encourages students to be flexible as they think about and evaluate different types of roofs. The teacher could eventually engage students in some manipulative activities, such as building different roofs out of balsa wood (or even Popsicle sticks) to test out their emerging theories about the functions of angles, lines, and triangles.

At this point, students have had a series of interactions with the content and have constructed a number of concepts and principles with the teacher and on their own. Students have integrated much of what they know about angles with their study of triangles and there is evidence from their talk that they are developing a deep understanding of the content and they know how it is useful. To complete the picture, it is important to help students become aware of *how* they have learned the content, to develop their sense of the powerful processes they can use to comprehend on their own.

Because of the richness of the concepts in any content area lesson, the development of process awareness is not easy. The best approach is a simple one that builds on what students understand about the content. Take some time to have students look back on the lesson and have them examine how they arrived at a particular understanding. In this lesson, five processes were important:

1. Reflecting on what is already known about key lesson concepts

2. Thinking about the role or function of the concepts in the outside world

3. Brainstorming for the processes and procedures important in learning the lesson concepts

4. Generating and answering questions

5. Applying lesson concepts to realistic problems

Not every situation requiring comprehension will involve all these processes. However, students need to be made aware that any and all of these processes are available to them as strategies for comprehending and communicating in content area classrooms.

SUMMARY

What we know about comprehension instruction makes the role of the teacher both important and complex. Communication is central to comprehension instruction. What teachers say to students becomes a pathway to understanding of the content and how to learn it. Therefore, teachers are critical mediators in building concepts and applications, as opposed to repositories of information who dump facts into receptive (or not so receptive) minds.

The techniques described and illustrated here represent opportunities for comprehension instruction in content areas. By adapting pre-reading and guided reading to different subject-matter purposes, teachers can create readiness and motivation and then carefully lead students to make their own meanings. If teachers treat these techniques as another set of dittos, however, they lead only to empty answer-giving or guessing what is in the teacher's head. Teachers are indeed the key to realizing the potential of comprehension instruction, developing deeper subject-matter understandings while building greater awareness for what it means to be literate and a good communicator in content areas.

SPECIAL PROJECTS

Course-Based

1. To develop in students an awareness for *how* to comprehend, it is important for teachers to talk with students about the processes being employed. This is complicated by the various kinds of labels used for comprehension (such as "literal," "interpretive," "applied," "textually explicit," "textually implicit," and "scriptally implicit"). Select or create a common language to use with students. Consider the need for students to understand the processes deeply and to use the processes strategically to comprehend subject-matter concepts.
2. Evaluate a textbook in your content area. What kinds of provisions are made for helping students comprehend? What assumptions are built into the activities provided with the text? For example, do the textbook authors assume that students are already capable of answering many different types of questions? Design a lesson based on one section of the text to illustrate how you will make decisions about:
   a. What content is important
   b. Which instructional activities will most assist students in comprehending the text

Field-Based

3. Plan a lesson devoted to comprehension instruction. Teach the lesson to a group of students. Evaluate your experience in terms of:
   a. Your original assumptions about what (and how much) content to emphasize
   b. The appropriateness of the comprehension activities you created
   c. How well students understood the content, learned how to comprehend, and were motivated to learn

SUGGESTED READING

These references offer additional examples of comprehension activities, similar to the ones presented in this chapter;

ALVERMANN, D. (1987). Learning from text. In D. Alvermann, D. Moore, & M. Conley (Eds.), *Research within reach: Secondary school reading.* Newark, DE: International Reading Association.

ANTHONY, H., & RAPHAEL, T. (1989). Using questioning strategies to promote students' active comprehension of content area material. In D. Lapp, J. Flood & N. Farnan (Eds.), *Content area reading and learning: Instructional strategies.* Englewood Cliffs, NJ: Prentice-Hall.

CUNNINGHAM, J. (1986). How to question before, during and after reading. In E. Dishner, T. Bean, J. Readance, & D. Moore (Eds.), *Reading in the content areas: Improving classroom instruction.* Dubuque, IA: Kendall/Hunt.

LANGER, J. (1982). Facilitating text processing: The elaboration of prior knowledge. In J. Langer & T. Smith-Burke (Eds.), *Reader meets author/Bridging the gap.* Newark, DE: International Reading Association.

OGLE, D. (1989). The know, want to know, learn strategy. In K. Muth (Ed.), *Children's comprehension of text: Research into practice.* Newark, DE: International Reading Association.

This chapter presents a good description of the content area teacher's role during comprehension instruction:

ROEHLER, L., & DUFFY, G. (1989). The content area teacher's instructional role: A cognitive mediational view. In D. Lapp, J. Flood, & N. Farnan (Eds.), *Content area reading and learning: Instructional strategies.* Englewood Cliffs, NJ: Prentice-Hall.

The following books consist of research reviews devoted to comprehension instruction:

DUFFY, G., ROEHLER, L., & MASON, J. (1984). *Comprehension instruction: Perspectives and suggestions.* New York: Longman.

FLOOD, J. (Ed.). (1984). *Promotion reading comprehension.* Newark, DE: International Reading Association.

MUTH, K. (Ed.). (1989). *Children's comprehension of text: Research into practice.* Newark, DE: International Reading Association.

REFERENCES

CARR, E., & OGLE, D. (1987). K-W-L plus: A strategy for comprehension and summarization. *Journal of Reading, 30,* 7, 626–631.

CONLEY, M. (1986). The influence of training on three teachers' comprehension questions during content area lessons. *Elementary School Journal, 87,* 1, 17–28.

GRAVES, M., & PRENN, M. (1984). Effects of previewing expository passages on junior high school students' comprehension and attitudes. In J. Niles & R. Lalik (Eds.), *Changing perspectives on research in reading/language processing and instruction.* Rochester, NY: The National Reading Conference.

GRAVES, M., PRENN, M., & COOKE, C. (1985). The coming attraction: Previewing short stories. *Journal of Reading, 28,* 7, 594–599.

HERBER, H. (1978). *Teaching reading in content areas.* Englewood Cliffs, NJ: Prentice-Hall.

HOETKER, J., & AHLBRAND, W. (1969). The persistence of the recitation. *American Educational Research Journal, 2,* 6, 145–167.

LANGER, J. (1982). Facilitating text processing: The elaboration of prior knowledge. In J. Langer & T. Smith-Burke (Eds.), *Reader meets author/Bridging the gap.* Newark, DE: International Reading Association.

MOORE, D., READANCE, J., & RICKELMAN, R. (1983). An historical exploration of content area reading instruction. *Reading Research Quarterly, 18,* 4, 419–438.

O'FLAHAVEN, J., HARTMAN, D., & PEARSON, P. D. (1988). Teacher questioning and feedback practices: A twenty year retrospective. In J. Readance & S. Baldwin (Eds.), *Dialogues in literacy research.* Chicago: The National Reading Conference.

OGLE, D. (1986). K-W-L: A teaching model that develops active reading of expository text. *The Reading Teacher, 39,* 6, 564–571.

RAPHAEL, T. (1984). Teaching learners about sources of information for answering comprehension questions. *Journal of Reading, 28,* 5, 303–311.

RAPHAEL, T. (1986). Teaching question answer relationships, revisited. *The Reading Teacher, 39,* 6, 516–523.

ROEHLER, L., & DUFFY, G. (1989). The content area teacher's instructional role. In D. Lapp, J. Flood, & N. Farnan (Eds.), *Content area reading and learning: Instructional strategies.* Englewood Cliffs, NJ: Prentice-Hall.

Teacher: Think harder, now! How could we pay for some of your solutions—you mentioned some and the text mentions some—for environmental pollution?

Students furrow their brows, stare into space, and put their hands on their chins, trying to think, but no one seems to be able to come up with an answer.

Scene observed in a ninth-grade science class devoted to solving environmental problems.

8

Reasoning and Problem-Solving

CHAPTER OBJECTIVES

After reading this chapter, you should be able to:

1. Describe various reasoning and problem-solving processes and explain their role in your content area.

2. Plan and teach a lesson emphasizing reasoning and/or problem-solving in which students' knowledge of the content is elaborated and enhanced and their sense of power and success with their own learning is increased.

RATIONALE

Reasoning refers to a collection of thinking processes (*Random House College Dictionary,* 1984). The word "reasoning" is often used synonymously with *critical thinking,* a term associated with what are called higher-level thinking skills such as analyzing, making comparisons, inferring, and evaluating (Ennis, 1987). *Problem-solving* is a specific form of reasoning in which students are given a situation (a problem) and are asked to fill in missing information (Bransford, Sherwood, & Sturdevant, 1987). The goal for solving a problem is usually given (for example, find X, figure out the identity of the murderer, identify the unknown compound), but key information necessary to accomplish the goal is missing and must be supplied by students. In contrast to Chapter 7, which is devoted to situations in which students require specific help with text comprehension, this chapter focuses on situations in which students can comprehend the text yet need help with beyond-text reasoning and problem-solving.

Though reasoning and problem-solving are considered pathways for students to reach their full potential (Nickerson, 1987), students rarely have direct opportunites in school to learn about reasoning and problem-solving, nor are they rewarded for engaging in those activities (Perkins & Simmons, 1988). Reasons for this are illustrated by the classroom dialogue at the beginning of this chapter. "Thinking" question are rarely easy— for teachers or their students. The answers are not readily evident in a textbook, nor are the processes or technqiues for finding the answers. Unfortunately, as students progress through the grades, more of their educational experiences are geared toward memorizing facts and fewer opportunities exist for thinking things out and challenging existing ideas (Goodlad, 1984).

CHAPTER ORGANIZER

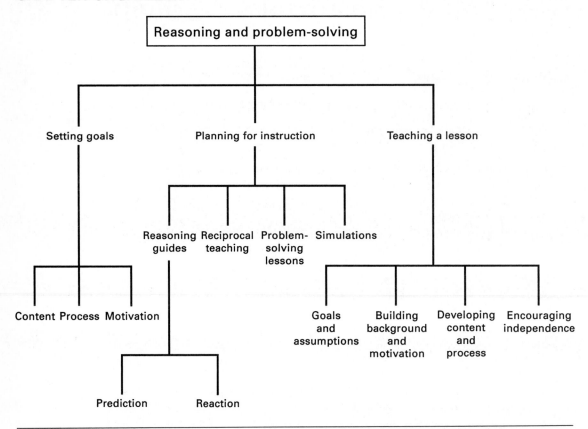

Teachers—as well as students—often throw up barriers to instruction devoted to reasoning and problem-solving. Reasoning and problem-solving techniques can be demanding on teachers and their students, and the processes underlying reasoning and problem-solving are complex. Further, critical differences in students, such as differences in learning style and in preference for some approaches as opposed to others, make it difficult for teachers to plan and teach lessons based on reasoning and problem-solving (Pressley et al., 1989).

Many students do not understand that learning is more than rote memorization; they feel secure when they are asked to fill in dittos or answer simple questions. Higher-level thinking, however, requires productive, generative thinking (Simon, 1980). The extent of risk and ambiguity with reasoning and problem-solving tasks is much higher than with most other classroom tasks (Doyle, 1984). For many students, the payoff is less clear and immediate and the tendency is to quit rather than to persevere (Perkins & Simmons, 1988).

Joel Gordon

Reasoning
and problem-
solving are
critical life-
long skills

The reluctance of teachers and students to engage in reasoning and problem-solving is unfortunate given the power of thinking, especially when factual knowledge is not very strong. Brown and Palincsar (1985) coined the term "intelligent novices" to describe students who may not possess prior knowledge required in a content area, but who know how to reason and go about acquiring the knowledge they need. Daily adult living is full of situations in which knowledge is sparse and reasoning and problem-solving are requirements. Viewed in this light, reasoning and problem-solving are critical, lifelong skills.

If reasoning and problem-solving are essential, and if teachers and students are reluctant to engage in higher-level thinking, how can effective instruction in these areas be developed? Answers to this question lie in teachers becoming more knowledgeable about reasoning and problem-solving processes and related approaches to teaching. Just as reasoning and problem-solving are keys for helping students put knowledge into action, knowledge about reasoning and problem-solving—and existing barriers—are keys for helping teachers wear down students' preference for low-level, memorization tasks, and for encouraging an appreciation for independent thought.

This chapter provides insight into instruction based on reasoning and problem-solving. It describes the goals for teaching reasoning and problem-solving, illustrates a number of instructional approaches, and portrays a lesson specially designed to emphasize reasoning and problem-solving in content areas.

SETTING GOALS

This section explains goals for reasoning and problem-solving. To reason and problem-solve effectively, students must be able to think in ways that are appropriate to each subject (a goal for content) and to vary their approach to reasoning and problem-solving in relation to different tasks they are asked to perform (a goal for process), and they must believe they are capable (a goal for motivation).

Content Goals

The content goal for instruction in reasoning and problem-solving is: to help students apply reasoning and problem-solving processes appropriately to the content. Accomplishing this goal requires that students have sufficient knowledge to reason and problem-solve and that teachers teach ways in which reasoning and problem-solving processes form subject-matter concepts and beyond-text principles.

In general, the more prior knowledge students possess, the more likely they are to engage productively in reasoning and problem-solving processes (Garner & Alexander, 1989). Put another way, students whose store of subject-matter knowledge is high are better able to reason and problem-solve appropriate in a content area (Anderson, 1984). Recall from Chapter 3 that students mentally store what they know in schemata containing hierarchically organized slots or categories (for example, the category "war" encompasses variations in battles across regions and time periods). When content knowledge is sufficiently high and well-organized, reasoning and problem-solving are aided in several ways.

When students are knowledgeable and they are presented with a situation that requires reasoning or problem-solving, information needed to respond to the situation is speedily accessed. Because they spend little time finding needed information, knowledgeable students can allocate more of their time to reasoning and problem-solving. A second way that knowledge helps involves learning: when knowledge is high but certain kinds of knowledge are lacking, the missing knowledge can be located and quickly slotted in so that reasoning and problem-solving can occur.

Having a store of content knowledge facilitates reasoning and problem-solving, yet knowledge alone does not enable a student to reason or problem-solve (Simon, 1980). Students must also learn ways in which reasoning and problem solving processes are applied to the content. The ability to apply what one knows is often determined by reasoning and problem-solving abilities. A simple science experiment illustrates this point. Students know from experience that adding two cups of water of the same temperature produces water that feels as warm or cool as the original cups of water. Yet, when they measure the separate cups of water with a thermometer, they predict that combining the cups will double the temperature, making the water twice as cold or twice as hot (Strauss, 1987). Students have some rich everyday experiences, yet they do not automatically use these experiences to engage in relatively simple reasoning.

Students can also be unaware of ways in which reasoning and problem-solving processes are subject-specific. What may be a powerful process in one area can be a weak strategy in another. For example, focusing attention on numbers is important in mathematics and history (for dates) but less important in literature. Flowery language and subjectivity may be important for some types of writing in English class, yet they interfere with communication in science, which values conciseness and objectivity (Bransford & Heldmeyer, 1983).

There are several ways teachers can make sure that students apply reasoning and problem-solving processes appropriately to the content of a lesson or unit of study. First, they must make sure students have sufficient prior knowledge. Assessing students' prior knowledge could take the form of a content area reading inventory (see Chapter 3) or the PReP plan (Chapter 6) prior to teaching. If students are lacking in prior knowledge, teachers should take some time to develop students' understanding of the content. As students begin to know more, they can apply reasoning and problem-solving processes in meaningful ways.

Process Goals

The process goal for reasoning and problem-solving is: to develop in students the ability to use reasoning and problem-solving processes strategically to perform many different kinds of tasks. Students can reason and problem-solve strategically when they are able to:

- Determine similarities between current and previous learning tasks.
- Access procedures or techniques that will lead to successful performance.
- Combine knowledge about content and process.
- Monitor their own performance to determine if they are making progress toward meeting goals.

Reasoning and problem-solving processes are ways to think about tasks. Ideally, reasoning and problem-solving processes assist students in figuring out exactly how they should perform a task and what knowledge they should apply. But students are asked to perform many kinds of tasks under many different conditions. For example, for some tasks, such as filling in a study guide, students may be required to open a textbook and write out answers; the tasks are clear and easily completed. For other tasks, such as preparing for a test, students' knowledge of the testing tasks is what they can glean from the teacher or assume based on instruction. Students have a much more difficult job reasoning and problem-solving when the task they must perform are not familiar or understood.

Reasoning and problem-solving processes are both *task-specific* and *general* (Pressley et al., 1989). Task-specific processes are often tricks for remembering. For example, students can memorize the notes on a musical staff (E-G-B-D-F) by memorizing the sentence Every Good Boy Does Fine. There are many different kinds of task-specific processes, but, as this example illustrates, task-specific processes cannot be applied very broadly.

General processes, in contrast, can be applied to various kinds of content and can work with a range of tasks. Figures 8.1 and 8.2 depict and illustrate general reasoning and problem-solving processes.

FIGURE 8.1

General Reasoning Processes

Clarification: Defining terms, analyzing arguments, and asking questions for purposes of clarifying or distinguishing concepts and generalizations under study.

> Kelly: What do doctors mean when they say that a disease is treatable but not curable? What is the difference?
>
> Brendon: Aids seems to be treatable. They can slow down the disease by treating it with drugs, but they can't get rid of it.

Induction: Building a set of rules or generalizations by examining facts, concepts, examples, or other generalizations.

> *Examples:* $6X + 4 = 4X + 12$ $5X + 15 = 2X + 27$
>
> 1. $6X = 4X + 12 - 4$ 1. $5X = 2X + 27 - 15$
> 2. $6X - 4X = 8$ 2. $5X - 2X = 12$
> 3. $2X = 8$ 3. $3X = 12$
> 4. $X = 2$ 4. $X = 4$

> *Rules:*   If numbers are on the left- and right-hand sides, subtract the number on the left from the number on the right. (Step 1)
>
> If like variables (X) are on the left- and right-hand sides, subtract the variable on the right from the variable on the left. (Step 2)
>
> If there is a variable on the left and a number on the right, divide the number on the right by the coefficient of the variable. Solve the problem. (Steps 3 and 4)

Deduction: Testing a generalization by examining facts, concepts, examples, or other generalizations.

> Teacher: Scientists say that earthquakes occur only in places where geological plates are able to rub together. What does the data say about their hypothesis?
>
> Jerry: The West Coast has a lot of earthquakes and they sit on two of the largest plates in the world.
>
> Sue: Yeah, the same is true about some areas of China and Russia.
>
> Teacher: Well, based on those regions the explanation holds up. What other kind of data would support scientists' hypotheses?

Transfer: Taking what has been learned (content and process) and applying it in contexts removed from the original learning context.

Directions: Match the persons with the issues. Place a "Y" in the box if you think the people that held segregationist or civil rights beliefs would support a specific issue. Place an "N" in the box if you think people with those beliefs would not support a specific issue. Be ready to defend your answers.

Person	Issues	Abortion	Capital Punishment	Television Sex and Violence
Segregationist				
Civil rights activist				

Source: Reasoning processes from R. Ennis (1987), A taxonomy of critical thinking dispositions and abilities. In J. Baron and R. Sternberg (Eds.), *Teaching Thinking Skills: Theory and Practice.* New York: W. H. Freeman.

FIGURE 8.2

General Problem-Solving Processes (Illustration Comes from Current Events)

Problem identification: Recognizing when a problem exists

"Heating oil prices are rising. The oil companies say it is because of the cold and refinery problems. The government says it is because of price gouging."

Problem definition: Deciding what is or is not a part of the problem

"The oil companies, the government and consumers are definitely involved."

Exploration: Considering a variety of processes that could be applied to the problem.

Induction/deduction

"I wonder if the oil companies can show evidence that they are not at fault. I wonder what evidence the government has to accuse the oil companies.

Transfer

"I wonder what kind of heat we get at our house and if it has become more expensive."

Acting: Selecting a process, several processes or some combination of content and process to solve the problem.

FIGURE 8.2 *(Cont.)*

"I'm going to watch the news for the next several days to see what kind of evidence emerges." or "I'm going to call our local oil company and see what they say."

Monitoring: Evaluating the effects of a particular approach, and modifying if necessary.

"The oil company said that the refinery is at fault. That didn't get me too far. I'll call the refinery and my Congress member to get more information."

Source: Problem-solving processes from J. Bransford, R. Sherwood, and T. Sturdevant (1987), Teaching thinking and problem solving. In J. Baron and R. Sternberg (Eds.), *Teaching Thinking Skills: Theory and Practice.* New York: W. H. Freeman.

Students are frequently naive in their approaches to reasoning and problem-solving. In one experiment, students were given a geometry problem to solve. Usually, they guessed wrong on the first try but arrived at an answer by the third try. When asked to say why their solution worked, most could say only "It just does." Finding not only a solution but also a problem-solving process would reduce the guesswork and chance of being wrong when solving future problems (Schoenfeld, 1985). Many students find that it is too complex to work simultaneously toward getting answers and developing their own reasoning and problem-solving abilities.

Students who are lucky enough to develop any approach to reasoning and problem-solving often rely on one approach for all situations, yet some situations require a different or more specific approach. Students commonly fail to check if the approach they are using is an effective one, preferring to simply work until they get an answer. Those who don't get answers adopt standard responses like "I don't know" (Perkins & Simmons, 1988).

Knowledge about general reasoning processes sometimes comes from previous experience. Consider the task of solving a word problem in mathematics. Students who are successful with word problems probably have encountered many other word problems in the past. They know how to examine the problem for key words and phrases that signal what numbers and mathematical operations are important. They not only have previously worked word problems to a successful conclusion, they also know (and can apply) many different approaches to different kinds of problems. Students who have not had similar experiences have not developed similar kinds of process-related knowledge and, as a result, will apply a single and often inappropriate approach to any kind of problem or will not know where to begin. Students who have learned to reason based on their experiences have developed the ability to use a reasoning process called "transfer" (see Figure 8.1).

Students also acquire knowledge about reasoning through instruction. Reasoning is often broken down into two broad categories: *induction* and *deduction.* Induction (also called "inductive reasoning") involves thinking from part to whole or from specifics to generalizations (Ennis, 1987). Consider the situation in which a crime has been committed, but no suspect has been arrested. A detective has to gather clues from many sources in order to arrive at a hypothesis about who may have committed the crime. The detective's inductive reasoning involves generalizing and creating hypotheses that explain the facts of the case.

When teachers opt for an indirect approach to instruction, inductive thinking is often the focus. Recall from Chapter 5 that an indirect approach is warranted when students already know something about the content of a lesson and are ready to develop their own generalizations and hypotheses based on facts and concepts. For example, if students are familiar with a controversial topic, such as the debate over capital punishment or the war on drugs, teachers can guide students in examining all the relevant facts and issues. The outcome of this inductive inquiry could be conclusions that students can justify and defend or even a debate.

In contrast, when teachers opt for a direct approach to instruction, deduction (or "deductive reasoning") is emphasized. Recall from Chapter 5 that a direct approach is desirable when students know somewhat less about a topic and could benefit from an explicit discussion about what they will learn. Deduction involves thinking from whole to part or from generalizations to specifics (Ennis, 1987). To understand deductive reasoning, consider the following example. A crime has been committed and a suspect has been caught. The defense hires a detective to prove that the suspect has been erroneously charged with the crime and the prosecution relies on the continued work of the police to make the charges stick. Both groups are responding to a single hypothesis: the suspect committed the crime. Yet each group seeks out its own specific facts (alibis, witnesses, and

Students should work simultaneously toward getting answers and developing their own reasoning and problem-solving abilities

Kathy Sloane/Photo Researchers

so forth). The deductive reasoning of the defense and the prosecution involves negating or supporting existing hypotheses (the charges) that explain the facts of the case.

To emphasize deductive reasoning, teachers discuss generalizations that provide an overview or framework for the content of the lesson, followed by a consideration of the facts and concepts that underlie the generalizations. For example, a seventh-grade science teacher began a lesson by talking about recent accusations against the Soviet Union as a major contributor to acid rain:

TEACHER: All right, I've told you about what people have been saying about the Soviet Union and acid rain. How do we figure out if the accusation can be supported or not?

JAYNE: We could look it up in the newspapers.

TEACHER: What kinds of things are newspapers in the United States going to say?

STEVE: They'll only report on the negative stuff !

TEACHER: That's possible. How do we get some accurate information on what the Soviets are doing?

JILL: Would somebody international, like the United Nations, keep that information?

Notice how this sceince teacher acts much like a judge during a trial, getting all parties to consider all points of view and sources of information as they engage in deductive reasoning.

Students benefit when they learn reasoning and problem-solving processes through instruction rather than through experience only. If students learn on their own, the danger is great that they will develop beliefs about reasoning and problem-solving that will limit their ability to be strategists (see the discussion about motivation below). Students who problem-solve independently often find one effective process and apply it to any learning situation, no matter what the task. Transfer can be blocked if students are not made aware explicitly of how processes can be applied from one situation to the next.

To keep this from happening, teachers need to take an active role in providing students with good instruction in reasoning and problem-solving. Helping students become strategists when reasoning and problem-solving requires a careful analysis of the processes students already know how to use. These processes can be built upon during instruction. Teachers should also (Pressley et al., 1989):

- Select a few strategies to teach.
- Use powerful methods of instruction, including extensive explanation, modeling, and practice.
- Reinforce and encourage use of strategies.

Motivation Goals

Motivation goals involve teaching students to: (1) understand the purpose and value of applying reasoning and problem-solving processes, and (2) persist in pursuing reasoning and problem-solving so that their efforts are successful.

In order to want to reason and problem-solve, students have to know the value of the

To accomplish these goals, reciprocal teaching employs four techniques students learn to use independently during classroom discussions. The four techniques are:

1. *Summarizing* (also known as *self-review*): deleting trivia or redundancy, selecting or inventing topic sentences, asking questions like "What is this passage about?"

2. *Questioning:* generating literal and interpretive questions at appropriate points, asking "What is happening?" or "Why is this happening?" in a short story

3. *Clarifying:* seeking out points where concepts are not clear, asking "Does this make sense?" or "Does this not make sense?"

4. *Predicting:* thinking about prior knowledge, asking "What do I already know?" and "What will happen next?"

Reciprocal teaching gets its name from the instruction used to teach these techniques. One interpretation of the word *reciprocal* is: "one party acts by way of return or response to something previously done by the other party" (Palincsar & Brown, 1985, p. 148). With reciprocal teaching, the two parties are the teacher and the student. The exchange between a teacher and student involves discussion about some subject and, usually, some text. One goal of the discussion, along with mastering the subject, is to help students become strategists in their use of the four techniques.

When reciprocal teaching is first used in a classroom, the teacher does most of the acting by modeling each of the four technqiues. The students respond by answering the teacher's questions and adding to the teacher's summaries, predictions, and clarifications. For example, in this excerpt, the teacher models the use of prediction as students are about to begin a new science unit:

TEACHER: The title of this chapter is "Animals without Backbones." Let's make some predictions. I bet this chapter is about some very unusual animals like sponges and bugs. Why do I say that?

DUANE: Those are animals that don't have backbones. You already knew that.

TEACHER: Right, I've had some experiences with those animals. Have you had any experience with similar kinds of animals?

BRENDA: We went to a restaurant once and my Dad ordered crab. (Other students say "Ugh!" and "That's gross!")

TEACHER: Did you see a backbone in that crab?

BRENDA: Just a hard shell.

TEACHER: That's interesting. Anyone have another example?

DARRELL: My dad ate squid once. It didn't have a backbone. (More student reactions.)

TEACHER: OK, that's another good example. We have sponges, crab, and squid. Let's make a prediction about what we will learn about some of these animals.

GRETCHEN: Where do they live?

TEACHER: Good question. Many seem to live in the ocean. What else?

DUANE: Which ones do people eat?

TEACHER: Very good. I'll remember to bring that up when we get to the worms (students groan). I would like to know how animals without backbones eat, breathe, and reproduce. Any ideas?

BRENDA: Some of them probably have gills like fish.

DARRELL: They probably eat other animals.

ROBERT: How the heck does a sponge eat?

TEACHER: Good question! Let's read the first section of the chapter to answer our questions and see if our predictions are right.

After a series of these experiences, students are given opportunities to assume the role of the teacher, that is, to lead discussions using the techniques. The teacher remains involved, but his or her role is determined by how the student performs as the teacher.

DARRELL: How do sponges eat?

TEACHER: Good question. You picked right up on one of our earlier questions. Who are you going to call on to answer your question?

DARRELL: Brenda.

BRENDA: They just sit there and wait for the food to come to them.

DARRELL: That's true. The sponge cells grab the food from the water.

TEACHER: To summarize, what are we learning about sponges from this section of the book?

DARRELL: Even though sponges aren't very complex, they still eat, respond to the outside, and reproduce.

TEACHER: That's right. The section goes on to show how other invertebrates are like the sponge in how simple they are.

DARRELL: Any clarifications?

ROBERT: Is the central cavity the same as a hollow sac?

At this stage, teachers tell students when they are doing well, or they help students refine their use of the technqiues.

Sometimes, the teacher returns to modeling a specific activity if greater refinement seems necessary.

TEACHER: Let's look at how we are asking questions again. Is it as important to ask "Are sponges very big?" as it is to ask "How do sponges protect themselves?" If we ask the first question, all we get is a "yes" or a "no" and we haven't learned very much. If we ask the second question, we get into how sponges are put together and what kinds of animals might want to harm or eat them. The second question leads us into more interpretation. Let's try to ask more of the second kind of question.

Gradually, as students take over more and more of the discussion, modeling is necessary only as a refresher.

With seventh graders, Palincsar and Brown (1984) found that it took at least twelve consecutive days of instruction before students could independently engage in these behaviors. Of course, this depends on the degree to which a teacher consistently applies the principles of reciprocal teaching, modeling the four techniques, releasing control to students, and refining students' discussion behavior when necessary. Additionally, this does not mean that students will automatically be independent with reciprocal teaching or show improvement in reasoning ability after twelve days. What the research suggests is that through persistent long-term instruction, students can learn to apply reciprocal teaching in ways that improve how they think and learn in a subject.

Special Considerations   While reciprocal teaching is another useful tool for reasoning, several cautions should be kept in mind. First, successful teacher modeling of the four techniques is key to the success of the approach. In an attempt to replicate Palincsar and Brown's (1984) findings, Mosenthal (1987) discovered that it is not that easy to maintain the quality of instruction with reciprocal teaching over long periods of time. Changes in the difficulty of text selections as well as the degree to which students are used to discussing with one another can make reciprocal teaching difficult to implement over the long haul. Mosenthal found that teachers had the most difficulty teaching and modeling when summarizing was the focus of instruction. In addition, the instruction tended to falter when teachers made abrupt shifts from teacher to student responsibility for the techniques.

There are several solutions to these problems. Teachers should be careful about combining passages that are too unfamiliar with techniques like summarizing that may be difficult and unfamiliar. As students master each of the reciprocal teaching techniques and learn where and when to use them, more and more difficult texts can be tackled. Where students are unfamiliar with how to discuss with one another, techniques for building discussion ability can be implemented (see Chapter 11). Further, teachers should be cautious about turning control for the lessons over to students before they are ready. If teachers see that students are experiencing difficulty with reciprocal teaching, it is best to assess where the approach is breaking down. For example, teachers may discover that their students do not know how to ask and answer questions very well. To bolster their questioning abilities, teachers might opt for combining some of the comprehension activities from Chapter 6 (such as the use of QARs) with the modeling that comes with reciprocal teaching.

Finally, because reciprocal teaching is a collection of generic yet powerful techniques, it is possible to focus on process at the expense of content; in other words, teachers could become so focused on developing the ability to reason via reciprocal teaching that content concepts take a backseat. To keep this from happening, teachers should prepare a content objective when planning a lesson involving reciprocal teaching.

Problem-Solving Lessons

Problem-solving lessons use problem-solving processes (that is, identifying and defining a problem, exploration, acting, monitoring) as a framework for content teaching. The goal of these lessons is to help students not only develop a better understanding of the content under study, but also grow in their specific problem-solving abilities.

Designing a problem-solving lesson takes careful planning. First, think about a problem (for example, in social studies, hunger in America; in mathematics, the long-term effects of the BIG numbers in the federal deficit; in health, the harmful effects of peer pressure). It is important to identify a content objective either before or after you design the problem so that a clear focus on the content understandings for the lesson can be developed and maintained. Having a content objective reduces the likelihood that teachers—as well as students—will get lost in the problem. Next, write a brief description of the problem. Include enough information so that students can grasp the problem and raise additional questions. The problem description does not need to include all the details of the problem. Part of the problem-solving process involves elaborating and expanding on the problem so that it can be better understood.

When teaching a problem-solving lesson, there are several different approaches from which teachers can choose. In some cases, teachers may prefer to lead students in a discussion of the problem, modeling important problem-solving processes:

TEACHER: How big is the problem of hunger in America? Does anyone have any idea?

MARCY: When we go to big cities these days, there seem to be an awful lot of homeless people.

JAMES: It sure is on the news all the time.

TEACHER: You are right. Those are some of the indicators, or signs that it is a big problem. Now to solve it, we're really going to have to delve into what the problem is all about. That's the first step in problem-solving: figuring out the nature and significance of the problem.

In other cases, teachers may wish to use the problem as a way of building interest in some text reading:

TEACHER: We've talked now about the problems related to homelessness and hunger in our big cities. Let's read in our text to see if anybody thought about that while the cities were being built in the early and later parts of this century.

Other teachers may want to use a problem as a springboard for students' research:

TEACHER: We're still kind of hazy on exactly what's causing the increase in poor people in the United States. Let's take a trip to the library to try to better understand what's happening. Remember, we're still in that part of problem-solving where we are trying to scope out the problem. Keep a lookout though, for possible solutions as you read.

This approach requires preparing students ahead of time for independent study and research (see Chapter 9).

To further illustrate the process of designing a problem-solving lesson, consider the dilemma of one vocational education teacher. His students were constantly in danger of hurting themselves with the machinery in the shop or on building sites. Lecturing about

FIGURE 8.7

Sample Problem from Vocational Education

Steve's Accident

Steve is working for a construction company. He runs the saw on a five-person crew working to finish the roof of a house. The crew is behind schedule and Steve is working hard to catch up. Steve's helper moves the rafters on and off the sawhorses. Steve cuts the rafters to size.

It is February and the weather has been wet and warm. The mud around the house is deep and slippery. The house is about 300 yards from the main road.

The saw is heavy and it is time for a break, but Steve sees that there are only a few rafters left. He has been setting the saw against his leg while he rests with his arm. As he starts up the saw for the next rafter, he forgets to move the saw away from his leg. The blade cuts into Steve's leg. If not treated properly, Steve will bleed to death. How can the crew work together to save Steve's life?

Source: Special thanks to Leon Hanson.

---

safety didn't help. Students easily forgot the lecture when they needed it most. To create a problem-solving lesson, the vocational education teacher began with the following content objective:

If you are well-prepared for safety, you could save someone's life.

Next, the teacher wrote a problem (see Figure 8.7) that presented students with an accident involving a saw.

In teaching the problem-solving lesson, the vocational education teacher introduced the problem and asked students if they had ever seen or experienced a similar accident. Several students related stories about parents who had cut themselves badly. The teacher explained that solving the problem would require making the following decisions:

- *Identifying* important aspects of the problem
- *Exploring* possible solutions
- *Acting on* or selecting the best solution
- *Evaluating* whether or not a solution is the best one

Next, the teacher began to model each of these steps. He asked students to list the parts of the problem that were most life-threatening to Steve (the bleeding, the location of the cut, the remoteness of the job site). He asked students to list some steps that might save Steve's life (stop the bleeding, run to call an ambulance, treat the victim for shock).

The teacher then reminded students that some cuts are worse than others and, with some cuts, people can bleed to death in as little as ten minutes. He suggested that a first aid book might help students prioritize what needed to be done. He divided students into their working crews (four or five students who worked together regularly), asking each crew to decide on the best set of steps to solve the problem.

When students communicated their solutions, it became apparent that many different types of solutions were possible. Students designated different roles for members of the crew (going for the ambulance, making a tourniquet), jobs that had to be done (getting the saw out of the way, ripping cloth to stop the bleeding), and even the time it might take to get the victim to safety. One group realized that if the wound were severe enough, the victim could not be saved unless the group cooperated. This kind of flexible thinking is the product of a well-planned problem-solving lesson.

To wrap up, the teacher discussed with students what they had learned. Students' responses indicated that not only had they fine-tuned their knowledge about first aid for cuts, they were more aware of what steps to take when any accident occurs. Most important, they understood the need to work as a team whenever a serious situation emerges. The teacher finished the lesson by having students speculate about how they would deal with other accidents that could happen in the shop or on the job site.

This example demonstrates many of the key features of a problem-solving lesson: applying problem-solving processes in relevant contexts, identifying important aspects of a problem, and exploring and communicating possible solutions.

Special Considerations   Like any reasoning guide, a problem-solving lesson by itself is no guarantee that students will develop the ability to problem-solve. When they engage in a problem-solving lesson, students practice problem-solving, but they may not gain a conscious awareness of how to problem-solve. To build an explicit understanding both of the content and the problem-solving processes under study, teachers should plan to explain and model clearly how a problem is being approached (for example, "This is where we figure out what is really important in this problem."). In addition, teachers should encourage review of the processes that were used in a lesson so that students will reflect on how problem-solving processes can be applied.

The problems teachers design for problem-solving lessons should meet several criteria: the problems should be as realistic as possible, should be related to the content under study, and should roughly match students' current abilities to reason and problem-solve. Problems that are contrived or overly difficult raise the possibility of doing problem-solving for its own sake rather than learning how to problem-solve to accomplish real purposes in realistic situations.

Teachers should also take advantage of the many opportunities students have for communicating a solution to a problem. For example, students could simply report to the class or they could move out into the world beyond the classroom, writing letters, attending local hearings, inviting speakers in to address the class, all as different ways of approaching a problem. The real potential of a problem-solving lesson is to help students become active problem solvers both in and out of school.

Simulations

Simulations are reasoning and problem-solving activities that engage students in various roles and small-group cooperation. It is useful to think of a simulation as a case study

Rhoda Sidney/Monkmeyer

Problem-solving lessons help students wrestle with real-life problems

(Jones, 1980). In a typical case study, students explore the problems depicted in a case, examining relevant documents and discussing among themselves what should or should not be done to solve the problem. The role of students is more like impartial judges, looking at things objectively and reaching decisions.

With a simulation, students assume a role that is integral to the case or problem at hand, while, at the same time, retaining the power and the responsiblity for solving problems and shaping events. The roles of students are diverse, with points of view formed subjectively and decisions reached through discussion and interaction.

To explain and illustrate the use of simulations, consider a social studies unit on Antarctica recently taught in seventh grade. In the past the teacher had taught the unit through lecture and readings from the textbook. She found that students rarely were able to develop an interest in this continent, which she found fascinating. She decided to create a simulation to build greater interest in the unit, to make students want to know more about Antarctica and geographical exploration.

A simulation contains three phases, the *briefing*, the *action*, and the *debriefing*. During the briefing, the teacher explains the mechanics and procedures for the simulation. This includes assigning roles, creating a scenario, and distributing materials. For the south pole simulation, the teacher decided to have students focus on one central question: Should the United States further develop the south pole? She chose four roles from which students could wrestle over the central question: businessperson, environmentalist, concerned taxpayer, and potential inhabitant. Students were presented *role cards* describing each of these roles (see Figure 8.8).

FIGURE 8.8

Role Cards for the Antarctica Simulation

Businessperson

You are Pat Gottrocks, head of Multinational Industries. You made your first fortune investing in high-risk mineral and oil exploration in Alaska and Texas. Now, you would like to turn your attention to the resources in Antarctica. To be on the safe side (so you don't lose money), you would like government support for any investments you might make.

Environmentalist

You are Kim Birdsall, founder of the Earth-Save Foundation. You are one of the few people who has actually visited Antarctica and studied its endangered wildlife. You are deeply concerned about the delicate balance between humans and the environment.

Concerned Taxpayer

You are Carol Penny, a concerned taxpayer. After paying nearly $1000 in taxes last year, you are upset about the number of government programs that seem to be a waste of money. You are in favor of progress, but *cannot stand* government waste. You don't want to see Antarctica become another chance for misusing taxpayer money.

Potential Inhabitant

You are Lee House and you would like to live in Antarctica. As a former member of the astronaut corps, you have decided that Antarctica is the last earthly frontier. You want to find ways to make Antarctica inhabitable, but are uncertain about how to make the continent safe for others.

During the briefing, students are also given a scenario and documents that provide the focus for the simulation. The following scenario was developed for the Antarctica simulation:

> You have been brought together as the Citizen's Committee on Antarctic Affairs to explore the feasibility of populating the Antarctica with American citizens. Next week, your committee will appear at a hearing before a select committee from the United States Senate to announce and explain your decision. Since this has been an especially controversial international issue, be prepared to argue your decision with evidence and vigor.

A well-developed scenario is vividly real and provides an opportunity for all the roles to interact. Note how the roles are also carefully constructed to provide some tension and potential for discussion.

FIGURE 8.9

Sample Document from the Antarctica Simulation

From: Alton D. Ross
         Douglas O. Hemmings
         Research Scientists at the U.S. Antarctica Base
         McMurdo Island on Ross Sea

To: Citizen's Committee on Antarctica Affairs

Re: Report on the national resources of Antarctica

- -

Potential Resources

Recent explorations point to an oil field larger than any encountered in North
America, a coal field larger than any other in the world, and large quantities of
rare minerals. Also important are pockets of copper, lead, iron, gold, and
manganese. There is considerable uranium available for nuclear power (to provide
local electricity or for export). The sea is full of krill, a shrimp-like creature high in
protein.

Problems

The main problems relate to getting people and supplies into and out of the area.
Ships can get through only from December to February. There are few suitable
harbors. Ships must be ready to move out at any time because of the weather.
Airplanes can move more easily, but airstrips on the ice shelf are in constant
repair. Heavy machinery often gets brittle and breaks.

To complete the briefing, students are provided a set of documents or some data. The
purpose of these materials is to help students better assume their roles and engage in the
simulation. For the Antarctica unit, the teacher created documents from two sources: the
social studies text and her own lecture notes. She selected material from the social studies
text only when it related to the central question of the simulation. The materials she chose
gave some basic information about the location and terrain of the continent. From her
notes, the teacher created an environmental report on weather patterns, geography, and
wildlife and a report on natural resources with respect to the potential and problems in
getting people and supplies in and out (see Figure 8.9). Another option (not exercised
here) is to obtain and provide some authentic original documents related to the scenario.
The choice of documents is very important; the more realistic the documents are, the
more seriously the students will engage themselves in the simulation.

The final activity in the briefing is to assign roles (by soliciting volunteers or through
teacher selection) and then placing students in groups to grapple with the simulation.

Prior to actually doing a simulation in the classroom, it would be wise to think carefully about small-group processes and group development (see Chapter 11).

The next phase is the action phase, also termed the *simulation event.* At this stage, teachers step back as students assume their roles and begin doing the simulation. Teachers serve as arbitrators, umpires, and instructors as the need arises. For example, students may get bogged down in what it means to take on a certain role or how to make decisions about the simulation. The teacher's job is to determine how the simulation is breaking down and then provide the necessary assistance. It is important for the teacher to avoid jumping in too soon or breaking in when teacher assistance is not necessary. Students tend to surrender control over the simulation and stop communicating with each other when teachers approach.

It is also important for the teacher to continue to emphasize the realistic nature of the simulation task. For the Antarctica unit, the teacher solicited the help of other teachers in the building to be the Senators for the hearing on Antarctica. Students were told that each of the groups would present their decisions and reasons and then the Senators would make a decision, agreeing or disagreeing with the groups. The effect on students was to provide a realistic audience. When students dropped out of their roles or lagged behind in completing the simulation, the teacher reminded them of the impending hearing and what was at stake in convincing the senators. This became a tool for the teacher in building and maintaining motivation.

The final phase, called the debriefing, provides students with an opportunity to reflect on the content and processes integral to the simulation. Teachers can go around the room asking students to explain their parts in the simulation and talk about problems they encountered and how they dealt with them. (In a sense, the Senate hearing in the Antarctica simulation served as a form of debriefing.) It is also useful, however, to have students look back on the experience and suggest ways the simulation could have been better. For example, following the Antarctica simulation, students wrestled with problems ranging from finding supplemental materials to involving students who could not or would not assume their roles completely.

Special Considerations   Simulations have a potential unmatched by many other types of instructional activities. Simulations are a vehicle for reaching out to the outside world; for engaging students in realistic types of reading, reasoning, and problem-solving; for communicating in diverse ways about multiple texts and sources of information.

But simulations also require some knowledge and skill. It is helpful if students have some frame of reference for activities in the simulation. In retrospect, it was difficult for some students to identify with one or more of the roles in the Antarctica simulation: students who have not directly experienced some aspects of the role they are taking on sometimes have a hard time. Teachers can help with this by thoroughly explaining the roles ahead of time during the briefing session.

Another difficulty stems from students' perceptions about what it means to assume a role. In the simulation research, a distinction is made between *role-playing* and *assuming a role* during a simulation (Jones, 1985). Role-playing is often associated with playing games. Simulations are easily sabotaged if students are expecting only fun and games. A simulation requires a deeper understanding and greater engagement—in other words, assuming a role as opposed to playing a role. Teachers can develop insight into what it means to assume a role by conducting some classroom demonstrations. The teacher, along with several other students, can assume roles in the context of a simulation while other students observe. Debriefings about this experience, as well as debriefings following other simulations, will help students learn how to assume a role. (Chapter 11 provides additional information about roles and responsibilities during small-group instruction.)

Finally, simulations require skills discussed in the previous chapter, the ability to question and respond to questions. Simulations will not work well when students assume a role but do not understand how to question one another in meaningful ways. If students are going to get the most out of simulations, it may be useful for teachers to study the current communication patterns in the classroom, observing students' facility with questions, and then engaging in some of the activities described in Chapter 13.

TEACHING A LESSON

Students need *direct opportunities* with reasoning and problem-solving if they are to achieve the goals laid out at the beginning of this chapter. Direct opportunities consist of "interaction with teachers, materials, and peers to hear about, see demonstrations of, and engage in guided and independent applications of the knowledge in question" (Perkins & Simmons, 1988, p. 319). Instruction that provides for opportunity is a prime ingredient.

Teachers also help during instruction by talking about their own thinking—what they do themselves when reasoning and problem-solving. By sharing experiences they have had—in their personal lives or even in planning a lesson—teachers demonstrate the thinking processes they have learned and want students to acquire. In reflecting, students not only look back on a task or the knowledge they have internalized, but also compare the processing they did with the teacher's processes (Collins & Brown, 1988). These are some of the guiding principles for instruction devoted to reasoning and problem-solving.

The following sections depict a lesson developed with these principles in mind. Though the lesson deals with teaching a short story in an English class, the principles can be applied to planning and teaching a lesson in your content area.

Goals and Assumptions

This lesson is based on the short story, "The Monkey's Paw," by W. W. Jacobs. The story is about a mummified monkey's paw that has the power to grant three wishes to its owner. The story begins on a cold and wet night when an old soldier brings the paw to a family— Morris White, his wife, and their only son. The first owner of the paw made two wishes and then wished for death. The soldier made his three wishes and wants to destroy the paw. Morris takes the paw for himself instead. After the soldier leaves, the family kiddingly wishes for £200, not expecting the wish to ever come true. The next day, the son is devoured by a machine at work. Compensation for the son's death comes to £200, the same amount requested in the first wish! The rest of the story deals with an attempt by Morris White and his wife to use the remaining wishes to bring their son back to life.

The intended audience is a heterogeneous group of tenth graders. Students are in the middle of a short story unit organized thematically—that is, a theme for each short story in the book has been selected to serve as a content objective, and stories have been sequenced so that content objectives can be related one to another. In thinking about "The Monkey's Paw," the first theme that came to mind was:

How people view their fate influences how they live their lives.

This seemed too abstract. It doesn't suggest an issue that students would directly care about. A more direct theme was chosen:

It is not always good to get what you wish for.

This theme was used as a guide in creating the activities that follow.

There are several features of the story that deserve consideration. First, the story is suspenseful: if students are engaged early in the story, the plot tends to make them want to read more. The story is also somewhat laden with unfamiliar language. The paw is described as "mummified" and a "talisman," and the old soldier has "bibulous habits." These words and phrases contribute to the atmosphere of the story or to insight about the characters. Some words are defined for students at the bottom of each page.

To capture students' attention before reading and to deal with some of the language, the teacher constructed the following semantic map:

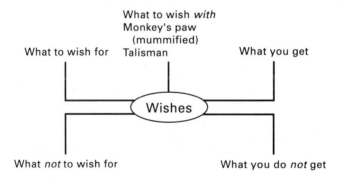

While the teacher cannot be sure exactly what students will insert under each of the headings, the map serves as a general framework, guiding discussion. Note that some of the unfamiliar words are already included on the semantic map (see Chapter 6 for more detail about how to teach vocabulary using a semantic map).

A prediction guide could help students fine-tune their focus on the story as well as motivate them and guide them through the reading (see Figure 8.10).

Note the assumptions here in using a prediction guide: the content is not very complex (though the unfamiliar language is addressed throughout the semantic map), and students possess some knowledge about the issues in the story. While few students have had much contact with a curse on a monkey's paw, they have all experienced wishing for

FIGURE 8.10

Prediction Guide for "The Monkey's Paw"

Part I: Place a check in the column labeled "You" if you think the statement is true. Think about one example from your own experience to support your opinion.

Part II: Now compare your answers with others in your small group. Place a check in the blank labeled "Your Group" if your group thinks the statement is true. Write one example beneath each statement to support your decisions.

You	Your Group	The Story	
_____	_____	_____	1. There is no such thing as magic.
_____	_____	_____	2. It helps to have a good luck charm.
_____	_____	_____	3. People who make wishes are often disappointed.
_____	_____	_____	4. Be careful what you wish for: it could come true!
_____	_____	_____	5. Wish for anything, but expect the unexpected.

Part III: Place a check in the column labeled "The Story" if you think the statement is supported by "The Monkey's Paw." If it is supported, write one example from the story for each statement.

---

something. The prediction guide draws on these experiences to build interest in the early stages of the lesson.

Notice also that the first responses to the guide are divided into "You" and "Your Group." This is done so that students can make individual decisions first before sharing what they think with other members of a small group. The advantage to this adaptation is that students can work independently to form an opinion before they wrestle over the ideas with others.

Building Background and Motivation

The teacher begins the lesson by asking several simple questions:

Have you ever wondered what it would be like if you had three wishes?
What would you wish for?

At the same time, the teacher writes the word "Wishes" on the blackboard to start the semantic map. Following a brief discussion in which students offer some examples of their wishes, the teacher poses a problem:

Is having everything you wish for necessarily a good thing?
Do you think having your wishes come true could cause some problems?

To play devil's advocate, the teacher mentions the difficulties of some lottery winners in leading a normal life. Note how this approach raises important issues in an interesting way before students read any of the story.

Next, the prediction guide is introduced:

TEACHER: Let's take a look at some other ideas about wishes and what happens to people who make them. Let's do Part I together. I'll read the statements and you decide whether you think they are true. If you think they are, place a check in the blank and think about a reason. Don't write a reason yet. Just listen and see if you agree.

The teacher adds one more thing:

TEACHER: And if any of these are unclear to you, please raise your hand and we'll talk about the statement.

This last direction is very important. It gives the teacher a way to cross-check the difficulty or abstractness of the statements. It also ensures that students all understand what is expected before the lesson progresses too far.

In completing the first part, one student questions the meaning of one of the statements:

BRENDON: I don't get number four ("Be careful what you wish for: it could come true!"). Why wouldn't you want a wish to come true?

TEACHER: That's a good question. What about our lottery example? Do you think all the lottery winners, with some of their bad luck, would want to make the same wish again?

SOME STUDENTS: Yes.

SOME STUDENTS: No.

TEACHER: That's one of the things you are going to have to decide. If you make a wish, is it always going to turn out the way you want, or should you be careful about what you wish for?

BRENDON: Oh, so if I wish my brother would break a leg? Just kidding.

TEACHER: That's a good example. You might kiddingly wish he would break a leg, but you would feel awful if it really happened.

The teacher takes time to clarify the statement, being careful not to lead students to one opinion or another.

As they progress through the guide, the class starts to assume that not all wishes turn out exactly the way the "wisher" intends. The teacher weaves this insight into a transition for the story:

TEACHER: All right, we have discussed how wishing does not always turn out the way we expect. We're going to read a story now called "The Monkey's Paw," in which the same thing happens. The story is about a mummified monkey's paw. Does anyone know what that is?

KELLY: Is it like a rabbit's foot?

TEACHER: Yes, it is a lot like that. It's a paw that has been cut off and preserved. The paw in this story has been preserved and it has a curse. Let's read about this paw and how it becomes involved in the wishes a family makes. Would anyone like to make any predictions about what might happen?

This transition not only builds on prior ideas, it provides a mini-preview for what students are about to read.

Developing Content and Process

After teaching several vocabulary words, the teacher alerts students to the words defined at the bottom of each page. Then, the teacher directs students to the part of the prediction guide labeled Part III:

TEACHER: Now I want you to read the story, but keep in mind these ideas we have been discussing. As you read, think about each of the statements again and whether or not the statements are supported by the story. Let's see if some of the predictions we made earlier about these statements are true based on this story.

Next, students read the story, recording their responses to the statements, and comparing what they think in small groups. The actual reading could occur in class or at home. At this point some teachers prefer to send the story home for homework because of its length (about nine pages). If the story is sent home, students will require several minutes the following day to record their responses and regroup. Have students briefly summarize what they learned the day before, if this kind of transition becomes necessary.

Disagreements often accompany the use of prediction guides, and this lesson is typical. There is general agreement among the class with all statements except the fifth one ("Wish for anything, but expect the unexpected"):

GEORGE: I don't think people in the story would agree with that. They didn't expect anything awful to happen.

MARTIN: Yeah, but they should have!

These disagreements are often ripe opportunities for teachers to help students understand reasoning and problem-solving processes:

TEACHER: Now wait a minute, you two. I am hearing opinions here, but not a whole lot to back them up. What did we say is important if we're going to learn to reason with one another?

BRENDA: You gotta have proof!

TEACHER: And what do we mean by that?

GEORGE: We have to use examples from the story or from our lives.

TEACHER: And what are we concerned with here?

GEORGE: We need examples from the story.

TEACHER: Good, now back up what you're saying.

GEORGE: If they knew something bad was going to happen, they wouldn't have made a wish on that paw.

MARTIN: They should have known, though, because the soldier said that the first owner wished for his own death.

TEACHER: OK, that's much better. You're backing up what you think.

Notice how, in this instance, the teacher doesn't try to resolve the disagreement, although that is also an option. At least for this lesson, the teacher has determined that it is more important for students to learn how to reason and problem-solve with one another. In other lessons, developing content may take more precedence. The choice of emphasis really depends on where students are in a particular unit, the topic of study, or the processes students need to acquire at different points in time.

This is not to suggest that content concepts should be overlooked when processes are being emphasized. In this lesson, the teacher frequently helps students refine their understanding of wishing and human motivation:

TEACHER: So, if the Whites could relive their experiences with the monkey's paw, do you think they would have done anything differently?

BRENDON: I don't think so. How could they have known that it (wishing) would kill their son?

MARTIN: It could have been even worse. Some people are so greedy, they would wish for more.

KELLY: Yeah. They might have even tried to outsmart the curse of the paw.

TEACHER: How so?

KELLY: They might have made a huge wish and then tried to stay out of trouble.

In getting students to make these kinds of predictions, the teacher also helps students draw some conclusions about the story, to bring some closure to this phase of the lesson. This is an important consideration. Prediction guides invite divergent thinking and discussion. It helps to pull things together, either when discussing individual statements or toward the end of discussing the entire guide.

Encouraging Independence

At this point in the lesson, the priority shifts to having students apply what they have learned, in terms of both content and process.

To apply students' knowledge of the content, many activities are possible. "The Monkey's Paw" has been made into a play several times. Students may wish to write their own dramatized version of the story and perform it, perhaps altering the ending. They could videotape or tape-record their dramatization. Students could try Morris White for the murder of his son, or prepare debate on whether myths and magic are real or fraudulent. Any reading, writing, speaking, or listening activity that encourages students to stretch and expand their understanding of the content is appropriate here.

To apply students' knowledge about process, recall the processes that run implicitly (and often explicitly) throughout the lesson: testing and clarifying generalizations, making predictions. The story is very powerful because the author encourages the reader's use of these processes through suspense. Students could practice their own use of these processes by writing some original suspenseful stories. Of course, this would require explicit discussion about how suspense is created in "The Monkey's Paw" and stories like it. For example:

TEACHER: When a writer creates suspense, hints are sprinkled throughout the story to keep the reader guessing. The hints have to be clear enough to let you know something frightening is coming, but fuzzy enough to keep you guessing. Can anybody think of this kind of hint from "The Monkey's Paw?"

ADAM: When they made the wish and the monkey's paw twisted in Morris White's hand, that was one. You could tell something scary was going to happen.

TEACHER: I felt the same way. Events like that make you predict and want to read more. Notice how the story is not full of those events. It is calm with everyone playing chess; the soldier tells his story and then the paw twists when they make the wish. It is the contrast from one event to another, with hints sprinkled in, that makes the story suspenseful. Now, let's write some stories for each other so we can try to create suspense.

Not every content area uses activities like this (though, wouldn't it be interesting to think about creating suspense in social studies, mathematics, or art?). However, the principle underlying these activities holds across the curriculum. Students become motivated and independent when they are given opportunities to creatively and flexibly apply what they have learned from a lesson devoted to reasoning and problem-solving.

SUMMAR

Students generally have few experiences with reasoning and problem-solving. This does not mean that students are unskilled. Rather, it means that teachers need to find ways to teach students how to reason and problem-solve. A sensible approach is one in which content and process are balanced so that reasoning and problem-solving occur in meaningful contexts. Thinking should not be isolated from important issues both in school and out. When this isolation occurs, motivation suffers.

Reasoning and problem-solving processes can be applied both explicitly and implicitly during instruction. When processes are explicit, teachers strive to develop in students an in-depth understanding of how to think on their own. This kind of instruction is built into techniques such as reciprocal teaching and problem-solving lessons. When processes are implicit, content knowledge is the focus and students practice processes implicitly. This kind of instruction is built into the use of reasoning guides and simulations. Taken together, these approaches provide teachers with a number of useful choices in reasoning, problem-solving, and communicating in content areas.

SPECIAL PROJECTS

Course-Based

1. Evaluate a textbook in your content area. What kinds of provisions are made for reasoning and problem-solving? What assumptions are built into the activities provided with the text? For example, do the textbook authors provide a number of "thinking-type" questions without guidance in how to answer them? Are special projects provided so that students can apply their reasoning and problem-solving abilities? Design a lesson based on one section of the text to illustrate your decisions about:
   a. What content is important
   b. Which instructional activities you will emphasize to help students learn how to reason and problem-solve

Field-Based

2. Interview a teacher about the reasoning and problem-solving activities he or she uses. Ask the teacher about the successes as well as the constraints involved in teaching students how to think in your content area.
3. Plan a lesson devoted to reasoning and problem-solving. Teach the lesson to a group of students. Evaluate your experience in terms of:
   a. Your assumptions about what (and how much) content to emphasize
   b. The appropriateness of the reasoning and problem-solving activities you created
   c. How well students understood the content, learned how to reason and problem-solve, and were motivated to learn

SUGGESTED READING

These book chapters describe reasoning and problem-solving activities similar to those discussed in this chapter:

NELSON-HERBER, J. (1985). Anticipation and prediction in reading comprehension. In T. Harris and E. Cooper (Eds.), *Reading, thinking and concept development* (pp. 89–104). New York: The College Board.

PALINCSAR, A., & BROWN, A. (1985). Reciprocal teaching: Activities to promote "reading with your mind." In T. Harris and E. Cooper (Eds.), *Reading, thinking and concept development* (pp. 147–160). New York: The College Board.

This chapter presents ideas about problem-solving lessons:

PAUL, R. (1987). Dialogical thinking: Critical thought essential to the acquisition of rational knowledge and passions. In J. Baron and R. Sternberg (Eds.), *Teaching thinking skills: Theory and practice.* New York: W. H. Freeman.

These books provide detailed information about designing and conducting classroom simulations:

JONES, K. (1980). *Simulations: A handbook for teachers.* New York: Kogan Page.

JONES, K. (1982). *Simulations in language teaching.* New York: Cambridge University Press.

JONES, K. (1985). *Designing your own simulations.* New York: Methuen.

These books are devoted to reasoning and problem solving. Several of these have chapters covering specific subject-matter areas:

BARON, J., & STERNBERG, R. (Eds.) (1987). *Teaching thinking skills: Theory and practice* (pp. 127–148). New York: W. H. Freeman.

HARRIS, T., & COOPER, E. (Eds.) (1985). *Reading, thinking and concept development* (pp. 147–160). New York: The College Board.

MARZANO, R., BRANDT, R., HUGHES, C., JONES, B. F., PRESSEISEN, B., RANKIN, S., & SUHOR, C. (1988). *Dimensions of thinking: A framework for curriculum and instruction.* Reston, VA: Association for Supervision and Curriculum Development.

RESNICK, L., & KLOPFER, L. (Eds.). (1989). *Toward the thinking curriculum: Current cognitive research.* Reston, VA: Association for Supervision and Curriculum Development.

This book may be of particular interest to mathematics teachers:

WHIMBY, A., & LOCKHEAD, J. (1986). *Problem solving and comprehension.* Hillsdale, NJ: Erlbaum.

REFERENCES

AMES, C., & ARCHER, J. (1988). Achievement goals in the classroom: Students' learning strategies and motivation processes. *Journal of Educational Psychology, 80,* 260–267.

ANDERSON, R. (1984). Role of the reader's schema in comprehension. In R. Anderson, J. Osborn, & R. Tierney (Eds.), *Learning to read in American schools.* Hillsdale, NJ: Erlbaum.

BRANSFORD, J., & HELDMEYER, K. (1983). Learning from children learning. In J. Bisanz, G. Bisanz, & R. Kail (Eds.), *Learning in children: Progress in cognitive development research.* New York: Springer-Verlag.

BRANSFORD, J., SHERWOOD, R. & STURDEVANT, T. (1987). Teaching thinking and problem solving. In J. Baron & R. Sternberg (Eds.), *Teaching thinking skills: Theory and practice.* New York: W. H. Freeman.

BROWN, A., & PALINCSAR, A. (1985). *Reciprocal teaching of comprehension strategies: A natural history of one program for enhancing learning.* Urbana: University of Illinois, Center for the Study of Reading.

COLLINS, A., & BROWN, J. (1988). *Cognitive apprenticeship and social interaction.* A paper presented at the annual meeting of the American Educational Research Association, New Orleans.

DOYLE, W. (1984). Academic tasks in classrooms. *Curriculum Inquiry, 14,* 2, 129–149.

ENNIS, R. (1987). A taxonomy of critical thinking dispositions and abilities. In J. Baron & R. Sternberg (Eds.), *Teaching thinking skills: Theory and practice.* New York: W. H. Freeman.

GARNER, R., & ALEXANDER, P. (1989). Metacognition: Answered and unanswered questions. *Educational Psychologist, 24,* 2, 143–158.

GOODLAD, J. (1984). *A place called school.* New York: McGraw-Hill.

HERBER, H. (1978). *Teaching reading in content areas.* Englewood Cliffs, NJ: Prentice-Hall.

JONES, K. (1980). *Simulations: A handbook for teachers.* New York: Kogan Page.

JONES, K. (1985). *Designing your own simulations.* New York: Methuen.

MOSENTHAL, J. (1987). Learning from discussion: Requirements and constraints on classroom instruction in reading comprehension strategies. In J. Readance & S. Baldwin (Eds.), *Research in literacy: Merging perspectives*. Chicago: The National Reading Conference.

NICKERSON, R. (1987). Why teach thinking? In J. Baron & R. Sternberg (Eds.), *Teaching thinking skills: Theory and practice*. New York: W. H. Freeman.

PALINCSAR, A., & BROWN, A. (1984). Reciprocal teaching of comprehension-fostering and comprehension-monitoring activities. *Cognition and Instruction, 1,* 2, 117–175.

PAUL, R. (1987). Dialogical thinking: Critical thought essential to the acquisition of rational knowledge and passions. In J. Baron & R. Sternberg (Eds.), *Teaching thinking skills: Theory and practice*. New York: W. H. Freeman.

PERKINS, D., & SIMMONS, R. (1988). Patterns of misunderstanding: An integrative model of science, math, and programming. *Review of Educational Research, 58,* 3, 303–326.

PRAWAT, R. (1989). Promoting access to knowledge, strategy and disposition in students: A research synthesis. *Review of Educational Research, 59,* 1, 1–42.

PRESSLEY, M., GOODCHILD, F., FLEET, J., ZAJCHOWSKI, R., & EVANS, E. (1989). The challenges of classroom strategy instruction. *Elementary School Journal, 89,* 3, 301–342.

Random House College Dictionary. (1984). New York: Random House.

ROSENHOLTZ, S., & SIMPSON, C. (1984). Classroom organization and student stratification. *Elementary School Journal, 85,* 1, 21–38.

SIMON, H. (1980). Problem solving and education. In D. Tuma & R. Reif (Eds.), *Problem solving and education: Issues in teaching and research*. Hillsdale, NJ: Erlbaum.

SHOENFELD, D. (1985). *Mathematical problem solving*. New York: Academic Press.

STRAUSS, (1987). Three sources of differences between educational and developmental psychology: Resolution through educational-developmental psychology. *Instructional Science, 15,* 275–286.

Studying consists of efficient, flexible ways for using your mind and your time.

Adapted from W. Pauk (1974). How to study in college, *2d edition. Boston: Houghton Mifflin.*

9

Studying

CHAPTER OBJECTIVES

After reading this chapter, you should be able to:

1. Describe the goals for studying in terms of content, process, and motivation.

2. Compare and evaluate the effectiveness of a range of study techniques.

3. Plan and teach a lesson in which students learn content as well as ways to study.

RATIONALE

When asked how they approach studying, some students respond with a shrug and others may name one of many study techniques, such as SQ3R or speed reading. Not many students perceive studying as an efficient and flexible way of learning.

Efficient studying involves making judgments about where information is located, what information is important, and how to go about recording and organizing the information for later retrieval and communication (Anderson & Armbruster, 1984). It involves decisions about when it is time to study (and when it is time to do something else) and how much time to spend (Pauk, 1984). Flexible studying involves a strategic awareness of which kinds of studying are appropriate for a particular situation (studying to write an essay is not the same as studying for a multiple-choice test), whether or not an approach to studying is working, and whether a different approach is warranted. Studying is not as simple as universally applying a favorite technique or a magic set of steps. Effective study does require simple and flexible thinking appropriate to the kinds of information and the tasks students need to learn.

Most students are ill-prepared when it comes to knowing how to study. In research on high school students in biology and social studies classes, it was found that students have a limited range of ways to study (Tierney, Lazansky, & Schallert, 1982). Many reported reading slowly, underlining or marking the text, rereading, and even memorizing entire chapters as methods they use when studying. While many of these activities are worthwhile (with the notable exception of memorizing entire chapters!), what is missing is a sense of how to study and to use study techniques purposefully. Though students are sometimes aware of one or two study techniques, they are naive about how to plan their

CHAPTER ORGANIZER

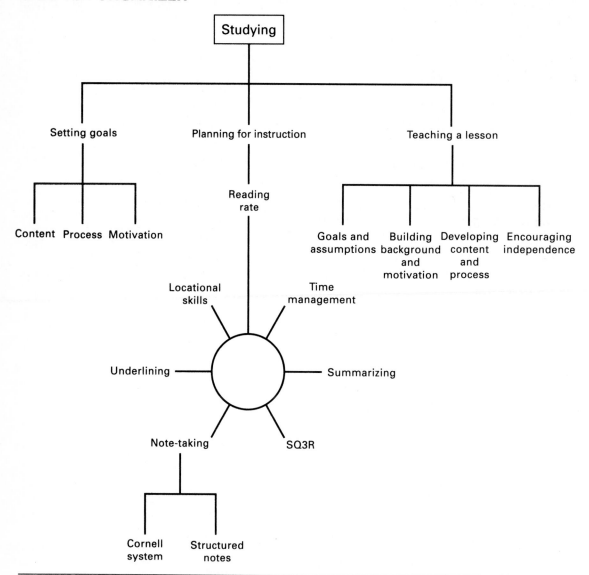

studying or to evaluate the effectiveness of a particular strategy. Many students experience difficulty even knowing when they have studied enough in preparation for a test.

Mature, strategic studying builds on many of the processes described in previous chapters. Students need to know which vocabulary concepts will aid them in understanding entire passages (Chapter 6). They need to be able to comprehend, reorganize, and elaborate on the concepts they encounter in textbooks (Chapter 7). They need to reason in

David M. Grossman/Photo Researchers

Though studying is a solitary activity, students do not study well without guidance

different ways, being analytical at one moment and creative the next (Chapter 8). What distinguishes studying from these other areas is that students are often alone when studying, yet teachers commonly assist with vocabulary learning, comprehension, and reasoning. As such, studying is the ultimate in beyond-text comprehension and student independence.

Though studying is a solitary activity, most students do not study well without guidance. Unfortunately, the typical approach to guiding student study does not work. Some teachers give students a study guide to be completed in class or at home. Study guides typically contain short-answer questions that focus on concepts the teacher or textbook author has chosen. Two problems underlie this practice: (1) questions rarely engage students' thinking, and (2) students never learn from their experience with the study guide how to study on their own. Students often complete study guides item by item (some wait until the teacher goes over the answers!), engaging in little, if any, thinking about how concepts are related from one question to the next (Langer, 1986).

Based on classroom research across the grades and the little students end up knowing about studying by the time they get to college, it is safe to say that most students receive only rare instruction in studying (Simpson, 1984). But effective study requires instruction. When students are taught how to study, they comprehend and recall more (Adams, Carnine, & Gersten, 1982) and their test performance improves (Nist, Hogrebe, & Simpson, 1985) in comparison with students who are simply left to their own devices.

Good instruction in studying is both contextual and explicit. Contextual instruction devoted to studying consists of focusing on the specific content and tasks students face in their classes. For example, if students are expected to summarize on a report or a test, they should learn to summarize while learning subject-matter content and in conjunction with completing other kinds of classroom assignments. Assignments in which students need to wade through vast amounts of information are ripe opportunities for teaching students how to study. Like reasoning, studying ability is not developed by pulling out skills and teaching them in an isolated fashion. Rather, students learn how to study best when it is incorporated into the content and activities of everyday teaching.

Instruction in studying should also be explicit. Explicit instruction in studying involves five steps (Adams, Carnine, & Gersten, 1982):

1. Providing purposes for the study strategy to be learned

2. Explaining the steps involved in using the strategy

3. Modeling for students the use of the strategy

4. Giving students practice and feedback, as they apply the teacher's models

5. Gradual fading of the teacher's role, as students demonstrate independence

These are the guiding principles of instruction throughout this chapter on studying. The chapter describes the goals for studying, explains strategies that students can learn, and presents an illustrative lesson based on studying.

SETTING GOALS

This section describes goals for studying. To study effectively, students must figure out for themselves what content is important, flexibly process information using an awareness of what tasks need to be performed, and grow in self-confidence that studying can help accomplish both in- and out-of-school purposes.

Content Goals

Content goals for studying can be summarized in a single statement: to help students determine for themselves what content is important to learn.

Previous chapters have emphasized the need to identify key vocabulary, to teach students about important content, and to help students generate beyond-text principles and generalizations. A guideline that has served throughout is to design lessons based on a content objective. Teachers use content objectives to shape what is important in a lesson, what concepts are stressed, and what beyond-text principles are developed.

Since studying is more of an independent activity (in comparison with activities described in previous chapters), the emphasis here is on how students can identify and apply their own content objectives. If students could learn to determine their own content objectives, their attention could be applied more specifically and purposefully to the content. Assignments requiring relatively more independence (such as long-term projects and independent or extra-credit study) could be completed with a more coherent focus.

How do students learn to develop content objectives on their own? Teachers need to model the process for students in a situation where the content is already familiar. As with reasoning and problem-solving, this requires selecting a topic and assessing students' understanding of the content (see Chapter 3). Or teachers can do comprehension teaching (Chapter 7) about the topic. Once students understand the content, teachers engage in a dialogue similar to the one below (taken from an English class):

TEACHER: How can we summarize what we know (or have learned) from this poem ("The Highwayman")?

ERIN: That people will make great sacrifices for someone they love.

TEACHER: How do we know that?

ERIN: Because Bess gives up her life for the Highwayman, who she loves.

TEACHER: Any other ways we can summarize?

JOHN: During a war, life isn't worth much.

TEACHER: Okay, why do you say that?

JOHN: Because the British were responsible for Bess and they killed the Highwayman.

TEACHER: Very good. Now, we have been summarizing the poem, but I want you to know that this is a step you can take even before you have read much of a story. Read a little bit and come up with a summary statement. I call the summary statement a "content objective" because it helps me focus on what I am reading, or what I want you to get out of a poem or a story. I think about a content objective and then, as I read, I try to see if the objective is still true. Sometimes, I change it. Sometimes, I find more evidence. If you think about a content objective, it could help you focus on and remember what you are learning. Let's practice with the next story in our book.

This dialogue illustrates a number of features that are important if students are to understand how to come up with their own content objectives. First, it is clear that students already comprehend the story and they know how to summarize (teaching students how to summarize is covered later in this chapter). Without enough knowledge of the content or the ability to summarize, students could not develop a concept for the term "content objective." Next, the technique students are learning, "creating a content objective," is given a label, its purpose is spelled out, and the activity is linked to something students already know how to do (summarize). Finally, students are given opportunities for practice. These steps—making sure students have adequate content knowledge, teaching students about content objectives, modeling their use, and providing practice—will help students develop independence in deciding what is important about the content they are studying.

Process Goals

Process goals for studying include: teaching students to flexibly focus their attention, record, and retrieve information so that they can successfully perform tasks that teachers—or others outside of school—ask them to do.

Effective study is dependent on knowledge of tasks that eventually must be performed (Anderson & Armbruster, 1984). Consider this example. At one extreme, high knowledge of a task could come from having a copy of an upcoming test. At another extreme, low knowledge could consist of knowing only that a test will be written with paper and pencil. Students who have the test copy potentially have an advantage in studying, but only if they know how to apply studying processes appropriately based on their understanding of what the tasks on the rest require.

For instance, suppose the test is on automobile repair and students will be given a series of cases (for example, the starter turns over but the car does not start or the brakes shudder when the car stops). Simply memorizing a series of facts will not be enough to pass the test. To be sure, knowledge of some facts will be necessary; of greater importance, however, will be students' prior experiences with similar situations and their ability to focus on, record, recall, and apply important concepts from those situations. Students who are strategists in their studying can predict the nature of the tasks they will be asked to

FIGURE 9.1

Processes for Studying

Focusing attention: Spending study time flexibly, allocating time to readings and tasks according to goals for learning.

"I had better crack the social studies book tonight. I want to read the chapter on inventions of the 20th century before our visit to the photography museum tomorrow. I can watch TV later and get ready for the algebra test tomorrow night."

Reorganizing and recording information: Deciding what is important, reconstructing and recording information so that it is easy to retrieve later on.

"I'll never remember all of this stuff for the test. I'll take some notes on the different inventions and then highlight the ones that made big changes in society so I can keep track of them better."

Retrieving information: Using recorded information for recall, adapting the information to subsequent classroom tasks.

"It's a good thing I took good notes on the inventions and why they are important. I can pull out big ideas first and back them up with facts for this essay (comparing and contrasting the impact of different inventions)."

---

perform, can analyze the tasks in terms of the content and processes they need to apply, and can adapt their approach to studying to ensure their success.

Figure 9.1 summarizes and illustrates the essential processes for studying through the "think-alouds" of one student.

Teachers are essential in showing students how to engage in these processes. Many teachers stumble on study processes through trial and error, often wishing someone had introduced ways to study earlier in their own education. Teachers help students prepare for the future by emphasizing processes for studying.

Motivation Goals

There are two motivation goals for studying: (1) to develop in students a sense of purpose in studying, and (2) to increase students' self-confidence in applying different study processes.

When students have positive attitudes toward the content and toward studying, they are more inquisitive and will work harder to complete classroom and homework assignments and to do well on tests (Estes & Richards, 1985). In other words, when they perceive a purpose for studying and are interested in the content, students will learn. On the other hand, without a sense of purpose, students can have knowledge of processes for studying, but they may not try to apply them. Again, teachers play a key role in teaching about effective study and in making sure students understand how to apply study processes to content.

Students will not study if they perceive themselves as being unable to study. Students who do study well tend to be confident about the tasks they need to perform, they have some knowledge of the content, and they believe they can succeed. Confidence in studying ability plays a significant role in whether or not students will be motivated to study (Alvermann & Ratekin, 1982). Given the potential problem of low student self-confidence, simply teaching students about studying is not enough. Teachers need to help students believe they can succeed by engaging in studying (Nist, Hogrebe, & Simpson, 1985).

PLANNING FOR INSTRUCTION

Although there has been a great deal of research on studying, educators continue to have difficulty in evaluating the effectiveness of one study technique versus another. The degree of effectiveness depends on what is going on inside students' heads (whether they are really thinking or simply going through the motions, whether they are processing the right kinds of information for what is expected of them). The following study techniques have shown some promise.

Note-Taking

Note-taking is a popular study technique. Contrary to general belief, there are some effective and some less effective ways to take notes. Generally, the more students move away from taking verbatim notes (copying down exactly what the book or the teacher says) to reorganizing and reinterpreting notes, the greater knowledge they will receive and retain (Anderson & Armbruster, 1984). Two approaches to note-taking are described here: the Cornell system and structured notes.

Cornell System   The *Cornell system* was developed at Cornell University as a means to record and master the ideas from discussions and textbooks (Pauk, 1974). The primary advantage of the Cornell system is simplicity. There are three steps:

Step 1. *Prepare for note-taking:* Use a large loose-leaf notebook. Draw a vertical line about 2½ inches from the left edge of several sheets. Notes (from classroom discussion, lecture, or textbook) will be written on the right side of the line. Later, key words and phrases will be written on the left side of the line (see Figure 9.2). Before taking new notes, review the notes that have been taken recently so that new notes can be connected to previous notes.

Teachers should help students believe they can succeed by studying

Alan Carey/The Image Works

FIGURE 9.2

The Cornell System for Note-Taking

After note-taking, reduce facts and concepts to concise key words, phrases, or summaries.	*During* class discussions or textbook reading, record notes in this space.

Step 2. *Take notes:* Record notes on the right-hand side of the notebook page in simple paragraph form. Focus on general concepts and principles as opposed to specific facts or details (although this recommendation could vary depending on whether, for example, the subject is social studies or mathematics). Separate ideas by skipping lines rather than using Roman or Arabic numerals or big and small letters. Try to capture the content clearly enough so that the notes will have meaning weeks and months later.

Step 3. *Review the notes:* As soon after taking notes as possible, consolidate the notes by rereading, clearing up any scribbles, and filling in any missing pieces. At this point, it may be a good idea to underline or highlight especially important information.

In the left-hand column of each page, reduce the more extensive notes to key words and phrases. Some students may prefer to create a semantic map or structured overview (see Chapter 6) as an outline in this space. The condensed and reorganized notes on the left serve as cues for the more elaborate notes on the right. To study the notes, cover up the right side of each page and use the key words or phrases to recall the more elaborate information. Verbalizing at this step tends to help with recall. Uncover the notes and verify that the information is intact and accurate.

Structured Notes   *Structured notes* are notes students take by using their understanding of text structure (Smith & Tompkins, 1988). Structured notes are graphic frameworks based on the text structure pattern with a text. Figure 9.3 contains several examples of graphics that could be used to help students develop structured notes.

To teach students how to take structured notes, begin with a simple pattern, such as time order. Discuss the purposes for taking notes, encouraging students to talk about their

FIGURE 9.3

Graphics for Use with Structured Notes

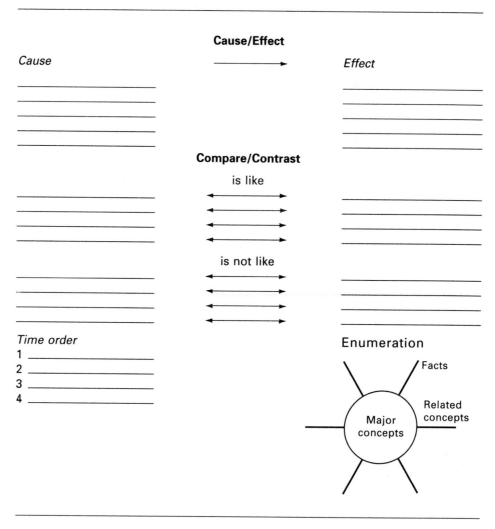

own experiences. Tell students that they will be learning about structured notes, a technique that will help them take better notes. Next, explain the differences between content and structure, noting that structure is the skeleton of a text and content is the flesh. Using a short passage with a relatively simple structure (such as time order) introduce the concept of text structure. Point out words that signal the structure in use (see Chapter 2).

Once students understand a text structure, introduce the graphic for that structure (Figure 9.3). Have students enter concepts from the text onto the graphic. Repeat the process with several more structures, explaining to students that they will eventually create their own structures. As students learn to fill in various types of structures, alternate passages with explicit signals and those where signals are more implicit. Encourage students to invent structures that will help them capture the concepts as well as the important conceptual relationships within different types of texts.

Special Considerations   Note-taking is a superior study technique when compared with activities such as filling in worksheets (Langer, 1986). With a typical worksheet, students are so focused on filling in blanks that they can miss major ideas or purposes. However, if students take notes mechanically or only gloss over what they have written, they can still miss important facts and concepts. The more students engage their minds during note-taking, the more they will remember and learn. Having students summarize and pose questions from their notes are just two ways of helping students grapple with their notes (Langer & Neal, 1987).

Summarizing

While summarizing is often assumed to be a single activity, the term actually stands for at least four activities, including:

1. Identifying/selecting main information

2. Deleting trivial information

3. Deleting redundant information

4. Relating main and important supporting information

When these activities are directly taught in the context of studying, students demonstrate improved recall of important information (Rinehart, Stahl, & Erickson, 1986).

While summarizing has already been discussed as a component of reciprocal teaching and reasoning (see Chapter 8), it is necessary to deal with the topic once more with respect to studying. Summarizing is a critical concern in any effort to help students learn how to study. Improving students' ability to summarize tends to produce benefits with other kinds of study activities. For example, improving summarization ability increases the quality of students' note-taking (Rinehart, Stahl, & Erickson, 1986).

Here are several tips for teaching summarization (Bromley & McKeveny, 1986; Shugarman & Hurst, 1986). One useful practice is to establish a purpose, explaining why summaries are useful (they improve comprehension, they say things in simpler, more concise terms). Another useful idea is to use demonstrations and simulations. Students can better grasp the summarization process if teachers use an overhead projector to walk students through the actual creation of a summary.

Provide opportunities for written as well as verbal practice. Give students copies of passages and have them write summaries. Begin with short passages and move on to longer passages. Vary the passages so that students get a feeling for how differences in text cause differences in their summaries. Provide examples of well-written and poorly written summaries, asking students to discuss strengths and weaknesses. For verbal summaries, have students summarize what has been said during classroom discussions, finding synonyms for words used by different speakers.

Another tip is to encourage adaptation. It is through adaptation that students gain confidence in their summarizing ability. Encouraging adaptation means being open to various ways of summarizing, but it also means working with students from what they understand (or do not understand) about summarizing. Some students need to begin by copying more than summarizing, but, through guidance and refinement, they eventually learn to create good summaries. Other students are ready to summarize in ways that represent and reorganize a text.

Finally, make a commitment to teach this study technique (many researchers recommend doing summarizing activities at least once or twice a week). Take the time as well as the opportunity to help all types of students become successful with summarizing.

Special Considerations   As a study technique, summarizing is most powerful when students receive instruction in how to summarize. As discussed in the last chapter, summarizing is not as easy as it might seem.

It is also important to think about the relationship between summarizing and the kind of assessment task students will eventually be asked to perform. Summaries are most helpful when the testing task involves recall of some kind (filling in blanks, providing a report), but summaries are not very useful if students will be asked to complete other more traditional testing tasks, such as true/false or multiple-choice items (King, Biggs, & Lipsky, 1984).

Underlining

Underlining (or *highlighting*) is one of the most popular study techniques. When compared with other techniques, it is equally effective in helping students recall information (Anderson & Armbruster, 1984).

Many students underline indiscriminately or without thinking about it. You have probably purchased a used textbook only to discover that nearly every line and passage had been highlighted by the previous owner. Underlining everything is not an efficient way to study. While this approach often feels like intensive study, it diverts valuable attention and makes study mechanical. It sidesteps the need to prioritize information when underlining so that essential content can be recalled and applied appropriately to later tasks.

Teachers need to provide specific instruction on how, when, and why to use underlining. Discussion about what will be required on a test or what information will help with class projects helps students focus in on what should or should not be underlined. To help students become strategists when underlining, pose problems such as: How would your underlining change if you were studying for an essay versus a multiple-choice test? If you were preparing for a brief oral report versus an extensive term paper? Discussion could center on a number of techniques—from pulling out more global information to seeking out specific facts or details—and how those techniques relate to different assignments and goals. Teachers can share their own experiences with underlining, the successes as well as the pitfalls.

Students should also become aware of how their own attitudes and opinions have an impact on what they underline. Teachers can assign an interesting text and an uninteresting text for reading and underlining. When students compare what they've underlined with what they've omitted, they learn how they are really in the driver's seat when it comes to deciding what is or is not important.

A practical problem is that, in many cases, students are not allowed to underline or otherwise mark up their school texts. Students still need to know how to underline, especially if they go on to college or are engaged in work where underlining might be useful. Teachers can show students how to underline other kinds of materials, such as course descriptions, study guides, and even notes they have taken. In addition, pages from textbooks can be copied so that students gain some practice with underlining.

Special Considerations   Teachers need to emphasize that underlining should always be followed by *timely review*. Timely review involves periodically scanning underlined material to check and refine one's understanding. Many students underline and then wait until the day before a test to review, only to discover that it is nearly impossible to reevaluate or ingest large blocks of underlined information. Review of underlined material on a regular basis, along with a final review just before a test, will prevent this from happening (Blanchard, 1985).

Improving students' ability to summarize produces many benefits

Elizabeth Crews

SQ3R

SQ3R is a systematic approach to studying. The approach works best with expository texts containing titles, chapter headings, and subheadings. SQ3R is actually a collection of study techniques that require students to preview a text and then generate and answer text-based questions. Invented by Robinson (1941), the initials SQ3R stand for:

- *Survey:* scanning the text to be read for a broad overview of the content, including the main points
- *Question:* forming questions about a text, making predictions about the information that might come from reading the text
- *Read:* reading the text, finding answers to the questions posed
- *Recite:* evaluating answers to questions raised, taking notes on important points
- *Review:* closing the text and covering notes, checking memory for main points

SQ3R has been popular in the past. It is likely that many students have been exposed to SQ3R by the time they reach high school.

Research suggests that, while SQ3R has rarely been evaluated, individual activities within SQ3R contribute to effective study (Adams, Carnine, & Gersten, 1982). For example, the positive effects of students writing and answering their own study questions is well-documented. Question-writing invites deeper text processing than simply reading the text (Anderson, 1980). Students who write their own questions tend to comprehend and retain more, in comparison with other approaches to studying (such as responding to questions on a teacher's study guide or worksheet) (Hayes, 1987).

To teach SQ3R, teachers explain the purpose of the approach and then introduce each of the study activities. Teaching students to *survey* involves showing students how to find out what a text is about and what kinds of information will be conveyed. The survey step often involves looking at titles, introductory paragraphs, headings and subheadings (if any), graphic materials (pictures, maps, charts, graphs), concluding paragraphs, and questions that may appear at the end of the reading. Teachers should demonstrate that the goal of this step is to arrive at a good general understanding of a text:

TEACHER: I can see from our survey that this chapter is going to be about the world economy, how economic decisions made in Europe or the Far East can influence what happens here. There are charts and graphs that compare different economies around the world and there is a list of import and export figures for the last ten years. We will probably be able to see how economies in different countries depend on one another.

As part of this step, students should also be encouraged to think about what they already know about the content.

The *question* step provides specific purposes for reading in SQ3R. Teaching students this step involves showing them how to restate all titles, headings, and subheadings as questions (Robinson, 1941). An example will help illustrate this technique:

Americans at Work: 1865 to Present
  becomes in question form
What did Americans do for a living in 1865?
  or
How have jobs changed since 1865?

Teachers and students write down questions that guide students as they read. Students should be encouraged to ask themselves what the questions mean and to make some predictions about possible answers to the questions.

The read, recite, and review steps are completed as part of a continuous cycle. During the *read* step, students read to answer the questions raised while doing the survey and question steps. Students typically follow this sequence: going from questions based on the title to those based on headings and subheadings. They work with one question at a time.

As students find an answer to a question, they move immediately to the *recite* and *review* steps. The recite step involves pausing and reflecting on an answer and monitoring and evaluating comprehension (asking, "Does this make sense?"). At this point, students can record brief notes for later review and study. The review step entails rehearsing the information so that it can be committed to memory. The student looks away from the text, thinks about the question under study, and tries to recall the answer. When this cycle—question, recite, review—has been completed with one question, students continue reading to find an answer to their next question.

Special Considerations   While SQ3R contains some powerful study techniques, the approach requires a certain amount of knowledge and skill. One criticism has been that systematic approaches like SQ3R are so rigorous and demand so much that they actually intrude on studying processes (Anderson, 1980). Without careful instruction, students could spend so much time trying to remember the individual steps or the meaning of the initials within SQ3R, they are unable to process the content. This can lead to problems with motivation.

Another source of difficulty comes from problems with asking and answering questions. SQ3R is not always supported by the structure or the content of the headings. In some cases, chapter headings may bear little relationship to the content of a passage or section (Anderson & Armbruster, 1984). To make reading and questioning productive within SQ3R, it is critical that students understand how to ask questions flexibly and in a variety of ways. Teachers should assess students' questioning abilities and consider using some of the questioning activities described in Chapter 7 before students learn to question under SQ3R.

Students also have a natural tendency to rush through their reading without wanting to stop. Teachers need to explain to students why it is important to take the extra time. The benefits include: self-monitoring, seeing if the material really makes sense, as well as committing facts and concepts to memory. Teachers should also model these steps, demonstrating how to form and answer questions, recite, and review.

The best way to work with SQ3R is to keep things simple. Focus on the quality with which students apply the approach. Encourage them to briefly survey a text before they read and make some predictions, to pause occasionally while reading to ask themselves a question. Encourage adaptation, helping students invent their own techniques and modifications. As they internalize SQ3R, or their version of the approach, students should become more knowledgeable and flexible in their studying.

Locational Skills

To some extent, *locational skills* were covered in Chapter 6 with respect to use of resources such as the dictionary or thesaurus. Locational skills are also necessary when using other general resources such as an encyclopedia, almanac, or atlas, or library resources such as the *Reader's Guide to Periodical Literature* (for magazines) or the card catalogue (for books).

A fundamental locational skill is the reader's own need to know. As discussed in Chapter 6, the best way to learn how to use different kinds of resources is when a real problem exists; when students need to know the meaning of a word or when an assignment takes them to a part of the world where they need to know more about the geography or the people. When confronted with a problem like this, many students won't use locational skills, relying instead on the teacher. If teachers teach students about locational skills and make resources readily available, students will find out what they need to know independently.

Dealing with locational skills is as simple as asking: "What resources will my students need to know how to use, given a specific lesson or unit of study?" Answers to this question can be divided into classroom-based resources and library resources. Classroom resources include students' textbooks, a dictionary, a thesaurus, and, in some cases, an almanac. Skills for using these resources include knowing how to use a table of contents and an index, matching a dictionary definition or thesaurus entry to the way in which a word is used, and following the more elaborate indexing systems found in many almanacs. Library resources include encyclopedias, the *Reader's Guide,* and the card catalog. Skills for using these resources include knowing how to use topic and subject headings, to interpret abbreviations and numerals (for volume and page numbers), and to navigate among the various collections in a library.

Teachers are often disappointed when they try to teach all these skills at once; when they turn students loose on a project, chaos is the result. Again, the important idea here is that locational skills should be taught only according to need. The content objective and the instruction chosen for a lesson or series of lessons dictates: (1) whether locational skills need to be covered, and (2) which locational skills need to be emphasized. It is important to examine the curriculum across the year to ensure that students are exposed to the kinds of resources and locational skills that will help them both in and out of school. Don't assume that everything students need to know is covered in their English class. There are resources and locational skills that are unique to different content areas.

The best approach to locational skills is one that is hands-on. In other words, the teacher demonstrates what he or she wants students to learn and then provides students with opportunities to practice and apply. For example, many students experience frustration when they are searching for a topic in an index, table of contents, or card catalog. They need to learn how to switch to another category label (for instance, "automobiles" instead of "cars") when they aren't successful. Teachers can teach students this important locational skill by taking students on a search through their own texts, modeling ways to find various topics and adapting to different category labels when the text uses different terminology. Next, students can mount their own searches with labels that the teacher supplies or that may be of interest to them.

It is simply not possible to illustrate here the many ways that locational skills might be integrated into content area teaching. In the final section of this chapter, a lesson is presented in which locational skills are developed through science content.

Reading Rate

The optimal *reading rate*, or the rate at which speed and comprehension are both at a maximum, varies for individuals and for different purposes and texts. Generally, the faster the reading rate, the lower the comprehension level. The reverse is also true. The slower the reading rate, the higher the comprehension level (*and* the less content covered) (Carver, 1982). Other factors such as the difficulty of the text and the degree of reader interest all affect reading rate comprehension level.

To test these principles, read the two passages in Figure 9.4 as fast as you can. Which are you able to read faster? Which are you able to better comprehend? Differences in the

FIGURE 9.4

Assess Your Reading Rate

Passage Number One

Want to keep an electronic eye on your business partner? Your baby sitter? Your spouse? You can do it—they'll never suspect a thing. To a world high on technology and short on trust have come spy gadgets for the masses, teeny-tiny cameras, tape recorders and other gee-whiz gizmos that were once only available to James Bond.

The proliferation of the gadgets has alarmed such groups as the American Civil Liberties Union. Federal legislation to increase limits on their use is pending.

"It's clearly a growing phenomenon," said Jan Goldman, a staff attorney for the ACLU in Washington, DC. "We're seeing technologies that once were in comic books and spy novels are now a reality. We're a very curious people and surely we want to know more and more about each other. But there have to be limits.

Among those who think current limits are strong enough is Ed Sklar, the president of the New York Company Spy Tech. From his office and showroom on the 80th floor of the Empire State Building, he enjoys a spectacular view.

—Anthony Gnoffo, Beyond the news, *Knight-Ridder Tribune News,* January 2, 1990

FIGURE 9.4 *(Cont.)*

Passage Number Two

A study of practice effects in recognition performance is reported. In each of two experiments, different conditions of training were followed by a critical final test. In Experiment 1, a yes-no was used on the critical test. During the training phase, some subjects were tested by the same method, either with or without item-by-item feedback, whereas others were given forced-choice tests. No significant changes in recognition accuracy were observed, either during the training trials or on the final test. However, feedback and experience with forced-choice tests both served to increase the bias toward positive responding. In Experiment 2, the forced-choice procedure was used on the critical final test. Either forced-choice tests or yes-no tests were given on the training lists. Again, there were no significant changes in performance. The absence of practice effects is attributed to the difficulty of identifying and implementing test-appropriate strategies.
—Abstract from Postman (1982)

---

rate with which you read the passages are probably due to differences in text difficulty and your own motivation.

Obviously speed-reading programs marketed only for the purpose of increasing speed do not tell the whole story. Good readers are able to vary their speed, speeding up when the material is not difficult and the demands for comprehension and recall are slight, and slowing down when the need to comprehend is critical or even when the material is enjoyable.

Rather than emphasizing speed with students, it is better to encourage flexiblity. To learn how to be flexible, students can learn to selectively *skim* reading materials. Skimming involves making several passes during reading, once to get the general idea or gist of what a reading selection is saying, another time to ingest chapter headings, boldfaced print or captions beneath pictures and diagrams, and once more to carefully read selected paragraphs (Pauk, 1974).

Skimming is fairly easy to learn with a little practice. Once students get the feeling for how to skim, they can learn how to make adjustments for different kinds of materials and purposes. For example, students need to skim materials differently when faced with the task of sorting out books for a term paper versus learning the content of a school textbook. Skimming through several novels (for characters and plot) is a way to select a book for pleasure reading or to prepare a critique. In each case, students need to make decisions about how fast to skim and what information to process. Teachers can help students make these kinds of decisions by talking about the myths surrounding reading rates and then demonstrating the flexibility and ease of skimming.

Time Management

It may seem strange to deal with an issue like time management in a text devoted to content reading instruction and communication, but time management is basic to studying (and, indeed, to all the activities discussed in this book).

Many people study by using a general technique called *persistent procrastination*.

The technique consists of working persistently for an hour or so, stopping, and procrastinating for several hours before returning to work. Another way to implement this technique is to avoid working until the last possible moment, and then to work feverishly into the night to complete the task. This is a not-so-efficient form of time management.

Many students have mastered only parts of this technique, getting pieces of work done but never completing it or waiting until the last possible moment without turning things in. It is no wonder this happens. Look at the models of time management we often provide them!

Students are programmed into a schedule at school but are rarely given opportunities to learn how to manage their time—time inside and out of school for both schoolwork and recreation. Time management is a fairly sophisticated study technique. It involves decisions about when to complete different kinds of tasks, which tasks to do first, what resources to use, how much time to spend, whether to work with others, and whether to learn pieces at a time or everything all at once (Pauk, 1974). Many students simply do not give themselves enough time to do everything they want or need to do. A common problem in many households is the student who pleads to watch a special show on television only to be faced with several hours of homework just before bedtime, a time when the mind begins to shut down. A real service teachers can provide is to get students to reflect on how they can help themselves with a sensible plan for time management.

To teach students about time management, begin by talking with them about reasons for planning how they spend their time. Discuss how having a plan actually frees people to think more about the activities they are doing and less about being squeezed for time. Point out that time management means never having to miss recreational activities because homework isn't done: both homework and recreation are programmed in.

Teach students how to make a simple schedule. Have them brainstorm for all the activities they need to accomplish in a typical day, noting the activities that occur on a daily basis and those that come up every several days. Make sure they include schoolwork, work around the house, as well as any recreational activities. Have students create a master schedule, incorporating this information (see Figure 9.5).

It is also a good idea to teach students to take notes about the assignments they receive from various teachers. Many teachers assume students already know how to do this. The poor return on many homework assignments suggests that students do not incorporate this step into their scheduling. Homework notes should include information about short-term as well as long-term assignments.

Helping students plan their time wisely is only the first step toward successful studying. Frequent and timely discussions about revising schedules, as well as what to do when they violate schedules, will help students develop a reasonable approach to time management. Teachers can plan their own schedules with students, demonstrating the difficulty as well as the rewards involved in successful time management.

TEACHING A LESSON

This section presents a science lesson in which students are simultaneously taught how to study. In reading this section, think about how the ideas presented in this chapter apply to planning and teaching a lesson in your content area.

FIGURE 9.5

A Sample Master Schedule

Time	Monday	Tuesday	Wednesday	Thursday	Friday	Saturday	Sunday
3PM	Band practice	Play rehearsal	Band practice	Play rehearsal	TV	Football game	Spend time with family
4PM	Band practice	Play rehearsal	Band practice	Play rehearsal	TV	Football game	Catch up on homework
5PM	Work	TV	Work	TV	Dinner	Dinner Work	
6PM		Dinner		Dinner	Date, Social activities		
7PM		Study and homework		Study and homework			
8PM	Dinner		Dinner				
9PM	Study and homework	TV	Study and homework	TV			
10PM		Bed		Bed	Bed	Bed	
11PM	Bed		Bed				

Goals and Assumptions

This lesson is adapted from a science unit about respiration (Anderson et al., 1987). A goal of the unit is to help students go beyond memorization to understand scientific explanations. To achieve this kind of learning, the unit is designed to help students reshape or abandon misconceptions they have held before in favor of scientific concepts. This learning process is referred to as *conceptual change* (Anderson & Roth, 1989).

The lesson selected from the unit deals with a single central question (from Anderson et al., 1987):

What happens to the food we eat?

Note how the question balances students' interests (eating) with their need to understand science content. The content objective for the lesson is for students to understand the following scientific explanation:

We need to eat because food is our cells' only source of energy.

The intended audience is a seventh-grade, mixed-ability class. They have already learned that food, not water, sunlight, or vitamins is the way our bodies get energy. They are now ready to examine specific ways food is processed by the body.

The teacher assumes that most students know little about what happens to food once it enters the body. She guesses that many know about the stomach and intestines and that feces are a product of eating, yet few are aware of how food enters the bloodstream or is used by the cells.

The goal of reorganizing what students understand is consistent with learning processes associated with studying. Note-taking was chosen as a way for students to reconstruct and record what they learn. The Cornell system was chosen for its ease and flexibility. Students need to take notes from a variety of sources, including text passages, discussions using overhead transparencies, and labs.

Building Background and Motivation

The teacher prepares students by discussing purposes for note-taking:

TEACHER: We're going to learn a lot of interesting things today about eating and what happens to our food. Before we start, I want to show you a way to take notes so that you can think about and remember what we are learning. This is a good way to keep track of what you own interests and understandings as well as a way to get ready for our labs and tests.

Notice how the teacher's comments are focused on both the students' personal and their academic concerns.

Next, procedures for using the Cornell system are introduced and demonstrated. Teachers may wish to use both a notebook and an overhead for this demonstration. The notebook is used to show students how to draw lines and format their own notebooks. Overhead transparencies serve to show students specific ways notes are entered. For example, to start the lesson on food, the teacher tells students to enter the central question for the lesson on the left-hand side of the notes:

TEACHER: This is where we are going to record the questions we raise for ourselves, what we are trying to learn. Some of the questions will come from me, some will come from the book, and others can come from you. On the right-hand side, write down any observations or explanations that help us answer these questions.

This is a change from the typical approach to the Cornell system (taking more elaborate notes first, summarizing and raising questions later), but it is a useful adaptation. Raising the questions first helps students focus their attention and develop good scientific explanations.

The teacher introduces the scientific content for the unit by asking students the central question for the unit:

TEACHER: What happens to the food we eat?
GEORGE: It goes into your stomach.
TEACHER: Then what happens?
KATIE: It goes into your intestines and then it comes out.
MARIA: Gross!

The teacher discovers that many of her original assumptions were correct, that students have some general knowledge about what happens to food, yet little specific awareness.

Developing Content and Process

Often, the most difficult part of note-taking is keeping students committed to the activity. That's why it is important to review periodically with students how to take notes, encouraging students to share what they have written, and teaching them to review and refine what they think.

Students should be encouraged to take notes while reading the relevant chapter of the science test. Prior to the reading, teachers might wish to model the note-taking they want from their students:

TEACHER: Let's look at the first section of the chapter together. Remember, we're trying to find out what happens to our food. Let's see if we are given any answers. (Reads the first few paragraphs.) I'm going to summarize now. It says we need to eat because food helps us live and that food is our cells' only source of energy. The part about helping us live is pretty general. The part about our cells tells *how* our body uses food. That starts to answer our question. Let's write down "Food is our cells' source of energy." That's how I would like you to take notes. Think about the question and find information that gives us some answers.

After students read more, the teacher asks for volunteers to read the notes they have taken:

TEACHER: Anyone like to share their notes? George?

GEORGE: I found out that there are parts of food our body can use and some parts that our body can't.

TEACHER: How does that help answer your questions?

GEORGE: They (the different parts of the food) don't go to the same places. The food our body doesn't use goes right through us!

TEACHER: That's good. You picked up some information that can help us.

As students learn how to take notes, they also develop a more detailed picture of how the body breaks down food so that it can be converted to energy for the cells.

This approach is also useful for discovering misconceptions students might have:

TELLY: So the blood gives us everything we need.

TEACHER: What does the blood do? What does the blood have to do with what happens to our food?

TELLY: It breaks it down?

TEACHER: No, that happens in the stomach and in the intestines. How does the blood help get the food to our cells?

TELLY: Oh, I see. Blood takes the food to the cells. Blood isn't like (the same as) food.

The teacher helps the student replace his misconceptions with a scientific explanation for the role of blood in food transport.

Encouraging Independence

Independence with note-taking comes when students can prepare and review their own notes for their own purposes.

For this lesson, this means that students should eventually be able to raise their own central questions and seek out, record, and refine their own notes leading to scientific explanations. Accomplishing this brings us back to the point made several times in this section of the text, that students need to be shown how to ask and answer questions. Many of the questioning techniques presented in the previous chapters can lead to achieving this goal.

The twist here, however, is that students also need to ask questions that are important from a scientific perspective. Helping students do this requires insight about how scientists ask and answer questions about the world. Scientists are more interested in providing functional explanations than in fleshing out idiosyncratic, small details. When students (and, sometimes, their teachers) are new to asking and answering their own scientific questions, they tend to focus on either trivia or technical minutia. All subject-matter teachers can develop independent note-taking skills in their students by modeling ways to focus attention appropriately and to record, reorder, and communicate important content concepts.

SUMMARY

Effective study is one of the more independent activities students need to be able to do. Unfortunately, most students do not know how to study efficiently or productively. Teachers need to model good studying techniques, if students are to learn what it means to study. Underlining, summarizing, and note-taking are among many techniques that have been developed for effective study. These techniques help students flexibly focus their attention, record, and retrieve information. Students who know how to adapt their studying techniques to different subject matter are likely to be successful learners and communicators in content area classrooms.

SPECIAL PROJECTS

Course-Based

1. Using the ideas presented in this chapter, select, adapt, or invent a studying approach that works for you.

2. Create an approach to studying that could work in conjunction with some of the other activities described in this book (for example, vocabulary, comprehension, reasoning and problem-solving, writing, and discussion).

Field-Based

3. Using the ideas in this chapter, design a lesson or series of lessons that you could use to teach students flexible ways to study.

4. Create a time management plan for yourself and share it with students. How can you help them organize their time flexibly to achieve their goals?

SUGGESTED READINGS

The following articles provide additional information about the instructional activities presented in this chapter:

ALVERMANN, D., & HAYES, D. (1986). Instructional strategies that induce useful study skills. In E. Dishner, T. Bean, J. Readance, and & D. Moore (Eds.), *Reading in the content areas: Improving classroom instruction.* Dubuque, IA: Kendall-Hunt.

COTTIER, S., & BAUMAN, S. (1985). A study skills unit for junior high students. In W. J. Harker (Ed.), *Classroom strategies for secondary reading.* Newark, DE: International Reading Association.

MEMORY, D., & MOORE, D. (1985). Selecting sources in library research: An activity in skimming and critical reading. In W. J. Harker (Ed.), *Classroom strategies for secondary reading.* Newark, DE: International Reading Association.

ORLANDO, V. (1986). Training students to use a modified version of SQ3R: An instructional strategy. In E. Dishner, T. Bean, J. Readance, & D. Moore (Eds.), *Reading in the content areas: Improving classroom instruction.* Dubuque, IA: Kendall-Hunt.

TAYLOR, B. (1986). A summarization strategy to improve middle grade students' reading and writing skills. In E. Dishner, T. Bean, J. Readance, & D. Moore (Eds.), *Reading in the content areas: Improving classroom instruction.* Dubuque, IA: Kendall-Hunt.

This book contains a variety of practical ideas about studying:

GRAHAM, K., & ROBINSON, H. A. (1984). *Study skills handbook: A guide for all teachers.* Newark, DE: International Reading Association.

These books on studying are classics:

HERBER, H. (1985). *Developing study skills in secondary schools.* Newark, DE: International Reading Association.

PAUK, W. (1974). *How to study in college,* 2d edition. Boston: Houghton Mifflin.

ROBINSON, F. (1961). *Effective study.* New York: Harper & Row.

This article provides an extensive review of the research on studying:

ANDERSON, T., & ARMBRUSTER, B. (1984). Studying. In P. D. Pearson, R. Barr, M. Kami, & P. Mosenthal (Eds.), *Handbook of reading research.* New York: Longman.

REFERENCES

ADAMS, A., CARNINE, D., & GERSTEN, R. (1982). Instructional strategies for studying content area texts in the intermediate grades. *Reading Research Quarterly, 18,* 1, 27–55.

ALVERMANN, D., & RATEKIN, N. (1982). Metacognitive knowledge about reading proficiency: Its relation to study strategies and task demands. *Journal of Reading Behavior, 14,* 3, 231–241.

ANDERSON, C., & ROTH, K. (1989). Teaching for meaningful and self-regulated learning of science. In J. Brophy (Ed.), *Advances in research on teaching.* Greenwich, CT: JAI Press.

ANDERSON, C., ROTH, K., HOLLON, R., & BLAKESLEE, T. (1987). *The power cell: Teacher's guide to respiration* (Occasional Paper No. 113). East Lansing, MI: Michigan State University, Institute for Research on Teaching.

ANDERSON, T. (1980). Study strategies and adjunct aids. In R. Spiro, B. Bruce, & W. Brewer (Eds.), *Theoretical issues in reading comprehension.* Hillsdale, NJ: Erlbaum.

ANDERSON, T., & ARMBRUSTER, B. (1984). Studying. In P. D. Pearson, R. Barr, M. Kamil, & P. Mosenthal (Eds.), *Handbook of reading research.* New York: Longman.

BLANCHARD, J. (1985). What to tell students about underlining . . . and why. *Journal of Reading, 29,* 3, 199–203.

BROMLEY, K., & MCKEVENY, L. (1986). Precis writing: Suggestions for instruction in summarizing. *Journal of Reading, 29,* 5, 392–395.

CARVER, R. (1982). Optimal rate of reading prose. *Reading Research Quarterly, 18,* 1, 56–88.

ESTES, T., & RICHARDS, H. (1985). Habits of study and test performance. *Journal of Reading Behavior, 17,* 1–28.

HAYES, D. (1987). The potential for directing study in combined reading and writing activity. *Journal of Reading, 19,* 4, 333–352.

KING, J., BIGGS, S., & LIPSKY, S. (1984). Students' self-questioning and summarizing as reading study strategies. *Journal of Reading Behavior, 16,* 3, 205–218.

LANGER, J. (1986). Learning through writing: Study skills in content areas. *Journal of Reading, 29,* 5, 400–406.

LANGER, M., & NEAL, J. (1987). Strategies for learning: An adjunct study skills model. *Journal of Reading, 30,* 2, 134–139.

NIST, S., HOGREBE, M., & SIMPSON, M. (1985). The relationship between use of study strategies and test performance. *Journal of Reading Behavior, 17,* 1, 15–28.

PAUK, W. (1974). *How to study in college,* 2d edition. Boston: Houghton Mifflin.

POSTMAN, L. (1982). An examination of practice effects in recognition. *Memory and Cognition, 10,* 4, 333–340.

RINEHART, S., STAHL, S. & ERICKSON, L. (1986). Some effects of summarization training on reading and studying. *Reading Research Quarterly, 21,* 4, 422–438.

ROBINSON, F. (1941). *Effective study.* New York: Harper & Row.

SHUGARMAN, S., & HURST, J. (1986). Purposeful paraphrasing: Promoting a nontrivial pursuit for meaning. *Journal of Reading, 29,* 5, 396–401.

SMITH, P., & TOMPKINS, G. (1988). Structured notetaking: A new strategy for content area readers. *Journal of Reading, 32,* 1, 46–53.

TIERNEY, R., LAZANSKY, J., & SCHALLERT, D. (1982). *Secondary students' use of social studies and biology text.* Champaign, IL: University of Illinois.

Spencer Grant/The Picture Cube

Students get motivated when they have an audience for their writing

during instruction. It is difficult to conceive of a situation in which all five writing processes would be emphasized in a single lesson. At the same time, it is difficult to conceive of situations in which a single writing process would be emphasized exclusively in a single lesson. Remember, for real writers, writing usually starts with one or several writing processes but skips around as writers develop and refine their ideas. When planning, it is important for teachers to think about which aspects of writing are appropriate, given the purposes and goals of a lesson and where students are in their thinking.

As you read the following sections, think about ways to combine and adapt the writing instruction to your own teaching.

Pre-Writing

Pre-writing is a process of discovery, finding out about writing topics, audiences, and purposes. For some writers, pre-writing is an elaborate mental rehearsal of possible ideas and insights. For others, pre-writing is a time for mapping ideas on paper or note-taking, jotting down characters or arguments, plots or structures. Often, writers talk to themselves or to others, working out ideas orally before transferring them to paper. Eventually, these activities blend into drafting, the formal structuring of thought onto paper. The purposes of pre-writing are to brainstorm and elaborate ideas for writing, but also to constrain and control, to focus in on intentions in order to produce a working first draft (Murray, 1985).

The following sections describe practices that shape and influence pre-writing: writing assignments, freewriting, and reader response.

Writing Assignments   Depending on how they are structured, *writing assignments* are either the barrier or the support to students' writing.

Some researchers argue that teachers should never assign what students write (Calkins, 1986). Many teacher-led assignments "stimulate" writing but they do not get students deeply and personally involved in writing. Worse yet, students become accustomed to writing only when teachers make them write. This creates a dependence on the teacher that blocks students' self-identification of topics and, ultimately, students' independent writing.

To break the cycle of teacher assignments and student dependence on teachers for writing, Atwell (1987) advocates guiding students in developing their own topics as part of pre-writing, a kind of self-assigned writing. Teachers model ways to think about and brainstorm their own topics and then show students how to list and develop their ideas:

TEACHER: What could I write about today? Let's see, I've been thinking about writing a story about the last sleep-out we had in my best friend's back yard. That's a long time ago. Maybe I won't remember everything. What about my last birthday party? I turned thirty and my friends gave me a real hard time. That was fun! How about my trip to Florida to visit my parents? I'm not sure everyone would be interested in that, but I would like to write about it for myself.

The process of breaking away from teacher-led assignments isn't easy, especially for older students who have grown accustomed to writing only when teachers tell them to write. Continuous modeling and persistence, however, can encourage students to become more independent.

Many teachers decide to continue assigning writing for several reasons. Some teachers prefer to give students some structure, especially when students are working with unfamiliar concepts. Other teachers want students to become more independent but realize that writing assignments are a temporary necessity until students learn more about the process of pre-writing.

Research suggests that the best kinds of writing assignments are those which are negotiated between teachers and their students (Rasinki & DeFord, 1986). The reasons for this are simple: students feel they have more of a stake in the writing and they are in a better position to assess their own prior knowledge about the writing topic and envision possible audiences and purposes. Jenkins (1986) offers four questions to guide the design of classroom writing assignments:

1. *Are the directions clear?* A good assignment states or implies a topic, a purpose, and an audience.

For example:

Convince your parents that you really should be given more freedom to make decisions on your own.

Not:

Write about some of the decisions you have made lately.

2. *Does the assignment allow the student to speculate before focusing on the topic?* A good assignment encourages brainstorming, reflection, and pre-writing. Poor assignments set restrictive time limits and focus more on length than substance.

For example:

Write down all the ideas you can, predicting what you think will happen in our science lab. When you publish the findings of our lab, compare your predictions (hypotheses) with what you actually observed.

Not:

By the end of the hour, write a report on our lab findings. Your report should be a minimum of 3 pages long.

3. *Is the assignment free from wrong assumptions about what students know or have experienced?* A good assignment is based on knowledge or experiences that students already have.

For example:

Now that we have studied the social conflicts that led up to the 1960s protests, let's explore the social conflicts we have today. Choose a social issue that interests you and persuade the class that this issue is worth their time and commitment.

Not:

Discuss the inadequate training procedures of technicians at nuclear power plants.

4. *Is there enough freedom in the assignment to allow students to find something personally interesting?* A good assignment invites student involvement.

For example:

To prepare for our study of families, interview your parents about what it was like to grow up in their family. Brainstorm for some interview questions that are interesting to you. Think about how you will prepare a report for us in our classroom "family."

Not:

Write a report on the history of your family.

Freewriting   *Freewriting* is a pre-writing technique devoted to putting ideas out on paper as quickly as possible. Freewriting, also known as "fastwriting" (or "fastwrites"), simply involves writing for ten or fifteen minutes without stopping. *Focused freewriting* occurs when the teacher asks students to respond to specific topics, such as an idea, an object, a poem, a story, or an event (Draper, 1979). Having students create structured overviews or semantic maps (see Chapter 6) is one way to stress focused freewriting.

Peter Elbow, originator of the freewriting concept, provides the following guidelines: "Go quickly without rushing. Never stop to look back, to cross something out, to wonder how to spell something, to wonder what word or thought to use, or to think about what you are doing. If you can't think of a word or a spelling, just use a squiggle or else write 'I can't think of it.' Just put down something . . . the only requirement is that you never stop" (Elbow, 1973, p. 3).

Freewriting supports the purposes of pre-writing by taking away, for a time, the pressure most students feel about producing a written product in the classroom. When writing, many students worry about grammar and spelling while trying to figure out what to say. When students attempt to simultaneously produce and edit a piece of writing, the result is often a blank page, or the incoherence that characterizes many classroom writing assignments.

Freewriting is nonediting. It is a procedure for producing thoughts and ideas and putting them on paper. With regular practice, it breaks students of the habit of producing and editing at the same time and it breaks down blockages to thinking and writing.

Freewriting results in two kinds of written product: garbage and ideas that develop a subject and a purpose. It is inevitable that some of the writing produced during freewriting will be of poor quality or won't make sense. On the other hand, the free flow of ideas that occurs during freewriting enables students to refine and integrate those ideas. The next task for students is to separate the garbage from the good writing, the random thoughts from the thoughtful insights, and edit to create a finished piece of writing (Elbow, 1973).

Reader Response   An area of emerging research concerns *reader response,* through writing, to content area materials. Simply defined, reader response consists of ways for students to explore and extend what they have read in informational and narrative texts (Rosenblatt, 1978). The opposite of reader response is *text-based response.* In many classrooms, text-based response is the way most students write in reaction to their subject-matter reading. Text-based response usually consists of taking notes or providing short-answer responses on a ditto page. In comparison studies, students who had been exposed to reader response learned significantly more from their reading and produced more complex kinds of writing than students who engaged only in text-based response (Newell, Suszynski, & Weingart, 1989).

Pre-writing is the perfect stage to focus on reader response. The goals of reader response are to encourage students to (1) develop a personal reaction and (2) elaborate on the meanings they have tentatively generated in their reading. To illustrate reader response, compare the following essay assignments designed to evoke response to a short story (adapted from Newell et al.),

Assignment 1

Describe Lois's feelings about her father. As you write, think about your reaction to her feelings. What about the story made you feel as you do? Also, try to compare what happened between Lois and her father with your own observations and experiences, that is, to things you have read, talked about, seen on TV, or lived through yourself.

Assignment 2

Prove the statement that Lois lost faith in her father. Support this idea by drawing on specific examples from the story. You must use the story to back up and prove your points.

These assignments represent contrasting views of where meaning resides. Assignment 1 reflects the belief that meaning is in the reader, that is, the reader is primarily personally responsible for constructing meaning from a text. Assignment 2 reflects the belief that meaning is in the text, that is, the text provides all the clues necessary for interpretation and all the reader has to do is read the clues and extract the meaning. Assignment 1 invites reader response, while assignment 2 focuses on text-based response. It should come as no surprise that reader response writing assignments invoke more thoughtful and reflective kinds of pre-writing than text-based assignments. This thought and reflection often translates into rich and integrated written interpretations (Newell, Suszynski, & Weingart, 1989).

The principles underlying reader response can be applied broadly to writing activities across the curriculum. Whenever asking students to write, always consider ways to elicit a more personal reaction to the content. For example, while preparing a report on environmental pollution in science, students could include perceptions about pollution in their immediate environment (around their homes, at school, in their neighborhoods). In mathematics, students could write stories about situations in which probability made a difference in their own decision-making. In physical education, students could draw on their own experiences with sports to write about how the mind relates to body movements when playing sports. The more teachers think of ways to incorporate reader response, the better the quality of students' pre-writing and learning from content reading materials.

Drafting

Drafting is the term given to the physical act of writing. Though some writing occurs during pre-writing activities, the generation of ideas is the focus. That some ideas are recorded during pre-writing is a concern, but it is not the central concern. When attention turns to drafting, it is time to put thoughts and ideas on paper.

There are many different approaches to drafting. It is not possible to illustrate them all here (a list of resources appears at the end of this chapter). Instead, two techniques have been chosen to cover the major functions of writing: journals across the curriculum for expressive writing, and guided writing for transactional and poetic writing. As these techniques are described, think about how you could design other approaches to drafting in your content area.

Journals Across the Curriculum   Through *journal-writing*, students learn to think and speculate on paper. Across the curriculum, journals can be used for such diverse subject-matter activities as jotting field notes during a science lab, offering personal opinions about historical events and periods, and figuring out a new set of plays for soccer or volleyball. Journals can be the place for students to express any new set of ideas they encounter or create in a subject (Fulwiler, 1986).

The key to using journals successfully lies in developing subject-matter purposes for journal-writing and giving students frequent opportunities to write in their journals. It is particularly important for teachers to write alongside students to demonstrate firsthand the potential of journal-writing. For example, during class a mathematics teacher might pause for a few moments to think and write about cases in which estimation affects daily decisions. He or she could then ask students to write in their journals for a few moments about their own personal experiences with estimation.

Music teachers might ask students to keep *listening journals* (Fulwiler, 1986). In these journals, students record their daily experiences with music. From time to time, the teacher can have discussions about music quality and form based on students' experiences and tastes.

How do teachers stimulate students to start and keep journals? One way is to describe the journal to students as a cross between a diary and a class notebook (Fulwiler, 1986). Like a diary, a journal is written in the first person (for example, "I think the Rolling Stones are the best!"). Like a class notebook, the focus is on subject-matter concepts students would like to remember or further explore. Students should be encouraged to use journals to expand their thinking, to experiment and play with ideas. Once students have been shown how to write in their journals, some teachers prefer to leave journal writing open-ended: students write in the journals as the need or whim arises. Other teachers give students journal writing assignments, using them to start the day's lesson or for reflection when important concepts emerge during class.

A controversial topic concerns the extent to which teachers should read or grade journal writing assignments. Some teachers believe that journals, as expressive writing, should be absolutely private. However, those teachers who do read student journals can provide some useful feedback to help students get the most out of their journal writing. For example, in the beginning it is not uncommon for students to be too literal or factual, or to have trouble knowing what to write. Teachers who pick this up can encourage students to speculate and expand their thoughts.

Another reason for looking at journals has to do with accountability: some students will not do assignments without a tangible reward, like a grade. To resolve this problem, some teachers offer grades based on quantity. For some teachers, this means that a full page of journal writing every day equals an "A," three-quarters of a page is a "B," and half a page is a "C." Other teachers count pages, with 100 pages equaling an "A," 50 pages a "B," and so on. Still other teachers like to balance the need for students to maintain privacy in their journals with the need to have a grading system. In these classrooms, students use a paper clip or piece of sticky notepaper to separate sections that are for the teacher from sections that are personal and for the student.

Journals are not for everyone. For teachers and their students, journal writing requires a certain amount of flexibility and persistence. However, in classrooms where journal writing has been successful, students are afforded many unique and creative opportunities to explore and share subject-matter insights in ways not addressed by other forms of writing or communicating.

Guided Writing   *Guided writing* consists of a set of practices that teachers use to explain, model, and assist student writing especially during the drafting stage. Guided writing consists of:

- Modeling the activities students are to accomplish during the writing
- Providing students with examples of the writing they are about to do
- Teaching students how to organize information gathered during pre-writing
- Encouraging students to put ideas on paper, reserving revision and editing decisions until later
- Discussing what students should do when a draft is finished, such as checking work for potential areas of revision and editing

Not every writing situation calls for the careful kind of guidance described here. In some cases, teachers will want students to write with a minimum of teacher intervention so that they can develop greater independence. When either the content or the writing task is particularly unfamiliar or complex, teachers should think about and apply principles of guided writing.

Principles of guided writing shaped the following dialogue in which a social studies teacher shows middle school students how to write letters, one from a northern child and another from a southern child at the height of the Civil War:

TEACHER: We said that the northern child might feel badly about slavery and want to convince the southern child that slavery is wrong. We have to think carefully about how we get those ideas into a letter. Do we just say: "Dear Jess, I think you stink for having slaves?"

RICK: No, we can't say it that way!

TEACHER: Why not?

RICK: He won't listen. He'll just get mad.

TEACHER: OK, how about this? "Dear Jess, I hear you have slaves on your farm to help out. I also hear they work hard. In the North, people get paid for the work they do. Do you ever think how the slaves feel, working hard and not getting any money?" Is this a good way to start?

KATHY: It's better because you're not accusing him.

TEACHER: Right. I'm also trying to give reasons for my opinions. Did you see how I used an example from my own experience? We're trying to be civil, but we're trying to convince him to listen to us too.

Note how this teacher asks students to compare nonexamples and examples. This helps students get a clearer picture of both the audience and how to organize the writing for persuasion. In this next segment, the teacher asks students to think about the audience again, this time to encourage the use of informal writing:

TEACHER: Now, this is interesting. When we've tried to persuade before, it's been in school and in essay form. But this is a letter. It should be more informal. How do we make it more informal?

RICK: We could talk about our families.

TEACHER: That's good. That would make him more comfortable. What else?

SUSAN: We could just write freer.

TEACHER: What do you mean "write freer"?

SUSAN: We write more like we talk, not worry as much about saying things exactly right, just get the ideas out.

TEACHER: Good suggestions. That's always a good idea when we just start to write like we're doing now, but it's especially a good idea when we're writing a letter like this one.

Through guided writing, teachers help students clarify, extend, and reformulate not only what they know about a subject but also what they are learning about writing.

Guided writing requires a careful analysis of what students are expected to accomplish while writing. For example, suppose students were presented with the following writing task in a vocational education class:

> Your company wants to buy a machine you think is too expensive and can't perform as well as a cheaper machine that works much better. Choose a machine that you know well and write a report to your boss on the advantages of one machine over another.

To accomplish this task, students need some content knowledge (the features of one machine in comparison with the other), they need to be able to envision an audience (a tough versus an understanding boss), and they need to know how to write a report involving a comparison between the machines. Teachers should think about how they would complete the task (for example, get information about the machines, describe the boss, find some examples of similar kinds of reports). Teachers guide students by making this thinking public, explaining potential ways of completing the task, modeling how someone might brainstorm and draft a a report, and then turning the task over to students for completion. Principles of guided writing are extremely important to consider whenever students need some additional assistance in putting their thoughts down on paper.

sion

The process of revision is often confused with the process of editing. *Editing* consists of polishing mostly at the sentence level and involves error detection and correction. *Revision,* on the other hand, focuses on how a writer solves problems related to the process of putting thoughts on paper (Fitzgerald, 1987). Revision means to view again, to look at a piece of writing with a fresh eye and perspective in order to create greater clarity (Moore, 1986). Given these definitions, students can distinguish revision concerns from editing concerns. If the need is to clarify the written message by reformulating and extending ideas, then students should revise. If, however, the need is to polish and correct misspellings and grammatical errors that could interfere with communication, students should edit.

Several problems can make it difficult for students to revise. First, if during pre-writing students have not spent much time clarifying their intentions, revision can be hampered. During pre-writing, students should make decisions about content, purpose, and form. Lack of thinking in any of these areas undermines a student's ability to conceive of some clear criteria for revising (Fitzgerald, 1987). Second, students may try to focus on too much at once during revision. Students who attend to content and form at the same time tend to get bogged down, especially when content knowledge is weak or the form chosen conflicts with the content (for example, when a student chooses to write an evaluation of a science lab in the form of a narrative). A third kind of problem occurs when students are unable to revise from a reader's perspective (Flower et al., 1986). When students are too egocentric in their revisions, they often fail to see conflicting concepts and other problems that affect the clear representation of ideas in a piece of writing.

Some students have a good sense of what to revise, but they lack a clear understanding of how to change things. Together, teachers and students play a role in developing both the what and the how of revision. Research suggests that revision skills and the quality of writing simultaneously improve when teachers and students communicate with one another and provide feedback during revision (Hillocks, 1982).

Two approaches—writing conferences and peer response groups—engage teachers and their students in communication devoted to revision.

Writing Conferences   *Writing conferences* are opportunities for writers (teachers and students) to ask each other questions, to help one another with emerging texts (Calkins, 1986). Writing conferences typically involve two people—a teacher and a student or two students working together—both of whom are engaged in discussion and decisions about a recently created draft of a piece of writing. Donald Murray (1985), one of the originators of classroom writing conferences, suggests that an essential ingredient is active listening. Murray suggests that any writing conference should begin with students speaking first, so that both the teacher and the student are informed about the thinking that produced a particular piece. That way, the teacher knows what needs to be taught and the student knows what needs to be done before the next draft.

Lucy Calkins (1986) describes four kinds of writing conferences, each devoted to different revision concerns. *Content conferences* focus on the subject or topic of a piece of writing. During content conferences, teachers ask and respond to questions about content and, ideally, help students expand and elaborate on their drafts. The emphasis in these conferences should be on what students *do* say as opposed to what students *do not* say. In other words, it is the teacher's job to comment first on what students actually produced rather than moving too quickly to get students to add more information. The following excerpt from a content conference in a mathematics class illustrates this principle:

Writing conferences are opportunities for teachers and students to help with emerging writing

Tony Velez/The Image Works

TEACHER: I see that you find it hard to estimate whether you have enough money when you're buying things for your mother at the grocery store. I've had the same problem. How do you do it?

MARK: I round up to the nearest dollar. So, if I buy milk and it costs $1.59, I call it $2.00. That way, I'll have enough money at the check-out and maybe a little more for candy.

TEACHER: How does your mother feel about that?

MARK: She gets mad sometimes because I don't buy everything on her list. But I think she estimates differently than I do. That's why I'm writing her this letter. I really would like her to know how and why I estimate things the way I do. Maybe I should say more about that.

Note how the teacher avoids doing too much of the talking, being curious while trying to elicit from the student what he or she already knows or has discovered or learned (in this case, that there are different ways to estimate). Conducted in this way, content conferences empower students, putting them in control of the writing, as opposed to making them feel their drafts are skimpy or aren't good enough.

Design conferences help students make the structure or the form of their writing match the subject. During design conferences, students make decisions about whether their topic is too large for a single piece of writing, whether the form they have chosen

Some of the best kinds of publication come from ideas embedded in real-life subject-matter contexts. It is useful to start a publication idea with the question: "What kinds of *public writing* are related to this content area?" Public writing includes the writing people do to communicate with one another while on the job. It also involves personal or even poetic writing that is meant for a public audience. The public writing embedded in careers is varied, from preparing reports and evaluating data to writing stories and plays that have a lasting effect on an audience. While an important kind of publishing that occurs in most classrooms consists of oral or silent sharing, public writing undertaken for real (or realistic) purposes and audiences prepares students for the writing challenges they will face in the outside world.

Once an idea for publication has been chosen, the next step is to help students understand how writers go about creating the desired piece of writing. This involves attention to (1) pre-writing, having students think carefully about the purpose, the audience, and the form of the writing; (2) guided writing and revision, showing students writing samples and modeling for them ways to write and refine their writing; and finally, (3) editing and publication, helping students see their efforts culminate in a written product. If students are treated genuinely as writers on the road to publication, they will want to write and will learn to love seeing their words come alive in the faces of their readers (Willinsky, 1985).

EVALUATING WRITING

Teachers often become squeamish when it comes to the topic of evaluating students' writing. When the instructional emphasis is on authentic writing tasks, on real communication and real audiences, grading seems an intrusion that reverts attention to the teacher.

Teacher input is very valuable in the evaluation process. As developing writers themselves, teachers have learned many things about writing and how writing works in a content area. Through evaluation, teachers pass on what they have learned as well as help students monitor their continuing progress with writing. One method some teachers use to evaluate student writing is primary trait scoring. (Another method involves the use of portfolios and is discussed in Chapter 12.)

Primary trait scoring involves ratings based on the essential features of a piece of writing: the special blend of audience, purpose, and form (Lloyd-Jones, 1977). This approach to evaluating writing is useful in both communicating to students how they are progressing and deriving grades (Woodley & Woodley, 1989). Primary trait scoring follows a simple, five-step process (Cramer, 1982):

1. *Select a writing task for students to perform.* This task should be a reality-based writing task. It could take the form of describing some object or event, or it could involve creating a persuasive argument or telling a story based on facts and concepts in the subject.

2. *Determine the specific criteria on which the scoring is to be based* (for example, accurate use of content concepts, an awareness of how writing functions and is organized in the discipline).

3. *Determine the criteria that describe high, middle, and low levels of achievement.* For instance:
   High: Accurate and functional use of content concepts. An organizational pattern is used purposefully to convey content.
   Middle: Accurate as well as some inaccurate use of content concepts. Some attempt to organize information, but not always successful.
   Low: Difficult to determine what concepts are being communicated. Disorganized writing with little sense of purpose tied to learning in the subject.

4. *Ask students to complete the writing task.* Talk with students about the writing task, offering information about how the writing will be evaluated. Provide students with some uninterrupted time to complete the writing.

5. *Evaluate students' writing.* Score their writing as high, medium, or low using the criteria identified.

Results and what they mean can be communicated in writing (for example, "Your rating was in the middle. Better find out more about x" or "Let's talk about how you organized this"). Some teachers prefer giving this kind of feedback during writing conferences.

FIGURE 10.3

A Primary Trait Scoring Guide

	Low		Middle		High
Audience					
Shows awareness of audience	2	4	6	8	10
Appropriate to the writing task	1	5	10	15	20
				Audience score: _____	
Purpose					
Clearly stated	1	5	10	15	20
Appropriate to the writing task	1	5	10	15	20
				Purpose score: _____	
Form					
Linked to purpose	1	5	10	15	20
Error-free	2	4	6	8	10
				Form score: _____	
				Total score: _____	

Additional comments: _____

_____

Primary trait *scoring guides* facilitate communication with students about their writing (Cooper, 1977). These guides can be relatively easy to construct. Teachers need only identify the crucial features of a written assignment and then apply a sliding (1 to 5, 1 to 20, or even 1 to 100) scale related to each of the features. An example of a scoring guide appears in Figure 10.3.

To illustrate how the scoring guide works, imagine that students are given the task of persuading big industry to take more responsibility for fighting pollution. If students clearly identify an audience (Exxon, a public utility, Lee Iacocca) and it is clear that the audience consists of a company (or representative) from big industry, they receive higher credit within the audience category. If students clearly state a purpose and it is relevant to the writing task (to convince and persuade), they receive higher credit within the purpose category. Finally, if students relate the purpose to the form (for instance, providing reasons for their persuasive argument) and their writing is error-free (few spelling or punctuation errors, correct usage), they receive higher credit within the form category.

Experiment with primary trait scoring both to improve your own awareness of how your writing assignments work and to communicate with students about the kinds of progress they are making.

TEACHING A LESSON*

Rosaen (1990) describes several ways that teachers provide instructional support for writing. Once teachers have made careful planning decisions about writing, they need to help students learn to capture ideas and manipulate them. To do this, it is often necessary to downplay the need to arrive at a perfect product in favor of using writing to explore thinking. Other times, teachers may want to develop students' understanding of how to write, simultaneously building their self-confidence and control. Teachers guide and direct students while still encouraging them to make their own decisions throughout their writing.

The following sections depict an approach to writing in physical education devoted to these principles. As you read, think about ways the principles applied here relate to teaching and learning in your content area.

Goals and Assumptions

When students enter a physical education class, they are usually hyperactive, with their minds only on physical activity. Though physical education teachers often try to reshape the environment, gymnasiums are not exactly conducive to sitting-down, paper-and-pencil activities. So, why consider writing instruction in a physical education class?

One reason is to break down the negative stereotypes about physical education, that thinking is rarely connected to physical activity. Writing, as a vehicle for thinking, could be a way for students to explore relationships between their minds and their bodies. A second reason is to help students think clearly about how physical activity develops lifelong fitness and health.

*Special thanks to Cindy Armbrustmacher, a physical education teacher.

The physical education teacher who created the following lesson was concerned about students going through the motions in physical education class without thinking about the implications of what they were doing. She observed many of her students eating junk food in and out of school. Many were over their recommended weight. Few exercised on their own. Concerns about what she observed led to this content objective:

Physical activity and healthy nutrition will give you a long life and a healthy lifestyle.

Or, stated as a central question:

How do people get healthy and stay that way?

The lesson described here (actually a series of lessons) was devoted to creating a better understanding of the relationship between physical activity, nutrition, and good health in a high school physical education class. To develop this understanding, the teacher decided to come up with a writing activity that, more generally, connected the head to the body and, more specifically, helped students use writing to consider how physical activity and good nutrition produce better health.

After considering a number of possibilities, the teacher came up with the idea of a *physical activity journal.* Students could use the physical activity journal to set personal goals, lay out strategy during competition, and visualize complex physical activities. An important goal was to get students to assess their own level of physical activity over a period of time (for example, counting up the hours of television-watching versus brisk walking) and then make some decisions about their fitness and health.

Building Background and Motivation

To prepare students, the teacher discussed the importance of keeping in good shape, including maintaining an ideal weight and getting enough exercise. She asked about difficulties in achieving fitness goals:

TEACHER: How do you know if you're getting enough exercise?
MIKE: I think I get too much sometimes.
TEACHER: What makes you say that?
MIKE: When we're out on the basketball court, it's easy to forget the time. All of a sudden, you look up and you feel wasted!
TEACHER: That's a good example of what we're talking about. Does anybody worry about not doing enough?
VALERIE: I work all the time and even though it feels busy, I don't feel like I'm exercising. I get too tired.
TEACHER: That's a good distinction between work and exercise. They're not always the same thing. James?
JAMES: I just love to eat!

Next, the teacher shared some of her own struggles:

TEACHER: I used to diet a lot. But I would go down and then I would go back up in my weight. It was really hard sometimes to tell if I was making progress.

After this initial brainstorming session, the teacher was ready to introduce her idea:

TEACHER: I'd like to try something with this class, where we keep track of our physical activities and what we eat for a period of time. We're all, even me, going to keep a physical activity journal. We'll try to solve this problem of not knowing just how much physical activity we are doing and whether or not we're taking good care of ourselves.

Now she was ready to talk with students about the content and processes that would support the use of the journals.

Developing Content and Process

The content of the journals was to be developed through a collaborative process. The class decided collectively what to write and then came together every Friday to compare and discuss what they had written.

Several accommodations were made for the physical education setting. It was decided that none of the writing would be done in the gym. The gym just wasn't conducive to writing. The teacher discussed setting aside a regular time at home or in a study hall for uninterrupted recording of both physical and nutritional activities. All agreed that they would get the most out of the journals if everyone invested some time. The teacher gave a brief and adapted view of writing processes, emphasizing the need to think before writing, to write quickly and purposefully, and to review to see if any ideas were left out or might need to be changed.

This physical education class was graded. Grades were usually based on attendance. Arrangements were made for students to receive credit for a set number of journal entries (daily for an "A," every other day for a "B," once per week for a "C"). Along with these external incentives, the teacher continually emphasized intrinsic rewards in terms of improved conditioning, weight control, and self-esteem.

Using her own journal entries, the teacher modeled for students the kinds of writing that were possible in the journals. She carefully recorded both the kinds and the duration of physical activity. She wrote down the kinds and quantity of food she ingested. She reflected on what the total picture meant for the health and fitness of her own body, telling about disappointments in downing a huge piece of cheesecake and victories in staying with an exercise routine.

When students came together to share their activity journals, they paired up and talked about their recent experiences. Many provided helpful hints to each other for exercise or diet. The teacher was able to assess informally the physical and health habits of her students and then plan and implement the appropriate kinds of physical activities for other class sessions in the gym.

Encouraging Independence

Through the activity journals, many students discovered some surprises about themselves. Some realized they were shoveling much more junk food into themselves than they previously thought, accompanied by very little exercise. Some discovered that they were getting a good amount of exercise, but their nutrition wasn't good enough to support all their physical activity. These students tended to feel tired all the time. Getting students to act on these realizations became the focus for encouraging independence.

The teacher suggested that some students might wish to continue the activity journals for the rest of the semester, to see if, acting on the self-awareness they now had, they might improve on their fitness. Other students, she suggested, might wish to devise and evaluate a plan for building lifelong fitness and use the activity journals to keep track of their progress. Students liked the idea of having options. By the end of the semester, students were using the activity journals not only to keep track of their own fitness, but also to interview family members about their own histories of physical activity and nutrition. It began to appear that even if not all students would continue to keep the journals beyond the class, most students had developed an ongoing concern with their own health and fitness.

SUMMARY

Through writing, students learn to generate their own knowledge and to communicate with a wide array of audiences both in school and out. Far too often, students are made to feel that teachers are the only ones who provide a purpose and an audience. This can lead to lifeless, mechanical writing. Ideally, writing provides students with a powerful vehicle for developing and responding to multiple purposes and audiences, in many different forms.

When teachers plan and implement writing instruction, they need to emphasize authentic writing tasks, shaped by subject-matter concerns. Attention to the design of writing assignments and to pre-writing activities helps students get started. As they write, teachers guide them, helping shape and direct the content and form. Revision and editing conferences encourage students to take the time to refine their writing. An emphasis on publication gives students reasons to write.

Following the principles and activities outlined in this chapter will not always be easy. But, as the physical education teacher's experience attests, the results can be rewarding with respect to the communication that blossoms in a content classroom.

SPECIAL PROJECTS

Course-Based

1. Design a writing assignment that focuses on an out-of-school audience. What special provisions must you make to help students complete this kind of

assignment? How will you (and/or students) evaluate what students produce? What kind(s) of feedback will you give students on their writing?

Field-Based

2. One of the challenges of teaching writing in school is to balance the need to give students plenty of specific feedback against the reality of large classroom numbers. With a class you are observing (or teaching) in mind, devise a plan for making sure that each student gets the needed feedback while using all available human resources (teacher and students) as well as techniques (for example, peer editing, writing conferences).

SUGGESTED READING

This book provides a research-based account of the state of writing in public schools:

APPLEBEE, A. (1981). *Writing in the secondary school.* Urbana, IL: National Council of Teachers of English.

These books provide practical information about teaching writing:

ATWELL, N. (1987). *In the middle.* Portsmouth, NH: Heinemann.

CALKINS, L. (1986). *The art of teaching writing.* Portsmouth, NH: Heinemann.

GRAVES, D. (1983). *Writing: Teachers and children at work.* Portsmouth, NH: Heinemann.

MURRAY, D. (1985). *A writer teaches writing.* Boston: Houghton Mifflin.

ROMANO, T. (1987). *Clearing the way: Working with teenage writers.* Portsmouth, NH: Heinemann.

TSCHUDI, S., & YATES, J. (1983). *Teaching writing in content areas: Senior high school.* Washington, DC: The National Education Association.

This book offers a comprehensive review of research on writing:

HILLOCKS, G. (1986). *Research on written composition.* Urbana, IL: ERIC Clearinghouse on Reading and Communication Skills, and the National Council of Teachers of English.

These books discuss recommendations for how teachers can respond to and evaluate student writing:

FREEDMAN, S. W. (1987). *Response to student writing.* Urbana, IL: National Council of Teachers of English.

GOODMAN, K., GOODMAN, Y., & HOOD, W. (1989). *The whole language evaluation book.* Portsmouth, NH: Heinemann.

PROBST, R. (1988). *Response and analysis: Teaching literature in junior and senior high school.* Portsmouth, NH: Heinemann.

This chapter gives a good description of ways authentic writing tasks shape thinking and learning:

HULL, G. (1989). Research on writing: Building a cognitive and social understanding of composing. In L. Resnick and L. Klopfer (Eds.), *Toward the thinking curriculum: Current cognitive research.* Alexandria, VA: Association for Supervision and Curriculum Development.

This is a good reference for both teachers and students when making editing decisions:

STRUNK, W., & WHITE, E. (1979). *The elements of style.* New York: Macmillan.

REFERENCES

APPLEBEE, A. (1981). *Writing in the secondary school.* Urbana, IL: National Council of Teachers of English.

APPLEBEE, A., LANGER, J., & MULLIS, I. (1986). *The writing report card: Writing achievement in American schools.* Princeton, NJ: Educational Testing Service.

BRITTON, J., BURGESS, T., MARTIN, N., MCLEOD, A., & ROSEN, A. (1986). *The development of writing abilities (11–18).* New York: Macmillan.

CALKINS, L. (1986). *The art of teaching writing.* Portsmouth, NH: Heinemann.

COLLINS, J. (1981). Speaking, writing and teaching for meaning. In B. Kroll & R. Vann (Eds.), *Exploring speaking-writing relationships: Connections and contrasts.* Urbana, IL: National Council of Teachers of English.

COOPER, C. (1977). Holistic evaluation of writing. In C. Cooper and L. Odell (Eds.), *Evaluating writing: Describing, measuring, judging.* Urbana, IL: National Council of Teachers of English.

CRAMER, R. (1982). Informal approaches to evaluating children's writing. In J. Pikulski & T. Shanahan (Eds.), *Approaches to the informal evaluation of reading.* Newark, DE: International Reading Association.

DIPARDO, A., & FREEDMAN, S. (1988). Peer response groups in the writing classroom. Theoretic foundations and new directions. *Review of Educational Research, 58,* 2, 119–150.

DRAPER V. (1979). *Formative writing: Writing to assist learning in all subject areas.* Berkeley: University of California, Berkeley, Bay Area Writing Project.

DUNN, S., FLORIO-RUANE, S., & CLARK, C. (1984). *The teacher as respondent to the high school writer* (Research Series No. 152). East Lansing: Michigan State University Institute for Research on Teaching.

ELBOW, P. (1973). *Writing without teachers.* New York: Oxford University Press.

ELBOW, P. (1981). *Writing with power.* New York: Oxford University Press.

FITZGERALD, J. (1987). Research on revision in writing. *Review of Educational Research, 57,* 4, 481–506.

FLOWER, L., HAYES, J., CAREY, L., SCHRIVER, K., & STRATMAN, J. (1986). Detection, diagnosis, and the strategies of revision. *College Composition and Communication, 37,* 1, 16–55.

FULWILER, T. (1986). Journals across the disciplines. In E. Dishner, T. Bean, J. Readance, & D. Moore (Eds.), *Reading in the content areas: Improving classroom instruction.* Dubuque, IA: Kendall-Hunt.

GRAVES, D. (1983). *Writing: Teachers & children at work.* Portsmouth, NH: Heinemann.

HARSTE, J., SHORT, K., & BURKE, C. (1988). *Creating classrooms for authors: The reading-writing connection.* Portsmouth, NH: Heinemann.

HEALY, M. K. (1980). *Using student writing response groups in the classroom.* Berkeley University of California, Berkeley, Bay Area Writing Project.

HILLOCKS, G. (1982). The interaction of instruction, teacher comment and revision in teaching the composing process. *Research in the Teaching of English, 16,* 261–278.

HULL, G. (1989). Research on writing: Building a cognitive and social understanding of composing. In L. Resnick & L. Klopfer (Eds.), *Toward the thinking curriculum: Current cognitive research.* Alexandria, VA: Association for Supervision and Curriculum Development.

JENKINS, C. (1986). The writing assignment: An obstacle or a vehicle? In E. Dishner, T. Bean, J. Readance, & D. Moore (Eds.), *Reading in the content areas: Improving classroom instruction.* Dubuque, IA: Kendall-Hunt.

LAMPERT, M. (1986). *Knowing, doing, and teaching multiplication* (Occasional Paper No. 97). East Lansing: Michigan State University, Institute for Research on Teaching.

LLOYD-JONES, R. (1977). Primary trait scoring. In C. Copper & L. Odell (Eds.), *Evaluating writing: Describing, measuring, judging.* Urbana, IL: National Council of Teachers of English.

MOORE, S. (1986). Revising writing in the content areas. In E. Dishner, T. Bean, J. Readance, & D. Moore (Eds.), *Reading in the content areas: Improving classroom instruction.* Dubuque, IA: Kendall-Hunt.

MURRAY, D. (1985). Teaching the other self. In T. Newkirk (Ed.), *To compose: Teaching writing in the high school.* Washington, DC: The National Institute of Education.

National Assessment of Educational Progress. (1981). *Reading, thinking and writing: Results from the 1979–80 national assessment of reading and literature* (Report No. 11-L-01). Denver: Educational Commission of the States.

NEWELL, G., SUSZYNSKI, K., & WEINGART, R. (1989). The effects of writing in a reader-based and text-based mode on students' understanding of two short stories. *Journal of Reading Behavior, 21,* 1, 37–58.

PARKER, R., & GOODKIN, V. (1987). *The consequences of writing.* Portsmouth, NH: Heinemann.

RASINSKI, T., & DEFORD, D. (1986). Students and their writing: Perceptions, motivations, and behaviors. In J. Niles & R. Lalik (Eds.), *Solving problems in literacy: Learners, teachers, and researchers.* Rochester, NY: The National Reading Conference.

ROMANO, T. (1987). *Clearing the way: Working with teenage writers.* Portsmouth, NH: Heinemann.

ROSAEN, C. (1990). Improving writing opportunities in elementary classrooms. *Elementary School Journal, 90,* 4, 419–434.

ROSENBLATT, L. (1978). *The reader, the text, the poem.* Carbondale: Southern Illinois University Press.

SCARDAMALIA, M., & BEREITER, C. (1986). Research on written composition. In M. Wittrock (Ed.), *Handbook of research on teaching.* New York: Macmillan.

SHELL, D., MURPHY, C., & BRUNING, R. (1989). Self-efficacy and outcome expectancy mechanisms in reading and writing achievement. *Journal of Educational Psychology, 81,* 1, 91–100.

SQUIRE, J. (1984). Composing and comprehending: Two sides of the same basic process. In J. Jensen (Ed.), *Composing and comprehending.* Urbana, IL: National Conference on Research in English, and the ERIC Clearinghouse on Reading and Communication Skills.

WILLINSKY, J. (1985). To publish and publish and publish. *Language Arts, 62,* 6, 619–623.

WOODLEY, J., & WOODLEY, C. (1989). Whole language, Texas style. In K. Goodman, Y. Goodman, & W. Hood (Eds.), *The whole language evaluation book.* Portsmouth: NH: Heinemann.

2:00 The bell rings. Students settle down and you start your discussion. Most students seem interested and you congratulate yourself on another good beginning.

2:15 Help! Students are restless. You try to insert questions into the discussion to get them involved. Several students are yawning, some are whispering.

2:20 You switch gears, getting students ready for a small-group discussion activity. Some students are staring out the window. You give students directions. They move into their small groups.

2:35 Time for students to report on what they have done. Several groups have still not completed the activity. You think, "Why is this taking them so long?"

2:42 With scant minutes left in the period, you try to wrap up the discussion.

2:45 The bell rings. Students stream out as you remind them about the homework. Another day over.

Lesson experienced recently in an English classroom.

11

Discussion

CHAPTER OBJECTIVES

After reading this chapter, you should be able to:

1. Describe the goals for discussion in terms of content, process, and motivation.

2. Explain how creating a classroom learning community can help foster effective discussion practices.

3. Plan and teach a lesson in which discussion skills and expectations are developed simultaneously with the teaching of subject-matter concepts.

RATIONALE

The description of a class period in the life of an English teacher illustrates why discussion is a difficult issue in most classrooms. The constraints of time and the need to cover content often deal a lethal blow to many meaningful discussions before they even get started. Another constraint on discussions is that they involve an entire range of communications skills. Teachers and students spend many hours developing and practicing ways to discuss.

It has become common lately to focus on classroom discussion only in terms of small-group, cooperative discussions. *Cooperative learning* is a form of discussion used with small groups (Johnson, 1981). The approach was developed in the mid-1970s and has grown in popularity, if not classroom practice, ever since. Because of gaps between ways some teachers currently teach (for instance, in rows, with teachers doing most of the talking) and what it takes to implement cooperative learning (teaching students how to work and discuss with one another), some teachers don't want to think about structuring small-group discussions. For some teachers, it is difficult to place greater responsibility for discussion on students, to let go of the traditional teacher-as-authority role in favor of teacher-as-facilitator (Conley, 1987). Unfortunately, because cooperative learning has been so strongly identified as *the* classroom discussion technique, the rejection of cooperative learning sometimes evolves into a disavowel of *all* discussion techniques.

Classroom discussions are one of the more important ways students come to understand a subject. Discussions serve diverse social as well as academic purposes. Through discussion, teachers and students establish a supportive environment for

CHAPTER ORGANIZER

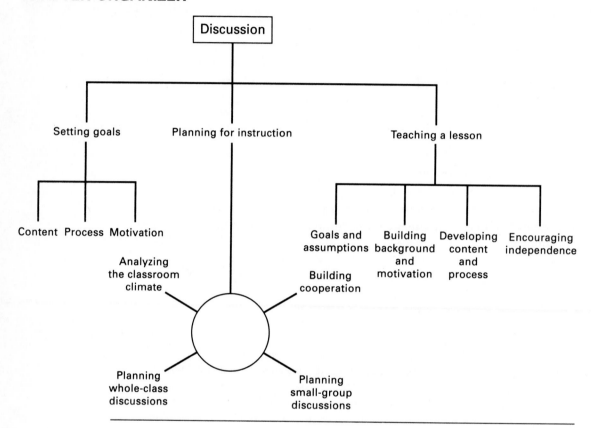

learning. They come to agreement on rules and expectations for how things are to be learned and how people in the classroom are supposed to treat each other. Through discussion, students reveal themselves, and teachers can build bridges from what students know to what they need to know both inside and outside of school.

The forms of discussion available to teachers are diverse. When students are new to a topic or the topic is unusually technical or unfamiliar, it makes sense to lecture. In other cases, small-group, cooperative discussions are called for because the content is ripe for students to disagree, read, and write together to come to consensus. Other times, students discuss in pairs or they work alone and do not discuss at all, depending on the content and processes under study. Ideally, classrooms should engage in diverse forms of discussion across the year, changing from time time according to needs that emerge in the curriculum.

Research has identified discussion practices that make a difference in the quality and cohesiveness that develops within large and small groups. Not surprisingly, effective discussion begins with the teacher. Recall from Chapter 7 that recitation is the most typical form of classroom discussion. During recitation, teachers ask a question, a student responds, and the teacher either asks another question or offers feedback. An assumption about recitation has been that the student answering questions as well as students who are listening to the exchange are able to learn from the exchange. Unfortunately, there is no evidence that students who listen can internalize concepts as well as those who present the concepts themselves. Low achievers especially do not do well with whole-class discussions because they are adept at disengaging themselves from the class (Mills et al., 1980).

Whether a teacher adopts an authoritarian versus a more democratic style also influences the quality of discussion. Authoritarian teachers exercise and maintain power in the classroom by being serious and by making and enforcing rules. They can even create the image of a well-ordered, pleasant classroom, despite the fact that students can feel alienated and do not see themselves as participants. This kind of environment severely limits the potential for students to learn and grow from working with many types of individuals, a skill students need to thrive both in and out of school.

Teachers who are more democratic, on the other hand, tend to be adept at giving students a sense of belonging during discussions. These teachers often discuss the importance of participation, they talk about what to do when classroom conflicts arise, and they are in a better position than their more authoritarian counterparts to teach students adaptability when working with different types of people. Their classrooms may be noisy and not so neat and orderly, and there can be tension and stress. When given opportunities to learn how to work and discuss with one another, students need to practice responsibility and they will make mistakes and experience difficulty in controlling their own behavior. The payoff comes through persistence. Teachers who invest the time and energy in helping students learn how to discuss and cooperate will produce students who are well-prepared to face the academic and social challenges of the future (Delamont, 1984).

Students are important players when it comes to the quality of classroom discussion. Most classrooms are competitive, and students tend to rank each other both academically (with respect to success in a subject) and socially (according to perceptions of attractiveness or popularity). Students who are ranked high by their peers tend to dominate discussion. Students with a lesser rank tend to be passive (Cohen, 1986).

When they have multiple opportunities to talk and to interact during many types of discussions, students learn. Those who do not talk will not learn as much or as well as those who have more frequent opportunities to participate. Many teachers want equal opportunities for discussion and learning in their classrooms. Unfortunately, the stereotypes that students apply to one another often get in the way (for example, "Let's not listen to her. She never gets the right answer!"). Often, these stereotypes go unchallenged. Sometimes, teachers unintentionally support the stereotypes by calling on popular students or students who always seem to have the answer. When stereotypes are allowed to prevail, classroom discussion only enforces the negative notions students carry about one another.

Teachers who commit to full participation in classroom discussion must also be committed to breaking stereotypes. Students learn how to learn from each other. Rather than using discussion as a way to rank-order and divide their students, teachers can use discussion as a vehicle for pulling various groups together, helping students find strength and insight in their own differences.

This chapter is devoted to discussion practices that encourage full participation. It describes the goals for discussion and explains planning and teaching decisions underlying different kinds of discussion.

SETTING GOALS

Goals for discussion consist of developing a good environment for talking and learning about school subjects, building awareness of how to work with others, and encouraging positive relationships and a sense of belonging.

Content Goals

The content goals for discussion are to: (1) use discussion to teach subject-matter concepts, and (2) create a better understanding of diversity in thought and opinion.

In a book about classroom discussion, Alvermann, Dillon, and O'Brien (1987) describe three different types of discussion. (One type consists of *subject mastery*, helping students comprehend the content of a lesson.) To foster subject mastery, teachers alert students to important terms, they guide students through the learning of new concepts, and they help students apply what they have learned. These discussions tend to start with a focus on the content but broaden to consider implications of the content in the outside world.

A second type of discussion is *issue-oriented*. During issue-oriented discussions, students listen to understand others' beliefs and feelings about a topic. They analyze and evaluate, sometimes changing their own beliefs and feelings as a result. During these discussions, the content tends to function as a springboard for talking about issues that emerge. These discussions help students appreciate not only the perspectives of the authors they are reading, but also the perspectives of students and others around them.

A third type of discussion engages students in *problem-solving*. Recall from Chapter 8 that problem-solving is a specific form of reasoning in which students read and study in-depth about a problem and devise a number of possible solutions. The problems students talk about are embedded in the content but, ideally, also have genuine linkages to the real world. For example, students might start by thinking about a problem raised by the author of a text, and, through discussion, come to understand how that problem affects everyone at some point in life.

All three forms of discussion are powerful tools in helping students learn content and learn about each other. Through these forms of discussion, teachers can decide on a particular emphasis, whether on subject-matter, issues that affect students personally, or both. These decisions are facilitated when teachers have a clear focus on the content. In other words, it helps to have a content objective in mind (see Chapter 5) before making decisions about discussion. For example, when the content objective tends to be technical or full of unfamiliar concepts, a discussion emphasizing subject mastery might be the best approach. If, on the other hand, the content objective raises for students a host of personally interesting issues, then an issue-oriented discussion might be appropriate.

In issue-oriented discussions, students share beliefs and feelings about a topic

Elizabeth Crews/The Image Works

Finally, if the content objective poses or suggests problems both in and out of school, teachers may want to emphasize problem-solving during discussion.

Process Goals

The process goal for discussion is to help students understand how to "do" discussions, talking and working together. Figure 11.1 identifies the discussion processes related to this goal.

At the beginning of the year, students enter classrooms with their own ideas about discussion. Often, the understanding students have is different from what the teacher wants or expects. For example, students may be used to insulting each other, especially in situations in which someone is succeeding or receiving praise. This can make it difficult, if not impossible, to hold most kinds of classroom discussions. A teacher could plan a lesson dealing with interesting and controversial issues only to have the lesson fall apart because students do not know how to discuss in a way that is supportive of one another.

Sometimes, discussion practices at home and at school dramatically differ. For example, Heath (1982) studied discussion accompanying storybook reading at home and compared those discussions with discussion practices at school. In three communities, Heath found three separate types of discussion: (1) a "mainstream" pattern in which parents use questions to help children relate what they already know to what they are

FIGURE 11.1

Discussion Processes

Giving ideas and opinions

Offering support for ideas and opinions

Being an active listener

Speaking in turns, giving others a chance

---

reading, (2) a "passive" pattern in which parents lead children to their (the parents) own personal meaning, and (3) a "participatory" pattern in which parents tell stories and children are encouraged to tell stories of their own or sing songs.

Knowing that these patterns exist helps teachers make good judgments about how to help students build on their home-based discussion experiences. Through their parents, some students have learned a great deal about how to discuss in school. They have learned to answer questions that require connections and explanations and they know how to listen. For these students, discussion practices are consistent between home and school, and teachers need simply to reinforce the processes that parents have already taught.

Students from passive or participatory discussion backgrounds, however, present some unique challenges. Students used to passive discussion at home can be reticent or withdrawn during classroom discussions. They usually have not been exposed to many different forms of discussion. Students used to participatory discussions at home can be competitive and overly aggressive during classroom discussion. They can be labeled discipline problems early in school, when the real issue is that home and school discussion practices differ. This is unfortunate because these students may have learned to be unusually creative with language.

Teachers need to talk with these students about how to engage in discussion processes. Passive students should be taught how to offer and support opinions, and they need to experience a variety of successful discussions. Participatory students who are overly aggressive must learn to adapt their creativity in language to talking about books and other learning materials in school.

Teachers also need to reflect carefully about their own understanding and application of classroom discussion processes. For many teachers, it is easy to offer opinions and ideas but not so easy to be an active listener or even take turns with students (Conley, 1986). The more teachers and students communicate with one another about discussion processes, the more likely it is that students will become successful learners.

Motivation Goals

Motivation goals for discussion are to develop in students (1) better self-understanding of how they work with others, (2) a sense of belonging, and (3) more positive whole-class and intergroup relations.

Teachers build in students greater self-understanding and a sense of belonging by striving for a classroom *learning community* (Putnam & Burke, 1991). A learning community is an open, active, and fair environment in which to learn. Teachers who are successful in creating a classroom learning community are directly responsible for what happens in their classrooms, yet their role is distinctly different from the traditional, authoritarian role of teachers who spend most of their time chastising students and maintaining order. Rather than focusing on how to react to student disruptions, the learning community teacher proactively builds and maintains a support system. Discipline *is* part of a learning community teacher's job, but the emphasis is on supporting students in their learning, and dealing with disruptions quickly and fairly so that instruction can continue.

Classroom learning communities share the following characteristics (from Putnam & Burke, 1991):

1. Sense of common needs and purposes

2. View of peers as colleagues and collaborators

3. Questioning attitude, a desire to embrace rather than avoid problems

4. Recognition of similarities in other groups

5. Reflection of past actions

6. Value placed on helping and being helped

7. Celebration of accomplishments

When teachers incorporate these principles into their daily instruction, the students' lives are enhanced both inside and outside the classroom, as students learn about themselves, how to work with one another, and how to draw strength from each other's differences.

More positive whole-class and intergroup relations come from experience with specific kinds of group experiences. In classroom-based research, it has been found that cooperative groupings promote better social relationships, improved self-esteem, and higher achievement in comparison with competitive groupings and individualized work (Slavin, 1980). *Cooperation* exists in a group (whole-class or small-group) when assignments are set up so that students succeed only by helping each other succeed (as in a relay race or many kinds of dramatic productions). *Competition* exists when assignments are set up so that some students succeed only when others do not (such as when students are given a higher grade for handing in an assignment first and a lower grade for handing in an assignment last). In many classrooms, competitive assignments outweigh the cooperative ones (Johnson et al., 1981).

When competition reigns, students can become aggressive toward one another, striving to beat each other rather than learning how to work together. To be sure, students need practice with competition to survive in today's competitive society. Knowing how to work cooperatively, however, not only helps students feel better about themselves and others, but also prepares them for the teamwork and creative problem-solving so important for their future success.

PLANNING FOR INSTRUCTION

The movement to examine classroom discussion is still fairly young. For quite some time, the emphasis has been on developing discussion techniques. More recently, the focus has shifted to finding ways to adapt various techniques to classroom practice. The following sections are organized to deal with four topics related to adaptation. The first two sections describe ways to analyze the existing classroom climate and build cooperation. The second two sections deal with adaptations for whole-class and small-group discussions. As you read, think about adaptations you will need to consider for your students and content area.

Analyzing the Classroom Climate

Classroom climate is a term used to describe important environmental variables that shape the tasks of teaching and learning (Doyle, 1986). Classroom variables include the extent to which teachers and students share common understandings about discussion and whether cooperative tasks and relationships are valued and practiced. Classroom climate has the greatest impact on teachers' and students' perceptions, their reasons for working (or not working) together, and their basic ability to have classroom discussions.

Schmuck and Schmuck (1988) have made some useful recommendations for analyzing the climate of a classroom. Through observations, surveys, and personal interviews, teachers can explore student perceptions about classroom climate. Figure 11.2 presents some questions that could be used by teachers to explore the climate of their classrooms.

An advantage of using these questions is that teachers and students can find out just how close they are to establishing a classroom learning community. Teachers and their students may already have a sense of common needs and purposes but might discover that they need to do some work on recognizing and appreciating diversity or that they need to explore or return to thinking about what it means to help one another.

The disadvantage of these questions is that the answers may reveal a wide disparity in their student perceptions about cooperation and what it takes to have a positive classroom climate. Teachers who fear this outcome may ignore the answers or simply not ask the questions. In addition, students' perceptions about classroom climate can differ markedly from those of their teachers. The difference in teacher and student perceptions is one reason for the emergence of a *hidden curriculum* in many classrooms, where students and teachers go through the motions of learning but no real learning takes place.

To turn a negative, the fear of what students think, into a positive, avoiding the pitfalls of a hidden curriculum, teachers should talk with students about the issues raised by the questions in Figure 11.2. By talking explicitly about classroom climate issues, teachers and

students with note-taking skills (Chapter 9), or guide students through the writing process (Chapter 10). Whole-class discussion is for generating ideas, providing transitions, and forming conclusions. Whole-class discussion is most appropriate for uncovering misconceptions, demonstrating skills and procedures, and covering some fairly simple facts or concepts in a short amount of time. Whole-class discussion alone is generally *not* effective as a vehicle for covering complex content in-depth. In more complex situations, it is better to combine whole-class discussion with small-group and individual work.

The success of a whole-class discussion depends on the level of cooperation teachers and students have been able to establish as well as the diversity of students in terms of their knowledge and beliefs (Alvermann, Dillon, & O'Brien, 1987). Substantial diversity often means that teachers need to work harder at managing the classroom and ensuring that every student has a chance to participate. While a classroom filled with eager students possessing a variety of ideas may seem like a teacher's dream, this situation requires special plans to manage and process all the information these students generate, and a great deal of time to develop whole-class cooperation.

A lack of diversity in students means that some kinds of whole-class discussion could fall flat. For example, one social studies teacher tried to hold an issue-oriented discussion in a class where students held similar views on capital punishment. The discussion faltered within a scant four or five minutes after nearly all the students agreed that it is best to "fry" inmates on death row. The discussion became more lively only after the teacher offered

During whole class discussions, teachers have to work extra hard to ensure every student gets a chance to participate

Sven Martson/Comstock

some examples of how capital punishment was applied mistakenly. Though whole-class discussion with docile students may seem more manageable and appealing, it also means careful planning for when discussions run dry.

The next sections offer specific ways to plan for the success of your whole-class discussions.

Organizing for Whole-Class Discussion   Classrooms need to be organized intentionally for whole-class discussion. Making a map of the classroom is one of the best ways to do this. Figure 11.3 presents "maps" reflecting some ways classrooms are typically organized.

Choosing among these configurations involves some thoughtful decision-making. These are advantages and disadvantages associated with each type of configuration. In choosing the right configuration for you and your class, it is important to consider options for whole-class discussion (there will probably be a mix of teacher- and student-directed discussion) and the amount of eye contact and mobility available to teachers and students. If the teacher can't move around the room, for example, it becomes difficult to talk with or listen to students in the farthest reaches of the classroom. If students are placed in a configuration where productive talk with one another is nearly impossible, then options for whole-class discussion are limited to teacher talk, and discipline problems often

FIGURE 11.3

Some Common Ways of Organizing for Whole-Class Discussion

Traditional

```
x x x x x x
x x x x x x
x x x x x x
x x x x x x
x x x x x x
x x x x x x
      T
```

Aisle in the middle

```
x x x      x x x
x x x      x x x
x x x   T  x x x
x x x      x x x
x x x      x x x
x x x      x x x
```

Horseshoe or semicircle

```
      x x x x x x
   x x              x
  x                  x
 x                    x
x                      x
x                      x
x                      x
x                      x
x          T           x
```

Lab or shop tables

```
x x x    x x x    x x x

x x x    x x x    x x x

x x x    x x x    x x x
          T
```

Key

T = Teacher
x = Students
▬ = Blackboard

emerge. The teacher should be able to observe students easily from all areas of the room. Students should be able to see the teacher and any frequently used equipment (blackboards and screens) or displays (maps and charts) (Emmer et al., 1984).

In the *traditional* configuration, everyone's attention is directed to the front of the room. Teachers can make eye contact when asking questions and they can watch for disruptions. However, this configuration also makes it possible for some students to hide from the teacher, "molding" their bodies to the backs of the students ahead of them. In addition, it is difficult for students to talk with one another productively (though many find ways to turn around and talk with one another *un*productively). The traditional configuration limits opportunities for students to direct questions or responses to other members of the class.

Some teachers choose to divide the class into two sections with an *aisle in the middle*. There are two variations on this configuration: students face the front of the room or they face the aisle. This configuration opens up the front and back of the room for whole-class discussion. The teacher can move readily from the front blackboard or overhead projector to the back, and it is easier to make eye contact than in the traditional configuration. Disadvantages include the following: skirmishes could develop among students who face into the aisle, some students could withdraw from the teacher or from other students, and, if the class is especially large, it can be difficult for the teacher to move around the sides of the classroom.

The *horseshoe*, or *semicircle*, configuration has many advantages. Eye contact is possible between the teacher and students, and students can see each other. Because the class is focused both inward and to the front of the class, a combination of closeness and cooperation is promoted. Students have fewer options to withdraw, which can make some students uncomfortable, though others appreciate being able to participate more readily. A disadvantage of the semicircle is that it can be hard to manage. While some students see this configuration as an opportunity to be productive during discussion, others may see it as a way to avoid work. A reason for this is that the semicircle represents a radical departure from the traditional configuration to which so many students have become accustomed. Developing some expectations with students for how they work and discuss in the semicircle can help offset this problem.

For science or vocational education, the *lab*, or *shop table*, configuration is a real asset. Since students are already seated at worktables, transitions are quicker and easier in comparison with some whole-class settings where students move from chairs and desks to workstations around the room. However, for teachers in other areas, such as English, mathematics, or social studies, lab tables can be a miserable experience. Since the tables are affixed to the floor, there are no options for altering the whole-class configuration. The lab tables tend to create small groups within the whole-class setting; students may interact readily with one another at the expense of whole-class discussions.

The configuration that is best for a class depends on what a teacher plans to do with students during whole-class discussion and the kind of environment the teacher wants to create. The teacher must choose carefully, because the configuration a teacher selects is the foundation for successful whole-class discussion. Some teachers alter the classroom configuration throughout the year as expectations become more established and cooperation makes some configurations more possible.

Developing Whole-Group Expectations   Once decisions have been made about the appropriate configuration for whole-class discussions, teachers need to think about activities for developing whole-class group expectations. The goal of these activities is to create both a sense of belonging and an understanding for how work is accomplished during whole-class discussion.

Schmuck and Schmuck (1988) describe orientation activities that can foster whole-group development. The activities are:

1. Students form two circles, one inside the other. The circles walk slowly in reverse directions. As students pass one another, they say a brief word of greeting to break the ice.

2. Students locate someone in class they know and they talk about something they have in common. Next, students find someone they do not know or someone about whom they are curious and they find out a few things about them. Finally, students locate someone with whom they would like to work and they talk about previous classroom experiences (some examples) when working together was especially positive or rewarding.

3. Students complete a series of simple tasks (such as introducing themselves to one another, filling out forms) in pairs or small groups. Change the pairing or group membership as each task changes and have students introduce and say something about themselves with each change. Talk with students about their experiences. Did some students or groups communicate acceptance or rejection? Discuss what it means to feel a sense of belonging or rejection in a class. Plan with students how the class can develop a sense of belonging for themselves and any new members.

4. Students prepare a biography of another student in the class. The whole class works together to prepare an interview format from which the biographies are written. Students pair off with one another to interview and prepare biographies. This activity culminates in a booklet reflecting the class biography.

Developing expectations for how work is accomplished involves setting norms. Recall that norms are expectations for how the class is run. The key to norm development is to encourage students to invest in the behaviors that will support whole-class discussion. Norms for whole-class discussion include:

- Everyone will have a chance to speak.
- Everyone has the responsibility to listen.
- Each student will respect the other's opinions.
- Everyone will raise hands and take turns.

Early in the year, teachers need to introduce these norms and talk with students about why they are necessary. Rather than lecturing students, it is best to get them involved in coming up with positive norms, raising practical examples of what happens when discussions and other classroom activities are not rule-governed (students cut each other off, someone has a good idea that is never communicated, the need of the class to take advantage of everyone's ideas, and even safety concerns). Some teachers place these norms on a large piece of paper for reference throughout the year. Others have students sign a contract stating their agreement with class discussion rules.

A number of activities can be used to practice and reinforce the norms for whole-class discussion. For example, teachers can have students paraphrase a speaker's last point before beginning a new point. This will not only slow the pace of a discussion to manageable levels, but also help students actively listen to what others are saying. It is also helpful to role-play situations in which whole-class norms are needed or typically break down. As the year progresses, students can take responsibility for planning and conducting mini-, whole-class discussions. After each of these experiences, it is important to talk about what it is like to participate in or manage large groups so that everyone feels a sense of belonging (Schmuck & Schmuck, 1988).

Conflicts will emerge. Students will forget to take turns; they will cut each other off in midsentence. Some will pursue their own interests, talking or giggling among themselves in the middle of a discussion. Resist the urge to clamp down on students, since this can reverse the process of norm development begun earlier in the year. If whole-class discussion norms are developed collaboratively and teachers discipline students autocratically, the result can be a power struggle that continues throughout the year. Instead, it is better to talk with students during orientation about what to do when conflicts emerge and be persistent in reminding students about the norms and how they relate to what is happening currently. For example:

TEACHER: I see that you (two students) are talking with one another without being a
    part of our discussion. What rules did we agree we would follow for our
    discussions?
JEREMY: Everybody should participate.
TEACHER: That's right. Now, we can't continue unless you decide to participate with
    us. You need to make a choice about whether or not you want to be part of our
    discussion, and that means whether or not you want to be part of our class.
    What do you want to do?
JEREMY: We'll participate.

Keep in mind that this sort of exchange does not happen casually. It is built on mutual agreement between teachers and students on how the class will run its own discussions. If orientation and norm development activities have been successful, a teacher can rely on substantial amounts of peer pressure and personal responsibility to resolve these conflicts and continue the process of building group expectations.

Managing Whole-Class Discussion   There are many tips or techniques that can ease the task of managing whole-class discussion. The concern here is not only for holding a well-organized, cohesive discussion. Teachers also need to consider ways to ensure broad participation and adapt discussions to the content being covered.

One of the more important techniques is to use a seating chart. Seating charts are invaluable for learning students' names and for keeping track of patterns of involvement. Some teachers ditto several copies of the seating chart for each class. Whenever a teacher calls on a student or a student answers a question, the teacher places a mark next to the student's name. Using this system periodically, the teacher can detect whether students are getting more versus fewer opportunities to participate in comparison with others. This can be particularly helpful in cases where some students tend to withdraw from instruction.

Guiding and shaping discussion takes a certain amount of forethought. Preparing discussion questions ahead of time and developing study guides with discussion in mind are ways to plan for whole-class discussion. It sometimes helps to try out discussion questions on someone before using them with students. A friend or spouse can react to the task you are about to spring on students. For example, if you plan to have students brainstorm about concepts like "justice" or "revenge," ask a friend how he or she might respond to those concepts. The response can give a rough indication of what students might say and how you will need to respond.

Other factors to consider involve student deviations from a topic, particularly when excitement is high. Changing the focus or pace of a discussion usually helps with this problem. Teachers can use questions to direct students back to the topic or they can slow the pace to refocus.

Teachers should also think carefully about the number and types of questions they ask. Teachers have a tendency to ask too many questions when one good discussion question may be all that is necessary (Dillon, 1984). With too many questions, a teacher may feel greater pressure to cover content and could inadvertently forget about students. Teachers should also use a variety of questions, noting whether students are well- or ill-prepared to answer them. Discipline problems that emerge during discussion could be due to students not knowing how to answer a teacher's questions. If this is the case, it would be wise to spend time talking about questions and how they fit into a discussion (see Chapter 6).

Finally, teachers should practice *wait time* during whole-class discussion. Research has shown that when teachers wait three to five seconds after asking a question, it gives students the time they need to process the question and think about an answer (Tobias, 1982). With wait time, teachers get more higher-level answers, and more answers from a broader range of students. In addition, students appear more confident in their responses, they interact more with other students, and they ask more questions on their own (Rowe, 1974).

Reflection and Evaluation of Whole-Class Discussion   Another consideration for whole-class discussion involves *reflection* and *evaluation*. Since whole-class discussion is based on cooperation, it is best to engage students in these activities.

To accomplish this, teachers can ask themselves some of the questions they used to analyze the classroom environment: "How did it go?" "How often did students talk or listen to one another?" Teachers can also use students to evaluate interaction patterns, asking questions such as: "Were some students called on more or less than others?" These questions can help teachers provide opportunities for response that are more evenly dispersed.

Alvermann, Dillon, & O'Brien (1987) have developed the idea of a *bipolar evaluation* for discussions. The idea is based on research in twenty-four content area classrooms. To use the evaluation, teachers and students circle the response that seems most appropriate for what happened during a discussion. Some items are materials-based (How well is the textbook being used?). Other items focus more on the behavior of participants in the discussion, the degree of fairness in a teacher's calling pattern, and the extent to which students feel supported by the teacher and other students.

Figure 11.4 contains one example of a bipolar evaluation for a whole-class discussion. Try using this evaluation as a jumping-off point for reflecting with students on progress in learning how to do whole-class discussion.

FIGURE 11.4

Evaluating Whole-Class Discussion

Directions: Circle the sentences that best describe what happens during our discussion.

What we read is used to make a point when we discuss.	What we read is rarely mentioned.
We ask questions about the text and answer them by reading or paraphrasing from the text.	The text is mentioned, but we never look in the text to ask or answer questions.
During discussions, we get to talk about what we know.	During discussions, we talk only about what is in the book.
If we do not understand a question, our teacher repeats the question or says it in a different way.	If we do not understand a question, the question is never repeated or explained.
Our teacher tries to call on everyone.	Our teacher calls only on favorite students.
When we answer a question well, our teacher lets us know.	When we answer a question well, our teacher hardly ever tells us that we did well.
I am very comfortable answering most any kind of question during our discussions.	When we have our discussions, I am always afraid I will be called on.
When we discuss in class, I can count on other students to help and support me.	When we discuss in class, I am afraid of what other students might think of me.

Planning Small-Group Discussion

Teachers should consider several factors before deciding to use small-group discussion (Cohen, 1986). First, learning or curriculum tasks should involve thinking on a conceptual level as opposed to memorizing facts or learning a procedure. Curriculum tasks that support small-group discussion are challenging, typically allow for more than one answer or more than one way to solve a problem, encourage different students to make different contributions, and involve communication through reading, writing, speaking, or listening. Tasks that do not support small-group discussion are just the opposite: there is usually only one right answer, the task can be completed satisfactorily by one person, or it involves memorization or routine learning. Given this description, a task involving controversy, like studying how statistics are used to mislead, might be good for a small-group discussion; having students define vocabulary words would not.

A second consideration for small-group discussion concerns whether teachers have prepared their students and provided them with the resources necessay to complete small-group discussion assignments successfully. *Preparation* includes developing classroom cooperation, making sure students have the appropriate intellectual and social skills for group work. *Resources* include legible instructional materials and good instructions.

There are many other factors to consider. There are many forms of small-group discussion; teachers need to make decisions about choosing the method, organizing the classroom, determining membership, developing group expectations, and managing and evaluating group work. Decisions based on each of these issues are addressed in the following sections.

Choosing a Method for Small-Group Discussion   Research over the past ten to fifteen years has identified and developed at least four different types of cooperative, small-group discussion. The type teachers choose depends on their particular goals and purposes, as well as the other forms of instruction that have been chosen (such as whole-class discussion or various kinds of classroom work and tasks). The methods available for small-group discussion are:

Student Teams—Achievement Divisions (STAD).   The teacher presents a lesson on some topic, and students work in teams to help each other master the content (Slavin, 1988). Teams consist of high-, average-, and low-achieving students. They help each other by discussing concepts, drilling each other, working problems, and comparing answers. Following team study, students take individual quizzes or tests. After the first week, during which a base score is obtained, average scores for each individual are calculated. Gains in each student's quiz score for a particular week above his or her average score are also calculated. For example, a student whose average is 80 but who scores a 90 has a gain of ten points for a given week.

The amount an individual contributes to his or her team is determined by the amount the student's quiz score exceeds her or her average. Students earn one point for their group, up to a maximum of ten points, for every point they go over their personal average. Every student has a chance to contribute to the group's success. Because the group interaction—students helping one another—is the vehicle for achieving success, conditions are created for cooperation. Teachers often award certificates of achievement based on the successful performance of various teams.

ANNA: We compared their reasons so we could decide who is right.

TEACHER: That's right. That's how we settle disagreements in our groups. We listen to everyone's opinion and reasons and we decide.

Eventually, through exchanges like this one, students gain an awareness of how to solve their own problems during small-group discussion. As students become more capable, teachers gradually "fade" into the background (see Chapter 5), monitoring and offering support when needed (Barnes & Todd, 1977).

Teachers need also to help students with the pacing of their discussions. Giving students time limits (which should be flexible) and designating a timekeeper are ways to pace the group. Inevitably, some groups will finish discussing before others. The first job is to find out if the groups who are finished have completed all their tasks and are ready for what will happen when the whole class reconvenes (for example, reporting back to the class on their group's deliberations). Next, teachers need to provide options: talking quietly, moving on to some new work, or even observing another group in action, without interfering. Avoid giving students busywork to keep them occupied. If students perceive they are being penalized for finishing early, small-group discussion will increase in length but not necessarily improve in quality. Be ready with some positive alternatives for when students finish discussing productively.

Reflecting on and Evaluating Small-Group Discussion   One of the first rules for reflecting on small-group discussion is to use every available opportunity to point out when quality work in groups has led to deeper understandings and better cooperation. Praise can go a long way in motivating students and reinforcing small-group expectations.

With small-group discussion, it is important to integrate reflection with evaluation. Students are almost always concerned about grades, and it is not uncommon for teachers embarking on small-group discussion to hear the refrain "Are we getting graded for this?" Some teachers choose to respond with grades for group work or even prizes for group cooperation (Vacca, 1977). The criterion for grades or prizes is often how well students address the norms for small-group discussion. Some teachers develop expectations and grade or reward students without offering opportunities for students to reflect on their own performance. When this happens, students cannot be expected to improve and refine their group discussion skills. If, on the other hand, teachers integrate grades or rewards with reflection, students are held accountable and also receive feedback they can use for improvement.

How does an integrated approach to small-group reflection and evaluation work? Figure 11.8 shows a simple checklist (adapted from Morris, 1977). Teachers can copy checklists like this one for each classroom group and then attach the checklists to a clipboard. While monitoring, teachers fill out a checklist for each group, making brief comments. Teachers can assign point values to each of the criteria (for example, twenty-five points apiece for each question/item on the checklist, and partial or full credit depending on how students are performing). To engage students in reflection, the final step is to hand the checklist to the group for further discussion, problem-solving, and refinement.

FIGURE 11.8

Checklist for Reflection on and Evaluation of Small-Group Discussion

Group members: _____

	Yes	No
Did everyone get a chance to talk?	_____	_____
Were group members listening to each other?	_____	_____
Were group members asking questions?	_____	_____
Did group members give reasons for ideas?	_____	_____

Some teachers prefer not to grade, wishing instead to communicate that small-group discussion is a reward in and of itself. For these teachers, small-group reflection is still a priority. In this context, the checklist becomes a vehicle for students to rate and discuss their own performance without having to depend on the teacher's observations.

SPECIAL CONSIDERATIONS

Ensuring broad participation—in cooperation and in different forms of discussion—has been a theme of this chapter. Making it happen requires attention to some special issues.

Teachers are responsible for creating conditions that encourage participation. Calling on some students and not others, and allowing students to call out answers at random are two ways teachers may inhibit full student involvement. Using a seating chart to monitor student participation patterns and teaching students about cooperation are two ways to build an environment for whole-class discussion.

In small-group discussion, teachers may experience anxiety over allowing students to take more responsibility for their own learning. This anxiety often emerges in situations where teachers and/or students are inexperienced with group work or a teacher's style has tended to be more authoritarian in the past. This problem is resolved mainly by working through the stages for building cooperation. As students grow in their discussion skills, teachers' anxiety decreases and they can begin to "let go," gradually transferring some of the control to students.

Another set of issues involves students. Some students refuse to participate in discussion. Forcing students to become involved can undermine cooperation. Students are only too quick to note contradictions set up when teachers say "I want to give everyone a say in what we do here, and I am going to make sure everybody does it." At the same time, it becomes nearly impossible to build a sense of a classroom learning community if some students do not participate.

Solutions to this dilemma lie in finding out causes and providing options. Some students may be new to a school or class and may need support in becoming a part of the classroom. Other students feel separated on the basis of low status—students reject them or treat them poorly because of low achievement or their social or ethnic backgrounds. Students who feel isolated can be brought into discussions gradually through the process of developing norms. Almost every student has felt new to a group at some point. Talking about those experiences helps unify a class in identifying with feelings of being isolated. This makes it possible to brainstorm ways everyone—the teacher as well as students—can encourage and support involvement.

Give reluctant students time to observe discussions, having them do the same work as students in small groups but without benefit of the discussion. Talk with them about the advantages of being in the group, and encourage them to involve themselves when they are ready. Given the interest and controversy that often emerges in small groups, even the most reluctant students will join in and participate.

TEACHING A LESSON*

In this section, a lesson in high school music is described. Unlike previous lessons, this lesson focuses more on developing group processes than on building an understanding of content. Read and reflect on this lesson carefully as you consider your own approach to classroom discussion.

Goals and Assumptions

Both early and older adolescents love to tease one another over their performance in just about any endeavor. This can be particularly true in a music class, where some students may be accustomed to musical performance and presentations but most students are only used to listening to the radio or concerts and not performing themselves. The central goal of this lesson was: to get students comfortable with talking about, if not performing, music in front of their peers. The teacher decided to address this goal through a combination of group development activities and rich curriculum involving comparisons of old and new music, in-depth studies of compositions and the life histories of composers, as well as translations of older music and different styles (for example, marches and operas) into newer compositions (disco, rock and roll, rap).

Twenty-eight tenth- and eleventh-grade students were in the class. They were taking the class as an elective.

*Special thanks to Bill Hare, a music teacher.

Building Background and Motivation

The teacher began by discussing the curriculum he had planned. Once he laid out all the possibilities, he asked students for their input. The class came up with an impressive list of possible activities, including musical presentations based on their favorite musical group or artist and even vocal performances.

To continue building background for the lesson, the teacher posed a problem:

TEACHER: These are some great ideas. But, if we're going to accomplish any of them, we're going to have to think about how we're going to do it—in other words, how we're going to treat each other when we're doing different kinds of performances, presentations. . . .

SUSAN: We'll treat each other OK!

TEACHER: I'm sure everyone will try to. But let's work on some agreements that will help us make sure everyone feels comfortable doing what we have planned.

Susan is motivated, but the teacher can't be sure yet that all the students have developed either the awareness or the skills to support the activities. At this stage the teacher avoids being negative.

Developing Content and Process

Instead, the teacher moves right on to the development of norms and expectations:

TEACHER: Let's try a dry run for how we might talk together. James, you come up to the front of the class.

(James, a usually motivated and talkative student, complies.)

TEACHER: What I want you to do is stand next to me and stare at the class for a moment.

(James stares at the class. They stare back, puzzled as to the purpose of the activity. The class is dead silent.)

TEACHER: Do they scare you at all?

JAMES: Nope!

TEACHER: You're not nervous?

JAMES: Nope!

TEACHER: All right! Let's give James a hand for getting up here!

(The class claps)

The teacher invited several more students to repeat the process before he provided some observations and explanation.

TEACHER: You were really good to the people up here—in fact, really careful about not giving them a hard time. Why was that?

GEORGE: It could be you up there!

TEACHER: What do you mean?

GEORGE: You really felt for them. I was thinking that it was good that it wasn't me!

TEACHER: Part of it, I bet, was that you were treating them the way you would want to be treated?

ALL: Yes!

TEACHER: That's one of the things I was trying to get across with this activity, that it really helps someone's performance if you offer them the support and attention that you would want for yourself. Let's write that down as one of our rules to live by when we do this unit.

(The teacher writes the rule on the blackboard)

Several other rules were developed in this fashion, with the teacher involving students in role-playing and guiding them in thinking about rules that would allow everyone to take risks but at the same time feel comfortable in the group.

Encouraging Independence

To accomplish the upcoming activities, students will need to develop the ability to think through some problem situations as they come up. Recall that conflict is an inevitable part of group development. To encourage student independence in addressing conflict, the teacher posed some possible scenarios:

TEACHER: Suppose one of you gets up and makes a presentation, but someone out there tries to distract you—you know—starts giggling and pointing.

MARVIN: I would take him out!

(The class laughs!)

TEACHER: You'd sure feel that way, wouldn't you! But we're trying to work together as a group, and if you take him out, that might send us all into a big mess. What other things could we do?

SUSAN: You could just remind him of the rules.

TEACHER: You mean, the ones we made?

SUSAN: Yeah.

MARVIN: But that won't make them stop. What if they won't listen?

TEACHER: Then maybe I have to help. Remember, I'm part of this group too. If somebody's causing trouble, we all have to do something and I can't just leave it to you. Now, let's discuss actions I might have to take.

The teacher continued by discussing choices the unruly student could make: to choose to remain a part of the group, to abide by the group's rules, or to leave and not be a part of the class activities. The teacher played up the importance of feeling a sense of belonging and talked about the disappointment the class as a whole would feel if someone could not cooperate.

This dialogue not only helps students understand the nature of their commitment to a group, but also gives them problem-solving strategies to use when an individual within the group falters. By conducting the dialogue against the backdrop of a motivating curriculum in a classroom where belonging was emphasized, this teacher prepared his students well for creating a supportive communication environment.

SUMMARY

The need to create a supportive environment for communication applies to all the activities described in this book. Classroom discussion is not restricted to either whole-class or small-group settings. In any setting, students can benefit from group development activities with a specific focus on discussion.

Developing a positive classroom climate and cooperation among students is a basic goal. Beyond this, discussion activities need to be adapted to the purposes and content in which students are to be engaged. In any process of group development, conflict is inevitable. Teachers who accept this notion and who have developed clear expectations with students are better able to assist in problem-solving when problems emerge. Moving students to more productive stages requires thinking about the interaction between curriculum and group development activities. A motivating curriculum tends to create a good environment for group development.

Fast-paced, stimulating, and engaging classroom discussions are every teacher's dream. Being persistent with the ideas described here could help many teachers make this dream a reality.

SPECIAL PROJECTS

Course-Based

1. Having read the book to this point, you probably have developed several content reading lessons (unless, of course, you are skipping around among chapters!). Using one of the lessons you have planned, brainstorm for the special discussion needs or problems that you will have to address in teaching the lesson. Come up with a plan for teaching students the norms and expectations necessary to participate in the lesson.

2. Chapter 13 describes unit planning. Read Chapter 13 and design a unit. Then, using principles described in this chapter, develop an approach to discussion that is integrated with the goals and activities you have prepared for your unit. How will you orient and involve your students? How will you keep them participating throughout the unit?

Field-Based

3. Observe a classroom in your content area. First focus on the students. Who participates during discussion and why? Are there clear patterns of participation among the students? Now direct your attention to the teacher. How would you describe this teacher's style? Is it more authoritarian, providing few opportunities for student participation, or is it more democratic? Does the teacher adapt his or her style and the types of discussion activities according to differences in topics, students, or tasks?

SUGGESTED READING

This book provides useful information about creating a classroom learning community:

PUTNAM, J., & BURKE, J. B. (1991). *The classroom learning community: Organizing and managing instruction in cooperative groups*. New York: McGraw-Hill.

This book offers practical advice and many good examples for both whole-class and small-group discussion:

ALVERMANN, D., DILLON, D., & O'BRIEN, D. (1987). *Using discussion to promote reading comprehension*. Newark, DE: International Reading Association.

These books provide practical information on how to organize the classroom for small-group discussion:

COHEN, E. (1986). *Designing groupwork: Strategies for the heterogeneous classroom*. New York: Teachers College Press.

EMMER, E., EVERTSON, C., SANFORD, J., CLEMENTS, B., & WORSHAM, M. (1982). *Classroom management for secondary teachers*. Englewood Cliffs, NJ: Prentice-Hall.

JOHNSON, D., JOHNSON, R., HOLUBEC, E., & ROY, P. (1984). *Circles of learning*. Alexandria, VA: Association of Supervision and Curriculum Development.

These articles offer comprehensive research reviews on the effects of cooperative small groups:

JOHNSON, D., JOHNSON, R., & MARUYAMA, G. (1983). Interdependence and interpersonal attraction among heterogeneous and homogeneous individuals: A theoretical formulation and a meta-analysis. *Review of Educational Research, 53*, 1, 5–54.

SLAVIN, R. (1980). Cooperative learning. *Review of Educational Research, 50*, 2, 315–342.

SHARAN, S. (1980). Cooperative learning in small groups: Recent methods and effects on achievement, attitudes, and ethnic relations. *Review of Educational Research, 50*, 2, 241–271.

REFERENCES

AARONSON, AND OTHERS (1978). *The jigsaw classroom*. Beverly Hills, CA: Sage.

ALVERMANN, D., DILLON, D., & O'BRIEN, D. (1987). *Using discussion to promote reading comprehension*. Newark, DE: International Reading Association.

BARNES, D., & TODD, F. (1977). *Communication and learning in small groups*. London: Routledge & Kegan Paul.

CAZDEN, C. (1988). *Classroom discourse: The language of teaching and learning.* Portsmouth, NH: Heinemann.

COHEN, E. (1986). *Designing groupwork: Strategies for the heterogeneous classroom.* New York: Teachers College Press.

CONLEY M. (1986). Teachers' conceptions, decisions and changes during initial classroom lessons containing content reading strategies. In J. Niles & R. Lalik (Eds.), *Solving problems in literacy: Learners, teachers and researchers.* Rochester, NY: The National Reading Conference.

CONLEY, M. (1987). Grouping. In D. Alvermann, D. Moore, & M. Conley (Eds.), *Research within reach: Secondary school reading.* Newark, DE: International Reading Association.

DELAMONT, S. (1984). *Interaction in the classroom.* New York: Methuen.

DILLON, J. (1984). Research on questioning and discussion. *Educational Leadership, 42,* 50–56.

DOYLE, W. (1986). Classroom organization and management. In M. Wittrock (Ed.), *Handbook of research on teaching, third edition.* New York: Macmillan.

EMMER, E., EVERTSON, C., SANFORD, J., CLEMENTS, B., & WORSHAM, M. (1984). *Classroom management for secondary teachers.* Englewood Cliffs, NJ: Prentice-Hall.

GALL, M., & GALL, J. (1976). The discussion method. In N. Gage (Ed.), *Psychology of teaching methods.* National Society for the Study of Education, Seventy-fifth Yearbook, Part I. Chicago: University of Chicago Press.

HEATH, S. B. (1982). Questioning at home and at school: A comparative study. In G. Spindler (Ed.), *Doing the ethnography of schooling.* New York: Holt, Rinehart and Winston.

JOHNSON, D. (1981). Student-student interaction: The neglected variable in education. *Educational Researcher, 10,* 5–10.

JOHNSON, D., & JOHNSON, R. (1986). *Learning together and alone,* 2d edition. Englewood Cliffs, NJ: Prentice-Hall.

JOHNSON, D., MARAYAMA, R., JOHNSON, R., & NELSON, D., & SKON, L. (1981). Effects of cooperative, competitive, and individualistic goal structures on achievement: A meta-analysis. *Psychological Bulletin, 89,* 1, 47–62.

MILLS, S., RICE, C., BERLINER, D., & ROSSEAU, E. (1980). The correspondence between teacher questions and student answers in classroom discourse. *Journal of Experimental Education, 48,* 3, 194–204.

MORRIS, R. (1977). *A normative intervention to equalize participation in task-oriented groups.* Unpublished doctoral dissertation, Stanford, CA.

PUTNAM, J., & BURKE, J. B. (1991). *The classroom learning community.* New York: McGraw-Hill.

ROWE, M. (1974). Wait-time and rewards as instructional variables. *Journal of Research in Science Teaching, 11,* 81–94.

SCHMUCK, R., & SCHMUCK, R. (1988). *Group processes in the classroom,* 5th edition. Dubuque, IA: Wm. C. Brown.

SHARON, S., & SHARON, Y. (1986). *Small group teaching.* Englewood Cliffs, NJ: Educational Technology Publications.

SLAVIN, R. (1980). Cooperative learning. *Review of Educational Research, 50,* 2, 315–342.

SLAVIN, R. (1988). Cooperative learning and student achievement. In R. Slavin (Ed.), *School and classroom organization.* Hillsdale, NJ: Erlbaum.

STANFORD, G. (1977). *Developing effective classroom groups.* New York: A&W Visual Library

TOBIAS, S. (1982). When do instructional methods make a difference? *Educational Researcher, 11,* 4, 4–9.

VACCA, R. (1977). Selected small group variables and their influence on performance. In H. Herber and R. Vacca (Eds), *Research in reading in the content areas, the third report.* Syracuse, NY: Syracuse University Reading and Language Arts Center.

WEBB, N. (1984). Stability of small group interaction and achievement over time. *Journal of Educational Psychology, 76,* 211–224.

assessment issues (such as interpretations that emerge from day-to-day experiences with a student). Teachers' subjective experience involves daily decision-making, analysis, and reflection.

This chapter presents some ways to assess what students have learned. Like previous chapters, it describes goals for content, process, and motivation, linking them whenever possible to instructional goals described earlier. Finally, the chapter illustrates assessment decisions through use of a portfolio approach.

PLANNING FOR ASSESSMENT

The following sections describe decisions related to assessment of content, process, and motivation goals. As you read, think about your own goals for assessment in your content area.

Assessing Content Learning

Assessment of content learning focuses on the extent to which students truly understand what they have been taught.

Demonstrating a deep understanding of the content involves more than performance on some set of test items (such as true/false exercises or even an essay). The trouble with more traditional approaches to assessment is that they typically emphasize fill-in-the-blanks, all-or-nothing performance while offering little insight about the knowledge students have acquired or their ability to apply it. When students really understand something, many outcomes are possible. Students gain new information, discover connections to existing knowledge, restructure ideas and concepts to create new interpretations, and adapt what they are learning to various uses and purposes (Norman, 1982). For instance, naive conceptions or misconceptions in science and mathematics can be transformed into more appropriate or accurate conceptions (Anderson & Roth, 1989; Wiser, 1988).

What kinds of assessment capture these levels of understanding? Anderson (1990) suggests that assessing understanding requires attention to three factors: knowledge, actions, and context. *Knowledge* refers to the extent to which new information has been integrated with other existing ideas. Most traditional forms of assessment deal with knowledge in isolation. *Actions* refer to what knowledgeable individuals do with the information being learned. In other words, the knowledge students learn is not static or inert. Experts in school and out use knowledge to guide their actions. Finally, *context* refers to the real-world situations in which knowledge is applied.

Figure 12.1 depicts some sample content assessment questions for use in mathematics. Question 1 deals with the knowledge dimension, calling on students to relate what they knew previously to what they are learning currently. Question 2 focuses on actions students might take on the basis of what they have learned. Question 3 encourages students to see the application of what they have learned within various contexts. Questions 4 and 5 offer opportunities for the teacher to evaluate students as they write and discuss.

FIGURE 12.1

Sample Content Assessment Questions

---

1. People use *statistics* every day. Which of the following situations involve statistics? Circle all that could be correct and give reasons.

   Doing an opinion poll   Comparing sales prices   Counting traffic fatalities

   Buying a car   Giving grades at school   Buying car insurance

2. How could you use statistics to plan for college? Explain your answer.

3. What kinds of statistics could be useful in the following situations?

   - Determining the favorite after school activity of teenagers
   - Comparing the test performance of two social studies classes
   - Finding out how one student did on a test in comparison with others
   - Predicting the sales of a compact disc two months from now
   - Finding out the most common age for people to get a driver's license
   - Determining the life expectancy of males and females

4. Statistics frequently appear in news articles. Write a news article in which statistics play a role.

5. Using statistics, discuss the positives and negatives of the food in the cafeteria.

Assessing Process Learning

Assessments geared to process learning focus on students' abilities to reason and explain, select appropriately from among a number of available processes, and shift and adapt according to the success or failure of a particular approach to learning (Snow, 1989).

Traditional approaches to assessment offer little with respect to process learning. A major obstacle to process assessment is that learning processes are not easy to discern. Test makers design tasks that get students to produce or reveal evidence of thinking. Multiple-choice tests are among the most popular ways to assess process learning. Unfortunately, a response to a traditional multiple-choice item tells little about how students are processing information (Petrie, 1986).

Consider this example (from Ennis & Millman, 1985). Suppose a teacher created the following item:

Explorers on a planet are attempting to decide whether the water is safe to drink. Which statement is more believable?

A. The health officer says, "This water is safe to drink."
B. The soldier says, "This water is safe to drink."
C. Both A and B are equally believable.

Elizabeth Crews

Getting students to talk about their answers adds insight to the processes they are using during assessment

A test taker could easily pick any one of the three answers and we would know something of how he or she *performed*. We would not know, however, the kinds of *processing* he or she might have applied, a critical factor in judging the plausibility of any of the responses. For example, though item A is the most logical response, a test taker might choose item B or C, depending on his or her view of the training a soldier receives.

The challenge for teachers in process assessment is to be aware of the variety of strategies students use to handle different types of tasks, to make invisible processes become more visible (Siegler, 1989). Meeting this challenge means coming up with alternative forms of assessment that stimulate students to verbalize and demonstrate how they are thinking. Several ways to do this have already been discussed in Chapter 3.

Effective process assessments encourage students to judge the credibility of information while requiring them to justify their decisions. For example, having students write reasons or think out loud while discussing answers to a test would add insight about processes students are using. Teachers can also engage students in retrospective reports, asking "How did you come up with that answer?" or "Walk us through the way you thought about that."

In conducting process assessments, teachers should watch for evidence of flexible thinking. Are students' answers to questions arbitrary? Are responses reasonable, given the evidence at hand? Are students truly aware of the processes they are using or are they simply going through the motions?

FIGURE 12.2

Sample Process Assessment Questions

---

1. Which of the following best describes the motive of the murderer in "The Cask of Amontillado"?

   a. He was angry about being embarrassed by Fortunato.
   b. He wanted to get caught.
   c. His family was feuding with Fortunato's family.
   d. Fortunato was wealthier and more popular.

   In the space below, tell why you think your answer is the best one:
   _____
   _____
   _____
   _____

2. If you came to something you did not understand in a story, what could you do to figure it out?

3. Describe what you could do if you wanted to find out more about murders and how they are solved.

4. Describe what you could do if you wanted to know more about what it's like to be a writer.

5. What would you need to do to write a screenplay for "The Cask of Amontillado"? Describe how the writing of a screenplay might be different from the writing of the short story.

6. With a partner, discuss some of your favorite stories. Talk about what makes them so enjoyable. Is it the story itself? The way it was read?

Figure 12.2 presents some process assessment questions prepared for an English class. Question 1 requires students to choose among several plausible answers and to justify their thinking. Question 2 focuses on a student's ability to apply a process when he or she gets stuck (recall fix-it strategies from Chapter 3). Questions 3 and 4 encourage students to think about actions they could take to learn more. Whatever the approach to process assessment, a goal is to help students confirm for themselves the strategies that are available in learning new information. Again, questions 5 and 6 provide opportunities for writing and discussion.

Assessing Motivation to Learn

Motivation assessments are designed to test students' willingness to expend effort, their tendency to act based on what they are learning, their motivation to continue learning, as well as their interest and self-confidence (Snow, 1989).

developed in solving different problems, and stories and pictures that evolve from mathematical reasoning. In music, a biographical portfolio could include audio and video recordings of various performances and collections of compositions.

Range of works portfolios aim for a diversity of samples. A range of works portfolio could include some biographies, and it might also incorporate various kinds of student- as well as teacher-selected artifacts. For instance, students should be encouraged to build as complete a picture of themselves as possible as they progress through the school year. Some teachers start this process by taking students' pictures and affixing them to the portfolios. Students are asked to select anything during the year that best reflects the range of their learning: published works, performance on tests, media presentations, and even computer work. Teachers play a role by guiding students in thinking about their work, helping them assess their progress, and helping them select samples that illustrate the breadth of their success.

Reflection portfolios are organized to document important changes, challenges, and successes in students' work. With reflection portfolios, teachers make a conscious effort to encourage students to apply a critical eye to their work. Teachers and students talk with one another and try to achieve consensus about what counts as good work, given the goals and the challenges of a subject. With this approach, students use portfolios to collect their work. Periodically, they are required to turn in a number of their best works for discussion and review (and even a grade).

The choice of an approach to the content of portfolios really depends on the goals and purposes a teacher has in mind. Teachers engaging students in the writing process for the first time might appreciate the message built into the biographies of works approach: good work evolves over time. With younger students and a diverse curriculum, the range of works option might offer just the right amount of flexibility. For older students, reflection portfolios offer opportunities to further develop and refine their own sense of growth and quality.

Using Portfolios for Assessment

In comparison with traditional assessment techniques, portfolios can be messy. That's where a teacher's decision-making comes in. To use portfolios appropriately, teachers must find ways to develop, monitor, and evaluate their own decisions (Valencia, McGinley, & Pearson, 1990).

The first step in using portfolios is to establish a focus (Valencia, McGinley, & Pearson, 1990). For example, teachers might ask some questions about students to guide themselves in focusing on important instructional goals. For example, some questions to ask might relate to how well students are developing and applying an understanding of the content:

Can students use their newly acquired content knowledge to

- Articulate what they know?
- Gain new insights?
- Apply what they know to new situations?

Other questions might focus more on process:
How well are students able to use communication processes to

- Learn new vocabulary concepts?
- Guide and monitor their own learning?
- Think critically and solve problems?
- Study and understand content materials?
- Compose a piece of writing for different purposes and audiences?

A third set of questions might stress motivation:
Are students motivated enough to

- Make connections between themselves and the content?
- Communicate with others about what they are learning?
- Want to learn more?

Teachers may want to emphasize several or many of these kinds of questions as a basis for portfolio assessment decisions. It is neither necessary nor desirable to examine all possible dimensions of a portfolio. Instead, teachers should strive for a balanced effort over time, stressing content dimensions during some assessment opportunities and process or

Portfolios work best when students are involved

Peter Bates/The Picture Cube

motivation dimensions at other times. Student can also be involved in the effort, posing and responding to their own questions.

Once a focus has been established, it is necessary to make decisions about how to rate or react to portfolios. This set of decisions reflects a continuum as opposed to a set of absolutes. Thus guidelines are more appropriate than specific rules. Several illustrations should help.

Suppose that a teacher wants to assess the degree to which students are applying new content knowledge. Ideally, portfolios should show evidence that students are integrating prior knowledge with new knowledge; that is, writing assignments should show evidence of new knowledge stated in students' language and combined or contrasted with previously known information. In science class, portfolios might reveal struggles to overcome misconceptions alongside new learnings. Teachers could rate the quality of students' portfolios in terms of their content knowledge on a general 1-to-10 point scale, with 1 point representing regurgitation or inaccuracy and 10 points reflecting an integration of content with prior knowledge. Alternatively, teachers could have students rate themselves, or teachers might write a short reaction about problems or their degree of satisfaction with students' success with the content.

Now suppose that a teacher wants to find out the extent to which students are able to select and modify various reading-to-learn and reading-to-communicate processes. In this situation, teachers could ask students to keep a log in their portfolios of what they do when they get stuck or do not understand something they are reading, writing about, or discussing. In reviewing students' portfolios, the teacher might discover common problems or processes on which students need to work. For example, many students might give up too readily when faced with certain kinds of assignments (such as writing for different purposes or solving problems on their own). Other students might face a particular strategy need (for example, how to select the most appropriate way to construct the meaning of an unknown vocabulary term). Rather than grading this kind of portfolio information, a teacher should treat it as an opportunity to make teaching and assessment decisions. Students who give up readily might profit from greater emphasis on motivation. More explanations and modeling during teaching will assist other students who are experiencing difficulty.

Be creative in making decisions based on portfolios. Include students in the decisions so that they gain opportunities to assess and refine their own work. With time, teachers and students can turn assessment into a meaningful and integrated part of instruction.

SUMMARY

Assessment is here to stay, for good or ill. At its best, assessment is an instructional tool, helping teachers develop insights about students and what they are learning. At its worst, assessment bypasses the complexities and realities of learning. Teachers are the foundation of responsible assessment; when they strive to create tests that reflect higher-level goals and processes, students grow and learn. Ongoing assessment provides teachers with a continually updated picture of what students know and what they are still struggling to understand. Through instruction, many concepts are learned and many are *half*-learned.

Assessment should reveal gaps in students' understanding. Good assessment information opens up opportunities for teachers to make learning more complete.

Portfolios provide one way to approach assessment. Organized in various ways and for various purposes, portfolios offer teachers and students both flexibility and structure. Teachers can zero in on the extent to which students are achieving important content, process, and motivation goals, and students can learn to reflect on their own progress. Well-conceived and thoughtfully implemented portfolios support decision-making for content reading and classroom communication.

SPECIAL PROJECTS

Course-Based

1. Using principles described in this chapter, design a paper and pencil quiz that follows a lesson you have planned. The lesson should use one of the activities explained earlier in this book.

2. Read Chapter 13 on unit planning. Devise an approach to assessment that is consistent with the goals for your unit.

Field-Based

3. Administer a test that you have designed based on principles described in this chapter. To what extent did you learn about students' performance? How much did you learn about how students process information?

SUGGESTED READING

The December 1989 issue of the *Educational Researcher* is devoted to assessment issues.
The April 1989 issue of *Educational Leadership* focuses on changes in thinking about assessment.
The March 1990 issue of *Language Arts* describes various approaches to classroom assessment, including the use of portfolios.

These chapters offer a state-of-the-art explanations and classroom examples related to assessment:

FARR, R., TULLEY, M., & PRITCHARD, R. (1989). Assessment instruments and techniques used by the content area teacher. In D. Lapp, J. Flood, & N. Farnan (Eds.), *Content area reading and learning: Instructional strategies*. New York: Prentice-Hall.
VALENCIA, S., MCGINLEY, W., & PEARSON, P. (1990). Assessing reading and writing. In G. Duffy (Ed.), *Reading in the middle school*, 2d edition. Newark, DE: International Reading Association.

REFERENCES

ANDERSON, C. (1990). *Addressing scientific understanding*. A paper presented at the annual meeting of the American Association for the Advancement of Science, New Orleans.

ANDERSON, C., & ROTH, K. (1989). Teaching for meaningful and self-regulated learning in science. In J. Brophy (Ed.), *Advances in research on teaching,* Vol. I (pp. 265–309). Greenwich, CT: JAI Press.

ENNIS, R., & MILLMAN, J. (1985). *Cornell critical thinking test.* Pacific Grove, CA: Midwest.

FREDERIKSEN, J., & COLLINS, A. (1989). A systems approach to educational testing. *Educational Researcher, 18,* 9, 3–7.

MCTIGHE, J., & FERRARA, S. (1988). Assessing student thinking: Work in progress in Maryland. *Teaching Thinking and Problem Solving, 10,* 4, 1–4.

NORMAN, D. (1982). *Learning and memory.* San Francisco: Freeman.

PETRIE, H. (1986). Testing for critical thinking. In D. Nyberg (Ed.), *Philosophy of education.* Normal, IL: Philosophy of Education Society.

SCHOENFELD, A. (1991). On mathematics as sense-making: An informal attack on the unfortunate divorce of formal and informal mathematics. In D. Perkins, J. Segal, and J. Voss (Eds.), *Informal reasoning and education.* Hillsdale, NJ: Erlbaum.

SHEPARD, L. (1989). Why we need better assessments. *Educational Leadership, 46,* 7, 4–9.

SIEGLER, R. (1989). Strategy diversity and cognitive assessment. *Educational Researcher, 18,* 9, 15–20.

SNOW, R. (1989). Toward assessment of cognitive and conative structures in learning. *Educational Researcher, 18,* 9, 8–14.

VALENCIA, S. (1990). A portfolio approach to classroom reading assessment: The whys, whats, and hows. *The Reading Teacher, 43,* 4, 338–340.

VALENCIA, S., MCGINLEY, W., & PEARSON, P. (1990). Assessing reading and writing. In G. Duffy (Ed.), *Reading in the middle school,* 2d edition. Newark, DE: International Reading Association.

WIGGINS, G. (1989). Teaching to the (authentic) test. *Educational Leadership, 46,* 7, 41–49.

WISER, M. (1988). The differentiation of heat and temperature: History of science and expert-novice shift. In S. Strauss (Ed.), *Ontogeny, phylogeny, and historical development.* Norwood, NJ: Ablex.

WOLF, D. (1989). Portfolio assessment: Sampling student work. *Educational Leadership, 46,* 7, 35–40.

"What kind of alternative is offered here? It is a model for planning teaching that encourages us to see lessons or units as good stories to be told rather than (just) sets of objectives to be attained."

From Kieran Egan (1986). Teaching as story telling. *Chicago: University of Chicago Press, p. 2.*

13
Unit Planning

CHAPTER OBJECTIVES

After reading this chapter, you should be able to:

1. Plan and implement a unit of study centered on content, process, and motivation outcomes.

2. Integrate content reading instruction with other systemwide as well as classroom-specific approaches to schooling and instruction.

RATIONALE

A *unit* is a plan of action for a series of lessons. Units of study are like stories to tell. Often, teachers are the storytellers, setting the stage, weaving together subject-matter plots, building conflict and excitement, and constructing endings or conclusions that make students learn, laugh, or express surprise. Students are also the storytellers, passing on teachers' stories to classmates and family, or using the stories, the content teachers have taught, to weave stories of their own, to make a career and generate new knowledge in the content areas taught.

The purpose of unit planning is for a teacher to *transform* his or her content knowledge and knowledge about students into powerful and coherent instruction. To transform knowledge into practice, teachers engage in acts of comprehension and reasoning (Shulman, 1987). Unit planning begins when a teacher grasps a set of concepts. The concepts are shaped and tailored until they can be grasped by students. The transformation of knowledge to practice is not passive: in order to comprehend and think through the curriculum, the teacher must wrestle with concepts. For example, rather than asking the question, "How will I teach the circulatory system?" an actively engaged science teacher might ask, "What is important to know about the circulatory system?" and "How will I help *these* students see connections to their own lives?"

Because of variations in content and students, unit planning is far from a linear process, where all possibilities can be anticipated. Recall Yinger's (1986) descriptions of instruction from Chapter 5. Planning and teaching decisions are more appropriately compared with a maze or mosaic than a straight line. Units are planned, crafted, and refined so that instruction can be intentional but adaptable. Like the construction of a mosaic, structure and detail are balanced with variety and spontaneity.

CHAPTER ORGANIZER

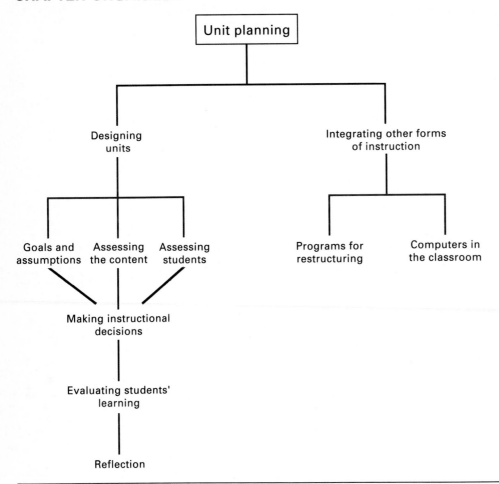

Unit planning plays a significant role in any teacher's approach to content reading instruction. Research has shown that when teachers construct units of study, they are able to integrate content reading and writing activities into subject-matter teaching more effectively than when they plan lesson to lesson. The reason for this is that unit planning tends to engage teachers in more careful reflection and synthesis. Teachers are better able to see connections between subject matter and literacy, finding ways to use reading and writing to promote deeper understandings (Pearce & Bader, 1986). Teachers who engage in thoughtful unit planning are more successful in helping their students achieve deep subject-matter understandings than are teachers who focus on one lesson at a time (Anderson & Roth, 1989).

This final chapter is about unit planning. A purpose of the chapter is to pull together many of the concepts developed in this book. Building on previous chapters, it describes

FIGURE 13.2

Sketching Out a Concept Map for a Unit

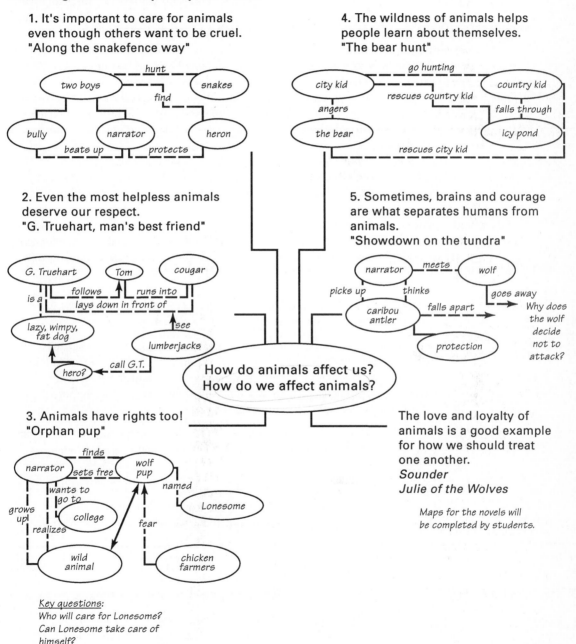

1. It's important to care for animals even though others want to be cruel.
"Along the snakefence way"

two boys — *hunt* — **snakes**
— *find* — **heron**
bully — *beats up* — **narrator** — *protects*

2. Even the most helpless animals deserve our respect.
"G. Truehart, man's best friend"

G. Truehart — **Tom** — **cougar**
is a — *follows* — *runs into*
lays down in front of
lazy, wimpy, fat dog
see — **lumberjacks**
hero? — *call G.T.*

3. Animals have rights too!
"Orphan pup"

narrator — *finds* — **wolf pup**
sets free — *named*
wants to go to — **college** — **Lonesome**
grows up — *fear*
realizes
wild animal — **chicken farmers**

Key questions:
Who will care for Lonesome?
Can Lonesome take care of himself?

4. The wildness of animals helps people learn about themselves.
"The bear hunt"

city kid — *go hunting* — **country kid**
rescues country kid
angers — *falls through*
the bear — **icy pond**
rescues city kid

5. Sometimes, brains and courage are what separates humans from animals.
"Showdown on the tundra"

narrator — *meets* — **wolf**
picks up — *thinks* — *goes away*
caribou antler — *falls apart* — Why does the wolf decide not to attack?
protection

How do animals affect us?
How do we affect animals?

The love and loyalty of animals is a good example for how we should treat one another.
Sounder
Julie of the Wolves

Maps for the novels will be completed by students.

Note how the teachers added *Sounder* and *Julie of the Wolves.* The stories in the literature anthology selected for the unit are not diverse enough in terms of gender (most are about boys) and culture (taken together, the stories do not reflect a range of diverse groups of people or individuals). The novels provide more diversity within the unit.

Developing Behavioral Objectives   Recall from Chapter 5 that behavioral objectives are used to identify process and motivation outcomes. Process and motivation provide access to the content. Well-conceived behavioral objectives are closely related to the content objectives developed for a lesson or unit. When writing behavioral objectives, it is important to be concise. Emphasize the issues and needs that will be of most concern as students progress through the unit. In many cases, a small number of well-conceived objectives is enough.

The English teachers developed process-oriented objectives by thinking about their general goals for students. Because they were concerned about making the literature relevant to urban students, the use of prior knowledge was a high priority. Because some of the students were poor readers, the teachers also wanted to emphasize metacognition and comprehension. The goals teachers had for writing implied a focus on various elements of the writing process. Finally, teachers wanted students to develop good discussion skills. These concerns were translated into the following behavioral objectives:

1. Given the task of reading a short story, students will brainstorm for experiences they have had that are similar to the situation in the story. The experiences students list must be relevant to the story.

2. While reading a short story or novel, students will summarize what they have read and make plausible predictions about what will happen next. Students' summaries will contain concepts identified as important in the reading (the teacher uses the concept map as a guide). Predictions will be supported by references to characters and/or previous events.

3. Given the task of writing a short story, students will use the elements of the writing process to produce a short story. The story will show evidence of thinking about audience and purpose and will be free of technical errors.

4. While discussing a short story or novel, students will actively participate and listen to others so well that they are able to guide their own discussion. The discussion will be entirely student-directed, without the need for teacher intervention.

One motivation-oriented objective was written, focusing attention on real-world applications of the content of the unit:

5. Given the task of doing something beneficial for animals, students will plan a project that either directly helps animals or increases awareness of the need for people to love and be loved by animals. The project should state a problem and specify a plan of action for accomplishing these goals.

Projects like this one are a good way to think about addressing motivation objectives within a unit (Cooter & Griffith, 1989).

With decisions made about content, process, and motivation objectives, now the teachers could turn to planning and teaching decisions.

Making Planning and Teaching Decisions   Now, it is time to select instructional activities, according to decisions about content, process, and motivation. Figure 13.3 presents one way to do this, by *charting* materials, objectives, and instructional activities. A chart is constructed by lining up reading materials, content objectives, and behavioral objectives. Content objectives, behavioral objectives, and reading selections are related to one another and sequenced by thinking about what content, process, and motivation outcomes need to be emphasized at certain points in a unit.

For example, in Figure 13.3, the behavioral objective related to using prior knowledge and experience was selected to go with the first story because teachers felt that making prior knowledge connections with the literature was a special priority early in the unit. The teachers planned to encourage students to talk about their relationships with animals, the effects of peer pressure, and times when they made decisions that were not popular with their friends. Later stories were matched with summarizing and predicting outcomes to prepare students for the eventual goal of leading their own discussions.

Just because one objective is being emphasized for one reading selection or set of lessons does not mean that others are being ignored. Prior knowledge is addressed in each of the lessons. Work with summarizing and predicting is ongoing.

Once objectives have been laid out, instructional activities can be selected. The behavioral objectives offer some guidance in how these decisions might be made. For example, the prior knowledge objective suggests work with semantic mapping (Chapter 6), K-W-L (Chapter 7), or prediction guides (Chapter 8). The objectives dealing with projects and writing imply work with the writing process (Chapter 10) or simulations (Chapter 8). Discussion objectives call for use of some of the techniques described in Chapter 11.

Figure 13.3 depicts the decisions the English teachers made in designing their unit. They thought about the nature of the reading selections, the content and behavioral objectives, and the special needs of their students. Again, these materials, objectives, and students are probably different from your own. What is important is the process for making these kinds of decisions.

Two more instructional decisions were made with this unit. First, teachers did not have class sets for *Sounder* or *Julie of the Wolves.* The teachers decided to read the novels aloud in two separate groups (remember, there were two teachers available, the special education teacher and the regular education teacher). They decided to have each of the groups prepare a "Siskel and Ebert–style" review of the books for the rest of the class. This would give real purpose to the discussion activities planned for this part of the unit.

To prepare students for these experiences, the teachers planned to work on discussion skills throughout the unit as well as have students write a *dialogue journal.* Recall from Chapter 3 that dialogue journals involve conversational exchanges about the content students are learning (Atwell, 1987). Students react to the content in the form of a

FIGURE 13.3

Charting Materials, Objectives, and Instructional Activities

Reading Material	Content Objective	Behavioral Objective(s)	Instructional Activities
"Along the Snake-Fence Way	It's important to care for animals, even though others want to be cruel.	Given the task of reading a short story, students will brainstorm for experiences they have had that are similar to the situation in the story.	Semantic maps K-W-L QARs Dialogue journals
"G. Truhart, Man's Best Friend"	Even the most helpless animals deserve our respect.	While reading a short story, students will summarize what they have read and make plausible predictions about what will happen next.	Reciprocal teaching (Summarizing, predicting, questioning) Dialogue journals
"Orphan Pup"	Animals have rights too!	Given the task of doing something beneficial for animals, students will plan a project that either directly helps animals or increases awareness of the need for people to love and be loved by animals.	Brainstorming Semantic maps Pre-writing, drafting, revising, editing, publishing Simulations Dialogue journals
"The Bear Hunt"	The Wildness of Animals helps us learn about ourselves.	Given the task of writing a short story, students will use writing processes effectively to produce a short story.	Pre-writing, drafting, revising, editing, publishing Dialogue journals
"Showdown on the Tundra"	Sometimes, brains and courage are what separates	While reading a short story, students will summarize what	Vocabulary development Prediction guide

Reading Material	Content Objective	Behavioral Objective(s)	Instructional Activities
	humans from animals.	they have read and make plausible predictions about what will happen next.	Reciprocal teaching (summarizing, predicting) Dialogue journals
Sounder	The love and loyalty of animals is a good example for how we should treat one another.	While discussing a novel students will actively participate and listen to others so well that they are able to guide their own discussion.	Discussion processes Simulations Dialogue journals
Julie of the Wolves	The love and loyalty of animals is a good example for how we should treat one another.	While discussing a novel, students will actively participate and listen to others so well that they are able to guide their own discussion.	Discussion processes Simulations Dialogue journals

letter to the teacher or to other students. The journals are exchanged, and teachers or other students respond with questions asking for clarification or elaboration ("Why did you think that *x* was a problem?"), comments ("I like the way you wrote about *x*), or suggestions ("Try to write more about what interests you next time"). The teachers hoped that the dialogue journals would help students learn how to evaluate and react to what they were reading.

Finally, the teachers created a rough time line for a typical instructional week.

FIGURE 13.4

A Tentative Weekly Schedule

Monday	Tuesday	Wednesday	Thursday	Friday
Announcements Overview of the week Pre-reading/pre-writing activities	Continue/complete story reading with reading strategies	Dialogue journals Work on pre-writing Drafting and discussion processes	Revision and editing Writing conferences	Novel reading Recreational reading and writing Recap/reactions to the week's activities

Planning a time line like this one, or even for an entire unit, is risky business. It is much harder to predict a time line for a unit when teachers are committed to giving everyone a chance to talk than it is when teachers do all the talking. The reward, however, is student engagement and motivation. With these considerations in mind, teachers speculated that it might take about five to six weeks to complete the unit (about one story per week). Figure 13.4 depicts their weekly schedule. The early part of the week was planned for literature and reading activities, the middle of the week was set aside for process writing, and the latter part of the week was devoted to novel reading and recreational reading and writing.

Evaluating Students' Learning

As Chapter 12 suggests, the evaluation of what students are learning should be ongoing. A unit should provide many opportunities for ongoing assessment.

Consider the English unit. Students were engaged in many different kinds of communication activities—reading and writing in response to literature, speaking with one another and to people in the community, and listening as students performed simulations and made presentations. Each of these activities provided an opportunity to evaluate students' work.

It may not be possible or desirable to derive grades from everything that happens in a unit. Observations and brief reviews of students' work and even student interviews provide an informal look at how students are progressing (see Chapter 3 for descriptions of

Observation can be very useful in evaluating students' progress

Joel Gordon

these techniques). The goal of *nongraded assessment,* reflected in activities like these, is to provide periodic "snapshots" of what students are learning and how they are thinking.

For *graded assessments,* other approaches are necessary. To figure out what activities might be graded, teachers should look at the behavioral objectives for clues. The objectives for the English unit focused on how students: (1) used prior knowledge, (2) summarized and predicted, (3) applied the writing process, (4) developed a project that benefited animals, and (5) engaged in independent discussion. The objectives also specified conditions under which these activities would be completed: while reading or writing short stories, and during and following discussion of a novel.

Creating evaluation criteria for grading requires some thinking about what tasks students will accomplish and what counts as proficient student performance. Atwell (1987) suggests that grades should be related to the growth students exhibit in the areas that are stressed during teaching. For example, the English teachers assigned points to the dialogue journals based on students' application of prior knowledge, the quality of their summaries and predictions, their concern for the audience, and the clarity and mechanics of their writing:

20%	Use of prior knowledge
20	Summaries
20	Predictions
20	Concern for audience
10	Clarity
10	Mechanics

To evaluate students' plans on behalf of animals, the following categories might be used:

20%	Identifying a problem animals face
20	Collecting information on the problem
10	Ordering that information
20	Developing a plan or a solution
20	Presenting the plan with clarity
10	Following customs of spelling, mechanics

"Siskel and Ebert" critiques based on the novels could incorporate concerns for the reality of the simulation and students' use of various communication processes:

25%	Content of the script
25	Realism of the roles
25	Concern for audience
25	Commitment (uses classroom time productively)

Other tasks in which similar thinking could be applied involve student participation in both whole-class and small-group discussion. Chapter 11 contains several observation sheets that could easily be used for student evaluation.

Some tasks might be evaluated more often than others (for instance, the dialogue journals). Some might be weighted more than others (such as the critiques). In the English unit, one-third of the credit was applied to reading-related activities (using prior knowledge, summarizing, predicting), one-third to writing-related activities (the dialogue journals, writing a short story), and one-third to the larger projects (reactions to the novels). Some teachers also like to apply a class participation grade, focusing on various ways students actively engage themselves and listen to one another.

Evaluation decisions are primarily in the hands of the teacher. However, it is crucial that teachers involve students in goal-setting and striving to achieve the goals developed for the unit. Teachers should talk with students about what areas they are going to emphasize and what they deem desirable growth in each area. Teachers can balance formal, performance-oriented activities like the ones described here with more informal, process-oriented activities like the ones described in Chapter 12. When students are unable to complete a task in an expected way, it is appropriate for teachers to change their evaluation plans in the middle of a unit. Effective assessment within units depends on teachers' ability and willingness to evaluate students flexibly.

Reflection

The purposes of reflection are to think about: (1) the extent to which students met the unit objectives and (2) how the unit, or subsequent units, might be adapted or changed to better meet students' needs.

The specific unit described in this chapter was actually taught during the fall of 1990. Several unexpected events altered the implementation of the unit. First, the teachers were confronted with larger class sizes than they had experienced in the past. In previous years, there had been thirty to thirty-four students per class; in 1990 there were over thirty-five students per class, and some classes exceeded forty students. A second related series of events also had an effect on the unit. To offset the effects of the large class sizes, some students were transferred into other middle school teams (groups of 4–5 teachers responsible for 150 middle school students). Other students transferred to *magnet schools,* schools offering specialized areas of instruction such as music, theater, the arts, and vocational education.

Frequent changes in the student population made it more necessary than ever to pay attention to the careful development of classroom groups and expectations (see Chapter 11). The idea of creating classroom biographies, while difficult to accomplish given the frequent changes in class membership, proved to be an important vehicle for helping students get to know each other and for providing a consistent focus in the early weeks of instruction. Students were extremely proud as they introduced one another. Some students, though too shy to read a biography, insisted on standing by a partner as the biographies were shared.

As teachers pondered moving into the literature in the unit, it became clear that some plans would have to be scaled back. In units of study, it is not an uncommon occurrence for teachers to bite off more than they can chew during the planning stages only to reduce the amount of material that students will read or the number and scope of instructional activities. The teachers decided to read the literature as planned but focus on a smaller number of reading and writing activities. Components of reciprocal teaching (see Chapter 8) would be emphasized, particularly predicting and summarizing. The dialogue journals would also be kept in order to focus on students' personal responses to the literature.

As the unit progressed, the teachers wrestled with several important questions: Should the stories and poems be read orally or silently? How could the teachers model the kinds of predicting and summarizing they wanted students to do? What are some ways to get students engaged in the journal writing and keep them engaged? Decisions about each of these questions were made in collaboration with students. Teachers and students discovered that some pieces of literature (especially those with lots of dialogue) merited oral reading. Teachers demonstrated how to perform versus merely read a story, and then teachers as well as students volunteered to read different parts. As teachers read, they modeled ways to summarize and make predictions. Gradually, students joined in with their own summaries and predictions.

The journal writing failed miserably during the first tryout. Students either had difficulty putting their thoughts down or quickly ran out of things to say. The teachers decided they needed to do some modeling of how to write journals and then support and reinforce students as they learned. The teachers discovered that it helped if students had a good understanding of the literature before they began writing. It also took some patience and persistence to acclimate students to writing independently. After several weeks of modeling and continuous feedback, students were accustomed to writing in their dialogue journals and giving as well as receiving feedback.

As students became comfortable summarizing, predicting, and reacting to the literature in the unit, it came time to consider evaluation. The teachers had already been assessing students' dialogue journals using the criteria mentioned earlier. The teachers decided to make another part of the assessment a traditional multiple-choice test, while another assessment would be based on "Siskel and Ebert–style" critiques. To prepare students for the multiple-choice test, teachers worked to develop students' awareness of question-answer relationships (see Chapter 5). Preparation for the critiques came, in part, from doing the dialogue journals each week. Students were unfamiliar, however, with how to perform an oral critique the way movie critics do on television. To help students get ready, the teachers videotaped several different types of televised movie critiques and watched them with students. Teachers and students anlayzed the formats for the shows (for example, on one show one critic gave an introduction, an excerpt of the movie was shown, and the critics took turns reviewing the movie). Students and teachers discussed ways to adapt the shows to the literature in the unit, "showing" excerpts by summarizing, creating posters, doing skits, or playing audio- and/or video-recorded dramatizations.

After students were given the multiple-choice test, they were divided into teams and given one week to select a work from the literature unit and prepare their critiques. The teachers facilitated students' work by helping them make decisions about the best ways to present their critiques. Not every team worked productively, so teachers also spent time problem-solving and reminding some teams about ways to work together.

From students' performance on the dialogue journals, the multiple-choice test, and the critiques, it was clear that they had learned many of the content objectives for the unit. Students demonstrated in many ways that they had a different understanding about human/animal relationships than they had at the beginning of the unit. Early in the unit, few students knew about very many animals other than domesticated ones; by the end of the unit they talked about some of the more exotic animals they had read about in the unit, including wolves, bears, and mountain lions. They also knew about the relationships of these animals with humans, for example, that wolves have an undeservedly bad reputation for attacking humans, and that wolves live in close-knit families. While students were not taught explicitly about the literary elements of a short story or play, they did demonstrate an awareness of those elements in their critiques and dramatizations.

For the most part, the unit "worked." Reasons include the teachers' emphasis on creating a supportive learning environment early on, including the development of clear expectations. The teachers also spent a great deal of time illustrating and modeling what they wanted students to accomplish. Adjustments and adaptations to instruction were considered regularly, especially when problems arose, such as enlarged class sizes and the difficulties students were having with writing. As the teachers prepared for the next unit, they tried to devise ways to better anticipate some of the glitches and bumps in the road that almost always accompany unit planning and teaching.

INTEGRATING OTHER FORMS OF INSTRUCTION

Unit planning does not take place in isolation from other educational approaches or concerns about schooling. This point is particularly important, given the recent explosion of staff development programs. The content of many of these programs has influenced what happens in many teacher preparation programs. Computers in the classroom, cooperative learning, clinical supervision, writing across the curriculum, and thinking and study skills programs are among the many educational approaches that are available.

Problems emerge when proponents of these programs, whether in or outside of schools, compete with one another. In some cases, distinctions are made between the fortunate teachers who have been "trained" and those unfortunates who have yet to be trained in a particular approach. Many teachers constantly struggle with the dilemma of putting all these ideas and practices into some coherent whole (Conley & Tripp-Opple, 1990).

A goal of the following sections is to demonstrate how content reading instruction can be conceived and implemented alongside two other educational initiatives that are currently having a considerable impact on schools: *programs for restructuring* and *computers in the classroom*. What follows is not an endorsement of any particular program. Instead, it is an attempt to recognize that teachers these days are bombarded with many instructional approaches and there is a need to synthesize, collaborate on, and explore what is best for students.

Programs for Restructuring

Around the United States, there is an entire family of programs that are devoted to restructuring, making fundamental changes ranging from entire school districts to individual classrooms. The programs go by many names: Madeline Hunter, ITIP, Clinical Supervision, Effective Schools, Site-Based Management, and Outcomes-Based Education.

Broader, more systemic changes involve decentralizing authority and decision-making so that teachers, administrators, and community members are able to identify critical issues and collaborate to create solutions. More specific restructuring occurs with curriculum and instruction, modifying what is taught and how instruction is carried out so that students achieve deeper subject-matter understandings and higher-level thinking skills (O'Neil, 1989).

Outcomes-Driven Developmental Model (ODDM) is one example of a total school restructuring approach (Vickery, 1990). ODDM is an attempt to reduce the fragmentation that characterizes the decision-making in many school systems. When there is a lack of consensus within a school organization on various policies or practices, the results can be quite damaging. For example, one school district purchased a new set of reading materials without any initial agreement on how the materials fit into the goals of the district's curriculum or any understanding of what teachers needed to know about implementing the materials. The new materials involved much more complex kinds of classroom discussion (for example, students asking each other questions, cooperative learning) in comparison to the types of discussion to which teachers were accustomed (for example, lecture, whole-class discussion). As more and more teachers and students experienced frustration, the reading materials were soon viewed as a complete failure.

Proponents of ODDM attempt to view school districts as a whole rather than a collection of parts. Teachers, administrators, and members of the community work together to develop a coherent vision of knowledge, beliefs, and aspirations, which are articulated in the form of desired student outcomes. An emphasis on creating communication networks and problem-solving procedures helps school districts proceed from a vision of policies and practices to ongoing changes in how decisions are made and how schools are run.

How content reading instruction is adopted by school committed to ODDM is a function of the degree to which consensus has been achieved around issues such as the organization of the curriculum and instruction. If a school committed to ODDM evolves a set of content, process, and motivation goals similar to the ones described in this book, then content reading instruction might be a good choice, along with other programs, for improving classroom practice. Some school systems, however, may not be at the stage where consensus has been reached. In that case, a simultaneous examination of subject-matter issues (deciding *what* to teach) and instructional issues (deciding *how* to teach) is necessary. Exploring the purposes for teaching in various disciplines (see Chapter 2) could help with curriculum questions, while the study of content reading instruction could assist with questions about instruction. In short, content reading instruction could be adopted in a school already committed to systemic restructuring or it could play a role in schools preparing for systemic change.

Madeline Hunter's (1984) program is an example of a specific approach to restructuring. Hunter's approach deals with decisions teachers make about desirable teaching behaviors and student outcomes. At the heart of her approach is a template for the design of effective lessons:

1. *Anticipatory set.* Activities in which teachers focus students' attention on what is to be learned.

2. *Objective and purpose.* Statements teachers make to students that explain the intent and outcomes of a lesson.

3. *Input.* Providing or exposing students to information to be learned.

4. *Modeling.* Demonstrating processes and/or products that students are expected to acquire or produce.

5. *Checking for understanding.* Determining whether students understand important content and what it is they are supposed to do.

6. *Guided practice.* Students practice what they are learning under direct teacher supervision.

7. *Independent practice.* Students practice what they have learned while the teacher "fades into the background."

Not all these categories are incorporated into every lesson. Instead, teachers are expected to use each of them as a basis for decision-making.

In many ways, Hunter's template for lessons is similar to the instructional framework described in Chapter 5. There are more steps or decision points to Hunter's template, but many of the purposes are the same. Like many of the planning and teaching decisions described in this book, Hunter's teacher decisions depend on what students know or do not know at any particular point.

If teachers are working in a district committed to Hunter's program but are also committed to the goals of content reading, it should not be difficult to integrate the instructional activities described in this book with Hunter's approach. Compare the purposes and categories in the instructional framework in Chapter 5 with the purposes and categories in Hunter's template. Think about which instructional activities best meet various purposes. For example, vocabulary activities such as the use of semantic maps and structured overviews (Chapter 6) could provide for an anticipatory set. Various comprehension (Chapter 7), reasoning (Chapter 8), and writing (Chapter 10) activities could assist with the input and modeling of information within a lesson. Techniques for studying (Chapter 9) might be useful during guided practice. Discussion activities such as cooperative learning (Chapter 11) could provide the right environment for independent practice.

Many other combinations are possible. These ideas should help teachers begin to integrate Hunter's approach with content reading instruction.

Computers in the Classroom

Computers are gradually changing the face of education. When computers first appeared on the educational scene, some thought they might replace teachers, textbooks, and instruction. Now, a little more than a decade into the personal computer revolution, researchers and teachers are still struggling to find productive ways computers can provide and enhance instruction (Sandery, 1989). As multiple roles for computers in schools become more clearly identified, the need will increase to integrate content reading instruction with computers in the classroom.

The purpose of the following sections is to (1) review the various kinds of computer programs used in schools, (2) discuss the relationship between computers and instruction, and (3) suggest ways computer-assisted instruction might become integrated with content reading.

Types of Programs   Many types of computer programs find their way into classrooms. Some have the potential for becoming indispensable tools; others are expensive and not very useful. This section presents a review of the major categories of computer software and provides suggestions for selecting worthwhile programs.

Word-processing programs (also known as *word processors*) are designed to help writers compose, revise, and edit text. Basic word processors support the typing of text and not much more. Deluxe word processors include spell checkers, a thesaurus, and even procedures for checking grammar. Word-processing programs facilitate the writing process by making various forms of real communication more readily accessible. Students can produce newspapers, recipes, stories, lists, diaries, and journals. For some younger students or students who experience difficulties with reading and writing, word processors can shift the focus from the mechanics of writing to the use of language to construct meaning (Moore, 1989). Word processors also support the development of study skills, helping students take notes from readings, reorganize notes taken by hand during lectures, prepare for various kinds of tests, and gather information for research reports

Content reading can be used to teach students about computers

Joel Gordon

(O'Byrne, 1989). Popular word-processing programs for students include Appleworks (Claris) and Bank Street Writer (Scholastic Publishing).

Data base programs capture and organize important concepts. For example, if cultures are being studied, a *record* (similar to electronic index cards) can be set up for each culture. Classroom discussions can set up *fields* (or categories) for the kinds of information to be gathered about each culture (such as art, religion, economy, government, and so forth) (Blanchard & Mason, 1985). Popular data base programs include PFS File (Software Publishing) for Apple II and IBM computers and compatibles, and Hypercard (Apple Computer) for the Macintosh. Students can use these programs to prepare their own data bases; professionally prepared data bases, incorporating encyclopedias, directories, and bibliographic references, are rapidly becoming available as resources for various reading, writing, and discussion activities (Hancock, 1989; Oley, 1989).

Computer simulations consist of programs that convey information by providing experiences that imitate reality (Blanchard & Mason, 1985). Simulations typically simplify complex situations or events and engage students in analyzing data, evaluating hypotheses, decision-making, and reflection. Simulations that work best are the kinds that support existing curricula. Some simulations are so self-contained and gamelike, often accompanied by complex manuals, that it is difficult to find ways to incorporate them. The Minnesota Educational Computer Consortium (MECC) is a good source of inexpensive simulations (see the address at the end of this chapter).

Networking software (also known as *electronic mail*) allows students to communicate with one another, within and between classrooms and schools. With networking software students can share stories, newspapers, letters, and reports. Teachers can use these materials as reading materials, thus helping students see connections between reading and writing (DeGroff, 1990). QUILL (D. C. Heath) is one example of software devoted to classroom and school networks.

Some programs have been developed for the convenience of teachers. *Electronic gradebooks* are used by teachers to simplify the process of student record-keeping. Most programs work by allowing teachers to create a roster of student names and then enter grades at will. Most electronic gradebooks allow various sorting procedures (alphabetical order, by exam or cumulative score) as well as simple statistical procedures (means, modes, standard deviations). One example of an electronic gradebook is The Apple Gradebook (Creative Computing Software).

There are several other categories of programs, often used in schools, that suffer from some notable limitations. *Readability programs* are one example. The Readability Program (Random House) estimates the readability of a passage entered into the computer by using six different formulas. Computer programs that estimate readability are subject to the same limitations as the formulas described in Chapter 2. The estimates are, at best, crude indicators of difficulty and they leave out any consideration of the reader (Duffelmeyer, 1985).

Other programs, devoted to *speed-reading* and *spelling,* are also problematic. Speed-reading programs typically allow the user to adjust the rate at which words appear on the computer screen. These programs may increase speed to a point, but developers have ignored the need to develop flexibility (see Chapter 9). Spelling programs run the gamut from words presented using computer-synthesized speed (students respond by typing the words on the keyboard) to games inviting student participation. This tends to isolate spelling as a separate topic, rather than giving students experiences with words in context.

Selecting software that can be integrated into the curriculum is not always easy. In many cases, it is not possible to review programs personally. Some local computer or software stores encourage potential users to try out programs before a purchase. Teachers who have an opportunity to review software for the classroom should consider the following questions (Balajthy, 1984; Rude, 1986):

- What kinds of content or process areas are covered?
- What kinds of activities are included? (game, tutorial, drill and practice, problem-solving, simulation)
- Are the activities interesting? motivating?
- What are the appropriate grade levels?
- What time is required to use the program?
- How are activities paced? (by the program? the student?)
- Does the program make use of appropriate, immediate feedback?
- How effective/coherent are support materials?
- How does the program relate to the rest of the curriculum?

Other considerations include the quality of the graphics and the price. Graphics that are fuzzy and uninteresting might make it difficult for students to use a program. Many programs are discounted in some stores and through mail order. It pays to shop around.

Teachers who cannot review programs in person will want to consult the computer magazines. These publications routinely provide reviews of new products for education. A list of these magazines is provided at the end of this chapter.

Computers and Instruction   Some software developers are learning to incorporate elements of good instruction into *stand-alone programs* (programs that teach without assistance of a human instructor!). Many educators are finding ways for computers to enhance the instruction that already happens in many classrooms.

In some cases, students working with computer-assisted instruction can learn more than students who learn by conventional methods. Mikulecky, Clark, and Adams (1989) used a computer to teach students concept mapping (see Chapter 6). The computer had been programmed to provide many important elements of instruction, including explanations and modeling devoted to (1) identifying key concepts in a biology text, (2) writing summary statements, and (3) mapping relationships among key concepts. In addition, the program guided students to practice each of these steps and offered corrective feedback. Students who used the program did better on two end-of-unit examinations than students who did not use the program.

Computers have shown promise in complementing traditional instruction (Woodward, Carnine, & Gersten, 1988). For example, some problems or simulations (such as predicting life expectancy based on health habits or solving international problems) can be too complex to accomplish by using conventional methods alone. Computers provide ways to manage, organize, and represent information. They help teachers and students focus more on content and tasks than on developing from scratch ways to present or learn from some forms of information (such as graphics, pictures, and other visual displays).

Another approach to computer-related instruction is that which teaches students how computers work (Kinzer, 1986). More and more, computers are becoming a kind of

FIGURE 13.5

Using Content Reading to Teach Students About Computers

Content objective: A spreadsheet is a flexible tool for arranging and calculating important values.

Literal level: Place a check by the statements made by the author of the manual. Be able to locate the place where you find the statements.

_____ 1. Visualizing your spreadsheet ahead of time helps you decide where to place different kinds of information.

_____ 2. Standard values determine how information is displayed.

_____ 3. Labels are left-justified in the default.

_____ 4. There are several standard formats for numbers.

Interpretive: The following statements could be reasonable interpretations based on the manual. Check any of the statements below that you think are implied by the manual. Be ready to identify information that supports your decisions.

_____ 1. The default column width is nine characters, but that can be changed on any or all columns.

_____ 2. Calculation of values either is automatic or can be done manually whenever you change values.

_____ 3. The loan schedule spreadsheet calculates across rows and then down columns, which is the opposite of the default.

_____ 4. When automatic calculation is selected, the program will automatically recalculate the values every time.

Applied: Place a check next to the statements you believe are correct based on the manual and your experience with spreadsheets. Support your answers with examples from both places.

_____ 1. A spreadsheet can represent any information that requires calculations.

_____ 2. A standard calculation for grades could be a fixed decimal format with no decimal places.

_____ 3. All spreadsheet standard values can be changed whenever you want.

_____ 4. You could set up a spreadsheet to keep track of your checking account deposits and withdrawals.

Source: Thanks to Genise Fries, a technology teacher.

---

subject matter as well as a tool for learning. To use computers, students need to understanding *keyboarding*, including typing as well as function keys, word processors, data bases, and, in some cases, computer programming. While learning about computers often involves hands-on participation, instruction sometimes depends on text materials (manuals, diagrams, and instructions) (D'Angelo, 1984). Learning about computers is also an opportunity for meaningful dialogue among students, with students collaborating to teach one another the inner workings and applications of computers and software programs (Webb, Ender, & Lewis, 1986).

Computers and Content Reading   Computers and content reading instruction can be integrated two ways: (1) using computers to enhance content reading, and (2) using content reading to enhance the use of computers.

Computers can enhance content reading by assisting with concept mapping (Chapter 6) and problem-solving and simulations (Chapter 8), and by helping students manage and organize information when studying (Chapter 9). Computers are also useful tools for writing instruction (Chapter 10), vastly expanding students' opportunities to engage in real communication. Computers can also serve as vehicles for discussion, as students talk with one another about what they are writing or learning to do on a computer.

Teaching the use of computers through content reading means directly applying the techniques described in this book to learning computer concepts and applications. For example, structured overviews, in the form of flowcharts, might be useful for vocabulary development or to illustrate the planning that accompanies computer programming. Comprehension activities could be adapted to help students internalize concepts found in computer manuals (for an example, see Figure 13.5). Instruction in reasoning and problem-solving could assist students in learning how to approach computer simulations. Taken together, computer-assisted instruction and content reading can become a powerful way to build content, process, and motivation outcomes and prepare students for a technological future.

SUMMARY

Planning a unit is a little like planning an epic story with sweeping themes and larger-than-life events and episodes. Assessing the content and students is a critical step in unit planning. Concept mapping and the development of objectives helps teachers make good planning and teaching decisions. Through the activities described in this chapter, teachers can become more intentional in their unit planning while preserving, if not fostering, flexibility and spontaneity.

Content reading instruction, if it is to be of any value, must be integrated with other approaches to curriculum and school restructuring. For example, computers can enrich content reading, while content reading can help students learn about computers. Synthesizing various educational innovations with content reading is one way to promote and refine effective classroom instruction and communication.

SPECIAL PROJECTS

Course-Based

1. At this point, you should be ready to design your own unit of study. Prepare a unit based on a group of students (for example, mixed group of tenth graders) who are about to study some "big ideas" in your content area. Follow the framework and procedures presented in this chapter.

Field-Based

2. Teach a unit you have designed. Reflect on its success or failure. How will you use information you have gained from teaching the unit to teach other units?

3. Find out about the various attempts at restructuring going on in your area. Are most of the attempts districtwide and systemic or specific to individual buildings or classrooms? In what ways is content reading instruction compatible with what is already happening? In what ways could content reading instruction be used to help set goals? To improve instruction? How would you plan a unit with the restructuring plans of a school or school district in mind?

4. Design a plan for using computers in your classroom. In what ways could computers be used to expand the potential of content reading? In what ways could content reading be used to teach the use of computers?

SUGGESTED READINGS

This book provides a useful framework for thinking about unit planning:
EGAN, K. (1986). *Teaching as story telling.* Chicago: The University of Chicago Press.

These articles discuss several different approaches to unit development:
COOTER, R., & GRIFFITH, R. (1989). Thematic units for middle schools: An honorable seduction. *Journal of Reading, 32,* 8, 676–681.
DILLER, C., & GLESSNER, B. (1988). A cross curriculum substance abuse unit. *Journal of Reading, 31,* 6, 553–561.

These are units of study available in mathematics and science:
FITZGERALD, W., WINTER, M., LAPPAN, G., & PHILLIPS, E. (1986). *Middle grades mathematics project.* Menlo Park, CA: Addison-Wesley.
ROTH, K., ANDERSON, C., & SMITH, E. (1987). *The power plant: Teacher's guide to photosynthesis* (Occasional Paper No. 112). East Lansing: Michigan State University Institute for Research on Teaching.
The annual catalogue for the National Council of Teachers of English (1111 Kenyon Rd., Urbana, IL 61801) has an extensive listing of literature units.

This book describes systematic school restructuring involving collaboration between schools and universities:

The Holmes Group. (1990). *Tomorrow's schools: Principles for the design of professional develop-ment.* East Lansing, MI: The Holmes Group.

This chapter discusses ways to integrate various specific staff development approaches within a school, including content reading instruction:

CONLEY, M., & TRIPP-OPPLE, K. (1990). Improving staff development through cooperation. In G. Duffy (Ed.), *Reading in the middle school,* 2d edition. Newark, DE: International Reading Association.

These books are excellent resources for ideas about computers and classroom teaching:

BALAJTHY, E. (1986). *Microcomputers in reading and language arts.* Englewood Cliffs, NJ: Prentice-Hall.

RUDE, R. (1986). *Teaching reading using microcomputers.* Englewood Cliffs, NJ: Prentice-Hall.

These books will help you make selections from among thousands of computer programs:

BLANCHARD, J., MASON, G., & DANIEL, D. (1987). *Computer applications in reading,* 3d edition. Newark, DE: International Reading Association.

HECK, W., JOHNSON, J., KANSKY, R., & DENNIS, D. (1984). *Guidelines for evaluating computerized instructional materials,* 2d edition. Newark, DE: International Reading Association.

The April 1989 issue of the *Journal of Reading* is devoted to new technologies and content reading.

PUBLISHERS' ADDRESSES FOR COMPUTER PROGRAMS MENTIONED IN THIS CHAPTER

Apple Computer
20525 Mariani Avenue
Cupertino, CA 95014

Claris Corporation
5201 Patrick Henry Drive
Santa Clara, CA 95054

Creative Computing Software
39 East Hanover Avenue
Morris Plains, NJ 07950

D. C. Heath Software
D. C. Heath and Company
Lexington, MA 02173

Minnesota Educational Publishing Computing
   Consortium
2520 Broadway Drive
St. Paul, MN 55113

Random House School Division
400 Hahn Rd.
Westminster, MD 21157

Scholastic Publishing Company
730 Broadway
New York, NY 10016

Software Publishing Corporation
1901 Landings Drive
Mountain View, CA 94043

SOURCES FOR REVIEWS OF COMPUTER SOFTWARE

Apple II Computers
A+ Magazine
Nibble

Color Computer III (Tandy)
Rainbow

IBM AND IBM Compatibles
PC World
PC Computing
BYTE

Macintosh Computers
Macworld
Macuser

General
Classroom Computer News
Educational Computer
Electronic Learning
The Computing Teacher

REFERENCES

ANDERSON, C., & ROTH, K. (1989). Teaching for meaningful and self-regulated learning of science. In J. Brophy (Ed.), *Advances in research on teaching*. Greenwich, CT: Jai Press.

ATWELL, N. (1987). *In the middle: Writing, reading and learning with adolescents*. Portsmouth, NH: Heinemann.

BALAJTHY, E. (1984). Reinforcement and drill by microcomputer. *The Reading Teacher, 37,* 6, 490–494.

BLANCHARD, J., & MASON, G. (1985). Using computers in content area reading instruction. *Journal of Reading, 29,* 2, 112–117.

CONLEY, M., & TRIPP-OPPLE, K. (1990). Improving staff development through cooperation. In G. Duffy (Ed.), *Reading in the middle school,* 2d edition. Newark, DE: International Reading Association.

COOTER, R., & GRIFFITH, R. (1989). Thematic units for middle schools: An honorable seduction. *Journal of Reading, 32,* 8, 676–681.

D'ANGELO, K. (1984). Computer books for young students: Diverse and difficult. *The Reading Teacher, 37,* 7, 626–630.

DEGROFF, L. (1990). Is there a place for computers in Whole Language classrooms? *The Reading Teacher, 43,* 8, 568–573.

DUFFELMEYER, F. (1985). Estimating readability with a computer: Beware the aura of precision. *The Reading Teacher, 38,* 5, 392–396.

EGAN, K. (1986). *Teaching as story telling*. Chicago: University of Chicago Press.

HANCOCK, J. (1989). Learning with databases. *Journal of Reading, 32,* 7, 582–589.

HUNTER, M. (1984). Knowing, teaching and supervising. In P. Hosford (Ed.), *Using what we know about teaching*. Alexandria, VA: Association for Supervision and Curriculum Development.

KINZER, C. (1986). A 5 part categorization for the use of microcomputers in reading classrooms. *Journal of Reading, 30,* 3, 226–233.

MIKULECKY, L., CLARK, E., & ADAMS, S. (1989). Teaching concept mapping and university level study strategies using computers. *Journal of Reading, 32,* 8, 694–702.

NOVAK, J., & GOWAN, D. (1984). *Learning how to learn*. New York: Cambridge University Press.

O'BYRNE, J. (1989). The personal computer: An information-based study strategy. *Journal of Reading, 33,* 1, 16–21.

OLEY, E. (1989). Information retrieval in the classroom. *Journal of Reading, 32,* 7, 590–597.

O'NEIL, J. (1989). Piecing together the restructuring puzzle. *Educational Leadership, 46,* 3, 4–10.

PIERCE, D., & BADER, L. (1986). The effect of unit construction upon teachers' use of content reading and writing strategies. *Journal of Reading, 30,* 2, 130–135.

RUDE, R. (1986). *Teaching reading using microcomputers*. Englewood Cliffs, NJ: Prentice-Hall.

SANDERY, P. (1989). Cutting the cords that constrain. *Journal of Reading, 32,* 7, 620–627.

SHULMAN, L. (1987). Knowledge and teaching: Foundations of the new reform. *Harvard Educational Review,* 57, 1, 1–22.

VICKERY, T. (1990). ODDM: A workable model for total school improvement. *Educational Leadership, 47,* 7, 47–50.

WEBB, N., ENDER, P., & LEWIS, S. (1986). Problem-solving strategies and group processes in small groups learning computer programming. *American Educational Research Journal, 23,* 2, 243–262.

WOODWARD, J., CARNINE, D., & GERSTEN, R. (1988). Teaching problem solving through computer simulations. *American Educational Research Journal, 25,* 1, 72–86.

YINGER, R. (1986). Examining thought in action: A theoretical and methodological critique of research on interactive teaching. *Teaching and Teacher Education, 2,* 1, 263–282.

APPENDIX A

Bibliographic Sources of Books of Interest to Readers in Content Areas

ABRAHAMSON, R., & CARTER, B. (1988). *Books for you: A booklist for senior high students.* Urbana, IL: National Council of Teachers of English.

CARLSEN, G. (1980). *Books and the teenage reader,* 2d revised edition. New York: Harper and Row.

CHRISTENSEN, J. (1983). *Your reading: A booklist for junior high and middle school students.* Urbana, IL: National Council of Teachers of English.

DONELSON, K. (1976). *Books for you: A booklist for senior high students,* 6th edition. Urbana, IL: National Council of Teachers of English.

DREYER, S. (1981). *The bookfinder: A guide to children's literature about the needs and problems of youth,* 2d edition. Circle Pines, MN: American Guidance Service.

GILLESPIE, J., & GILBERT, C. (1981). *Best books for children: Pre-school through middle grades,* 2d edition. New York: R. R. Bowker Company.

Junior high school library catalog, 4th edition. New York: H. W. Wilson.

LIPSON, E. (1988). *The New York Times parent's guide to the best books for children.* New York: Times Books.

MATTHEWS, D. (1988). *High interest—easy reading: For junior and senior high students,* 4th edition. Urbana, IL: National Council of Teachers of English.

MONSON, D. (1985). *Adventuring with books: A booklist for Pre-K—grade 6.* Urbana, IL: National Council of Teachers of English.

WOLFF, K., FRITSCHE, E., GROSS, E., & TODD, G. (1983). *The best science books for children.* Washington, DC: American Association for the Advancement of Science.

Magazines of Interest to Readers in Various Content Areas*

Art

Art and Man

Business

Career World
Penny Power

English/Language Arts

Merlyn's Pen
Plays
Read Magazine
Reflections
Scholastic Scope
Shoe Tree
Writing!

Foreign Languages

Bonjour (French)
Das Rad (German)
Qué tal? (Spanish)

Mathematics

Scholastic Math Magazine

Music

Piano Explorer

Physical Education

Kid Sports
Sports Illustrated for Kids

Science

Current Science
OWL
Science World
Young Naturalist Foundation

Social Studies

Current Events
Junior Scholastic
National Geographic World

* Many of these magazines are listed and reviewed in Richardson, S. (1991). *Magazines for children.* Chicago: American Library Association.

Index

Assessment:
  authentic, 72, 369
  content learning, 363–364
  dilemmas in, 362
  graded, 391–392
  guidelines for, 368
  motivation, 101–109, 366–368
  nongraded, 391–392
  objectivity, 362–363
  portfolios, 369–373
  standardized tests, 72–74
  subjectivity, 363
  text, 34–46
  words of caution, 368–369
Attitude scale, 102
  words of caution, 101
Attitudes, 89–92
  favorable, 89–90
  negative, 89–90
  Rhody Scale, 100–103
Authoring, 298

Behavioral objectives, 132–133
Bilingual Education Act of 1968, 69
Bilingual students, 69–71
  dialogue journals for, 70
  motivation of, 99–100
  multicultural backgrounds of, 70

Central questions, 131–132
Class profile, 126–128
Classification, 161–163
Classroom climate, 330–331
CLOZE procedure, 42–44
  words of caution, 42, 44
Coaching, 123–124
Communication:
  approach to content reading, 9–15
  with self and others, 10–12

Competition, 329–330
Comprehension, 55, 60–62
  applied, 62
  beyond text, 62
  constructing meaning, 6
  levels of, 190–195
  monitoring, 59
  processes, 182, 183
  scriptally implicit, 62
  text, 60–62
    textually explicit, 61
    textually implicit, 61
Comprehension instruction, 177–214
  cognitive approach, 179
  goals for, 180–184
  motivation, 179
Computer programs:
  data base, 398
  electronic gradebooks, 398
  networking software, 398
  simulations, 398
  speed-reading, 398
  spelling, 398
  word-processing, 397–398
Conceptual change, 281
Content, 5, 115
Content area reading inventory (CARI),
  73–79
  words of caution, 79
Content objectives, 129–132
Content reading:
  computers and, 401
  field of, 4
  goals of, 5
  resistance to, 14–15
Content teaching, 121–123
Context analysis, 158–161
Cooperation, 329, 331–334
  stages for building:
    conflict, 333–334
    norms, 332–333

411